Sun Chief

Etching by Elias M. Grossman, 1941.

Sun Chief

The Autobiography of a Hopi Indian

SECOND EDITION

DON C. TALAYESVA

Edited by

LEO W. SIMMONS

Foreword to the Second Edition by

MATTHEW SAKIESTEWA GILBERT

Foreword to the First Edition by

ROBERT V. HINE

Yale

UNIVERSITY PRESS

New Haven & London

THE LAMAR SERIES IN WESTERN HISTORY

The Lamar Series in Western History includes scholarly books of general public interest that enhance the understanding of human affairs in the American West and contribute to a wider understanding of the West's significance in the political, social, and cultural life of America. Comprising works of the highest quality, the series aims to increase the range and vitality of Western American history, focusing on frontier places and people, Indian and ethnic communities, the urban West and the environment, and the art and illustrated history of the American West.

Yale University Press books may be purchased in quantity for educational, business, or promotional use. For information, please e-mail sales.press@yale.edu (U.S. office) or sales@yaleup.co.uk (U.K. office).

Symbol design courtesy of Designer Wendell Sakiestewa.

Printed in the United States of America.

Library of Congress Control Number: 2013934187
ISBN 978-0-300-19103-5 (pbk.)

A catalogue record for this book is available from the British Library.

10 9 8 7 6 5 4 3 2 1

TO
ALBERT GALLOWAY KELLER

CONTENTS

CONCERNING THE ANALYSIS OF LIFE HISTORIES

ILLUSTRATIONS

FOREWORD TO THE SECOND EDITION
by Matthew Sakiestewa Gilbert

MY INTRODUCTION TO Don Talayesva's *Sun Chief* came in graduate school at the University of California, Riverside. I had a worn paperback copy of the eleventh printing (1971), which, like many other Hopi books I owned, had once belonged to my father. People back home on the Hopi Reservation in northeastern Arizona often talk about this book. Some have stories to tell about Talayesva's life, things not recorded in the book. As a Hopi student, I read *Sun Chief* with much enthusiasm and interest. Eager to learn about the Hopi, especially from one of our own, I carefully studied every page. I was fascinated by Talayesva's story, and I closely analyzed its contents, including the book's two photographs. I was especially intrigued with the cover photograph of Talayesva by Fred Eggan. I looked at this picture carefully. Wearing black pants, a ribbed white shirt, black leather shoes, and a beautiful Hopi sash around his waist, Talayesva stands confidently in front of a field, perhaps his own. His eyes, partially closed from the glare of the sun, peer forward, looking, waiting, ready to welcome all visitors to the Hopi world behind him.

When Yale University Press published *Sun Chief* in 1942, the Hopi were among the most researched indigenous peoples in the Americas. Although Hopi author Edmund Nequatewa had worked with editor

Mary-Russell F. Colton to produce *Truth of a Hopi* in the mid-1930s, white ethnographers and other scholars still dominated the field of Hopi studies. They viewed Hopis as "subjects" to be studied and written about, and they published their accounts in leading academic journals and in various edited collections. Anthropologists such as Mischa Titiev spent years interviewing Hopis, including Talayesva, on the Hopi Reservation. His highly regarded book on Old Oraibi informed other great works by Peter M. Whiteley and Jerrold E. Levy. Titiev, and those scholars who came before him, meticulously wrote down their observations and studied the ways of their Hopi informants. But while academics situated Hopis at the center of their scholarly inquiries, Hopis did not publish their own books or articles with university presses. Instead, they relied on white scholars to make their voices heard. And white scholars relied on the Hopi to validate their research, provide and interpret information, and bring a sense of authenticity to their work.

The success of *Sun Chief* set in motion a wave of similar books on the Hopi. In the years following its publication, other non-Hopi scholars and writers collaborated with our people to create autobiographies that sought to enlighten the public on Hopi history and culture. During this "as told to" era in Hopi studies, Vada F. Carlson recorded the life story of Polingaysi Qoyawayma to publish *No Turning Back* (1964), Louise Udall worked with Helen Sekaquaptewa to write *Me and Mine* (1969), and Harold Courlander edited Albert Yava's account to produce *Big Falling Snow* (1978). For many years, these publications, combined with *Sun Chief* and Edmund Nequatewa's *Born a Chief* (1992), were the most-referenced works on our people, but none of them were solely written or published by Hopis themselves. At this time, white scholars and other well-established authors were the ones who had the academic credentials and resources to publish books on our people. Even previous editions of *Sun Chief*, an autobiography, did not list Talayesva as the author. As a Hopi person, I always wondered about this. Why did the Press not list Talayesva as the author of his autobiography? Why was Leo Simmons's name the only one shown on the spine of the book? Perhaps this speaks to a time when Hopis did not publish their own accounts, or a time when university presses preferred to situate Hopis as "informants" rather than the authors of their own books.

The field of Hopi studies today, however, looks very different than it did in the first half of the twentieth century. Beginning with Frank C. Dukepoo, who in 1973 became the first Hopi to receive a Ph.D., Hopi scholars have ventured beyond the reservation to receive advanced degrees, and they have secured faculty appointments at colleges and universities across the nation. Hopis are now producing scholarship on the Hopi people, using the skills they honed in graduate school to rearticulate, and at times reinterpret, our history and culture. Some of these scholars are examining the Hopi language, sustainability, health, and a host of other disciplines. Young Hopi scholars such as Darold H. Joseph and Jeremy Garcia are developing culturally responsive and relevant curriculums to use in our schools on the reservation, and Trevor Reed is using his research to repatriate Hopi music, once archived in Columbia University's Center for Ethnomusicology. Taking the lead role in their research, these and other Hopi scholars reflect a new direction in Hopi studies. They represent the ways Hopis have benefited from works such as *Sun Chief* to better develop and write their own scholarship in the twenty-first century.

My work on the Hopi boarding school experience at Sherman Institute, an off-reservation Indian boarding school in Riverside, California, has been personally informed by *Sun Chief*. In November 1906, Talayesva and my grandfather, Victor Sakiestewa, left the village of Oraibi by wagon for Winslow, Arizona, where they boarded a Santa Fe train for Southern California. Together they attended Sherman Institute, a school that U.S. government officials designed to weaken Hopi and other American Indian cultures and to train Native students in industrial trades. They received the same class instruction; participated in similar extracurricular activities, including Protestant services; and returned to their village of Old Oraibi together. But after they arrived on the reservation, their lives diverged dramatically. My grandfather never felt content to be back at his village. He wanted to continue his education beyond the mesas and sought enrollment at the Carlisle Indian Industrial School in Pennsylvania and the Greenville Indian School in California. He eventually worked as a plumber in

Tuba City, Arizona, and encouraged his children to pursue their education at schools off the reservation, including the Ganado Mission School on the Navajo Nation in eastern Arizona. Talayesva, in contrast, kept close to home and attempted to reclaim his identity as a "traditional" Hopi and chief of the Sun Clan.

Talayesva's recollections of his life after his time at Sherman are full of many details. But one account in particular will always invoke pride in me as a Hopi person. In the summer of 1912, the Hopi experienced a severe drought. Crops suffered under the intensity of the sun, and the clouds did not provide rain. People wondered why this was so. Talayesva then remembered that before he went to school in California, Mennonite missionary Heinrich Voth had stolen Hopi "ceremonial secrets" and "carried off sacred images and altars" to the Field Columbian Museum in Chicago, and he had "become a rich man." Talayesva recalled that people at Oraibi were afraid of Voth and "dared not lay their hands on him" for fear of imprisonment. Talayesva referred to Voth as a "wicked man" who had treated the Hopi very poorly. But after Talayesva had been educated in a Western school and learned about the Protestant faith, he was no longer afraid of Voth or any other Christian missionary. And so that same year of the drought, he heard that Voth, now an old man, had stopped by Talayesva's mother's house for a visit. Talayesva was furious, and he went straight to the house and ordered Voth to leave: "You break the commandments of your own God," Talayesva said to him. "He has told you to avoid all graven images; but you have stolen ours and set them up in your museum." He then called Voth a "thief and an idolater" who would "never go to heaven."

The showdown with Heinrich Voth is significant for several reasons. In the past, readers of *Sun Chief* often focused on Talayesva's detailed accounts of Hopi ceremonies or the descriptions of his many sexual encounters. They wrote at length about his dreams and the tragedies that he encountered throughout his life. But in his confrontation with Voth, one is able to see Talayesva at his very finest. Here the young Hopi from Oraibi used the knowledge that he gained at school to rebuke and even chastise Voth for his un-Christian behavior. He turned the Christian Bible against the old Mennonite missionary and exposed his hypocrisy so others might see. He recounted specific passages in Voth's holy book and used them to his advantage. Voth, who was most likely surprised by Talayesva's intelligence and nerve, came from a line of people who considered Hopi adults to have the mental capacity of children. He did not expect this response from Talayesva or any other Hopi. "I knew the Hopi Cloud People despised this man," recalled Talayesva, "and even though he was now old and wore a long beard, I had a strong desire to seize him by the collar and kick him off the mesa."

Talayesva's desire to kick Voth over the mesa edge also speaks to the cultural tensions on the reservation during the early 1900s. Over the years, writers including Robert V. Hine, who wrote the first Foreword to *Sun Chief* in 1963, have often observed that Talayesva was "caught between two cultures." They portray the Hopi from Old Oraibi in a constant struggle between, on one hand, adopting or accepting American ways and, on the other, holding to Hopi beliefs and practices. While Talayesva experienced tensions between Hopi and Western culture, he also embraced these tensions to create a Hopi reality for himself in the twentieth century. Hopi culture, at least how Talayesva understood it, did not always stand in opposition to American values or practices, nor did it stay stagnant from time immemorial. He had the ability to adopt or adapt aspects of Western culture to fit with beliefs in Hopi society. He made Western culture work for him, but he also rejected and fought against it when it imposed on him certain cultural norms or expectations as a Hopi person.

Although Talayesva operated within the Western world, the tensions he experienced among his own people cannot be overestimated. These tensions were far more complicated and intense than the ones he encountered in the white world. In his book, Talayesva recalls that Hopis on the reservation became increasingly suspicious of him and his friendship with the book's collaborator and editor, Leo W. Simmons. They accused Talayesva of selling Simmons secrets about Hopi ceremonies and other religious practices. In response, Hopis at Oraibi started a rumor that Talayesva was receiving money from officials in Washington, D.C., for selling dead Hopi bodies. Even though anthropologists and other museum officials in Washington thought very highly of Talayesva, many Hopis back home remained unimpressed with him and his accomplishments. They despised him for sharing religious information with Simmons, and they ostracized him for telling privileged Hopi knowledge to the world. Every reader of *Sun Chief* should be cognizant of the reality that although Talayesva produced a remarkable book, he did so at great cost to himself and his village community.

While *Sun Chief* remains a valuable historical and cultural resource, it does have its limitations. In his book *God Is Red*, Lakota author and theologian Vine Deloria, Jr., once argued that Native autobiographies of the 1930s and 1940s, including *Sun Chief* and *The Son of Old Man Hat* (1938) on the Navajo, did not sufficiently "inform the modern American public about the nature of Indian life" or give people enough "information about Indians to make an intelligent choice as to how best to support Indian goals and aspirations." "Could these books have correctly informed the reader," Deloria asks, "on the struggle of the Navajo and Hopi against Peabody Coal Company at Black Mesa or explained the protest at the Gallup ceremonial?" Although *Sun Chief* is a fascinating account of a specific era in Hopi and American history, it fails to speak to the broader issues that Deloria raised. For example, at no point in Talayesva's narrative does he discuss the establishment of the Hopi tribal government in 1936, the single most important political development for Hopis during the 1930s. Instead, readers learn about Hopi culture and religious practices and superstitions. We learn about life as one Hopi lived it during and after the Indian Progressive Era, but we receive very little information to help us understand the larger issues of Hopi self-determination or the political and legal struggles Talayesva's people faced in the 1930s and beyond. For these discussions, one ought to read *Sun Chief* alongside the work of Hopi historian Lomayumtewa C. Ishii and non-Hopi scholars Justin B. Richland and Emily Benedek.

Today's reader should also know that in the more than seventy years since Talayesva published *Sun Chief*, much has changed for the Hopi. Although the people continue to practice their religious ceremonies and many still speak the Hopi language, the Hopi and Western worlds have become increasingly intertwined. This is evident in our tribal government, including our tribal courts, where Hopi individuals such as Fred Lomayesva, Patricia Sekaquaptewa, and Delfred Leslie, all of the Hopi Appellate Court, have adjudicated cases on the reservation by relying on Hopi tribal law that combines elements of Anglo-American legal practice with principles from Hopi custom and tradition. It is further evidenced in our growing tourist economy, our efforts in sustainable living, and advancements in telecommunications. Furthermore, as Leigh J. Kuwanwisiwma once said, the Hopi people are now "global," and no single factor has contributed to this more than the development of the Internet. Hopis today use the Internet to conduct business and to stay connected with people throughout the world. While Hopi artists were among the first to use the Internet to market and sell their work, Hopi activists of the present also regularly use websites, email, and social media to advance their agendas and to remind the people of cultural values and responsibilities.

Regardless of its historical and political limitations, *Sun Chief* remains a remarkable and honest account of Don Talayesva's life between 1890 and 1940. While it does not reflect life for all or most Hopis during this period, it provides readers with a window into the once-secluded world of the Hopi people. Scholars and students will no doubt continue to consult *Sun Chief* in the future. It will continue to be the focus of masters theses and doctoral dissertations. Professors and other instructors will assign it in their courses, and students will further argue and theorize about its contents. And a new wave of Hopi scholars will use *Sun Chief* to inform their work and critically analyze it from one of many Hopi perspectives. Surely, if Talayesva were still with us today, he would be amazed and perhaps even embarrassed by his book's popularity. But he would also be glad to see that his story was still being told to the Hopi and non-Hopi worlds that he knew so well.

FOREWORD TO THE FIRST EDITION

by Robert V. Hine

DON TALAYESVA BEGAN life in the womb as twins, but, through his mother's will to oneness aided by her firm belief in the powers of the supernatural, he was "twisted into one." That sentence written by an outsider, a non-Hopi, like myself, sounds faintly ridiculous. The remarkable thing about *Sun Chief* is that when Don tells his own story, the cultural outsider is swept along into acceptance. This occurs largely because *Sun Chief* is a warm, universally human account, shaving the empiricist of his condescensions, stripping the Anglo-American of his self-complacency. Late in his autobiography Don tells of a woman tourist bemusedly watching a Hopi ceremony at Walpi. In the press of the crowd Don rubs her leg, and the woman and her friends laugh at him, undoubtedly with overtones of superiority before a rude, sensual semi-barbarian. But in *Sun Chief* we stand with Don, smiling in his heart at the woman, firm in his own beliefs, and also saddened at what the white man's laugh is doing to his Hopi way of life. *Sun Chief* puts us inside Don, like his Spirit Guide, beside him throughout his life. Within its literary framework, we are convinced, removed from our pretensions, momentarily certain that the Spider Woman and the Two-Heart exist. What happens to the reader in Rousseau's *Confessions* or in *The Little Flowers of St. Francis* also moves him here: *Sun Chief* communicates a compelling human experience. Having read it, we have added Don Talayesva to the company of our private worlds.

And he in turn has admitted us to his world. We smell the mesa air, spiced with spruce and pine. On special occasions the corn meal powders our path. Our hair is washed in yucca suds. We purify "our clothes and bodies in the smoke of juniper and piñon sap." With an amazing attention to such details Don recreates his life. And with rich similes: "Black clouds rushed forth from the mountains—like warriors on a warpath. . . ." "We felt like a flock of sheep huddled together in a corner of a big corral after the wolves have been among them." Perhaps the harshness of the environment ("dry, wind-beaten, and worm-infested sand drifts," heat, drought, dust, and disease) intensifies the style. "Strong winds drove sand into my face and eyes, filled my ears and nose, and made it difficult to eat my lunch without catching mouthfuls of grit. My clothes were often heavy with sand and chafed me as I walked; and my hair was caked with earth so that I could hardly reach the scalp with my fingernails." Yet, as with his flock ("I loved my sheep and knew the face of every one"), he cherished his land, his by birth and by choice. When he leaves the mesas, the vividness of his writing suffers; when he returns, the spruce and the piñon and the dusty sand hills are sensed again.

As viewed from a scientific, semi-Christian, Anglo-American society, Don's life contains both appealing and unappealing characteristics. There are elements of the stereotyped Hopi here—peaceful and secure, slow to anger, calm in the face of difficulties, cooperative and submissive to the good of the group, deeply attached to his way of life, culturally integrated and serene. All of these in some measure exist in Don, and they are appealing qualities. But Don is other things, too—superstitious, fearful, gossipy, occasionally lazy, lewd in his humor, excessively sensual, and dishonest with his wife. In short, he is a human being, confusing, baffling, contradictory. The value judgments which we attach to each of his traits are, of course, largely dependent on the society from which they are viewed. The matter is further complicated by the fact that Don in many of his attributes may not be typical of his Hopi culture. And, finally, what may have been representative of Hopis in 1900 may not be typical of them in 1963. These qualifications are essential to an examination of the various aspects of Don's life.

Take, for example, his religion. Don's commitment to Christianity was of doubtful depth, in spite of his testimonials to Jesus at the Y.M.C.A. In comparison to the lasting impact of his initiations into the Hopi ceremonies, his excursion into Christianity was pale and meaningless. It was a means to an end, tied to his temporary flirtation with the white man's way, his momentary wish that "there were some magic that could change my skin into that of a white man." It lasted for only a few years, was in no sense a conversion, and provided at most a foil for his moving dream-revelation on the truth of the Hopi gods. After this crucial night's spiritual journey, Christianity for Don became increasingly suspect, effective perhaps "for modern Whites in a good climate," but bringing the Hopis only drought and disease. When Christian preachers tell the Hopis they should fear destruction in a great flood, Don comments ruefully that he has prayed for rain all his life and the one thing he is sure he will never see is a flood in Oraibi. "Other gods may help some people," Don concludes, "but my only chance for a good life is with the gods of my fathers. I will never forsake them, even though their ceremonies die out before my eyes and all their shrines are neglected."

Don remains a religious man with an abiding reverence for the transcendent or supernatural. "If a person has no religion to follow he lives no better than a dog," he wrote. A Spirit Guide, like a Christian guardian angel, stands beside him, admonishing and protecting. Beyond his Guide is a vast pantheistic world of gods and spirits. Once they walked the mesas, like Greek gods on Olympus; but now they are less physically evident though equally powerful to influence the life and death of man. Don has faith, in the Tillich sense of concern for the ultimate. But as the white man's religion inundates the mesas and the Hopis grow more and more aware of the Protestant-Catholic society which surrounds them, Don's religious plight becomes increasingly similar to that of an ancient Jew in Egypt or Babylon, and, like Moses or Judas Maccabaeus, he holds the more tenaciously to his traditional beliefs.

The white man's education had a greater effect on Don than the white man's religion. His schooling gave him a command of English, thus making *Sun Chief* possible, and taught him something of the world, late and soon—at least he refers to men as soon as Miles Standish and late as Adolph Hitler. "I had learned many English words and could recite part of the Ten Commandments. I knew how to sleep on a bed, pray to Jesus, comb my hair, eat with a knife and fork, and use a toilet. . . . I had also learned that a person thinks with his head instead of his heart." (It is hard to know how much irony is concealed in that last sentence.) At Sherman Institute in Riverside, California, he added accomplishments as disparate as debating, football yells, square dancing, baking bread, tailoring, telling dirty stories, and presumably more experience in thinking with his head rather than his heart. But he was not convinced. He was like a clock spring wound tight. At the New Oraibi day school they had cut his hair and burned his old clothes and given him a new name. At the Keams Canyon boarding school they fed him hash and prunes and tea, none of that "good Hopi food"—like piki bread or dumplings made of blue corn meal—which came for him to symbolize the ways of his fathers. More important, the white man's education spoiled him for making a living in the desert. At least as a young married man, he worried over such a result, fearing, although able-bodied, to be unable to support a wife. Like the white man's religion, his education might prove unusable on the rigorous mesas. So he broke the watch spring, loosened the tension. He let his hair grow long, stored his "citizens' clothes in a gunnysack," and eventually taught his son that dancing the Katcina ceremonies was far more important than learning.

In his sex life, too, Don suffered conflict, his Hopi mores contrasting with Protestant ascetic morality. As a child he was led to believe that sex was the most important function of his body. Even intercourse with animals and masturbation were tolerated. The Katcina clowns he loved were given to joking that, next to eating, love-making was the greatest joy of life. And as an older man such pleasures even included extramarital "private wives." None of these were ideas to be tolerated in the Christian code, especially not by the missionaries like the Mennonite H. R. Voth on whom Don heaped such abuse. To escape the white man's gaze, "to make love without fear of sin or a rawhide" was one of his aims. And he succeeded rather well; he had an extraordinary number of affairs with women, everywhere from California to the brothels of Winslow, and he detailed these experiences in a proud if not boastful manner. In his promiscuity and sensuality was he typical of his Hopi society? Although the answer to that question is complicated and requires a great deal more information than is now available, it seems reasonable tentatively to assume that he was not. To begin with, he frankly admitted to the classification of "naughtiest boy in the village." His father in a measure of desperation saw that Don was given a double thrashing at initiation time. And, as Clyde Kluckhohn has pointed out (reviewing the book in the *American Anthropologist*), there is more than a suggestion of latent homosexuality.

If Don is not sexually typical, he is, nevertheless, gifted with insight into the nature of women and love. "The love making business," he wrote, "has two aspects, sometimes making a man very happy and sometimes worrying his life out." The happy element may well have come from sound reasoning: "I learned that unless one is sure of himself the last word with a wife is not worth the trouble." Here, as in the following lines, Don proves himself a most profound commentator on the female sex. "Women are like the wind, blowing first from the east and then from the west. The sooner a man learns this the better. He must expect his wife to make quick changes from joy to sadness and back to joy, in spite of anything that we can do. She can be more stubborn than a mule and harder to control than either wind or weather."

In each of these broad aspects—religion, education, sex—the contrast between Don's Hopi customs and the white man's ways are the nub of his book. Don is basically hostile to white men, "wicked, deceitful people," as he called them, who made us feel "that we were no better than dung." True, he is cooperative in some ways, and he finds working for anthropologists, like Leo Simmons, pleasant and materially rewarding. "I found it much easier to talk in the shade for cash than to cultivate corn and herd sheep in the hot sun." But his eyes had seen the destructive acid working in the white presence, most particularly as a result of missions and schools.

Actually the early years of Don's life were a critical period in Hopi-white relations. The tribe had been missionized by the sixteenth- and seventeenth-century Spaniards, but the effects had been negligible, for the Hopis had always proved peculiarly resistant to cultural infiltration. After 1890—the year of Don's birth and about the time H. R. Voth, the missionary, arrived—the rugged Hopi mesas felt the first effective white penetration. Serious prospects of Christianization and Americanization among their people produced a rift which grew as deep as the pit in Don's vision of the underworld. While still a boy he, considering himself a part of the Friendly faction, threw stones at boys of the Hostile persuasion, suggesting the way modern boys might fight a presidential campaign on a fourth-grade playground. But the Hopi problem ran much deeper than national politics, leading in 1906 to an ultimatum, a demarcation line, the evacuation of the Hostiles, and the establishment of the new Hopi settlement at Hotavila. Don's reactions to the whites were formed against this historically critical period. He was a Friendly, recognizing the desperate necessity of cooperation; he was at the same time tragically aware that accommodation meant erosion of the Sun Trail. The final result of this apparent contradiction was his sophisticated judgment that white men, like the Hopi, were both good and bad. Among them were respectable individuals "who could be trusted and who never discredited our Hopi beliefs and customs," but also there were low-class whites whom he called "dump-hole people." This recognition of individual differences based initially on a distrust of the whites gives the whole story of *Sun Chief* an aura of authenticity; we never feel that Don is saying something merely to please his white inquisitors; and we are relieved when, as in the Wowochim initiation, he refuses to reveal ceremonial secrets. The drawing of the line reflects a level of integrity which strengthens all the comments he is willing to make.

Perhaps Don's honesty returns us to those universal human qualities which shine through *Sun Chief* quite unaffected by scientific interest in acculturation. Professor Simmons tells us that it is important to note in each situation whether Don is a creature, a creator, a carrier, or a manipulator of the mores. We could ask in another way how Don as one particular human being answers the besetting, catholic questions of life and death, how he establishes the essential relations with fellow men and with a transcendent being, how successfully he can balance a sense of the elemental tragedy and humor in life.

Don related himself to his community through an overwhelming acceptance of its traditions. The older generations were the teachers and preservers and Don paid dutiful attention to their words. The lessons were clear—walk the Hopi Trail in peace, work hard with the sheep and the corn, eat the Hopi food, pray to the Hopi gods, observe the ceremonies, and be continent till four days after the final dances. Such a tradition-directed society might be expected to conceive of time as natural and organic, based upon the rising of the sun or the running of spring sap. As Don said, "there were proper times for planting, harvesting, and hunting, for ceremonies, weddings, and many other activities. In order to know these dates it was necessary to keep close watch on the sun's movements." Time meandered through the generations, the seasons deceptively changing within the changeless years, like the band of the Colorado River seen from the rim of its great canyon. Time was not a line but a spiral in which the end brought one close to the beginning. Don was a traditionalist and time, his unhurried companion. After all, there was no reason to believe the future would be any better than the past when one remembered, facing back, that the gods themselves had once walked the earth and, facing forward, that the modern world offered such dubious items as Bull Durham and Mentholatum and cornflakes and aspirin. He had tried all of these progressive products and remained dubious. Once when ill, he was being taken in an automobile to a doctor and, after begging his Guardian Spirit not to drop him on the road and hoping against hope that his act would be as effective as the traditional spreading of corn flour on the footpath, he weakly sprinkled a little meal from the window of the speeding car. The new ways, like the automobile, might be a positive detriment to known potent practices.

Don's account is full of comedy, but humor is a fragile cultural export, and the jokes, especially the practical ones, frequently escape us. Sometimes we only laugh at Don, as when he prescribes sexual thoughts as a cure for hiccoughs. Sometimes the fun seems coarse and earthy; and then we tend to be embarrassed by our own Puritanism and understand how the presence of the whites spoiled the play whenever Don danced as a clown Katcina. But then there are moments when the humor, though culturally oriented, still proves magnificently universal. At dinner just after his marriage Don's mother-in-law solicitously hovered over him and did the work of unrolling his tamales. "Perhaps she will do this for me always," he thought. "But I was mistaken; at breakfast I had to unwrap my own tamales." Or a bit earlier, Don prepared himself for the tip-to-toe ritual bathing of the bridegroom at the hands of the bride's womenfolk—and worried because he was ticklish. Such are Don's wry twists of unintentional, candid, artless humor.

And finally, there is the human tragedy, particularly surrounding the deaths of his four children, one baby after another succumbing until the tears on Don's brown face unite in one deep gully of grief. Sometimes he told of those tears ("We cried and cried and stayed up all night"). But more often the anguish comes in stark scenes revealing like a flash bulb the father beside his dead child: "I knelt and uncovered my little daughter, running my hands over her cold body; and when I touched her chin, the mouth opened." At each successive birth he dreamt for the baby, expecting again that his new son might make a good sheepherder and a "first-class lover of the girls," that his new daughter might wear Hopi clothes and comb her hair in the squash-blossom style. And he carried each bundled hope to a common grave where the small wrapped corpses lay one beneath the other. "Long after, whenever I passed within sight of the grave of my children, a lump would rise in my throat, and it seemed that my anger and grief were more than I could bear."

Sun Chief is, thus, an extraordinarily introspective and revealing autobiography. It cannot be taken alone as evidence of Hopi society, but alone it unquestionably reveals a human being in depth. Such personal revelations are unusual in the history of western America. Mention Sarah Royce on the overland trek or Lewis Garrard on the Santa Fe trail or a Mormon like John Lee, and there are few left. The white man in the West has been little concerned with inner revelations. (He was either introspectively impotent or too busy.) And the

Indian, for quite different reasons, has been equally reticent. The sum total of American Indians who have opened their lives and thoughts to the white man's printed page is perhaps no more than four—a Winnebago, *Crashing Thunder* (ed. Paul Radin); a Kwakiutl, *Smoke from Their Fires* (ed. Clellan S. Ford); a Navajo, *Son of Old Man Hat* (ed. Walter Dyk); and *Sun Chief.*

Crashing Thunder is much shorter and less revealing than the others; *Son of Old Man Hat* (the Navajo) and *Smoke from Their Fires* (the Kwakiutl) both, however, make interesting comparisons with *Sun Chief.* The Navajo's narrative covers only his youth, to the age of twenty; the Kwakiutl's nearly an entire life, to the age of seventy. But even the latter seems deficient in the mature wisdom of Don's senior years. All three works have an earthiness; sex life is openly discussed; and a certain joy in the green of spring pushes through. But the Navajo and Kwakiutl are much more pragmatic; their chants and ceremonies are viewed matter-of-factly without an expression of spiritual feelings so characteristic of Don. With the exception of the Kwakiutls' concern for the potlatch tradition, the elders' advice in the two other books often reads like *Poor Richard's Almanac* ("when you've acquired stocks you have to work on them day and night") compared with the more philosophic Hopi Trail theme of Don's story.

Sun Chief has proved continuously popular, having thus far run through four printings. In the fields of anthropology and ethnology it has been a basic reference in a host of monographic studies; it appears in such general works on the Hopi as Laura Thompson's *Culture in Crisis;* and it is at this moment being translated into German. On its first appearance in 1942 both professional and non-professional journals were expansive in their praise, though many reviewers cautioned against the assumption that Don was a typical Hopi and pointed out that, even if he were, his material had been filtered by selection and arrangement through the mind of a white college professor. Similar worries bother many of those now working close to the tribe, especially since the impression of Don's sexual life, if taken as representative, could reflect harm on the group as a whole. But these criticisms have never overshadowed appreciation of *Sun Chief*'s ethnologic accomplishment and lively charm.

It is the human quality to which we at last return. Time after time in simple, beguiling ways Don throws us completely off our scientific track of relating his life to Hopi mores or cultural conflicts. We forget our original intent to dissect his customs and ideas; his mesa ceases to be an anatomy table; and in place of a cadaver we have a living man, imaginative, humorous, and tragic, so filled with contradictions and illusions that analysis must in desperation restrict itself to only a portion of the whole. Edward Sapir has said that cultural autobiographies "have a disappointing way of dying in the meshes of the tapestry which they are commanded to enliven." If this is the rule, it is proved in the exception, for Don Talayesva and his Hopi scene are as alive as flesh, dreams, and tears.

Riverside, California
January 1963

PREFACE

THIS IS A FRANK AND intimate account of fifty years in the life of Don C. Talayesva of Oraibi, Arizona. It attempts to describe how he came to be the person that he is, and how he thinks, feels, and behaves. It is a comprehensive case history, reported in the first person, for those who are interested in the development of personality in relation to society and culture.

Don definitely feels that this is his book. When the manuscript was read back to him to be checked for errors, he said: "I am living my life over again. I am surprised that I have done this, and I'm proud of myself." When it was suggested that a few delicate items might be deleted for personal reasons, he replied, "No. You have insisted that without the complete record of my life our work would be wasted."

There are two sections in the Introduction: the first on "The Project and the Procedure" which provides a detailed account of how the data were obtained and organized and the purpose for which they are to be used; and the second on "The Hopi in Oraibi," which presents a brief sketch of the people, their physical environment and social organization, and their way of living. The autobiography, consisting of fifteen chapters, constitutes the narrative. There is also a preliminary discussion of the analysis of life histories. Appendices give an example of situational analysis, a small sampling of typical legends and myths such as Don heard as a boy, and a guide to the Hopi kinship system in which practically all persons mentioned in the narrative are identified with respect to residence, clan affiliation, and relationship to Don. There is also a sample of Don's composition which enables the reader to see how the material has been treated in the text. A special study of dreams is planned for a later publication.

The project was planned and accomplished under the auspices of the Institute of Human Relations and the Departments of Anthropology, Psychiatry, and Sociology at Yale University. It was financed chiefly by the Institute of Human Relations. I am particularly indebted to Professor George P. Murdock, Chairman of the Department of Anthropology, and to Professor Mark A. May, Director of the Institute of Human Relations, for guidance in research and for continuous encouragement. Many pertinent criticisms and valuable suggestions were also received from Professors Maurice R. Davie, Eugen Kahn, Albert G. Keller, and Bronislaw Malinowski.

I am also indebted to Dr. Paul W. Preu of the Department of Psychiatry at Yale for his coöperation in a field trip to Oraibi in the summer of 1938. Professor John Dollard and a class of graduate students used the manuscript in a seminar in 1940 and made valuable criticisms. Dr. Amos B. Hulen, Ruth Chapman, and Clara Thurber also read parts of the manuscript and made helpful suggestions. Elizabeth H. Simmons was a constant source of encouragement and assistance. The engraved etching was contributed by Elias M. Grossman. Geoffrey Gorer rendered invaluable editorial assistance and made some excellent modifications in the selection and organization of the data. For secretarial assistance, and not infrequently for counsel, I wish to thank Laura C. McCarthy. My deepest gratitude, however, is richly deserved by my Hopi brother, Don C. Talayesva. Without his rigorous honesty, wholehearted coöperation, and willingness to suffer some public censure, the task could not have been accomplished and might have been interrupted in its most critical stage. It was his life, and it is in a very real sense his book.

L. W. S.
Yale University,
February 1942.

INTRODUCTION

The Project and the Procedure

THIS WORK STUDIES one individual in contact with two cultures which are in strong contrast and considerable conflict. He spent approximately the first decade of life in conservative Hopi society, the second in the American educational system, the third "by choice" in the culture of his childhood, varied in the fourth and fifth decades by more or less incidental digressions again into the society of Whites. Our interest is in what manner of man the two cultures made of him and what we can learn from his experiences.

The subject was selected from an alien society, and within a culture greatly contrasted with our own, in order to insure objectivity and to emphasize the molding impact of culture upon personality. "While it is probably impossible—certainly so without a saving sense of humor—to stand off and get a cool view of ourselves and our own entanglements, anyone can observe with detachment the life of peoples [or of a person] remote in time, space, or behavior from his interests."[1]

The objectives of the study are fourfold: *First,* to prepare a relatively full and reliable account of an individual's experience and

---

1. A. G. Keller, *Man's Rough Road* (New Haven, Yale University Press, 1932), p. 25.

development from birth on—to write a comprehensive life history as an experimental technique in the investigation of personality problems. *Second*, to accumulate and arrange in natural order (the order in which it was experienced) a substantial body of concrete and relevant data on an individual in a "primitive" society for the purpose of developing and checking hypotheses in the field of culture and its relation to personality development, or of the individual and his role in cultural change. The record is, therefore, socially and culturally orientated throughout. Although the lens of investigation is focused on the individual in his environment, particular effort is made to see in what way society and the mores frame every incident of personal experience. A *third* objective was to attempt at least a partial interpretation of the individual's development and behavior by means of available techniques and sources of investigation. It was considered highly desirable to try to make sense out of one person's behavior as a demonstration of what can be done with more extensive research and techniques of analysis. This was a task to pursue as far as time and ability permitted, but with no expectations of completion. The *fourth* objective was systematically to utilize the investigation for the formulation of generalizations and the testing of theories in the field of individual behavior with respect to society and culture; and to share the data and research project with others engaged in similar inquiries. This is not to imply that the most pertinent data can be accumulated for testing general hypotheses that are at the time imperfectly formulated; but some collection of materials is essential for the formulation of theories. It provides a backlog of data; it lessens the labor of securing additional material; and it provides very essential contextual information. There will be less need for this, perhaps, when we have more life histories which are adequate for personality analyses. In this publication an effort has been made to realize the first two objectives and to make a start on the third, but the fourth is reserved for further investigation.

An important reason for delay in the fourth objective is that it appeared incompatible to prepare a case history and develop test cases for and against hypotheses at one and the same time. A life history would seem to require that attention be focused on the individual under study and that the materials be organized about his chronological development, while the testing of hypotheses requires that attention be focused on theory and that the materials be arranged and proportioned in a different order. No satisfactory compromise seemed possible for the achievement of both goals in the same presentation.

One further reason discouraged the arrangement of the initial materials in the form of theory testing—the subtle danger of indoctrination of the data. There is no doubt that the interests and personal biases of the investigator project themselves into his material and probably even influence the subject in the responses which he makes, as well as distort the presentation and analysis of the data. An individual's life is so complex and the processes of transcription and interpretation are so flexible that an astute investigator with a theory to prove or disprove may possibly extract from a naïve informant an approximately desirable answer, at least by symbolic implication, to any inquiry which relates to so general a subject as the dynamics of personality development. With present techniques of investigating and recording life-history materials, it is sometimes easier for an investigator to deceive his reader, and even himself, than for the informant to lie successfully to him. Perhaps the best safeguard to this scientific hazard is to become fully aware of it, stand shy of hypotheses until a substantial body of data has been assembled, first organize the material in its natural context, and only later begin the testing of hypotheses when a substantial bulk of the data is well documented.

Since there is no common agreement yet as to what life histories should be like when the study of personality development is the objective, and since there was no satisfactory model to follow at the time, it was decided to make the initial investigation exploratory in "dragnet" fashion and gather data on any and every topic that appeared to be significantly related to the individual's growth and development. If the first objective was to be a life history, then it seemed that the dominating interests of the individual, in the order in which they were experienced, should determine the presentation of material and regulate the general proportion of space and emphasis on each item. The ideal objective was to mirror the developing personality in such accuracy and detail, and so frame it in its environment, society, and culture, that the reader in moving through the pages might "see" the infant emerge from conception, grow into manhood, and play his adult role, and might come to understand to a certain degree how it happened and if possible how it felt. The truest objective test of the personality sketch is for the informant in reading the document to be able to say, "That's me," for his associates in Hopiland to identify him in most of the details of his life, and for the general reader, who later meets the man, to be able to conclude, "He is just as I expected to find him."

I met Don C. Talayesva in June, 1938, as a result of correspondence with Dr. Mischa Titiev of the Department of Anthropology at the University of Michigan. After two weeks' acquaintance at Oraibi, Don rented me a room in his house, permitted me to employ his sister as housekeeper, and agreed to work for me as informant in a general cultural study projected to fill in the gaps in the data of the Hopi literature for the files of the Cross-Cultural Survey at the Institute of Human Relations. He was to receive thirty-five cents an hour whenever we were engaged in formal interviewing. Whenever, from the start, he described an item in the customary cultural pattern, he was asked specifically what his own experience had been. His conversations were recorded as nearly verbatim as possible, and he was permitted to wander from the subject as much as he pleased, provided he was relating personal experiences. Considerable interest was shown in every personal incident, but all moral judgments of praise or blame were studiously avoided. After about four weeks he was told that his own story was of much greater interest to me than a general description of his culture—a decision which seemed to please him. As his confidence in me developed, he spoke more frankly about himself, sometimes going back to include items that he had left out in former accounts. In the last week of July Don and Chief Tewaquaptewa at Oraibi let it be known that upon request I might be considered for adoption. Within a few days the Chief did adopt me as his "son," and Don adopted me as his "brother" and therefore a member of the Sun Clan, an event which improved my status in the village and made it appropriate for me to be instructed in some subjects which were regarded as clan and tribal secrets.

Increasing interest was shown in Don's personal experiences, and he was finally informed that I wished to record them as a complete and permanent record of one Hopi, to be preserved in Yale University, and that part of it might, with his permission, be published. It was emphasized that the job was to be done chiefly for professional people and that the task would take several years. It was explained in great detail that the project would be entirely worthless for professional use unless the account could be absolutely true and as complete as possible, with no items omitted on grounds of propriety. He was a little frightened at first but pleased that his personal experience was regarded so highly, and said that if he had realized its importance he would have tried to remember more of the details and would have kept notes. But very soon he stated that the ceremonies were secret and that he would never be able to impart them to anyone; for he would get into trouble with other Hopi and with his gods if he told these things. It was agreed that he would not be required to impart any ceremonial information that was not already published, but that he might be asked about his personal experiences in certain ceremonies which were on record. He agreed to this plan without realizing all its implications, since he did not know what had been published; neither was I familiar at that time with all available information.

Many hours were spent at work in Don's house, or in herding, cultivating, caring for horses, hauling stone, attending dances, or traveling from place to place in a car. There was much opportunity to act as a "participating observer." Don was taught to report on the events of the day, together with his mental and emotional reactions to them; and these were recorded in diary form with the understanding that he would keep his own diary after my departure and receive seven cents a page for it. In this preliminary phase of diary work he was instructed to include as nearly as possible everything that had happened during the day, and he was rewarded with praise when he included the smallest details. An effort was made to approximate "free association" in the diary account, in that he was to write whatever came to his mind and as many pages as he desired. All communications were carried on in English, in which Don was exceptionally fluent for a Hopi of his age. He started his writing in September, 1938. After about a year of detailed, often highly significant and sometimes monotonous accounts of such routine as going twice a day for horses and eating three meals, listing all items in the menu, reporting every conversation with other people, etc., he was requested to leave out certain types of material and concentrate on others.

In January, 1940, I made another trip to Oraibi and spent seventeen days in his house in intensive interviewing, checking information gathered earlier, having him repeat many of the major experiences of his life, and filling in gaps in the accounts. Up to this time about 350 hours had been spent in interviewing, and he had written about 3,000 pages of diary in longhand. Rapport was very satisfactory and much new information was obtained; but near the end of my stay some difficulties arose over the question of information on the ceremonies.

Don had seen a book in the possession of Dr. Fred Eggan which was published by George A. Dorsey and H. R. Voth in 1901,[2] and which described the Soyal ceremony in elaborate detail. I again produced this book and unwisely pressed Don for comments on certain details of the ceremony. He became morose and remarked, "What I do in the Soyal is secret. When you ask me about that it sets the people against me." When more details were sought, he became evasive and finally stated that he could not go on. Discouraged, I reminded him that the account had been published for nearly forty years and that unless he could tell me a little more of his personal experience with the Soyal I would have to depart immediately. When there was no response, I settled financial accounts with him, told him good-by, and stated that I would probably leave New Oraibi the next morning, earlier than he had expected me to go. He appeared quite sad but not angry.

2. Publications of the Field Columbian Museum, Anthropological Series, Vol. III, March, 1901.

While I waited for mail in the post office in New Oraibi at six-thirty in the afternoon, Don entered and seemed pleased to be invited to ride with me to his home. On the way he said, "I am surprised that you are leaving so early. I must have done something to hurt your feelings this afternoon. If I did anything that grieved you, I am very sorry." He finally suggested that if I returned to his home that night he would try again to answer my questions.

In the evening we began with Dorsey and Voth's account. Don examined the pictures and drawings of the altars and seemed distressed, making such remarks as, "This is awful. It makes me unhappy. That man Voth was a thief. The secrets are all exposed." He looked long at the picture of his uncle, Talasquaptewa, who had the part of the Star Priest, but made no comment. When asked, he specified the different parts that he had performed in the ceremony, and looked long at the Soyal altar showing the War Priest, Star Priest, and altar equipment. Finally he said, "That is the picture of the exhibit in the Field Museum that has caused all the trouble." When we came to the section in the book that described the Powamu ceremony and its altar, he declined to look at it very carefully, stating that he had no right to know these secrets. At this point an important officer in the Soyal ceremony came into the house and the interview was abruptly ended. Most of the account was read to Don the next day and he corrected a few very minor details and related some of his personal experiences. In discussing page 25, for example, he said that he had drunk the "special medicine" many times, and that it had a bitter taste and was very powerful for health, strength, and long life. He agreed that he had often touched the sacred stone to his heart to make him strong, and that with a little medicine in his mouth he had taken a pinch of the clay and gone annually to his house to rub it over the breast, body, arms, and legs of every member of his family. When over a year later the account of this ceremony in his life history was read to him, he was again rather sad, made no comment at all except to correct three slight inaccuracies, and at the end of the chapter remarked with some bitterness, "That guy Voth was clever."

In March, 1941, Don came to New Haven and spent two weeks with me. At this time the entire narrative, in more extensive form than here published, was read to him slowly and he made corrections and occasional comments which were incorporated. Don had then written about 8,000 pages of his diary in longhand.

The account is, therefore, a highly condensed record in the first person, and almost always in Don's own words or in words which he readily recognized in checking the manuscript. The report is not free narrative, but selected and condensed narration, interwoven with additional information obtained by repeated interviewing. It is greatly abbreviated and often reorganized. Possibly not more than one fifth of the data are published here, but the remainder is for the most part monotonous repetition of the daily details of life, legends, and additional dreams. After literally thousands of inquiries had been made, when on one occasion there was a long pause on my part, Don laughed and said: "Now it is my turn to question you. Can't you think of anything else to ask?"

The style is often disjointed still, but further smoothing on my part would detract from its individuality. Indeed, the question may be argued whether there has been too much of this or too little. In general the materials are left more nearly in Don's own form of expression in the account of his early life up to marriage and much more condensed beginning with the chapter on maintenance. The direct quotations are not to be regarded as strictly literal, but in the latter part of the narrative, where materials are drawn from the diary, it is my opinion that they are very nearly verbatim. Many of the conversations reported even from birth and early childhood are, no doubt, close approximations in that they are highly patterned, and Don consulted his aged relatives on many points. Furthermore, Don has a remarkable memory which has often astonished me when I have been able to check it.

The humor and pathos appear coarse in places, but both were spontaneous and genuine; indeed, so much are they a part of the man and his culture that many of the fine points can be seen only through Hopi-conditioned eyes. This fact I discovered chiefly by reading the completed manuscript back to Don, letting him correct the errors, and recording his hearty laughter and somber silences.

Some parts of the account still appear a little strange and unreal to me, when I am away from Don and Hopiland for a while. But when I come again into close contact with him and his culture, they ring true. I fear, therefore, that the only way the reader can become convinced of the validity of certain passages is to know Don for himself. And to many this is entirely possible, for he wishes to win new friends.

The story ends with Don in Oraibi. He considers his trip East as the crowning event of his life, and there is no question but that it made a deep impression upon him; but he will have to live again in Hopiland before it can be studied in proper perspective.

To specialists in culture and personality problems I wish to emphasize that the task is unfinished. The data have been gathered and prepared with great care, checked and counterchecked for accuracy in details, but the interpretation of the data in terms of personality development has only begun. Although the present document is a greatly abridged account, no type of information that seemed pertinent to the investigation has been consciously ignored and a complete file of the original records is available for study. Moreover, Don is still coöperating by recording his daily experiences, and may provide additional data for proof or disproof of particular hypotheses. The material is offered at the present time in the hope that experts in the various approaches to the study of individual behavior in social and cultural perspective will see fit to criticize and coöperate in the formulation of hypotheses, the testing of theories, and the extraction of principles that may have more general application.

The Hopi in Oraibi

Oraibi, the home of Don C. Talayesva, is reputed to be the oldest continuously inhabited town in the United States. It is a pueblo of terraced, flat-topped, earth-roofed, and connected stone dwellings built upon a bleak and barren rock ledge on a high, arid plateau— a southern extension of Black Mesa—in Arizona, 100 miles east of the Grand Canyon and approximately 60 miles north of the Santa Fe Railroad. Here for 800 years or more the Hopi Indians have managed to survive amid droughts, famines, disease, and predatory raiders and to maintain their ethnic and cultural integrity to a considerable degree in spite of Spanish conquerors, Catholic priests, Protestant missionaries, and many benevolent but often ill-advised agents of the United States Government. At the time of Don's birth (1890) the population of Oraibi exceeded 1,000. Forty miles to the west was Moenkopi, an Oraibian settlement of probably 200 persons who lived on the banks of the Little Colorado River and returned to the home village to fulfill their ceremonial obligations. To the east of Oraibi on First and Second Mesas were 6 other Hopi pueblos which, in 1890, had about 1,500 inhabitants. On the easternmost, or First Mesa, was also situated the pueblo of Hano, inhabited by Tewa Indians who had intermarried with the Hopi.

Although of heterogeneous origin, the Hopi—believed to be descendants of prehistoric cliff dwellers—speak a dialect of the Shoshonean branch of the Uto-Aztecan linguistic stock, and reveal typical Indian racial characteristics in their reddish-brown skin, high cheek bones, broad faces, and straight black hair. The men are short, averaging five feet four-and-one-half inches, and are well framed, hard muscled, and agile. The women are about five inches shorter and when young are rather fair-skinned, lithe, and graceful; but as they grow older they become portly, though almost never clumsy or lazy. The Hopi are a peace-loving people, as their name implies ("Hopi" means peaceful people), and display good fellowship and humor, but they maintain a poise which reflects courage and self-confidence. Whenever they were attacked by marauding Apache, Navahos, and Utes, they defended their homes on the mesa tops with great valor and have even made devastating counterattacks, although armed with nothing better than wooden clubs, sinew-backed bows, and reed arrows tipped with flint or obsidian.

Life has been hard on this sandy, rock-laden, and semibarren plateau 6,500 feet above sea level. With precipitation averaging scarcely ten inches a year, water is a chief problem for survival. Rainstorms are confined mainly to midsummer and often occur in torrential downpours, which cause considerable damage to the soil and the very scanty vegetation. In March and April strong windstorms tear growing plants to shreds, fill the few springs with sand, not infrequently bury scrub trees and houses, and literally move fields of sand and soil about over the desert. Sage, yucca, scrub cedars, greasewood, cactus, and other semidesert plants afford very little food, have small utility for building purposes, and provide scant fuel, which must, at that, be carried several miles to the village.

Since it is essential to cover much territory in search of subsistence—piñon nuts, juniper berries, mesquite beans, prickly pears, and many other wild seeds, roots, leaves, and fruits—travel and transportation are vital problems, and the Hopi have become famous for their ability to cover long distances on foot and with considerable speed. Until recently, and quite often even now, all the food and fuel and much of the water, occasionally in the form of ice blocks, had to be laboriously borne to the mesa top on human backs with the aid of carrying straps or blankets. The beams used for the roofs of houses were transported many miles and all the brush and adobe and much of the building stone had to be lugged, or more recently hauled, up the mesa.

The native fauna—bear, deer, antelope, cougar, wildcat, badger, wolf, fox, and coyote—have long been too scarce to provide an important source of food supply; but they are eagerly hunted with religious ritual, killed in communal drives with bows of oak and flint-tipped arrows, or recently with firearms, and are highly prized for their furs, hides, bones, and meat. Foxes, coyotes, rabbits, rats, and prairie dogs are also hunted in parties, slain with curved throwing sticks, and eaten with considerable relish. Animals were once trapped in flat stone deadfalls and birds caught in horsehair or yucca-string snares. Fowls are rarely eaten, insects or serpents are never used for food, and fish are not available. Dogs are domesticated but almost never eaten. Turkeys are domesticated and highly prized for their plumes, which are used in the ceremonies. Hawks and eagles are kept in captivity part of the year and their feathers employed for making the sacred prayer sticks, called *pahos,* and for sacrifice to the gods. They are never eaten.

Long and arduous journeys, with elaborate ritual and ceremony, were formerly made to procure salt. Clay and various materials for native dyes are borne long distances for the making of pots and other utensils. Twigs from small bushes are stripped of their bark, dried, dyed, and woven into plaques and baskets for domestic use.

The native fare is predominantly vegetarian. Every herb is carefully studied for its food values and medicinal properties. Cultivated plants like maize, beans, squash, watermelons, and sunflowers are staples. They are carefully planted in the sand drifts and gullies, closely guarded from worms, insects, and windstorms, and cultivated through floods and droughts with the utmost diligence and patience. Corn is truly the "staff of life." Centuries of selection have produced a type of corn and cotton that can germinate and mature within a very short time.

The Spanish priests—first known to the Hopi in 1540—built a chapel and residence at Oraibi in the early part of the seventeenth century but were all massacred in a general uprising in 1680, and the Catholic church never reopened its mission. While the Hopi rejected the religion of the Spanish priests, they kept their peaches and apricots and adopted their sheep, burros, and horses, which produced fundamental changes in their system of maintenance. But in spite of these and more recent improvements under the supervision of the United States Government, life is still very hard at Oraibi. An individual born there of Hopi parents in 1890 was destined to live a life in very close contact with a raw, harsh, and difficult environment.

The organization and division of labor include practically every person in Oraibi with the exception of very young children and extremely incapacitated adults. Daily work is highly conventionalized, being based chiefly on sex and less definitely on age and special aptitudes. Formerly the men protected the village from raiding enemies and some of them were organized into a military system. Men engage in the more energetic outdoor occupations such as hunting, herding, farming, and fuel gathering (both wood and coal). They also do the heavier work in housebuilding, make extensive expeditions for hunting and trade, perform most of the ceremonies, and regulate civil and political activities. In the village much of the men's work centers in the *kivas*—underground rectangular chambers which serve as a combination of chapel, lodge, assembly hall, men's sleeping quarters, and clubhouse. Here they card and spin wool and cotton, weave blankets, heavy black *mantas* (women's dresses), kilts, and belts. They make moccasins and beads in the kiva, manufacture and repair tools and weapons, prepare paint, cut hair, tan hides, carve Katcina dolls, and repair the sacred masks and other ceremonial paraphernalia. A few Hopi men are silversmiths. It is also in the kiva that the men relate stories and legends of their tribe, play indoor games, practice songs and Katcina dances, and perform the secret and esoteric parts of their elaborate religious ceremonies. The healing arts are in the hands of the men, except for midwifery and the application of herbs, poultices, and hot stones, and even these treatments are more often carried out by them.

The women's activities center in the homes which they own and usually occupy throughout their lives; residence is matrilocal and marriage monogamous. Women perform most of the housework, cook, care for the children, grind corn—great quantities of it—cultivate garden patches, and assist in housebuilding or repair. They bring almost all the water from springs and cisterns, dry peaches and vegetables, care for the chickens, plaster the earthen floors and stone walls of the houses—both inside and out—watch over the stores of food, and manufacture pots and baskets. Although men weave all the native clothing, women often sew and repair their own and their children's dresses, many of which are now purchased from local traders. Women also engage in considerable trade and barter. Since they own the cultivated land under the supervision of the clan and village chiefs, they claim most of the produce and equipment that are brought into the household. The men possess their own jewelry, personal equipment, farming tools, horses, herds, and ceremonial paraphernalia. But women also own some herds, horses, field houses, and orchards, although they almost never engage in herding or in heavy farm work.

Work parties, consisting of men, women, or both, are very popular. Men coöperate in clearing and fencing fields, planting, harvesting, sheep shearing, clearing the sand out of springs, coal digging or wood gathering, kiva repairs, and weaving wedding outfits. They also go in parties on hunting and trading expeditions. Women form parties for grinding corn, repairing houses, cooking for feasts, sewing, making pots and plaques, and cultivating the gardens. Groups of men and women coöperate in housebuilding, cleaning out springs, harvesting crops, sweet-corn bakes, and in expeditions for the collection of plants for food, yucca roots for head washing, materials for the manufacture of pots and plaques, and fagots for fuel.

The Hopi possess neither a federal government nor a supreme chief. Each pueblo is politically independent, although on rare occasions of great public calamity the chiefs of different villages meet for discussion, prayer, and occasionally for combined action. Within a pueblo authority is chiefly theocratic and is vested in a council of hereditary clan chiefs, who are also heads of religious fraternities and often of kiva organization. No sharp distinction is made between religious, civil, and secular duties. Succession to office, like inheritance, almost always follows the female line. A man's sister's son, not his own son, succeeds him in office, with some right of selection accorded to the previous incumbent. Certain members of the council hold special offices, and the Village Chief, who is usually head of the Bear Clan, directs all council activities and exercises a right of veto on proposals coming before the council. In Hopi theory the Village Chief owns in trust all the land around the pueblo, all the houses, and the crops; the people are considered to be his "children" and call him "father." Therefore, he decides all disputes about land and most of those about property. He is required to keep a "good heart" and not to become angry, lest the people suffer. A Crier Chief makes public the decisions of the council and announces impending ceremonies as well as other public functions. A War Chief (*Kaletaka*) assists the Village Chief in the supervision of affairs and in the settlement of all disputes. Laws are traditional and unwritten, infractions are few, and penalties are rare—other than ridicule and social ostracism, which can be very sharp. There are no courts, no policemen, and no fines except those imposed by the agents of the United States Government. Theft in former days was very rare indeed; and murder by violence is practically unknown. Disagreements, arguments, and troubles of various kinds do arise to upset the community but they manage to get themselves settled without overt danger to anyone, perhaps owing to the strong traditions against violence. The decisions of the council and Village

Chief are regarded as final by everyone; indeed, individuals say they would have to leave the village if the Chief ordered them to do so. The political functions of the village are entirely in the hands of the "hierarchy" of hereditary priests operating under religious sanctions, for its council is chiefly a religious body, which, in order to maintain its purity of mind, does not meddle in quarrels unless absolutely necessary.

There are practically no generally recognized class demarcations that have much bearing upon social participation. However, certain clans are regarded as more important than others by reason of the offices or ceremonies which they control and of traditional accounts of what they have contributed to the welfare of the village.

Every adult male is a member of a kiva group—there were once thirteen or more in Oraibi—which represents another formal type of organization in Hopi society. Membership in a kiva group is usually arranged by the ceremonial father. Don became a member of the *Tawaopi* (Sun Hill) kiva through his ceremonial father, and later inherited ownership of the kiva through his uncle, Talasquaptewa. It is in this kiva that the Soyal ceremony has been performed in recent years. Membership in a kiva is never confined to one clan, for ceremonial fathers are never of the same clan as their sons. Although much economic and social activity goes on in a kiva, its main use is for the performance of ceremonies. During a ceremony members of a kiva who are not participants move out, since most of the ritual is secret. Women are not allowed in the kivas—except the Marau kiva, which they own—unless to attend Katcina dances or as special participants in a ceremony.

In each pueblo the Hopi are organized into exogamous, matrilineal clans, which usually extend throughout the tribe, are totemically named, and are loosely linked into phratries, which are likewise exogamous. Each clan is composed of one or more lineages, closely associated with a "household." The individual's ceremonial and daily life is regulated by a more or less systematic classificatory system of kinship (Crow type), which is based in part upon genealogical relationships. Residence is matrilocal, and descent, inheritance, and succession are matrilineal. Beyond the basic differentiation of relatives the Hopi have numerous methods of extending the range of kinship, and an individual may be potentially related in some manner to the majority of persons in both the village and the tribe. In many instances there are multiple forms of relationship which the individual may utilize as he chooses. There are also means of extending kinship to other clans and even tribes by adoption and by the recognition of relationship through the same totemic names.

The kinship system is fundamental to both the social organization of the Hopi and the participation of the individual in his society. It regulates most of his interpersonal relations and may be said to afford a sort of blueprint of his "social personality." It establishes his potential status and role, formulates an elaborate network of relationships between himself and scores or even hundreds of other persons, provides standardized formulas of social interaction, and insures for him numerous rights, privileges, and obligations which are in part reciprocal. It also specifies and conventionalizes the degree of permissible approach and necessary avoidance in more intimate personal affairs such as early childhood dependency, parental and sibling relations, courtship and marriage, and participation in fraternal life, as well as in economic, ceremonial, and recreational activities. No person in Hopi society ever makes use of all his kinship prerogatives: he reciprocates in many, probably neglects a majority, exploits a few, and is in turn exploited. Whenever two or more individuals meet in Hopi society, the first act is to establish the relationship of each to the other, and from there on behavior usually follows a customary and almost ritualized course. Indeed, in the association of men with women, neglect to establish the fact of relationship may lead to critical consequences, as in the case of Don's first love affair.

The importance of kinship in the regulation of personal behavior appeared so obvious in the present study that information on this point was gathered in considerable detail and an effort was made to construct a "social map," or kinship chart, which would indicate the relationship to Don of every individual who plays any important role in the life history. It also proved useful to develop a key formula descriptive of the various categories and degrees of relationship involved, so that the reader could look up the name of any person in an alphabetical list and see roughly what relationship he held to Don.[3]

The Hopi have peopled the imaginary world with hosts of supernatural agents. In fact, they hold that nearly everything in nature possesses spirits, and that some of them are far more powerful than others. Their reverence for their dead relatives and communion with them also suggest ancestor worship. In Hopi belief all prosperity depends upon propitiating the deities. Crude rock shrines are erected to them in the villages and fields and at far-distant places; and some shrines are equipped with figurines and images. Within an environment where survival is difficult at best, almost as much effort is expended in worship as in work. "If we could pick the threads of religion from the warp and woof of Hopi life there apparently would not be much left."[4]

In briefest summary, according to Don and other Oraibians, the Hopi gods may be listed in the following order of importance. The Sun is the highest god. He ("Our Father") is believed to be a strong, middle-aged "man," who makes daily journeys across the sky, lights and heats the world, and sustains all life. In the far-distant oceans to the east and west live two aged goddesses of hard substance (Hurung Wuhtis), who still answer Hopi prayers. Associated with the Sun are the Moon and Star gods (both male and female) who assist him in his important work. Eagle and Hawk deities also live in the sky and look after the interest of the people. Lesser sky gods are the wind, lightning, thunder, rain, and rainbow deities. Serpent deities live in the springs and control the water supply. Below these gods in rank are the Six-Point-Cloud-People, departed ancestors who visit Oraibi in billowy clouds and drop a little rain on the parched lands. Masau'u, the god of fire and death, is master of the underworld of spirits but resides also in shrines near the Hopi villages. He is a restless nightwalker who carries a firebrand and guards the people while they sleep. Muyingwa lives below the earth with his wife and looks after the germination of all seeds and the growth of plants. The old Spider Woman (who is

3. For a guide to kinship see Appendix, pp. 451–465.

4. Walter Hough, *The Hopi Indians*, p. 71. 1915, Cedar Rapids.

also the Salt Woman) lives with her grandsons, the Twin War gods, in a shrine near each village, but resides also at many other distant places. She, with the War gods, protects the interest of all good and faithful Hopi. There are a Corn-Mother and her Corn-Maidens who watch over the maize plants, and the Mother-of-Wild-Animals who rewards the hunters with game. The Katcinas, ancestral spirits, are in contact with the Oraibians six months of every year and promote the prosperity of the village with their masked dancing and by conveying the prayers of the people to the more important gods. Every person also has a Spirit Guide who may protect him from danger and direct his course throughout life. In addition to these and other well-known supernatural agents there are many unidentified spirits—both benign and malignant—who frequent Oraibi and must be avoided, coerced, or propitiated.

The Hopi ceremonies are extremely complicated, predominantly religious, and usually performed for the express purpose of insuring rain, promoting the growth of crops, and safeguarding health and long life. Each ceremony has a special place in the calendar, is associated with a fraternity which is responsible for its observance, is "owned" by a particular clan which provides the Chief Priest, and is performed in a certain kiva. Membership in a fraternity is made up of different clansmen whose induction involves elaborate initiation rites. Although a few persons are accepted through trespass into tabooed areas or by treatment for disease by a ranking priest, new members are usually sponsored by ceremonial "fathers" or "mothers."

When Don was a small boy there were at least thirteen fraternities in Oraibi. The Katcina society included all persons above the age for initiation (seven to eleven years). Some Katcinas were also inducted into the Powamu fraternity to serve as "fathers and mothers" of the Katcinas. The Wowochim with its three related fraternities—Ahl, Tao, and Kwani—was exclusively for men, and membership in one of them was necessary for adult status in the tribe and for active participation in the Soyal ceremony. The Soyal fraternity consisted of Wowochim men, with the Village Chief as High Priest, and a few women who held very special positions. The Snake, Antelope, Blue Flute, and Gray Flute fraternities were responsible for the more important ceremonies performed in the summer months. There were also three women's societies—Marau, Lakon, Ooqol—which performed ceremonies in the fall to celebrate the harvesting of crops. Formerly there were "clowning" fraternities, although persons could perform as clowns without being members of them. Also, there were once "curing" fraternities, or at least a "Fire Fraternity" (Yaya) for the treatment of burns. Old Tuvenga was a member of this society. There was likewise a Kaletaka or Warrior fraternity, the qualifications of membership in which required the taking of a scalp and nightly vigilance in guarding the village. Talasvuyauoma was the War Chief of this society. It is commonly asserted that the Bowakas, evil-minded witches who possess "two hearts," have a secret fraternity where they frequently meet at night to promote mischief. At one time there was an "eye seeker" society (Poboctu), engaged in healing diseases and in counteracting the evil influences of the Bowakas.

In addition to the more serious ritualistic ceremonies, there are social ceremonies such as the Buffalo, Butterfly, and Eagle dances, which are performed in fall or spring to bring moisture and insure good crops. Every ceremony consists of secret, esoteric, and very complicated rituals performed in the kiva—e.g., smoking, fasting, prayers, songs, dances, medicine making, and altar worship—and at public dances, and the running of foot races or the performance of rituals in the plaza or at sacred springs or shrines. Strict continence is required of all actual participants during the ceremony and for four days thereafter. Many ceremonies are concluded with feasts and the distribution of food or other gifts. Some ceremonies are repeated on a smaller scale semiannually. Considerable social pressure is brought to bear upon the leaders of the ceremonies to keep pure minds and hearts, to perform the rituals letter-perfect, and thus to protect the people from misfortunes.

The Hopi ceremonial year may be said to begin in late November with the opening of the Wowochim ceremony, which is associated with the generation of new fires, the worship of Masau'u, and the initiation of new members, which customarily occurs every four years. The elaborate initiatory rites symbolize the change from youth to manhood. The Wowochim is performed by the Wowochim, Ahl,

Tao, and Kwani fraternities and is believed to portray what happened in the underworld and how the Hopi managed to escape. New fire is kindled by drill in the Kwani kiva, while the High Priest of the Kwani fraternity impersonates Masau'u, after which offerings are carried to the shrines of this great god of fire and death.

The Soyal ceremony follows soon after Wowochim in December and is under the direction of the Soyal fraternity. All Wowochim, Ahl, Tao, and Kwani members coöperate and, in fact, all officials and clan chiefs participate. Everyone in the village is deeply concerned in the performance of this elaborate ceremony, the making of *pahos,* and the offering of prayers and sacrifices for the welfare of everything in Hopi life—indeed, in the whole world. The ceremony is associated with the winter solstice and the Sun god, who is believed to control all life and to perform the same ceremony at his southern "house" before returning north. There is a simpler summer-solstice ceremony performed annually by the chief of the Sun Clan. Don has participated in the Soyal for thirty years, has been an important official in it as Chief of the Sun Clan, and now owns the kiva in which it is performed. He probably knows the entire ceremony in all its elaborate detail and certainly regards its performance as the most important obligation in his life.

The Powamu ceremony, observed in February, is controlled by the Chief of the Badger Clan with the assistance of the Katcina Chief. It consists of growing beans in the kivas, keeping vigils, the performance of an elaborate ritual, the initiation of children into the Powamu and Katcina fraternities, and welcoming large numbers of returning Katcinas. The deity of germination is impersonated by the Powamu priest, and the emergence of the Hopi from the underworld is dramatized—particularly the origin and migrations of the Badger Clan. The Powamu ceremony is said to be held in order to melt the snows, banish cold weather, and prepare the fields and gardens for planting. A fine growth of bean sprouts is regarded as a good omen for a rich harvest.

From December until July, and particularly from the conclusion of the Powamu ceremony, both masked and unmasked Katcina dances are very popular in all the villages. There are no prescribed dates for these dances. During the winter months they are usually held at night within the kiva but in summer they are performed in the plazas and last all day. A dance is sponsored by an individual who wishes to receive a special blessing such as recovery from a disease, or to insure the prosperity of the entire village. The dances are under the supervision of the High Priest of the Katcina fraternity, who is also Chief of the Katcina Clan. He is assisted by a "Katcina father" of the Powamu society, and other "fathers" are likely to participate in the ceremony. The Katcina dancers are men, although they impersonate women. Don maintains that in these dances he has enjoyed the greatest pleasures of his life.

In July is observed the Niman or farewell dance of the Katcinas. This is a home-coming festival for Hopi everywhere. It is an especially happy day for the children, for the Katcinas bring great loads of corn, beans, melons, peaches, and other gifts to them, including new Katcina dolls and brightly painted bows and arrows. This is the dance at which the brides of the year make their appearance and the men break spruce boughs from the costumes of the Katcinas and plant them in their fields with prayers for their crops. The Katcinas depart westward and are not seen again until the next December. On the following day the sacred eagles and hawks are strangled and prayerfully dispatched to their "home."

In August of even-numbered years, according to the Christian calendar, the Snake and Antelope ceremonies are performed jointly, alternating with the Blue and Gray Flute ceremonies in odd-numbered years. They are for the propitiation of the Snake deities and to insure plenty of spring water and abundant rain for the maturing crops. The ceremonies dramatize the legends of the Snake Clan and the Snake Priests gather their "elder brothers"—rattlers, bull snakes, and others—wash them ritually, and carry them in their teeth during the public dance. They are then released with prayers to convey to the Rain deity. Only the pure in mind and heart can dance successfully with the very wise and sacred snake in his mouth. In the Flute ceremony a pilgrimage is made to the spring, a ritual is performed, and a priest dives to the bottom of the pool to bring up pahos and ritual objects. Then the procession returns to the village and performs at the shrines in the plaza, accompanied by the blowing of an old and sacred flute. Although Don tried to become a member of the Snake society by trespass, going into the territory where the men were hunting snakes, he failed twice.

In September of even-numbered years the Lakon, or Women's Basket dance, is performed; and in October of odd-numbered years the women's Marau and Ooqol ceremonies are observed. All three ceremonies have much in common and are said to be held in honor of the goddess of germination. Altars are set up in the kivas where the elaborate rites are observed. The ceremonies conclude with a Basket dance in the plaza and the public distribution of various small gifts—plaques, baskets, household utensils, food, and other articles. Competitors wrestle vigorously for these gifts. Although Don's grandfather, Homikniwa, was Assistant Chief Priest of the Ooqol, Don has never participated in these ceremonies other than as an interested spectator and competitor for the gifts.

Even at the time of Don's birth (1890) factions had arisen in Oraibi which threatened to disrupt the ceremonies. These culminated in the "Split" in 1906 when many people moved to Hotavila. The ceremonies were gradually discontinued until now only the Powamu and the Soyal are observed at Oraibi with anything like their complete ritual. But in recent years many of them have been revived in Hotavila where the Oraibi people attend, often as envious spectators.

Don's life spans the period in which the ceremonies have disintegrated and the old village of Oraibi has dropped in population from more than 1,000 to about 125. He is keenly aware of the fact that the ceremonies will never be revived in their traditional purity and that Old Oraibi will soon be another pueblo ruin. But he holds steadfastly to the orthodox teachings of his uncles and fathers as the "only way of life" for him and is a conservative and loyal supporter of the Village Chief.

For a comprehensive bibliography on the Hopi see George P. Murdock, *Ethnographic Bibliography of North America*. Yale Anthropological Studies, Vol. I, pp. 142–145. New Haven, 1941, Yale University Press.

Autobiography

I

Twins Twisted into One

WHEN WE WERE WITHIN our mother's womb, we happened to hurt her. She has told me how she went to a medicine man in her pain. He worked on her, felt her breasts and belly, and told her that we were twins. She was surprised and afraid. She said, "But I want only one baby." "Then I will put them together," replied the doctor. He took some corn meal outside the door and sprinkled it to the sun. Then he spun some black and white wool, twisted the threads into a string, and tied it around my mother's left wrist. It is a powerful way to unite babies. We twins began, likewise, to twist ourselves into one child. My mother also helped to bring us together by her strong wish for only one baby.

My mother has described how carefully she carried me. She slept with my father right along, so that he could have intercourse with her and make me grow. It is like irrigating a crop: if a man starts to make a baby and then stops, his wife has a hard time. She had intercourse only with my father so that I could have an easy birth and resemble him.

She refused to hold another woman's child on her lap and took care not to breathe into the face of small children and cause them to waste away. She had nothing to do with the tanning of skins or the dyeing of anything lest she spoil the goods and also injure me. When she grew big, she was careful to sit in such a way that other people would not walk in front of her and thus make my birth difficult. She

25

would not look at the serpent images displayed in the ceremonies, lest I turn myself into a water snake while still in her womb and raise up my head at the time of birth, instead of lying with head down seeking a way out.

My father has related how he took care to injure no animal and thus damage my body. If he had cut off the foot of any living creature, I might have been born without a hand or with a clubfoot. Any cruel treatment of a dumb beast would have endangered my life. If he had drawn a rope too tightly around the neck of a sheep or burro, it might have caused my navel cord to loop itself about my neck and strangle me in birth. Even if I had been able to free myself from the cord, I might have remained half choked and short of breath for a long time.

Whenever I made movements in the womb, my mother was encouraged to expect an early and easy birth. She worked hard at cooking, grinding corn, and bringing water, so that her body would be in trim for labor. My father fed her the raw flesh of a weasel and rubbed the skin on her body so that I could be active and come out swiftly, in the way that sly little animal slips through a hole.

I have heard that I had a hard birth. It began in the early evening of a day in March, 1890. Since the exact date was not remembered, I could never have a birthday. When my mother's face darkened and she felt the expected pains, she settled down on the earthen floor in the third-story room of her Sun Clan house. She had sent my five-year-old sister Tuvamainim with my little brother Namostewa to a neighbor's house. Namostewa was about two years old and still nursing.

My grandfather (mother's father, Homikniwa of the Lizard Clan), who lived in the same house with my mother and father, has told me how he climbed the ladder to the third floor where my mother lay. There he rubbed her belly and turned me straight to come out. The power in his hands helped her womb. His presence encouraged her, too, because he was the best medicine man in Oraibi. My father, Tuvanimptewa of the Sand Clan, also came in to help, which was rather unusual for a Hopi husband. He soon sent for Nuvaiumsie, an experienced old midwife and a member of his father's linked Water-Coyote Clan. As soon as she came, she heated water in a clay pot over coals in an old-fashioned fireplace in the southwest corner of the room.

In labor, according to all reports, my mother moved over on a pile of sand which was especially prepared for my birth, rested herself on hands and knees, raised her head a little, and began to strain downward. My father and her father took turns standing over her with their arms around her belly, pressing down gently and trying to force and shake me out. If I had refused to come, more and more pressure would have been applied, but no Hopi doctor would have opened her body to get me.

I was a big baby. I caused a lot of trouble and took a long time coming out—head first. Old Nuvaiumsie is said to have taken me fresh and crying from my mother. She cut my navel cord on an arrow to make me a good hunter, folded back my end of the cord, and tied it about a finger's length from the navel to keep out any fresh air. She used a piece of string from my mother's hair, which was the proper thing to do. If she had not tied the cord securely, fresh air would have entered my belly and killed me. My mother was given some small twigs of juniper to chew and some juniper tea, in order to strengthen her and to hasten the discharge of the afterbirth.

My grandfather, my father, and Nuvaiumsie examined me closely. Sure enough, I was twins twisted into one. They could see that I was an oversize baby, that my hair curled itself into two little whorls instead of one at the back of my head, and that in front of my body I was a boy but at the back there was the sure trace of a girl—the imprint of a little vulva that slowly disappeared. They have told me time after time that I was twice lucky—lucky to be born twins and lucky to just miss becoming a girl.

Wrapping me in a cloth, they laid me near the fire and waited for my mother to free herself from the afterbirth. Nuvaiumsie is reported to have taken hold of the free end of the placenta cord and pulled gently, while my father stood behind my mother, held her around the waist, and shook her. She was told to stick her fingers down her throat and gag until she expelled the afterbirth. Finally it came out. Then my mother was placed near the fire in a squatting position on a low stool—perhaps the Hopi birth stool—so that the blood could drip upon the sand. She was given a drink of warm juniper tea to clear out the womb. A little later Nuvaiumsie bathed her in warm yucca suds, wrapped her in a blanket, fed her some warm corn mush, and had her lie on her side before the fire so that the bones could fit back into place. The old lady carefully swept up the sand and blood from the floor with a little broom, placed them with the placenta, the dirty rags, and the broom in an old basket, sprinkled the whole with corn meal, and gave them to my father to throw on the placenta pile. This he did at a special place near the southeast edge of the village, so that no person would step upon them and cause his feet to become sore and chapped, his eyes yellow, and his urine thick.

When all bloody traces of the birth were removed, my father hastened to the house of his mother's sister, Masenimka. He would have fetched his own mother, had she been alive. Masenimka came quickly, bringing a bowl of water, some corn meal, a piece of yucca root, two white corn ears, and some baby wrappings. She came with a smiling face and a happy heart, hoping thereby to bring me good luck and to insure my having a cheerful spirit.

Masenimka has related how she greeted me with tender words, washed my head in warm yucca suds, rinsed it with clear water, and bathed me from head to foot. She rubbed the ashes of juniper or sage bush over my skin to make it smooth and to cause hair to grow only in the right places. Then she pulled up her black dress (*manta*) to her thighs, rested me on her naked knees, and announced that I was her boy and a child of her clan. Chewing some juniper twigs, she spat upon my ear lobes and rubbed them to numbness. Then she pierced them with a sharp instrument and passed a thread through the holes to keep them open. She placed my arms by my sides, wrapped me in a warm baby blanket, and laid me on a wicker cradle made of a frame of bent juniper branches which was filled in with a network of small lemonberry stems and other twigs. There was a face guard of the same material. The cradle was padded with cedar bark or old clothes. A larger blanket was wrapped about me and the cradle and bound tightly with a string. Masenimka sat before the fire with me in the cradle upon her knees for a long time. Then she placed me on the floor near my mother and put an ear of corn on either side, one to represent me and the other my mother.

In the early morning hours when the cocks began to crow, Masenimka took a little finely ground corn meal and rubbed four horizontal lines, one inch wide and six or seven inches long, one above the other, on the four walls of the room. Then she resumed her seat by my mother and me and said, "Now, thus I have made a house for you. You shall stay here while we wait for you twenty days." Soon after she went to her own home and brought over some corn which she cooked with a few small twigs of juniper. This food was to make my mother's milk flow freely. Masenimka might have given her some unsalted gravy and some milkweed for the same purpose, since when that weed is broken the milk runs out.

Before the eastern sky had turned gray, the Sun Clan women propped two poles against the door that faced the rising sun and draped a blanket over them. This was to keep out the sun's rays from the birth chamber, for they were considered harmful until I had been properly presented to the Sun god. By breakfast many neighbors are said to have dropped in, taken a little food, looked me over, congratulated my mother, and expressed best wishes for my life.

I was bathed again by my godmother, Masenimka, who rubbed me anew with juniper ashes or the powder of a special clay found near the village. After my bath I was fastened back in my cradle and given the breast. My brother may have thought that I was stealing his milk, but he could do nothing about it. If my mother had been dry, I would have received the breast of a relative, fed upon finely ground sweet corn mixed with the juice of stewed peaches, been given a little gravy without salt, or perhaps some milk from the cows of the missionaries. If I had taken the breast of another woman, her own nursing baby might have discovered the theft of milk, worried, and even become nervous or sick. Babies are pretty wise about these things and quickly learn what is going on. I could not have taken the breast of another pregnant woman, for that might have caused my death.

For twenty days my mother was not allowed to eat or drink anything cold or salty, lest blood clot in her womb. All her food was cooked with juniper leaves. The fire in our room was kept going. No one was permitted to kindle other fires from it, for this fire belonged to me and such a theft would have made me unhappy. If it had become extinguished through accident, it would have been rekindled immediately, and that day would have gone uncounted. No food could be cooked on the coals themselves, although it might be cooked in a vessel over the fire. Neglect of this rule would have made me a "fire meddler" and caused me to play with fire carelessly in childhood. My father could not have intercourse with my mother during those twenty days, nor for twenty days thereafter. If he had done so before all the blood had drained from my mother's womb, a new baby would have been started which would have worried me, brought on sickness and nervous spells, and perhaps spoiled me for life. Had he attempted intercourse, the sisters and clan sisters of my mother would have interfered. If he had had intercourse with some other woman and then had an argument with my mother over it, that would have been almost as hard on me, for I would have sensed that something was wrong.

A routine was set up for me. Every morning I was unbound, bathed, rubbed with "baby ashes," and put back on the cradle. A little pad of cloth was placed at the back of my neck to keep me from becoming bull-necked and soft cedar bark was placed under my buttocks to drain off the urine. Someone probably cleaned me three or four times a day. I was always fed in the cradle and could move only my head a little in nursing. I do not know that anyone took saliva from my mouth and rubbed it on the nape of my neck to conceal my crying from the evil spirits, as is done with many Hopi babies.

When my navel cord dried and dropped off, it was tied to an arrow and stuck beside a beam overhead in the room. This was to make me a good hunter and to provide a "house" for my infant spirit in case I died, for my soul could then stay by the arrow in the ceiling and quickly slip back into my mother's womb for an early rebirth.

On the fifth morning I was bathed as usual, but with a special application of yucca suds to my head. My mother's head also was washed with the suds, and her body bathed with warm water in which juniper leaves had been boiled. Her clothes were changed and the soiled ones were taken to a near-by rock cistern and washed. After our bath my mother scraped off the lowermost of the four lines of meal from the walls of the room. She took the scrapings in her hand, and going to the edge of the mesa, held them to her lips, prayed for my long life, and sprinkled the meal to the rising sun. On the tenth and fifteenth days the same ceremony of bathing and prayers to the sun was repeated. If I had been the first baby, my mother could not have gone out before the sun on the fifth day and thereafter. Had she been too sick or weak to go, my godmother would have gone for her. The water with which our bodies had been bathed was carried to the placenta pile and emptied there.

On the twentieth day of my life I was named according to strict custom. About four o'clock in the morning Masenimka and her sisters, Kewanmainim and Iswuhti, and many other clan aunts—any woman of my father's clan and linked clans—came to our house to wash our heads again. Masenimka first washed the two "mother corn" ears in the yucca suds, rinsing them with fresh water. These were the ears that had been by my side since the night of my birth. Then she washed my mother's head, as did all her sisters in turn. Fresh water was poured over it, after which her hair was wrung out dry. They also bathed her arms and shoulders with warm water which had a few sprigs of juniper in it. Sweeping a little sand from the corner into the center of the room, they heated a stone, set it upon the sand, and laid yucca roots and juniper leaves on top of it. My mother stood with her right foot and then her left resting upon this heap of sand, stones, roots, and leaves while Masenimka bathed them. The entire heap was then placed in a tray along with the broom that was used to sweep the floor. The last of the corn-meal lines from each wall was scraped off and the dust thrown on the tray. A live ember from the fireplace was put on top and the fire permitted to go out. One of the women took the tray and its contents and some of the bath water and carried them to the placenta pile.

Within a few minutes the customary naming ceremony began. Masenimka unfastened the wrappings that bound me to the cradle, stripped me bare, and washed my head in a bowl of yucca suds. Then she bathed me from head to foot, rubbing on the "baby ashes." My head was rinsed in fresh water and each of my many aunts bathed me in the same manner, one after the other. The last one handed me back to Masenimka, who wrapped me in a blanket that had been warmed by the fire. My bath water—like my mother's—was handled with care and carried out to the placenta pile. During so many baths I probably cried a little, but no one has reported it.

Masenimka took me again on her left arm, picked up my "mother corn" ears with her right hand, waved them forward over my chest, and said, "May you live always without sickness, travel along the Sun Trail to old age, and pass away in sleep without pain. And your name shall be Chuka." Chuka means mud, a mixture of sand and clay. Masenimka and my father are of the Sand Clan, which made my name appropriate. This name was a sign to everyone that although I was born into the Sun Clan of my mother I was also a "child of the Sand Clan" and that my father and all his clan relatives had a claim on me. Each aunt repeated the ceremony and each gave me another Sand, Lizard, Earth, or Snake Clan name, but they have been forgotten. Even if I had never been told these things about myself I could be sure that they happened, for there is no other way for a new child to get a good name among the Hopi.

After the naming ceremony most of the women went back to their houses. But just before sunrise Masenimka placed me in a blanket upon her back and started with my mother to the edge of the mesa where they were to present me to the Sun god. Each took along a pinch of corn meal, and my mother carried my pair of mother-corn ears. They stopped with me southeast of the village where the trail leaves the mesa. This is a kind of "highway" of the Sun god, the main Sun Trail for the Oraibi people.

My mother took me with the cradle and blanket from Masenimka's back and placed me on the right arm of my godmother. Masenimka, thus holding me before the Sun god, breathed a silent prayer on a pinch of meal which she held in her right hand. Then she uncovered my face to the early dawn with her left hand in the proper way, rubbed some of the sacred corn meal between my lips, and threw the rest to the rising sun. She then sucked the meal from my lips with her mouth and blew it toward the east four times. Taking the ears of corn from my mother, she extended them toward the east with a circular motion from right to left and brought them close up to my chest four times. As she concluded she prayed again for my long life and called out to the Sun god the different names that I had received, in order that he might hear them and recognize me. It was my mother's privilege to take me in her arms and repeat the same ceremony, but it is not required by Hopi rules, and I have never learned whether she did it or not.

When we returned to the house where my father had just washed his own head in yucca suds, a big breakfast feast was served to relatives and friends. They were invited to eat *piki* (native wafer bread), boiled meat mixed with hominy, puddings, and other choice foods. Masenimka received a big load of food in payment for her services as my godmother and carried it home on her back. Many of my mother's sisters and clan sisters were present and were all called my "mothers," while the sisters and clan sisters of my father were called my "aunts." The Sun Clan men who came and ate were called my "uncles," while my father's brothers and clan brothers were all called my "fathers." Almost everyone praised my mother, made hopeful remarks about me, and predicted that I would become a good hunter, a fine herder, and perhaps a powerful healer, for I was a special baby—twins twisted into one. There was no doubt about this, for they could see the two whorls of hair on the back of my head, and those present at my birth told others how large and double-sexed I looked when fresh from the womb. All knew that such babies are called antelopes because these animals are usually born twins. It was anticipated, therefore, that I would have a special power to protect myself, do many strange things before the people, and be able to heal certain diseases, even as a boy. My mother, father, and grandfather made careful note of these signs and sayings and were prepared to fill my mind with them as soon as I could know anything.

I have learned little about my babyhood, except such treatment as is shared by all Hopi children. The first three or four months of my life were spent on my back on the cradle. Like other babies, my hands were bound securely so that I could not awaken myself by movements, and it is reported that I was a good sleeper. Even when awake I rarely had a chance to touch my face or body, and my legs were wrapped in blankets which prevented much kicking. The cradle was placed flat on the floor and the face guard was usually covered with a cloth to exclude flies, but this also kept me in semidarkness. The back of my head flattened itself against the cradle.

I had many kinds of soft food stuck into my mouth and I could get the breast almost any time I cried. My mother was almost always present but I could touch or nestle up to her very little, for I was off the cradle only to be cleaned or for a morning bath, and was rebound before nursing. Of course the people talked baby talk to me, passed me from lap to lap on the cradle, rocked or shook me to sleep on their knees, and often sang to me. I am sure my father and grandfather sang many songs with me on their laps at the close of the day, and before I could remember anything.

At mealtime my cradle was placed on the floor near the food, and first one and then another member of the family would chew up a morsel—piki, stewed meat, dried peaches, corn mush, cantaloupe or watermelon—and feed me from their fingers.

By early fall I was permitted off the cradle during the day and crawled naked over the earthen floor or rolled about in the sunshine on the roof of our winter house. I urinated any time and at any place, but whenever I started to defecate, someone picked me up and held me just outside the door. Dogs, cats, and my brother were my constant playmates. My sister became my nurse and often carried me wrapped in a blanket on her back. On other occasions my mother ground corn with me fastened to her back, or took me with her to the spring or rock cisterns for water. But she often left me to play on the ground under the watchful eye of her crippled brother, Naquima, who lived with us. I had now learned to suck my thumb, my "whole fist," reports my father. I had probably discovered pleasure in my penis, too, for every male child was tickled in his private parts by adults who wished to win smiles and sometimes to stop crying. No doubt other children, including my brother and sister, played with me in the same way.

Whenever the Katcinas danced in the plaza, my mother or some relative sat on the ground with me on their laps and held out my infant hands to receive gifts—peaches, apples, sweet corn, and other blessings.

From left to right: Homikniwa, Gladys, Hahaye (Don's Mother), Don in Mother's Lap, Ira, Naquima.

Before the snows came, we moved down the ladder to our winter house, where I could play on the floor all day and stay up by the fire at night until I wished to sleep. I still slept on my cradle after I had begun to walk and talk at about two. It seemed that I was restless without it. My mother has told me how I would drag it to her crying, "Ache," which means sleep. But several people have agreed that I was never a cry baby. I was healthy, grew rapidly, and surpassed other babies in size. I was still nursing when my mother gave birth to another child. This baby died, so I kept on getting the breast.

2

Childhood Crises and Early Memories

WHEN MY INFANT BROTHER died at birth something happened to my
mother's womb to prevent the coming of children for several years.
As a result I remained the "baby" and continued to nurse for a long
time. But my strange antelope ways were showing up fast. Before I
was two I climbed high on a top shelf to the surprise of my parents,
who said no ordinary child could do that. One summer day I crawled,
naked, into a water jar about three feet high. When they discovered
me in the jar they were frightened for fear I might drown. My mother
reached in and pulled on my arm, but I refused to come out and cried
to be left alone. She fussed with me for a while, then took up a hatchet
to strike the jar and crack it. My grandfather cautioned her, "You
know he is twins formed into one. He has a special power and will
come out when he wants to." They have reported that I kept close
watch on them and slipped out when they were not looking. Later
they found me lying in the sunshine drying myself. They had noticed
that whenever I was caught using my special power I appeared sad
and upset.

I often climbed about on the housetops like a mountain goat. It
seemed that I could go anywhere without getting hurt, because of
my antelope powers. But whenever I did fall and hurt myself a little,
somebody usually punished me with blows, just the same as if I had
been an ordinary child.

I would wander from the house out into the road and in front of the horses. My mother made a rope of rawhide, tied it to my ankle, and fastened the other end to a stone. I cried and cried but had to get used to it. One day when my mother started to grind corn she forgot to tie me. I took the rope and carried it to her. She laughed and said that I was a wise baby. When I got a little stronger I could move the stone a bit myself, but she noticed that and used a heavier one. Then one day my father lengthened the leash. That is one thing I have never forgotten.

When I was a little older I sometimes disappeared from the village and wandered into the gullies and among the large boulders. At first my parents worried, but later, when they missed me, they reminded each other that I had special power to protect myself. I could go almost anywhere on the mesa, choosing my course and finding my way back. Sometimes I gathered flowers, mostly wild sunflowers such as the deer feed upon, and ate a few like a young antelope. But my grandfather reports that I tried to hide my strange ways from other boys and that I must have known even then that I was a special person.

One day I became sick, shook with fits, foamed at the mouth, and stiffened out as if dead. My parents were frightened and took me to blind old Tuvenga of the Greasewood Clan, who was a fire doctor and also knew magic songs to sing over such an illness. They have described how he examined me closely and said that I had received this sickness from my mother who had been under the influence of an underworld man, a sorcerer, who had put magic antelope power upon her in order to win her favors. He said this had happened long before I was born, but that the trouble had been passed on to me. My mother said to the doctor, "If you will cure my boy, I will give him to you as your ceremonial son." Once more I was lucky. He sang his magic song over me and restored my life. Although blind, that old man had great knowledge and power. He said, "Now, my son, I have saved you from death. You are mine. I will protect you from the evil powers, and when you grow older, you will become eyes and feet to guide me wherever I want to go." I do not remember this trouble and treatment, but my mother and the old man kept them before my mind as soon as I began to pay attention to words.

A little later I was badly scalded. My mother had cooked some dumplings for breakfast and placed the clay pot by the door to cool. When she was not looking I bent over and reached my right hand into the pot. My left hand slipped, and my right arm went down into the hot dumplings. My mother hurried back with me to old Tuvenga of the Fire society. His daughter Honwuhti, who was also my father's clan mother, took me in her arms and walked the floor to comfort me. My doctor father had some juniper brought, cut it into kindling, and put it into the fire. When the sticks were blazing brightly he bit off the burning ends, chewed them up, and spat the bits into a bowl four times. Then he said, "My son, this will pain you a little, but it will help you too." He sucked my hand to draw out the fire and smeared the chewed charcoal over the burned places, remarking, "Now you will become well and strong. I am blind and partly paralyzed. Some day you will lead me about." Honwuhti took me in her lap and kept me in her house until the pain was gone and I fell asleep. When I awoke she gave me some good things to eat and took me back to my mother. I had learned a lesson—never to put my hands into hot places.

Old Tuvenga treated me like a real son. Whenever trouble came upon me my mother got his advice first. Often when he heard me playing in the plaza he would call me to take hold of his stick and lead him outside the village to relieve himself or to the Snake kiva to work. When difficulties arose at our house I would go over to Honwuhti's place where she gave me nice things to eat and let me watch her chickens. She was the kindest woman I knew and had the best food in her house. I often wished I had her for my godmother instead of Mase-nimka. Even my mother's sister Nuvahunka, who was also a "mother" to me, was not so kind and did not give me as many good things to eat, perhaps because she had three boys of her own.

My own mother was my best friend and my earliest memories are of her. She was always busy as a bee or an ant, cooking, grinding corn, bringing water, making baskets out of rabbit weed or pots out of clay. I well remember how my father frightened me over her when

I was perhaps three. It happened after the snow had disappeared in the springtime. We had moved back up the ladder into our summer house. My parents and I were sleeping in the same room where I was born. I was lying on a sheepskin in the northwest corner. When I awoke I heard struggling and felt the floor shaking. The noise and the movements made me wide awake. From the sounds that my mother was making I thought she was suffering and that my father must be killing her. I cried out and covered up my face and head with a blanket. Pretty soon they quieted down and my mother got up and came over to me with kind words. She lay down beside me, and I went back to sleep. The next morning at breakfast I felt angry, first at my father but later at my mother also, because she was still so kind and polite to him. The next night I slept with my grandfather in another room.

My brother worried me because we wanted the same things and fought over them. We both wanted to play with the big yellow dog and to claim the cat that brought in the young rabbits, small birds, and kangaroo rats. I especially wanted my brother's little bow and arrows and his top. One day when we both struggled for a sharp awl, he punched it into my left eye and nearly ruined it. I was never again able to see anything more than large moving objects with that eye. Nobody did anything about this accident.

My crippled uncle Naquima, who lived with us, was a good friend of mine. He often sat on the floor shelling corn or minding the babies for the neighbors. He and I were good pals from the first. He would tell me funny stories with his crooked mouth, making the words come out upside down. He would crawl about on his paralyzed legs, spinning tops or playing games with me. Sometimes he put me to sleep with his funny singing. He would take my side in most of my arguments with my brother, and although he punished me with blows a little himself, he never tattled when I got into mischief. He often picked lice off my head and played with my privates to give me pleasure. When we all sat on the floor around the family bowl of stew, he would pick out choice pieces for me. Sometimes I would strike poor old Naquima but I loved him too. I often slept on a sheepskin with him.

I kept wetting the bed clothing even when I was a good-size boy and probably four years old. My mother and father told me that this habit had to be stopped. But it seemed that in my sleep I forgot their warning. There was some talk about this among my relatives. My clan grandfather, Talasemptewa, the husband of my father's clan sister, warned me that if I did it again he would take me out in the early morning and roll me naked in the snow. The next time I forgot he did so, nearly freezing me. After a few nights I wet my bed again. He came and caught me, took me out southeast to one of the rock holes, let me down into the ice-cold water, and splashed it all over my head and back. I cried and cried; I stopped bed wetting too. He was one of the toughest men I knew. My real grandfather never did that to me.

There was another "grandfather," Talasweoma, the husband of another of my father's clan sisters, who was pretty rough to me. When it snowed we children rolled snowballs on the ground to make snow men. One morning before breakfast I was pushing a snowball downhill. This grandfather came up to me and caught hold of my hands. I was wrapped in a blanket but wore no other clothing except snow moccasins made of sheepskin. He stripped off my blanket, took hold of my wrists, put my arms around the snowball, drew me up close to it, and said, "Now I have caught you in a trap and today you are going to freeze up." While I stood hugging the snowball against my bare body, he laughed and told me to cry or I would die right there. Pretty soon I cried out. Then he let me go and said, "Now run home." At first I was not going to, but when he tried to catch me and bring me back to the snowball I ran all right. I heard that he laughed and told his wife, my "aunt," about it. She took my side, scolded him, and said that some day I would give him a lesson in return.

This man was terrible. He was always accusing me of some mischief, grabbing for my penis, and saying that he would cut it off. One day in the month of May he and his uncle, who was a very old man and my father's ceremonial father, corralled their sheep near the village on the southwest edge of the mesa. We children went out before breakfast to watch them castrate the rams and billy goats. Some of us were sitting on a rock near by. Talasweoma's son tied up and held the legs of the animals while he did the cutting. When breakfast time drew near he jumped up quickly, turned around, caught hold of my arm, pulled me into the corral, and said, "This is a boy I want to cut.

He is naughty. I caught him in my house trying to make love to my wife. I am going to castrate him. Then if he wants to live he cannot eat or drink for a number of days."

He fastened my hands together and drew up my legs in the way they tied the billy goats. While I lay on the ground, greatly frightened, he sharpened his knife carefully on a stone, watching me. He said, "Now after your balls are cut out, you will grow to be a nice-looking boy." The other children stood staring at me. I was crying. He got down over me, felt about my private parts, and tied a string tightly around them, just as he had done with the goats to check the bleeding. Then he took up his knife, rubbed it on a stone again, eyed me closely, and said, "Now your time has come." Seizing my privates, he rubbed his knife across them smooth with my body, as though he were cutting off everything. I struggled and yelled. But he was using the blunt edge of the knife. One of his grown sons took my side, saying, "Turn him loose; you will learn your lesson yet." This son unbound me and said, "Now, Chuka, when you get to be a big boy it will be your turn to do that to him."

That old man was laughing loudly when I started up the mesa in a fast run. I went crying to my mother. She said that he was my "grand-father" and that she could do nothing about it; but that when I became a big boy I could get even with him. She said that he had a right to tease me and that it showed how much he cared for me. His wife, who was my aunt, took my side, comforted me, and warned the terrible man that some day I would treat him the same way.

After I was four or five nearly all my grandfathers, father's sisters' and clan sisters' husbands, played very rough jokes on me, snatched at my penis, and threatened to castrate me, charging that I had been caught making love to their wives, who were my aunts. All these women took my part, called me their sweetheart, fondled my penis, and pretended to want it badly. They would say, "Throw it to me," reach out their hands as if catching it, and smack their lips. I liked to play with them but I was afraid of their rough husbands and thought they would castrate me. It was a long time before I could be sure that they meant only to tease.

My father never threatened me in that way. He was almost always kind and gentle. He let me sit by him while he carded and spun cotton or wool, or when he wove blankets in the kiva. Sometimes he took me to his field. He also let me ride about the village on a burro. In the evenings he took me on his lap and sang to me, stood me on the floor and lifted my feet up and down as in dancing, or told me stories. He also promised to teach me to be a good farmer and herder, and perhaps a weaver like himself.

My earliest memories of my real grandfather, Homikniwa, are full of kind feelings. I slept with him much of the time. In the mornings before sunrise he sang to me and told me stories. He took me to his fields, where I helped him to work or slept under a peach tree. Whenever he saw me make a circle on the ground he stepped cautiously around it, saying that he had to watch me lest I block his path with my antelope power. He kept reminding me of this power. He also took me through the fields to collect healing herbs. I watched him sprinkle corn meal and pray to the Sun god before picking off leaves or berries or digging medicine roots. Whenever mothers brought their sick children to our house, I watched him take their pinches of meal, step outside, pray, and sprinkle them to the Sun god, moon, or stars, and to his special medicine god. Then he would return to the patient, blow upon his hands, and begin his treatment. He was respected by all. Even Mr. Voth, the missionary, came to him to learn about plants and herbs. He taught the white man many things. He also taught me almost all I ever learned about plants.

Mr. Voth and the Christians came to Oraibi and preached Jesus in the plaza where the Katcinas danced. The old people paid no attention, but we children were told to accept any gifts and clothing. Mr. Voth never preached Christ to me alone but talked to us in groups. He said that Jesus Christ was our Saviour and suffered for our sins. He told us that Jesus was a good shepherd and that we were sheep or goats. We were to ask Jesus for whatever we wanted. Oranges and candy looked pretty good to me so I prayed for them. I said, "Jesus, give me some oranges and candy." Then I looked up into the sky but I never saw him throw anything down to me. Mr. Voth claimed that our gods were no good but the old people pointed out to us that when the Katcinas danced in the plaza it often rained. Even as a child I was taught that the missionaries had no business condemning our gods and that it might cause droughts and famine.

When I began to run around, I first wore shirts, without pants, which the missionaries gave us. We were told that Whites (*Bahanas*) did not like to see us naked. But we boys went without clothes most of the time unless someone warned us that Whites were climbing the mesa. We were always on the lookout for them. One day my father made shirts for my brother and me out of a couple of flour sacks. There was a beautiful deer's head printed on the backs. The other children stared at us with eyes shining, while we felt happy and up-to-date. But I was careless, and my mother sometimes scolded or spanked me for getting my clothes dirty. I did not seem to mind dirt.

In the summer Katcinas with great heads and fine clothes came into the plaza and danced. They almost never spoke but sang a great deal. An old man, called the Father of the Katcinas, sprinkled corn meal upon them, and our mothers carried loads of food to their resting place just outside the village. My father and others dressed as clowns and played funny jokes in the plaza. The Katcinas usually gave us gifts. At about sundown the old man, their "Father," asked them to go home and send us rain. They marched away toward the San Francisco mountains in the west. Everybody knew they were spirit gods.

In late summer when I was perhaps four, the men in the Snake and Antelope societies placed signs outside their kivas and our parents warned us to stay away. For several days the men came out in fancy costumes, lined up, and marched off the mesa in search of snakes. I wished to follow them and was told that some day I might be chosen as a Snake man. In the evenings the people told how many snakes had been caught and that some were large rattlers. We knew snakes were spirit gods who bring rains and never harm anyone with a good heart. We were told never to act silly and scream or yell like Whites when a snake goes toward them. My grandfather said that such foolish behavior spoiled the ceremony. When snakes were pleased with their treatment they were quiet and would bring rain as a reward.

On the last day of the ceremony great crowds of Whites and strange Indians came to Oraibi. They climbed over housetops, stood in doorways, and crowded into the plaza near the Snake kiva to see everything. Late in the afternoon the Antelope men entered the plaza in fine costumes and marched around the Snake house (*kisi*) four times, stamping their feet before it. Then the Snake members, painted and finely dressed, came with lively steps and circled the kisi in the same manner. Soon they were dancing with big live snakes in their hands and between their teeth. Some snakes wriggled and stuck out their tongues but others were quiet. My grandfather said later that dancers with the best hearts had the quietest snakes. When the serpents were placed in a circle on the ground they ran in every direction before the snake catcher could get them. Some Whites yelled and jumped back shamefully. A bull snake came toward me at the edge of the plaza. I did not cry but I was ready to run when the snake catcher picked it up. He was brave and had a good heart. I wanted to be a Snake man.

Every year at about the time of the first snow my grandfather said to me, "Grandson, this is a bad season. It is the time when parents have to watch their children closely. Don't be out after dark, don't go among unfriendly families, and don't sleep outside our own house. You might be captured by Two-Hearts (*Bowakas*), witches who would take you to their secret meeting place and make you a member of their underworld society. If that happened, you would hear death calls from time to time and would have to kill your own brothers and sisters, or some other relatives, in order to save your life. Sometimes these witches meet northeast of here in the valley where you see the cluster of large rocks. Don't go near that place. If you should ever be captured and carried away to the underworld kiva, the Two-Hearts will try to initiate you into their society. They will ask you, 'Whom do you choose for your secret ceremonial father?' Then you should answer, 'The Sun shall be my father.' They will then ask, 'Who shall be your ceremonial mother?' You should answer, 'The Corn Mother shall be my ceremonial mother.' If you remember to answer in this way they will release you and bring you back to the village, but they will try to persuade you to become a member and make you believe that you will be happy with them. You will be happy as a member of the underworld society only until you hear your death call. Then you will wander off alone and cry in the fields because you will have to betray your loved ones in order to prolong your own life. Now, my grandson, keep this in your heart and remember it always. Be very careful." My grandfather put piñon sap and soot on my forehead to protect me from the evil spirits that flock into Oraibi in December, but he said that this was of no help against the powerful Two-Hearts. He and others related how children could be touched by evil spirits or captured by Two-Hearts at night or even during the day when the wind blew hard. I was frightened and slept with him.

I also learned about Masau'u, the bloody headed Fire Spirit who guards the village at night and sometimes carries a torch. People said that to meet him face to face was a warning of death, and that to see even the fire was dangerous. My grandfather showed me where he lived in a shrine at the foot of the mesa. Everybody feared this god, so I feared him too and hoped that I would never see him or his fire.

When the Soyal ceremony was on in December, my uncle Talasquaptewa, the brother of my mother's mother, came out of the kiva early in the morning with medicine in his mouth and clay in his hands. Entering our house, he moistened the clay with medicine and rubbed a little on our breasts, backs, and limbs to protect us from sickness and death. A few days later, at sunrise, my mother took me to the east edge of the mesa with everybody else in the village to place prayer feathers on the shrines. These sacrifices bore messages to the gods in order to bring good luck. The people placed feathers in the ceiling of their houses and in all the kivas. They tied them to the ladders to prevent accidents, to the tails of burrows to give them strength, to goats, sheep, dogs, and cats to make them be fertile, and to the chicken houses to get more eggs. My grandfather fastened feathers to the branches of his fruit trees with prayers for better peaches, apples, and apricots. My father tied a prayer feather to my hair with a wish for my health and long life.

Later in the day male and female Katcinas with massive heads decorated with skins and feathers came into the plaza bringing gourd rattles, bows and arrows, and little bags of corn meal. They gave watermelons, piki, and other presents to us children. An old man sprinkled sacred corn meal upon the Katcinas while they danced and rubbed corn meal from their bags upon the four sides of the kiva hatchways. We were told that these spirit gods had come in answer to our prayers and to bring good luck. This was also the safest day for mothers to cut their children's hair without harm from evil spirits or Two-Hearts.

For four days the men went rabbit hunting. One afternoon the Soyal members came from the kiva naked, except for paint and loincloth, and went in single file to the second story of a special house (the Soyalmana's house). There four girls dashed cold water upon them to wash off the paint, while the men threw piki, squashes, watermelons, and other foods to the people who had gathered to watch. A race followed and there were Katcina dances and a feast. The old people said that all these things were important, that they pleased the gods and insured our lives.

One winter morning in February I saw a tall, strange Katcina (Hahai-i) coming into the village from the north side, blowing a bone whistle and uttering a long drawn "Hu-hu-huhuhu." When he entered the plaza women and children threw pinches of corn meal upon him and took sprigs of green corn and of spruce boughs from his tray. Two other Katcinas joined him near the kiva. Some men came out of the Powamu kiva where they were holding a ceremony, blew tobacco smoke on the backs of the Katcinas, and sprinkled them with corn meal. A number of different Katcinas, some running cross-legged (*hūūve*), came through the streets handing out gifts. Some of us received bows, arrows, rattles, and Katcina dolls (*tiku*). Other Katcinas came into the village bringing bean sprouts in baskets. We were in the plaza watching them. Suddenly my mother threw a blanket over my head. When she uncovered me the Katcinas were all gone and the people were looking up into the sky and watching them fly about— they said. I looked up but could see nothing. My mother laughed and said that I must be blind.

I later saw some giantlike Katcinas (Nataskas) stalking into the village with long, black bills and big sawlike teeth. One carried a rope to lasso disobedient children. He stopped at a certain house and called for a boy. "You have been naughty," he scolded. "You fight with other children. You kill chickens. You pay no attention to the old people. We have come to get you and eat you." The boy cried and promised to behave better. The giants became angrier and threatened to tie him up and take him away. But the boy's parents begged for his life and offered fresh meat in his place. The giant reached out his hand as if to grab the boy but took the meat instead. Placing it in his basket, he warned the boy that he would get just one more chance to change his conduct. I was frightened and got out of sight. I heard that sometimes these giants captured boys and really ate them.

A few days later my grandfather told me the story of the giants while I lay near him upon a sheepskin. He said: "A long time ago in Oraibi the children paid no attention to the old people, made fun of them, tied dirty rags behind their backs, and threw stones at them. They also took food from the smaller children and fought them. The parents tried to stop this mischief but could not.

"Now there were some Two-Hearts in Oraibi who disliked children and had cast a spell upon them to make them misbehave. They met in a kiva to make a giant who could eat them. Agreeing upon a plan, they sent the younger members to the woods for piñon gum. When it was gathered, the old men sat in a circle around the fire, smoked, and one old Two-Heart bowed his head with a silly laugh and said, 'I will make a giant. Watch me.'

"He took a gob of gum and molded it into a roll, smeared it with fat, covered it with a wedding blanket, and sang over it. While everyone watched, the gum made movements, sat up at the end of the fourth song, rapidly grew into a giant, and asked gruffly: 'Well, Father, what shall I do?' The old Two-Heart replied, 'The children in Oraibi are out of control. Go to the east mountain and build a house while we make a wife and children for you.' When he left the kiva, the old man made a giant woman and two children who set out after him.

"At sunrise the giant came back to Oraibi with a hatchet, spear, knife, and basket. He entered a house without knocking, caught a little girl, tied her up in his basket, and strode off with the child crying. The old Two-Hearts sat on their kiva and chuckled: 'This is what we wanted.'

"The giant returned each morning at sunrise until children became scarce. The parents were so worried that the chief took a couple of buckskin balls, two sticks, bows and arrows, went to the Spider Woman's house, and gave these things to the Twin War gods, asking them to slay the giant.

"The next morning the Twin War gods put arrows in their quivers, took their war outfits, and started to the village. The Spider Woman warned them, 'Don't play shinny on the way or you will be late.' When the giant saw them at the east edge, he said, 'Now I will take you boys home and eat you.' The Two-Hearts sat on their kiva and laughed behind their hands.

"The older boy struck his shinny ball so that it hit the giant on the forehead and knocked him down. In great surprise he jumped up, caught the boys, slung them in his basket, and started off the mesa. When he had gone some distance the older boy asked, 'May I get down to defecate, or shall I soil the basket?' 'And please, may I urinate?' said the other. But the giant paid no attention. A little later the boys warned that they could wait no longer. The giant let them down, tied a rope to each boy, and waited. They stepped behind a big rock, relieved themselves, untied the ropes, fastened one to their feces, and hid behind some stones.

"Growing impatient, the giant first urged the boys to hurry, then became angry, and jerked the ropes hard. The feces flew up and landed flat on his face, causing the boys to snicker. He then had a fight with the boys, finally took them to his house, and threw them into a very hot oven. His wife plastered down the lid with mud and set a heavy stone on top, after which she kindled a roaring fire. But the little gods smeared medicine over their bodies, urinated in the pot to keep it cool, and stayed there for the rest of the day and all night—telling stories to pass the time.

"At dawn, while the giant's wife ground corn in the next room, the War Twins pried off the lid, climbed out, caught the giant's sleeping children, put them in the pot, and hid in the house, laughing under their breath. The wife prepared breakfast and sat down with the giant to eat their own children. As they took full bites of the tender meat which dropped from the bones, the boys called out: 'You are eating your own children!' Then the giant fought again with the War gods; but they cut off his head as well as the head of his wife and dragged them into the village. Katcinas came later and took the heads away to use in scaring the children when they became naughty."

My grandfather told me how, when he was a boy, the giant female Katcina (Soyocco) entered the village and went from house to house looking for naughty children. She warned boys to behave, gave them a couple of sticks for a trap, and ordered them to catch mice. She gave girls a handful of baked sweet corn to grind into meal. Then she announced a date when she would return with the other giants for her reward of game and meal, or else the children. On that day the Nataska and the Soyocco Katcinas returned to the village from the west side—as many as eight Nataskas. They caught boys and girls and argued with parents who pleaded for their children and persuaded the giants to accept meat. My grandfather's talk was a great warning to me.

When I was four or five I was captured by the Spider Woman and nearly lost my life. One morning in May as I played in the plaza in my shirt my father said that he was going to his field. I wanted to go. But as he filled his water jar he said, "You had better stay here, my jar does not hold enough for us both." I began to cry. As he started down the south side of the mesa I followed along the narrow path between two great stones and came to the bottom of the foothill near the Spider Woman's shrine. My father had disappeared among the rocks. I happened to look to my left at a rock by the shrine where some clay dishes had been placed as offerings to the Spider Woman. There sat the old woman herself, leaning forward and resting her chin in her hands. Beside her was a square hole in the ground. She said, "You are here at the right time. I have been waiting for you. Come into my house with me." I had heard enough about the Spider Woman to know that no ordinary person ever sits by the shrine. I stood helpless, staring at her. "Come into my house," she repeated. "You have been walking on my trail, and now I have a right to you as my grandson."

My father had heard me crying as I followed him, so he asked a man whom he met coming up the mesa to take me back to the village.

As this man came around the corner of a rock the old woman disappeared. She had been sitting close by the pile of firewood that the people had placed on the shrine for her as they passed up and down the mesa.

I thought I had not moved, but when the man saw me I was standing right under the rock and was being drawn into the hole. The old Spider Woman has the power to do strange things. I had been caught in her web and could not step backward. When the man saw me he shouted, "Boy, get out of the shrine! The Spider Woman may take you into her house!" I laughed in a silly manner but could not move. The man rushed up quickly and pulled me out of the shrine. As he took me up the mesa I felt sick and was unable to play any more that day.

During the night I had an awful dream. The Spider Woman came for me and said that now I belonged to her. I sat up and saw her heel as she disappeared through the door. Crying, I told my parents that the Spider Woman was after me. Every time I closed my eyes I could see the old woman coming again. My father, mother, and grandfather talked about what had happened at the shrine and took turns watching me. Once when I cried and said to my father, "The Spider Woman will get me," he put his hand on my head and replied, "Well, my boy, you went too near her shrine. I fear you are hers now and that you will not live long."

I became weaker and weaker and felt only half alive. My grandfather tried to treat me, but his medicine did no good. On the fourth day my father and mother decided to take me to Shongopavi to a doctor specializing in that kind of sickness. They took turns carrying me the fourteen miles.

In Shongopavi we entered a corner house to see a medicine man named Yayauma. He prayed with the help of a pinch of meal that my mother gave him, examined me carefully, and smiled. My father and mother were worried. He said, "This boy has been caught in the Spider Woman's web. She holds him tightly." He asked my father, "Did you make a prayer feather for the Spider Woman at the Soyal ceremony?" My father hung his head for a while and said, "No, I don't think I made one for her then." The doctor replied, "That is causing this trouble. She will hold the boy until you make a prayer feather for her. If you love your boy, you had better do it right away. I hope she will let him go." "All right," said my father. Then the doctor rubbed my back and belly.

It was a Katcina dance day at Shongopavi. When the doctor had finished with me, my mother put me on her back and started to the house of our relatives. As she climbed the ladder to the roof of a winter house I saw the Katcinas resting near by. It seemed that they had cut off their heads and laid them to one side. They were eating and were using human heads and mouths like our own. I felt very sad to see those Katcinas without their own heads. When we reached home on the next day, before going to bed my father took some corn meal, went outside, and prayed to the sun, moon, and stars that they might protect us. That night the Spider Woman did not bother me and I slept until after sunrise.

At breakfast my parents and grandfather talked about the Shongopavi doctor and the Spider Woman. When we had finished our meal my father took some willow sticks and soft feathers and began to make the offerings. I was feeling stronger and sat beside him near the fireplace in the same room where I was born. He made two prayer sticks of willow, one male and one female, and fastened four soft prayer feathers to them. These he called pahos. He took another prayer feather and fastened a string to it, calling the string a breath. It took him a long time to make these offerings. When he had finished my grandfather said to him, "Take some food with the pahos to the shrine, and put a little mountain tobacco on the food; it may please the Spider Woman." My father left for the shrine with the offerings. I stood in the door of the third floor where I could watch. As he walked toward the shrine he sprinkled a path of corn meal upon which my spirit could step on its return to the house. At the end of the path he placed the breath feather and stuck the paho in the ground at the shrine. Placing the food near the fire-wood, he said, "Now, my son, I have brought this offering for your grandmother so that I may take you home. Grandmother, please release my boy. I will make a paho for you at every Soyal."

As my father returned from the shrine walking along the corn-meal path, I heard him talking to my spirit. He said, "Now, my son, I am taking you back home. Don't ever follow me off the mesa, or some bad spirit will get you and take you away." At the door he said, "Sit down." Thereafter I did not follow my father when he left the mesa and as a child I stayed away from the Spider Woman's shrine.

3

Learning to Live

I WAS MY GRANDFATHER'S favorite. As soon as I was old enough to take advice, he taught me that it was a great disgrace to be called *kahopi* (not Hopi, not peaceable). He said, "My grandson, old people are important. They know a lot and don't lie. Listen to them, obey your parents, work hard, treat everyone right. Then people will say, 'That boy Chuka is a good child. Let's be kind to him.' If you do these things, you will live to be an old man yourself and pass away in sleep without pain. This is the trail that every good Hopi follows. Children who ignore these teachings don't live long."

He told me that I was a boy after his own heart and that he could look into my life and see that I would become an important man, perhaps a leader of the people. I wanted to be a medicine man as he was, but he told me that I could not be a very good healer because I was not a member of the Badger Clan, nor even of the Snake Clan. They made the best doctors, but he thought I might become a Special Officer in the ceremonies. He advised me to keep bad thoughts out of my mind, to face the east, look to the bright side of life, and learn to show a shining face, even when unhappy. While I was still sleeping with him he taught me to get up before sunrise, bathe and exercise my body, and look around for useful work to do. He said, "Work means life. No one loves a lazybones."

Learning to work was like play. We children tagged around with our elders and copied what they did. We followed our fathers to the fields and helped plant and weed. The old men took us for walks and taught us the use of plants and how to collect them. We joined the women in gathering rabbitweed for baskets, and went with them to dig clay for pots. We would taste this clay as the women did to test it. We watched the fields to drive out the birds and rodents, helped pick peaches to dry in the sun, and gather melons to lug up the mesa. We rode the burros to harvest corn, gather fuel, or herd sheep. In house-building we helped a little by bringing up dirt to cover the roofs. In this way we grew up doing things. All the old people said that it was a disgrace to be idle and that a lazy boy should be whipped.

The importance of food was a lesson I learned early. My mother taught me never to waste it or play with it carelessly. Corn seemed to be the most important. A common saying was, "Corn is life, and piki is the perfect food." My mother-corn ears, which had been placed by my side at birth and used in my naming ceremony, were regarded as sacred and were kept a long time, but finally they were ground into meal and used for food before bugs got into them. Every family tried to keep a full year's supply of corn on hand and used it sparingly. There was always a pile of it in our house, neatly stacked in rows. A small supply of corn in a dry season was viewed with alarm, for to be without corn was a calamity. Whenever we shelled it we were careful to pick up every grain.

While the old people sat around shelling corn or spinning, they talked about the terrible famines that had come upon the people. It was sad to hear them. They said that on account of somebody's careless conduct the Six-Point-Cloud-People—our departed ancestors who live north, east, south, west, above, and below—refused to send rain and permitted droughts and famines. When the corn gave out the people prowled about the village looking for seeds and roots and scratched into trash piles for anything they could get. They scattered out over the desert digging for roots and wild potatoes. Some of them fell exhausted and died on their way up the mesa. Many people starved. Some stole food that others had stored, even digging tunnels under walls into neighbors' corn bins. A man might wake up in his own house and find all his corn gone but the first row. Some fled to the Santo Domingo Indians and traded their children for food.[1]

I have heard that when a man and his wife sat down to eat they would look at each other like wildcats ready to spring, and hold the hands of their children to keep them from eating. Think of that! Some children were kidnapped and eaten. Their bones and skulls were found later in the foundations of some of the old houses. I saw them. The old people said that we youngsters could never know what awful misfortunes had come upon our people. They were handing these warnings down to us so that we could some day pass them on to our children.

The last big famine came when my father was a little boy. He told me how his grandfather was fairly well off and had much food stored which kept his family from starving. I saw how important it was to have food on hand. We ate the old Hopi foods such as corn, beans, squash, chilis, spinach, and many wild plants. We never tired of them. Occasionally we ate the food of the white people such as flat flour bread and drank a little coffee. Only the rich Hopis had this white bread as often as twice a week. We were frequently reminded that the old Hopi food was best and that our gods preferred that we eat it.

In the spring the older boys went out with soft eagle feathers fastened on their heads to collect wild spinach, which they gave to their girl friends in exchange for other foods. Our parents took us smaller children out to watch the procession and to exchange our own foods. Ceremonial officers guided the boys and girls in this work and advised them that it was important in order to have good crops and plenty to eat. After the collection of wild spinach we always had a Katcina dance. By these ceremonies I learned to know that the gods had given us certain wild plants as special food.

We were taught that whenever anyone came to our house we should sweep a clean place on the floor, set out the food, and invite him to eat. It was only after the company had eaten that my father ever asked, "What can I do for you?" My grandfather said that we

---

1. For legends of famines, see Appendix, pp. 445–447.

must always observe this rule and feed visitors first, even when we were hungry or unhappy. I noticed that my mother and father stopped quarreling whenever company came. At mealtime we children were permitted to eat all that we wanted, but were told to behave and not to be greedy. It was no disgrace to break wind at mealtime or to laugh when someone else did. Whenever we went to a neighbor's house, we were told that we should eat their food to make them happy. It was proper to eat a little even when we were already full up to the neck. On a dance day we often ate ten or fifteen times.

As far back as I can remember, I noticed that my father, mother, and grandfather would take a little food before eating and put it aside. They said that it was to feed the Sun and other gods who protected us. Sometimes I heard them speak to these gods, inviting them to eat. They were especially careful to do this on dance days. Whenever my father asked the gods for anything, he fed them first. Sometimes he would take a bit of food, step outside and throw it to the Sun, then ask for something. We were told that there was no need to speak out loud in thanking our gods at the three daily meals. We could pray in our hearts: "Now this meal is prepared for me. I will put it into my body to make myself strong for work. May my Spirit Guide protect me."

Food was left on the graves, even the graves of very small babies who were buried among the rocks on the south and the northwest sides of the village. We children were not permitted to see a dead person or to go near the graves, but we could see our fathers taking food there in clay bowls.

I learned that it was important always to eat at mealtime. Once when my parents had scolded me, I sulked and refused to eat. After they had finished and gone out, I looked for the food that I expected them to leave for me, but there was nothing. I had tried to hurt their feelings, but I was starving myself. I ate at regular mealtime after that.

It was hard to learn what plants we could eat. Some of them were good for food and others for medicine, but still others were good for nothing save to make people sick or crazy. The locoweed would make even a horse crazy. I tried to remember the use of all the plants under my grandfather's instruction.

We liked meat and ate almost any kind that we could get. The old people showed us how to make deadfalls to catch kangaroo rats, prairie dogs, porcupines, badgers, chipmunks, squirrels, and turtledoves. The men used heavy rock deadfalls for trapping coyotes, foxes, wildcats, and other large animals. Sometimes they went long distances to hunt bear and deer. Whenever they killed a large wild animal they brought the carcass home, covered it with a wedding robe, smoked mountain tobacco before its nostrils, and asked for forgiveness. They also prayed to the godmother of wild animals to send us more game. They formed large parties on foot or horseback and hunted rabbits with dogs, clubs, and curved throwing sticks. We little boys made snares of horsehair to catch birds. I learned to catch bluebirds with a hair from a horse's tail set as a snare on the upper stem of a sunflower stalk, with a worm for bait. We also practiced shooting at birds and small animals with bow and arrows. But we were told never to kill any creature that we did not intend to eat.

Birds' eggs were not used for food, although chicken and turkey eggs were. We did not eat turkey meat but pulled out their feathers to make prayer sticks for the ceremonies. We were taught never to eat hawks, crows, eagles, snakes, lizards, ants, bugs, beetles, or terrapins. A few people ate dog meat, but some considered it a disgrace. We all ate horse, mule, and burro meat; but burro was the best. We watched the castration of rams and billy goats and ate the parts that were cut out. I liked this meat. We also castrated horses and burros, but we fed their parts to the dogs.

My father had fifteen burros that we used for hauling wood, water, corn, fruit, and other produce, and which I rode for pleasure. The men castrated the studs to improve their behavior and to make the meat fat and tender. We children watched from a distance when this was done, but the women stayed out of sight. It took a trained man to castrate a burro, and I thought that I never wanted to learn, for I pitied the poor animals. I was also sorry for a burro when I saw a man cut off its ears or tail as punishment for eating the crops.

Every fall the men who had cattle would drive them up to the lower shelf of the southwest mesa wall. Sometimes there were fifty or a hundred head. We boys would stand along the upper ledge and watch them butchered. The men shot them, knocked them on the head with an axe, or stretched them out with ropes and cut their throats. They would strip off the hides, drag them down to the trading post, and exchange them for the white people's goods. They cut up the meat and laid it out on the rocks to dry for winter food.

My father and uncles also corralled their herds on this ledge when they wanted to butcher a goat or sheep. Then early next morning we would go down, rope an animal, drive it up the mesa to our house, tie its four legs, stretch back its neck, and cut its throat, letting the blood run into a basin for the dogs. My father would drag the sheep in through the front door, strip off the hide, open up the stomach, and roll out the intestines on a sheepskin. Then he would cut up the meat and hang it on the wall of the house just outside the door to dry. My mother cooked the liver for lunch. We butchered every two or three weeks, whenever we could spare animals from the herd.

Food seemed most important on dance days. Our mothers fed the Katcinas and everybody had good things to eat. It was then, too, that the Katcinas presented their gifts such as watermelons, popcorn, hominy, mush, and piki. Those were happy days when children could be carefree and everyone was expected to be cheerful. At the end of the day the Father of the Katcinas sprinkled them with corn meal, made a farewell speech, and sent them to their homes in the San Francisco Peaks. He would ask them to send rain for our crops, and add, "Then our children, the little ones, will eat and surely be happy. Then all the people will live happily. Then our lives, reaching old age among our children, will be happily fulfilled." All this made it plain that food was necessary for life and happiness.

While I was learning the importance of food and trying to recognize the different things that were fit to eat, I kept going to my mother for milk and was still nursing at six. Whenever we boys set out to hunt kangaroo rats or other small game, I ran first to my mother, placed my bow and arrows on the floor, sat beside her, and drank from her breasts. The other fellows would say, "Come Chuka, come, or we will be late." "Wait, wait," I replied between draughts. But on account of their teasing, I finally gave up the breast in embarrassment. My mother did not wean me; I just decided to let her alone.

I also learned that water is as precious as food. Everybody appeared happy after a rain. We small boys rolled about naked in the mud puddles, doused each other with water, and built little irrigated gardens. In this way we used too much of the water from the little pond on the west side of the village where the women went to wash their clothes and the men to water their stock. Our parents scolded us for wasting water and once my mother spanked me on account of my dirty shirt.

During droughts we had strict rules for the use of water. Even small children were taught to be careful, and I saw mothers bathe their babies by spitting a little water upon them. By watching the old people I learned to wash my face with a mouthful of water—it is the safest way to wash without waste.

Sometimes water gave out. Then the men went with their burros to distant springs while the women stayed up all night taking turns to catch a little trickle that came from the Oraibi spring. My grandfather told me about the cistern that he had chiseled out of the solid rock to catch the rain that fell on the mesa shelf. He said that he had done this hard work when he married my grandmother in order that his children and his grandchildren might not suffer from thirst. My mother went daily to this well to fetch water. In winter she cut out chunks of ice from the rock ledges and brought them in on her back.

Whenever it rained, we were told to take our little pots and go out on the ledges, scoop up puddles, and fill the cisterns. There were about one hundred of these hewn out of the solid rock by our ancestors. The people pointed out that water is essential to life and taught us what to do out in the desert whenever we became so dry and thirsty that we could neither spit nor swallow. Then one should cut twigs off a cottonwood tree and chew them, eat the inner bark of the cedar, or hold dried peaches in his mouth.

The importance of water was impressed upon us by the way the old men prayed for rain and planted pahos in the springs to please the water serpents and to persuade them to send larger streams to quench our thirst. We were reminded that all the dances and ceremonies were for rain, not for pleasure. They were held in order to persuade the Six-Point-Cloud-People to send moisture for our crops. Whenever we had a good rain, we were told to show our happy faces and consider ourselves in favor with the gods. We made it a point never to praise the weather on fair, dry days. Whenever it rained during or just after a dance, the people praised highly those who had taken part in the performance. If a strong wind followed the dance, it was a sign that the people who had invited the Katcinas to come and dance had a bad heart or had done some evil.

We were told that there is health-giving power in water, and that it is a good practice to bathe in cold water, to wash our hands and faces in snow, and to rub it upon our bodies to make them tough. The old people said that warm water made wrinkles and shortened life. I saw them setting bowls of water outside to become ice-cold before using it for a bath. Some old men would go out naked and rub snow all over their bodies. My grandfathers, my aunts' husbands, often took me outside and rolled me in the snow on winter mornings. Talasemptewa did it many times. At first I thought he disliked me, but my mother explained that it showed he loved me and wanted me to grow up strong, healthy, and brave. I could see there was healing power in water, too, for my grandfather often had people drink warm water in order to vomit and clear out their systems. Sometimes he prescribed a person's own fresh warm urine for stomach trouble. Water then, like food, meant life and health and was a special gift from the gods to us in the desert. The gods could withhold rain when they were displeased, or they could pour it on us when they wanted to.

After food and water, fuel seemed hardest to get and fastest to go. Everybody was required to bring it in. People hardly ever came empty-handed up the mesa. If they had no other burden, they would lug up an armful of sticks and twigs. The men made long journeys on burros to get wood for cooking and for heating the houses and the kivas. Small chunks of coal were collected from the washes and gullies. Old men and women, some nearly blind, would go far out into the plains and return with bundles of brush and sticks on their backs. Whenever my father herded, he spent his spare time breaking dead bushes of juniper or greasewood, leaving them in little piles to be brought into the village on burros. Corncobs were saved for fuel. Dried sheep dung was used for cooking, heating, and baking pottery.

Whenever anyone passed the Spider Woman's shrine, he would make her an offering of a few sticks, for a little fuel was a worthy sacrifice. I brought armfuls of sticks into the village to please my mother and to win the praise of the old people.

Another important business was to keep track of the time or the seasons of the year by watching the points on the horizon where the sun rose and set each day. The point of sunrise on the shortest day of the year was called the sun's winter home and the point of sunrise on the longest day its summer home. Old Talasemptewa, who was almost blind, would sit out on the housetop of the special Sun Clan house and watch the sun's progress toward its summer home. He untied a knot in a string for each day. When the sun arose at certain mesa peaks, he passed the word around that it was time to plant sweet corn, ordinary corn, string beans, melons, squash, lima beans, and other seeds. On a certain date he would announce that it was too late for any more planting. The old people said that there were proper times for planting, harvesting, and hunting, for ceremonies, weddings, and many other activities. In order to know these dates it was necessary to keep close watch on the sun's movements.

My great-great-uncle Muute, who lived south of the Howeove kiva, was the Special Officer of the Sun Clan, and was called Tawamongwi (Sun Chief). He would sit at a certain place and watch the sun in order to know when it reached its summer home. It was the work of the Chief of the Flute society to guide the sun on its way. When the sun had arrived at its summer home, my uncle would say to the Sun Clan people, "Well, our great-uncle, the Sun god, has reached his summer home and now we must butcher a sheep and make prayer offerings for the sun, moon, and stars. We will pray hard to our Sun god, asking him to send rain and to keep away the bad winds that destroy our crops." On a certain evening he would gather material for making prayer sticks and meet with the Sun Clan men in our special Sun Clan house to smoke mountain tobacco and pray for rain. For four nights my uncle would sleep by himself in order to get rain for his people.

The next morning he and some of the Sun Clan men would return to the Sun Clan house, take off their shirts and shoes, sit on the floor, and light the pipe again, passing it from one to the other, exchanging kinship terms, and uniting their hearts in order to get their prayers through to the Six-Point-Cloud-People. They asked for rain, good crops, health, and long life. A few men from the other clans might come over and help make pahos so that their lives might be good and strong. They would work together, place the prayer sticks in a plaque, and set them aside. The trash was gathered up and placed in a little wash at the edge of the mesa where the rains could carry it into the valley and spread it out over the fields. When the pahos were finished, great quantities of food were placed on the floor and everybody was invited to come to the Sun Clan house to eat. There was always plenty of food on this day and everybody ate happily.

Before sunrise the next day my uncle took the prayer offerings over to the Sun shrine on top of a high mesa two miles northeast of Oraibi. He had to place the pahos on the shrine and pray for rain just as the Sun god peeped over the eastern horizon.

The old people said the sun was the most important. They said he could even replace lost teeth. I had a loose tooth in the front of my mouth one day in September when our family set out on burros to Shongopavi to see the Marau dance. We slept with our Sun Clan relatives that night. The next morning I was playing with a young clan brother, running after a ball. We collided and he struck me in the face with his forehead. I thought I felt a little stone in my mouth. It was the tooth. I ran into the house excited. My relatives consoled me, almost causing me to cry. They told me to go outside and throw the tooth to the Sun god, so that he would give me a new one. I said that I hoped he would give me a tooth as hard as a rock, and then threw the old one as far as I could. When I was teased about the missing tooth, I complained, "I should not have come here, the Shongopavi people are knocking out my teeth." The people laughed and laughed at this and repeated it many times.

Most of my time was spent in play. We shot arrows at targets, played old Hopi checkers, and pushed feather-edged sticks into corn-cobs and threw them at rolling hoops of cornhusks. We wrestled, ran races, played tag, kickball, stick throwing, and shinny. We spun tops with whips and made string figures on our fingers. I was poor at races but good at string figures. Another game I liked was making Hopi firecrackers. I mixed burro and horse dung, burned a lump of it into a red glow, placed the coal on a flat rock, and hit it with a cow horn dipped in urine. It went "bang" like a gun.

We hunted rabbits, kangaroo rats, and mice to feed to hawks and eagles. We also waged little wars with children of unfriendly families who were most opposed to the Whites. They criticized us for accepting gifts from white people and we called them Hostiles. Their children would upset our traps for turtledoves and try to torment us in every way. We had many fights with them, and my brother and I fought a great deal, even throwing stones at each other.

Sometimes we got into mischief in our play. One day when I was out with a gang of boys, I decided to play a trick. I defecated in the path. Now one could make water almost any place except in bed and against the house walls where it washed away the adobe, but a boy had to be careful where he defecated. During the day a woman stepped in the feces with her bare feet. Learning from some children that I was the guilty person, she came to our house complaining. My grandfather was quite angry and said that this had to be stopped. He had never licked me, but I was scared. He got a willow switch about three feet long, took me by the hand, and struck me four blows below my shirt. He ordered me never to repeat the act, and raised his arm to strike again, when I promised. He stuck the switch up in the ceiling near the arrow and my dried placenta cord. Later I tried to get it down. In about a week I received a second thrashing of eight stripes for the same offense. Then I learned to defecate in the proper places.

In winter we played in the kivas and listened to the long stories which the men told while they worked at spinning, weaving, and other jobs. They often picked out a boy to take messages and trade for them from kiva to kiva, and frequently I was chosen. The men would collect the things that they wished to exchange—wool, yarn, pieces of calico, leggings, and perhaps a sheep. Since a trader boy naturally could not carry a large animal, the owner would tie some wool from a sheep, or the hair of a horse or burro, on a stick to represent the animal. I would go from kiva to kiva showing the objects of trade. If a man wanted to purchase an animal or other large objects represented by a stick, he would make the trade and take the stick as proof of payment. Of course I had to remember the value of these objects and know exactly what the owner would take in exchange. It was great fun, and it also taught me to measure and to count.

I learned to count up to twenty with my fingers and toes. That was as high as we went. If, for example, we wanted to indicate forty-four, we would say "two twenties and four." Four was a lucky number, but we had no unlucky numbers. In measurement we said "one finger wide" for about one inch, "from the reach of the thumb to the middle finger" for about six inches, and "one foot" for the length from heel to toe. For long distances we counted in steps. I did not learn much about the weight of things at this time. Morning and afternoon were determined by the direction of the shadows, and we told time at night by the position of the moon and stars. Promises to pay at a future date were expressed in number of days, the state of the moon, or the number of moons.

One day while we were working in the kiva, someone came in with a Navaho blanket and offered to sell it for eight days' work at quarrying stone. My grandfather offered to do the work and took the blanket. He threw it to me and said, "Here, grandson, now we have a blanket." Gee! I was happy.

Sometimes it was fun to sit in the sun searching one another's heads for lice and cracking the catch between our teeth. We learned to catch beetles and put them in circles; we called them our "wild horses," but were warned never to hurt them, for the old people said they were good in treating some diseases. I never played with spiders because of their mother, the Spider Woman. I never teased the hawks and eagles staked out on the housetops, for we were told that they were spirit people.

We made necklaces out of horned toads and strung them around our necks. The old people said, "Don't tease toads too much; they are spirits and can help us." I could pick up a lizard or a horned toad in my hands and not feel afraid. I was taught to love them because my father belonged to the Sand-Lizard-Snake Clan. One time I was too rough with a toad, and it bit me. This taught me a lesson. I never tied a string to a toad and hung it around another fellow's neck; he might have slung the toad away roughly, angering it, and this would have been a disgrace. At first I used to pick up small snakes, but later I learned that this was not right. One day I killed a very small one, which was an awful thing to do.

We chased the chickens, threw corncobs at them, and shot them with our toy arrows. We encouraged roosters to fight for our amusement. My grandfather cautioned me that chickens are the chosen pets of the Sun god. "The crowing of the cocks in early morning is important," he said. "The Sun god put them here to wake up the people. He rings a little bell telling the roosters when to announce the coming dawn. They crow four times before daylight."

We often played with dogs and cats, and sometimes we encouraged them to fight. I had a dog of my own. My doctor father, old Tuvenga, had a white bitch with a black ear and a black spot over each eye. She gave birth to ten pups. The owner passed word around that whoever wanted a puppy should bring food for the mother. I was given first choice, and five other boys also chose male pups, but the little bitches were killed. We boys fed the mother well. The puppies opened their eyes and grew rapidly, fighting over their food. When they began to bite their mother as they nursed, my doctor father said, "Take the pups to your homes." I named mine Bakito (Setting Sun). When he learned his name, he would run to me when I called and jump up to kiss my face. He grew larger than his mother and made me proud of him as a hunter.

One day when I was wandering about the mesa, I found five baby kittens in a gully. I put them in my blanket and carried them to the house, where I gave three to my companions. Later one of mine disappeared, but the other grew up into the biggest cat I ever saw, and the best hunter. She looked like a wildcat, and when she had kittens of her own, she would go down the mesa and return with a rabbit to feed them. When I knew all about puppies and kittens, I asked my mother about babies, and how they came. She said that they were given to people by the two gods, Talastumsie and her husband, Alosaka. She said that Talastumsie would bring a baby and tell the mother to keep the child and raise it. My father said the same thing.

I had captive birds for pets. Once I caught some young wrens under a rock ledge and brought four of them home. The first day I killed houseflies to feed them, and the next day grasshoppers. Then I grew tired of working for them and gave them away. One day, when out in the field with my father, I saw a couple of burrowing owls run into a prairie dog's hole. I begged my father to dig them out with his hoe. We dug deep for them. They were queer-looking and made a peculiar noise. We took them home and fed them mice and kangaroo rats. It was hard to supply them with food, and finally I let them starve. When they died, I threw them away without even saying my prayers to them. This was a mean thing to do. Later I stole three mockingbirds from their nests, gave two to my playmates, and kept one as a pet. After a short time, however, the cat caught it one night. When I could find only the tail feathers, I cried.

I liked birds. My grandfather told me that all the songbirds are the Sun god's pets, put here to keep the people happy while they work. I liked to listen to the meadow lark, the robin, the mockingbird, and many others. The mockingbird mimics the songs of all other birds. Once I also heard one cry out like a jack rabbit caught in a trap. At one of the dances a clown imitated the mockingbird. He was clever and made the people laugh. First he mocked all the birds, then talked like a Navaho, a Havasupai, and a Hopi. He also imitated cattle, horses, sheep, and burros. Finally he mocked Masau'u, the Fire Spirit who guards the village at night. That call, like the cry of an owl, surprised everybody.

One spring my father made some pahos and went out to hunt hawks, taking me with him. When we came to the Eagle cemetery, we placed our offering on it and made a prayer to catch hawks. We went to Hotavila Valley looking for hawks, and found a young one in a tree out of its nest. When she tried to fly, my father chased her, leaving me behind. I was frightened and yelled for him, thinking a Navaho might capture me and carry me off. That was one thing that I did not want to happen.

I had a terrible fear of Navahos. I had been told time after time that they could not be trusted, that they were thieves and raiders who even taught their children to steal. The old people warned that they were like coyotes who travel at night, pillage our land, and carry off our goods. Everyone had a tale of woe concerning Navahos who had stolen sheep from his herd, corn and melons from his field, fruit from his orchard, and water from his well. They had also been known to steal Hopi children. So I had cause to be afraid.

My father finally caught the hawk and, carrying her gently in his hands, came back for me. Since we had found the hawk in the Bear Clan hunting territory, we had to take her to Chief Lolulomai's sister, Punnamousi. When I took her the hawk, the old lady told me that they had enough pets already—five eagles and three hawks tied out on the housetop. That year there were about thirty-five eagles in the village. She suggested that I return next morning and let her wash the hawk's head and name her. I was so anxious to keep the bird that I went early next morning. She washed the hawk's head in white clay suds—just like a baby—and named her Honmana (Female Bear). All hawks and eagles are given female names because we believe they are mothers. I took my hawk home and my father helped me tie a soft cotton string to her leg and stake her out on our housetop. I had to work hard hunting mice and kangaroo rats to feed my bird.

My uncles and fathers told me that the eagles and hawks are spirit people who live in a special home in the sky. Sometimes in the winter and spring these sky people are said to come to Oraibi as Katcinas, with heads like eagles, and to dance in the plaza. I had seen them do this. Whenever they came, the people made prayer offerings to encourage our eagle and hawk friends to bear offspring for the next year. I was told that at the right time of the year the Eagle Chief above sent his people down through a special hole in the sky to build their nests, lay their eggs, and hatch their young among the cliffs of the mountains and high mesas. Then the Hopis go out and catch their spirit friends, bring them into the village, and feed them upon their housetops. I knew that after the Niman dance, when the Katcinas are sent home for the season and when the quills are hard, these eagles and hawks should be "sent to their homes" with sacrifices and prayers.

When my hawk's quills grew hard, I helped my father "send her home." We first made little dolls for her and tied them to a cattail stalk. My mother made a little plaque about three inches wide. She took these things up to the housetop and said to the hawk, "These presents are given to you by the Katcinas. You will take them to your home tomorrow. These dolls are given to you so that you will have children and multiply. Your feathers will be kept here and used as our offerings to the Six-Point-Cloud-People."

The next morning after sunrise I climbed upon the housetop with my father and held the cotton leash while he threw a blanket over the hawk. Then he placed his thumb upon her windpipe and pressed hard. It seemed to take a long time for the hawk to "go home." When she became very still, we plucked her feathers and sorted them. We stripped off the skin and tied our prayer feathers to the wings and feet and around the bird's neck, so that she would forgive us and be ready to return and hatch young hawks the next year. Then we took her out toward the place where we caught her, to the Hawk and Eagle cemetery of the Bear Clan. We took along the small plaque, the dolls, a few rolls of blue piki, and a pointed stick. My father lighted a pipe of mountain tobacco and blew smoke over her body. We dug a hole about two feet deep, laid her to rest on the bottom, and sprinkled corn meal over her. Then my father made a speech: "Now we let you go free. Return to your people, for they are expecting you. Take these prayer feathers with our messages to the Six-Point-Cloud-People, and tell them to send us rain. We hope you will return next year and multiply." We then bade her good-by, filled the hole with earth, placed food near by, and stuck the stick into the little mound so that she could climb out and go home on the fourth day. Upon returning to the house, we gathered up the feathers, put them into a special box, and saved them to be used in making pahos.

As soon as I was old enough to wander about the village my grand-father suggested that I go out to the Antelope shrine and look for my deer people who were invisible to ordinary human beings. Sometimes I thought I could see antelopes who changed into people. Whenever I dreamed of antelopes in the village, my parents would say, "That is to be expected, for you are an antelope child." Then when I was perhaps five I would wander off a mile or two from the village to a place where sunflowers grew and where it was known that the spirits of deer and antelope gathered to give birth to their young and to feed on the sunflowers. It was a miracle that I could see these deer while others could not. I would return home with a bunch of sunflowers and with the juice of the sunflowers spread around my mouth. My grandfather or parents would remark that I had been feasting with my relatives and would probably use my special power soon to heal some poor person who was sick and unable to urinate.

My grandfather had already taught me how to heal such diseases and people had begun sending for me whenever this trouble came upon them. The first thing I did when working on a sick person was to put out my left hand with the palm up and pray, "Now my mother of the Antelope People, this sick person is in bad condition; come and cure his disease before I put my hands upon him; join with me and save his life."

After praying, I would rub him or her around the private parts and especially between the navel and the pubis. I would take piki, chew it, and feed it to the sick person from my fingers. My uncle, Talasquap-tewa, said that a twin like myself was in an unfortunate position be-cause sometimes such sufferers die in spite of all treatment, and then the person who had tried to help them feels responsible. But I seemed to be able to tell whether a patient would get well or die. Whenever I saw someone beyond help, I simply walked away, refusing to treat him. The old people praised my power to heal, but predicted that it would probably disappear as I grew into manhood. They warned me never to let the Whites know about it, because they would not be able to understand.

I had also learned to pick out the people whom I could trust. My own mother still stood at the head of the list. She was my best friend. Though always busy, she was ready to help any person who came to her. My father also was a good friend and taught me how to do many things with my hands. I liked him, except on a few occasions when he punished me. He worked hard in his fields and with his herd, and was one of the best weavers in Oraibi. He traded the garments that he wove for things for his family to eat and wear. My grandfather, who lived in the house with us, liked me best and spent most time in teaching me. I knew I could count on him. My uncle Naquima and my sister Tuvamainim were good pals to me, but my brother Namostewa was not much of a friend.

Outside of our household, Masenimka, my aunt and godmother who named me, was perhaps the most important. She often kept me at her house, but was hot-tempered and sometimes treated me unfairly. I liked to go to her place, nevertheless, because she fed me the white-flour food. Her family was rich; she owned turkeys and her husband owned the first wagon and team in Oraibi. I frequently went out with her little son Harry Kopi to hoe weeds. I occasionally slept at Masenimka's house, but whenever she became cross at me I returned to my own house. Sometimes she would even come and scold my own mother and father. But she was not stingy with her food; whenever she had something good to eat she would come and get me. She was my friend all through my boyhood, and took my side whenever anyone teased me. She was an important member of the secret societies too—of the Marau, the Lakon, and the Ooqol.

I could always count on my doctor father, old blind Tuvenga. We were like partners, helping each other every day. I led him about, acting as eyes for him, and he instructed and advised me. He was an important man in the ceremonies and a member of the Wowochim and the Fire and Snake societies. I expected him to take me into these societies some day. Solemana, old Tuvenga's niece, lived near by and was always very kind to me.

My mother had three uncles who enjoyed high respect in Oraibi—Talashungnewa, Kayayeptewa, and Talasquaptewa. Her great clan uncle, Muute, was the Chief of our Sun Clan, and a very important man. These four men showed great interest in me and never teased me. I was taught to pay close attention to their words. My father's brother Kalnimptewa also looked out for me and taught me to call him "father," just like my own father.

There was an old man named Bechangwa (the appearance of the rising sun) who came to our house often. My grandfather, Homikniwa, raised big, juicy, clingstone peaches that a toothless person could eat. So this old man came in the mornings for peaches and collected peach stones to plant. He would walk past me with his stick and say, "Good morning, good luck to you, my father." I did not like to be called father (*ina'a*) and showed that I was offended. One day my mother said to me, "Don't treat your son that way, Chuka. He used to have a father who belonged to our Sun Clan. His father was your great-great-uncle; that makes me his aunt and you his father. Try to treat your son better." After a while I grew used to having him call me father.

One person held in high respect was Lolulomai, the Village Chief (Kikmongwi), who was the "father" of all the people in Oraibi. Everybody was expected to look up to him and to obey his orders. He wanted to be friendly with the Whites, accept their gifts, and send us children to their school. He said that it was better to be educated and become civilized. My people were mostly on his side, but there was much arguing in the village on this subject. One time the Hostiles under the leadership of Yokeoma, a member of the Antelope society, imprisoned him in the kiva and would have starved him to death if the government agents had not come and rescued him. Lolulomai was the uncle of Tewaquaptewa, who was about fifteen years older than I and was expected to become our Chief some day. Tewaquaptewa and I were good friends. He too was my "son," since my great-uncle was his father. There were many other people in the village (about eight hundred) who were not very important to me. I did not even know many of them. I was told to keep away from the Hostiles.

By the time I was six, therefore, I had learned to find my way about the mesa and to avoid graves, shrines, and harmful plants, to size up people, and to watch out for witches. I was above average height and in good health. My hair was clipped just above my eyes, but left long in back and tied in a knot at the nape of my neck. I had almost lost one eye. I wore silver earrings, a missionary shirt or one made of a flour sack, and was always bare-legged, except for a blanket in cold weather. When no Whites were present, I went naked. I slept out on the housetop in summer and sometimes in the kiva with other boys in winter. I could help plant and weed, went out herding with my father, and was a kiva trader. I owned a dog and a cat, a small bow made by my father, and a few good arrows. Sometimes I carried stolen matches tucked in the hem of my shirt collar. I could ride a tame burro, kill a kangaroo rat, and catch small birds, but I could not make fire with a drill and I was not a good runner like the other fellows. At the races people teased me and said that my feet turned out so far that I pinched my anus as I ran. But I had made a name for myself by healing people; and I had almost stopped running after my mother for her milk.

4
Mischief and Discipline

I WAS FULL OF MISCHIEF and hard to manage. Therefore I was scolded, doused with cold water, rolled in the snow, and teased terribly. But we children were never denied food, locked in a dark room, slapped on our faces, or stood up in a corner—those are not Hopi ways. Sometimes the old people warned us that if we mistreated them our lives would be short; that if we imitated the snake dancers our bellies would swell up and burst; or that if we twirled a flat stick on a string to make a humming noise, a bad wind would come. Our relatives warned us that the Katcinas would bring no gifts to naughty boys and that giants would get us and eat us, or the Spider Woman would catch us in her web. My parents often threatened to put me outside in the dark where a coyote or an evil spirit could get me, a Navaho could carry me off, or the Whites could take me away to their schools. Occasionally they threatened to throw me into the fire or warned me that Masau'u the Fire god would appear in the night and cause my death. In this way we were taught to be watchful and to behave.

I also learned early to mark the people who could punish me. My parents whipped me some and so did my grandfather, Homikniwa— at least twice. My father's father, Lomayeptewa, died when I was a baby and my parents' mothers both died before I knew them. My father's brother and clan brothers, called my fathers, could whip me whenever either of my parents asked them. My grandfathers, the husbands of my father's sisters and clan sisters, played rough jokes on me and scolded me some, but never flogged me. The relatives that a boy needs to watch closest are his mother's brothers and clan brothers. They have a right to punish an unruly lad severely and almost kill him.

There was a time when my father and mother said that I needed a spanking daily, but they could not make me behave. Since blows seemed useless, one day they put some coals in a broken dish, covered them with cedar boughs, and held me under a blanket in the smoke. When I cried, smoke entered my throat and nearly choked me. They finally let me go but said, "The next time you get into mischief we will punish you the same way, but worse." It seemed to me that this was the worst punishment a child could get. When I warned my playmates to be careful and avoid a smoking, some listened and some laughed.

Sometimes my father said to his brother, "My boy pays no attention to my blows; you whip him." He would do a thorough job of it. One day, while playing with some boys near the Snake kiva, I killed a chicken with my bow and arrow. I was worried and went home. The owner, who was no aunt of mine, came angrily to our house with the dead fowl. My mother gave her the best hen she had, but asked for the dead one. Then she went to fetch Kalnimptewa, my father's brother. He came with a stern face and said, "Young man, I hear that you are out of control. I am going to smoke you." I tried to be brave. My mother set a dish of hot coals on the ground and covered them with green boughs. Kalnimptewa put my head into the smoke and covered it with a blanket. He held me there a long time, and I was choked so that I could not even cry. When he let me go, he said, "Now, kill another chicken, and I'll give you more." I promised to be good. This happened at about eleven o'clock in the morning, and I was sick the rest of the day and vomited a lot of black stuff.

One morning old Bechangwa, my "son," walked through the plaza on the way to his field, carrying a water jar on his back. I got behind him with a stick and hit the jar, cracking it. He turned quickly and exclaimed, "Who are you?" By then I was running for home. My mother gave him one of her best jars to make good the damage. She was angry and told Kelhongneowa (her mother's sister's son) that it was his duty to teach me a lesson. He caught me and nearly smoked me to death, causing my throat to burn for a long time. When he let me go, he said, "Now break another pot; there is one, break it!" Of course I didn't. This man had a strong sharp eye and almost never smiled. Whenever he looked at me, I felt afraid and thought about my behavior.

But instead of improving, I seemed to get worse. My father and grandfather excused my mischief a little, explaining that it was due to the antelope power in me because I was a twin. But even a threat of the giants failed to make me behave. I got into some new mischief almost every day. One day Archie, a clan brother, and I pulled all the tail feathers out of my godmother's turkeys. Whenever I saw an ugly-faced or snotty-nosed child I wanted to whip him. When it rained, I walked through the streets throwing mud into the windows at girls grinding corn. When women went down to the spring for water, I placed sharp sticks in the path for them to step upon with their bare feet, and watched gleefully from a hiding place. I persuaded other children to engage in mischief and sometimes licked them to make them join me.

Once I punished a boy severely, and almost scared him to death. We boys hunted for kangaroo rats in a melon field, and told Paul to watch the plants while we dug for rats. I passed by a little later and noticed that he had fallen asleep, shirking his duty. Discovering a sand snake coiled up, I said to myself, "Now I will teach this boy a lesson." I crept upon the snake like a cat, caught it by the neck, wet my fingers with spittle, and rubbed them along its back to quiet it. Then I slipped up to the boy and placed the snake around his neck, holding it just enough to save the lad from choking. He struggled and squealed like a pig and was soon wide awake. Then I told him to do his duty, but he ran for home. I did not get a whipping for this, but my parents heard about it and warned me never to do it again lest I injure either boy or snake, for mistreatment of snakes might bring bad luck.

Some time later I caught a bull snake and got my lesson. I spied the snake under some rocks in the shade at the Oraibi spring. Creeping up to it, I quickly grabbed it by the neck. It seemed frightened, coiled itself about my arm, and opened its mouth with a hissing noise. I spat in its face to soften its spirit and smeared saliva along its back. When it had quieted down, I thought, "Some day I may become a member of the Snake society and dance with one in my mouth. I will practice now." I started to take the neck of the snake between my teeth as the dancers do, but changed my mind and held it near my mouth. As I took a dance step, the snake coiled itself around my neck and nearly choked me. Greatly frightened, I broke its grip on my throat, threw it upon the ground, and seized a stone to kill it. I was trembling from head to foot and wet with sweat. Fortunately, as I raised the stone to strike, I suddenly changed my mind and said to myself, "It is wrong to harm this snake; I was teasing it and have only myself to blame." I left it alive and went up the mesa, thankful for the lucky thought that came just in time.

I wanted to become a member of the Snake society but was told that my doctor father, Tuvenga, was too old to take me in. Now there is a rule that when the society members go out to hunt serpents for the Snake dance in August they have a right to catch, and make a member of, any person whom they find in the field near by. One day I wandered out in that direction, hoping that they would catch me. I had made up my mind that if a Snake society man chased me, I would not run like a coward, but would stand and say to him, "Well, I am caught; I choose you as my ceremonial father." I was not lucky for the Snake men paid no attention to me.

As I grew larger, my father began sending me with my brother to herd the sheep whenever they were corralled near the mesa. We got into an awful fight in which my brother beat me up and nearly killed me. My mother decided that we had better watch the sheep alone on separate days. Then one day as I herded, a coyote came, sniffing the air and searching for a sheep. I ran to him with a stick, yelling to frighten him away, but he turned and came toward me. I struck at him, turned tail, and ran crying. If it had not been for my big dog, I might have been injured. Thereafter I was afraid to herd alone, so my mother asked a clan brother to accompany me.

When I had grown a little braver, my father went with other Hopis to trade beads for sheep. He left my brother and me to watch our flock and promised to give us some sheep of our own if we did not fight.

He exchanged one wampum necklace for thirty sheep and another string of beads for twenty-five. Returning home late one evening, he corralled the new herd near the village. Early the next morning we went out to see them. He gave my brother five animals and me four—two sheep and two goats. When I asked him why we did not receive an equal number, he replied, "You are not as good a sheep herder as your brother." I cried until he agreed to give me one more sheep to even matters. My little flock made me very happy and gave me more interest in herding.

We had great excitement one day not long afterwards. Tawalet-stewa, my uncle's middle-aged ceremonial son, became insane and ran wildly about the village, climbed on our house, and threatened us. My father and mother decided that we should leave until the trouble was over, so we departed for Shongopavi, our ancestral home. When my grandfather came home from his field, he found our house empty and followed us. On the way he found poor old Naquima, weary and tearful, sitting beside the road where he had dragged himself in an ef-fort to follow us. He picked up the cripple and carried him on his back to Shongopavi. Some days later, when the insane man had quieted down, we returned home.

Later the same man became violent again. As I was passing through the village, I saw him running about with a knife and axe. I ran into our house where Naquima sat alone on the ground. Since Tawa-letstewa lived in a house adjoining our own, Naquima was afraid and begged me to stay and protect him. I got down my bow and arrow and waited. The lunatic went to the kiva where the women were holding their Lakon ceremony, climbed down the ladder into their midst, and after some strange talk went up to his own father, who was present, and threw him to the ground. The women ran crying to the ladder and climbed out hurriedly. The important ceremony had been inter-rupted and spoiled.

The madman roamed about the village during the rest of the day and night. The next day the women refused to return to the kiva and asked Chief Lolulomai to permit them to call off the ceremony. It was never held in Oraibi again. The wild man continued to roam about the village with his hatchet and knife. He passed the old Chief, who was sitting on his housetop, and called out, "I am going to come up and kill you." He climbed up and struck the Chief a glancing blow on the head with his hatchet. The feeble old Chief fought for his life, threw the powerful lunatic off the roof, hurled a rock after him, and drove him into his own house, where he stayed until he recovered from his raving. During the fight I was in the house with Naquima, greatly frightened.

One night the next spring we were sleeping on our housetop when I awoke and went to the edge of the roof to make water. Looking over at the next house, I saw a man crawling along the roof. I slipped over to my mother and awakened her. As we watched together, the man stood up and began to run as if to jump off the roof. He stopped abruptly and said, "I am not a man, I am afraid to die." Then he ran again, put his head down on the edge of the roof, somersaulted over, and landed hard on the ground with a moan. People awoke and ran to him. I stepped over onto his roof, went to the edge where he jumped off, and looked down. His father and mother had come up and were standing over him, scolding him and saying, "Why did you jump off? You deserve to suffer." Men carried him into his house with a broken leg. A Hopi doctor came and bound it with splints. Later the missionary Voth tried to save the man's life, but the leg became infected and he died.

That summer when the Katcinas danced in the plaza, I was old enough to wonder about them. I had been taught from the first that the Katcinas are gods and all our gifts come from them. I loved them and liked to receive their gifts at the dances, but I began to notice that the rattles which they removed from their legs and gave us children at the end of every dance always disappeared within a few days. Although I searched everywhere, they kept disappearing, and this made me decide to pay close attention. I soon discovered that I was receiving the same ones from the Katcinas on different occasions, and I concluded that either the Katcinas or my parents were stealing them and giving them back again and again. One evening when the Katcinas had stopped dancing and were giving the rattles to the children, one of them offered his to me. I refused to take them. My mother came and said, "You will disappoint the Katcinas if you don't take the rattles." I felt offended and ran into the house, leaving the rattles on the ground.

Some time later, when there was to be a Katcina dance within two days, I found my mother in a near-by house, baking piki. I had entered unexpectedly and discovered that she was making red piki, the kind that I had always received from the Katcinas as a special gift. My mother seemed surprised and embarrassed. At last she said, "A Katcina was making piki here, but did not finish the work. I happened to come in and decided to help." I walked out, entered our house, and lay down on a sheepskin. I was upset because I had never seen anyone make that special red piki before. That evening at supper I was still unhappy and ate almost nothing. My mother noticed this and finally said, "My son, I told you the truth; the Katcina left that piki and I was finishing it." She offered to fry an egg to cheer me up, and went out and borrowed some eggs. The next day when the Katcinas were distributing their gifts to us I did not want any red piki. And to my surprise they gave me not red but yellow piki, and six boiled eggs, all colored! Then I was happy.

As I grew older I learned more and more about sex. My aunts (father's sisters and clan sisters) continued to show much interest in me and called me their sweetheart. The rough grandfathers kept teasing me about my penis and threatening to take it from me. They made me believe that it was the most important part of my body. Once on a dance day a fun-making Katcina ran into the plaza stark-naked. A clown caught him and asked him what he was doing. He replied, "I am chasing my penis and can't overtake it; it is always a little ahead of me. I think a person would die if he ever overtook it." The people laughed. The clowns frequently captured women and imitated the sexual act in the open plaza to entertain the people. On some occasions they fastened long gourd necks in front of them and pursued the women. Aunts would also chase their nephews and jokingly pretend to have intercourse with them. I was chased and handled in this way.

We small boys paid close attention to these matters. We also watched the animals about the village. Whenever a rooster chased a hen we looked closely and laughed. We called to each other to watch dogs, cats, goats, and burros when they mated. We also discovered that it was fun to play housekeeping with the girls and to make believe that we were their husbands, sometimes handling them.

The men joked together and told many stories about sexual intercourse. They drew figures on the rocks representing the sexual organs. I found a carving of this kind near the Buffalo shrine. There was an outline of a vulva with a coyote symbol and eight marks above it; near by was a drawing of the male organs, and above them the symbol of our Sun shield. I was told it signified that a man of our Sun Clan had had intercourse with eight women of the Coyote Clan. Somebody was boasting. My companions drew similar pictures on other rocks, some with arrows leading to sheltered places suitable for the act.

Old crippled Naquima had a favorite story which he told to make the people laugh and which I learned to repeat, imitating his funny voice and manners. He would say, with his mouth twisted to one side, "You see, on account of being paralyzed, I am unable to work in the fields and must therefore stay at home all day. Well, the single girls and the women divorced from their husbands get in need of a man, so during the day, while the men are away and few people are on the streets, they come to me one by one. . . ." The men would laugh and say, "Naquima, you must be a powerful man with the women; we had better castrate you." The women would take his part and remark, "Naquima, you are a fine-looking man; we will marry you and make pots and plaques to support our children."

While at work in the kiva the old men gave detailed accounts of their successes with women. We listened to these tales with eyes and ears wide open. They said there were magic songs by means of which a clever man could draw a woman to him against her will but that every word had to be pronounced correctly. Several of the old men were said to have this power. One of them shook all the time and had to move from place to place because the power was so strong in him.

I was about eight when old Tuvawnytewa of the Water Clan told us the story of the maidens with teeth in their vaginas. He said: "Once some beautiful girls lived in a house near Masau'u's home on the southeast side of the mesa. The Spider Woman, who lived near by, warned her grandson to stay away from these girls, for they were dangerous. But one day the boy wandered near the mesa wall and spied a maiden in a striped Hopi shawl with her hair fixed up in squash-blossom style, which made her charming. She stood by the rock where there was an easy way up, and beckoned to the boy. When they had talked together for a while, she invited him into her house, saying that she had some sisters who wished to see him. The boy had to leave then but promised to return soon. Hastening home, he found the Spider Woman sitting by the fire and told her about the beautiful girl. 'Well, my grandson,' said she, 'you have not listened to me. I have warned you that those girls are dangerous. They have sharp teeth like a saw that can bite through anything. When once they embrace a lad, he is lost.'

"But the boy seemed eager to keep his promise. Finally the Spider Woman said, 'Well, you must have some protection. Here are some wild lemonberries. Let's make a paste of them.' She ground the berries, mixed the meal with water, and made dough, out of which she molded a penis sheath, fitted it to her grandson, and said, 'Now don't let this slip off. Perhaps it will set their teeth on edge and wear them down.'

"Thus prepared, the boy went back. The girl was waiting and wondering why he was late. When he climbed the ladder with her to the second roof, he found forty pretty girls peeping through the door, all of medium size and light complexion. As he entered they clapped their hands for joy and fed him piki and watermelon, urging him to eat a plenty so that he would be strong. The girl who had enticed him to come said, 'Well, I have brought you here for pleasure, I will have you first.' All the other girls retired to another room. The vaginal teeth bit on the lemonberry sheath but soon they were worn smooth. This girl went out and another came in. When all had their turn the first girl came back and said, 'My sweetheart, you must have some strange power. Hitherto we have ruined our boy friends, but now all that is over.' The brave boy excused himself, stepped outside, threw his sheath behind a stone, and returned. When he had finished with them all again, they praised him and gave him a large bundle of piki to take home."

Whenever old Tuvawnytewa repeated this story, he would add, "You should beware of girls. If you must have one, then first collect lemonberries and take them to the Spider Woman." It was safest, he said, to have intercourse with a chicken, dog, or burro first. My father's brother, Kalnimptewa, told us that as a boy he tried burros with success and related how he was once caught in the act. I was afraid of dogs, however, because they can turn and bite very quickly, and also because I once saw two which could not separate. These old men made us believe that girls are even more dangerous, and insisted that any boy who had intercourse with a girl would stop growing and become a dwarf.

Some time before I heard the story of the maidens' teeth I had an awful experience with a clan mother. One morning while the men were in the fields I went to a clan brother's house to get him to hunt rats with me. He was away, and I found an unmarried clan mother about twenty years of age alone in the house. I stayed to play games with her on the floor. Finally she looked around, took my hand, and pulled me into the next room, suggesting that we take a nap. She lay on a sheepskin and drew me close to her. Soon she was touching my private parts which excited and frightened me. When I had an erection, she held me tightly to herself and breathed very hard. I tried to withdraw, and when she released me I saw blood on my penis and cried. Cleaning me with a cloth, she talked to me soothingly and begged me to tell no one. It was no pleasure to me. It was the first time that I had seen the black pubic hair, the blood frightened me, and I was terribly worried. I wondered if all women were like that. I ran home and told my real mother. She went over and talked with the girl who was her clan sister. I heard nothing more about the matter except that my mother called it a disgrace and said that I must keep it a secret. The woman treated me very nicely after that and even cooked many good things for me to eat.

One day when I was playing with a boy named Felix, we found one of his grandmother's hens on her nest. "Felix," said I, "let's make good use of that hen." We watched her until she cackled and came off. Then we caught her and took her down the hill to a good hiding place in the bushes. There we attempted intercourse with her, Felix following me. She tried to squawk, but we choked her off. When we were through she looked pretty weak and wobbly. "Well," I suggested, "she is nice and fat; let's cook and eat her." We killed the fowl, collected some greasewood sticks, and started a fire with matches which I had tucked in the hem of my shirt collar. While Felix sneaked up to his grandmother's place to get some piki, I plucked the bird. We had a good feast, but later our theft was discovered and my mother had to replace the fowl with one of her own. I got most of the blame because I was the older boy, but I did not get a smoking. We joked about the matter with our playmates, who boasted that they had done the same thing.

I had the reputation of being the naughtiest boy in the village. So when I was nine my parents decided to have me initiated into the Katcina society. Old Tuvenga had been selected as my ceremonial father but he was too old and feeble for this work and asked his nephew, Sekahongeoma, to take his place. Sekahongeoma's sister, Solemana, agreed to be my ceremonial mother.

In the month of February came the great Powamu ceremony. Solemana and my mother begged my father to let me be initiated into the Powamu society instead of the Katcina. The children are whipped on their admission to the latter, and my mother seemed anxious for me to escape this suffering. After much discussion with my father she said, "Solemana has come here to ask which ceremony our boy is to attend. You are the father and you should decide that question. She is waiting for you to speak." My father finally raised his head and answered, "Well, when I decide what ceremony our boy shall attend, the matter will be settled; no one may discuss it with me again. I want him to join the Katcinas and be whipped. You have complained time after time that you are getting tired of his mischief. So you have no right to back down now. It will do him good to be whipped soundly and learn a lesson. We can pray to the Whipper Katcinas to drive the evil from our boy's mind, so that he may grow up to be a good and wise man. Don't you agree with me?" My mother and Solemana began to weep, but finally they agreed and Solemana went home. I did not cry then; I only smiled. My ceremonial father also begged four times for me to be admitted into the Powamu, but my father steadfastly refused. My brother, since he was considered a quiet, good-natured boy, had been taken into the Powamu.

As the days passed, the ceremonial officers went into the kivas more and more. I began to worry about the flogging. I had seen boys after their whipping, and although they would tell me nothing I knew that it would be pretty bad. But the Katcinas were said to strike a boy only four times with the yucca stems, and I thought I could stand that. I made up my mind that I would set my teeth to grin and bear it, for other boys had been brave enough to do it.

On the morning of the sixth day of the ceremony Solemana came and took me to her house, where she bathed my head in yucca suds, plastered my face with meal, and gave me a white ear of corn and a new name—which I have forgotten. At the same time she repeated a prayer for my health and long life. Early in the evening Solemana and Sekahongeoma took me to the Marau kiva, where there was a long line of boys and girls with ceremonial fathers and mothers. People were standing in the plaza and on the housetops watching. I was naked, except for a small blanket around my shoulders, and carried the white corn ear given to me at the naming ceremony. When we reached the south end of the kiva hatchway, my ceremonial father and mother sprinkled corn meal on the natsi or insignia of the society, a yucca plant set in a clay pedestal.

Having climbed down the ladder into the dimly lighted kiva, each ceremonial father and mother sprinkled corn meal on a brown sand painting with symbolic designs on the floor north of the fireplace.[1] At the southeast corner of this large mosaic was a smaller one, representing the Sipapu—the opening in the earth within the Grand Canyon from which the human race emerged. On each side of the square Sipapu mosaic were laid an ear of corn and a celt. Above it, suspended from the roof of the kiva, was a string to which were attached ancient white beads and many old eagle wing feathers, and from the lower end of the string was fastened a small quartz crystal. I could not remember all I saw at the time but I was to review it often thereafter.

1. The details of the sand paintings and ritual are given in H. R. Voth, *The Oraibi Powamu Ceremony* (Anthrop. Series, Field Mus. Nat. Hist., 1901), Vol. III, No. 2, pp. 67–158. They are also checked by Don.

The ceremonial fathers and mothers sprinkled corn meal on both the large and the small sand mosaics, after which I, like the children ahead of me, was told to step into a yucca ring or wheel, made of four lengths of several yucca leaves tied together with a hawk feather attached at each of the four knots. Two men squatting on opposite sides raised and lowered this yucca ring four times for each of us, expressing the wish that we might grow up to manhood and live happily to old age. Then we were taken to the north side of the kiva.

When we were all in the kiva, the Katcina Chief and his assistant entered with trays upon which lay pahos and some corn meal. Standing between the ladder and the fireplace, they lit a pipe and smoked, frequently glancing up as though expecting someone. Suddenly a great man, a god, descended the ladder in a white blanket, carrying in his left hand a netted gourd, four corn ears, and a wooden implement about fourteen inches long and resembling a knife; in his right hand was a long crook to which were fastened an ear of corn and some corn-meal packets. He was Muyingwa. In the kiva all were very quiet until an old man asked the god whence he came. He replied in a slow voice and with a long speech to the effect that he had come from the four corners of the world below to tell the Oraibi children about the ceremonies and the Hopi way of life. He stepped forward, sprinkled us with sacred water from his gourd, and ordered the Katcina Chief to see that we were whipped with yucca to enlighten our hearts and lead us over life's road.

The god then departed and four Coyemsie Katcinas arose from their hiding place in the southeast corner of the kiva, rapidly encircled the small mosaic four times, and finally stopped with a Katcina on each of the four sides. Each Katcina in turn picked up the ear of corn lying before him in one hand and the celt in the other, reached both arms around the string of beads and feathers suspended over the mosaic, exchanged the corn ear and the celt from hand to hand, came and touched us candidates with them, and replaced them on the floor. Then all four returned to the southeast corner of the kiva and everybody waited in silence.

Presently a loud grunting noise, a rattling of turtle shells, and a jingling of bells were heard outside. Two Ho Katcinas and a Hahai-i ran around the kiva four times, beat the roof with whips, jumped upon it howling, and came hurriedly down the ladder. The Ho Katcinas were painted black with large white dots all over their bodies and small, soft eagle feathers stuck on the paint. They had great black masks with a few white marks upon them, protruding eyes, very large mouths, and paired horns. On their heads they wore large eagle feathers pointed backward and downward. Around the hips each had a belt of leather painted green and a kilt made of the hair of horses' manes dyed red. On their upper arms were green leather bands, to each of which was fixed an eagle tail feather; and on each leg below the knees were fastened a turtle-shell rattle and a number of bells. Their feet were clad in moccasins and each carried a yucca whip. The Hahai-i Katcina wore a large mask with triangular holes for eyes and mouth, wings on the sides, and a bunch of feathers on top. He was dressed in a black manta, white buckskin wedding moccasins, and a darkly bordered blanket, and carried an extra supply of yucca switches in his arms. This Katcina represented a woman, and I thought he was one at the time. The Ho Katcinas took positions on the east and west sides of the large sand mosaic while the Hahai-i Katcina stood at the southeast corner with his yucca stems. Some of the children were already crying, but I was not. The Ho Katcinas kept grunting, howling, rattling, trampling, and brandishing their yucca whips.

Soon a boy was placed on the large sand mosaic and received four yucca blows which he bore bravely. Then Sekahongeoma placed me, naked, on the mosaic, holding my right arm high over my head and telling me to protect my private parts with my left hand. If a ceremonial father wishes to do so, he may let the boy get two stripes, then pull him out of reach of the Whipper and receive the other blows on his own bare thighs. My ceremonial father failed to do this, letting me take the four blows full force. I stood them fairly well, without crying, and thought my suffering was past; but then the Ho Katcina struck me four more times and cut me to pieces. I struggled, yelled, and urinated. Solemana cried out for me, and Sekahongeoma finally pulled me away. Blood was running down over my body. The people in the kiva shouted angrily at the Katcina Whipper and asked him whether he did not know how to count four stripes. When they let me go, I wrapped the blanket around my painful body and sat down. I tried to stop sobbing, but continued to cry in my heart—and paid little attention to the other floggings.

After all the children were whipped—there were about twenty-five of us—the Hahai-i Katcina stepped on the very much spoiled sand mosaic, bent forward, raised his ceremonial kilt, and was severely flogged by both Ho Katcinas, after which they flogged each other in the same manner, which afforded us some satisfaction. The Katcina Chief and his assistant then handed some corn meal to the Ho Katcinas and the three left the kiva, encircled it four times, and disappeared. After they had gone, the Powamu and Katcina chiefs warned us never to tell uninitiated children what we had seen.

I was taken out of the kiva and to Solemana's house to be fed some stew before I was led home and put to bed on a sheepskin. The next morning when I awoke, the pelt had stuck fast to my body, so that when I tried to get up it came with me. I cried and cried and had a dreadful time freeing myself, even with the help of my father. The wounds were awful, and everyone could see that there would be permanent scars. My mother reproached my father for his cruelty. He had told the Katcina Whipper to give me a double thrashing and had instructed Sekahongeoma not to protect me. Katcinas in varied costumes wandered about the village all day and many of them distributed gifts to us.

That night everybody went to the kivas to see the Katcinas dance. I accompanied my mother to the Mongwi kiva, where we sat with many others on the raised portion, watching. When the Katcinas entered the kiva without masks, I had a great surprise. They were not spirits, but human beings. I recognized nearly every one of them and felt very unhappy, because I had been told all my life that the Katcinas were gods. I was especially shocked and angry when I saw all my uncles, fathers, and clan brothers dancing as Katcinas. I felt the worst when I saw my own father—and whenever he glanced at me I turned my face away. When the dances were over the head man told us with a stern face that we now knew who the Katcinas really were and that if we ever talked about this to uninitiated children we would get a thrashing even worse than the one we had received the night before. "A long time ago," said he, "a child was whipped to death for telling the secret." I felt sure that I would never tell. My wounds became infected and caused me several days of suffering. I kept thinking, too, about the Katcinas whom I had loved. Recalling the occasion when I had caught my mother making red piki, I asked her how it had happened that the Katcina gave me yellow instead. She laughed and laughed, but finally told me that she had traded her red piki for yellow in order to keep me fooled. I was told that since I now knew about the Katcinas I would receive no more special gifts from them. But my father made me a bow out of juniper root. This bow was not very strong but the arrows he made were excellent. My ceremonial father gave me a good, strong bow and arrows tipped with metal.

I watched from a housetop one afternoon and saw the dreaded giants coming into the village with their lassos. They accused the children of bad behavior and threatened to take them away and eat them. I saw them rope one boy from a housetop and release him only after his parents had pleaded for his life and given good meat in his place. They stopped at Honwuhti's house, calling Mattima, a lad who was known to behave badly. While they were seeking this boy, I quickly climbed down and ran to the Howeove kiva. Hurrying down the ladder, I rushed to the corner where my father was carding wool. The men in the kiva noticed my excitement and asked the cause. "The giants have come," said I. "They are after Mattima now, and I want to escape." The men laughed and said, "Well, boy, you are not in the safest place. This kiva is the home of the giants. They may come here and catch you any minute." More frightened than ever, I jumped up and started out. My father caught hold of me and said, "Chuka, these men are teasing you. Don't run away." My heart was leaping up and down as I turned and looked at an old man named Tewahongnewa. He said, "You stay right here, my boy, and if those giants come we will protect you." Then the others promised to keep the giants out. So I sat down close to the old man and was quiet. He was the ceremonial son of my father's uncle, and one of the finest men I ever knew.

Some of the men left the kiva to see what happened to Mattima, but I stayed there until sunset. When a man returned, he remarked, "That boy was tough. He picked up his little bow and arrow and shot one of the giants in the face. He was aiming another arrow when a giant roped him. Then he shook with fear, for the giants were angry and threatened to carry him off and roast him for a feast. It was a long time before his parents could persuade them to accept a piece of meat and release the boy. He cried and promised to behave hereafter. The giants warned him that if they had to return for him he would be unable to escape." The men talked about disobedient children and someone remembered that once a child whom the giants caught actually died of fright. I was grateful for their protection.

I began to pay more attention to the stories of the old people and learned much about the world, gods, and spirits.[2] At night we were talked to sleep with true accounts of our ancestors in the good old days when the gods lived near Oraibi and mingled with the people, when the spirits were visible to the naked eye, and when the Katcinas appeared in person and without masks. My father and grandfather were good storytellers and so were my great-uncles, Talasquaptewa and Kayayeptewa, and my father's brother, Kalnimptewa. My ceremonial father also answered many questions for me and gave me good advice on how to get along with the spirits and gods. My mother had some very good stories about witches who turned themselves into animals and about animals who were really people. She also had a sad story about how she once died, traveled westward to the home of the dead, and talked to some of her relatives. Other people told of dying, traveling over rough country to the home of our dear ones, and returning to life. Many old people told of dreams in which they wrestled with evil spirits and even with gods. We often heard people talk in secret about how some relative had been initiated into the society of witches and spent most of his time doing mischief—bringing sickness and death upon other members of his family. The talk about witches was the most frightful, especially when we were told that our closest kin and best friends might be Two-Hearts. The stories I liked best were about the Twin War gods and their grandmother the Spider Woman who then lived northwest of the village.

2. See chapter on Legends in the Appendix.

Groups of boys and girls would go to the houses of the old people and beg for more stories. Sometimes we stayed in the kiva where the men worked in order to hear some blind old man recite the story of the Hopi from the beginning of the world up to the present and predict what would happen in the future. But whenever we begged for stories in the summertime we were refused; and our elders warned us that people who spent their time talking when they should be working in the fields are almost certain to be bitten by rattlesnakes.

My fathers and uncles showed me the ancestral masks and explained that long ago the real Katcinas had come regularly to Oraibi and had danced in the plaza. They explained that since the people had become so wicked—since there were now so many Two-Hearts in the world—the Katcinas had stopped coming in person and sent their spirits to enter the masks on dance days. They showed me how to feed the masks by placing food on their mouths and taught me to respect them and pray to them.

In accordance with strict Hopi rule, I killed rabbits with my bow and arrows and gave them to my ceremonial father and mother. I also learned that it was proper to hoe and chop weeds for my ceremonial father and to help him in other ways. My relatives said, "You owe your ceremonial father a great deal because he will advise you and take your part in arguments, and some day he will take you into the higher societies. When you are a man, he will help make wedding garments for your bride, and if he happens to have sheep, he will give you two or three for the wedding feast." They said that if my real father ever neglected me, my ceremonial father would help me out, and that he would never whip or punish me.

I thought of the flogging and the initiation as an important turning point in my life, and I felt ready at last to listen to my elders and to live right. Whenever my father talked to me I kept my ears open, looked straight into his eyes, and said, "Owi" (Yes). One of the first rules was to rise earlier, run to the east edge of the mesa, and pray to the Sun god to make me strong and brave and wise. My father also instructed me to go to the foothills and run for exercise, and to bathe in the spring, even in winter. The races at sunrise were too hard on me, so I asked my father what other plan I might follow. He advised me to sit on the housetop before sunrise and pray to the Sun god as he appeared in the east. That suited me better; and one night in a dream I saw a strange being coming to me in the form of a middle-aged man and as white as snow. He kept his face hidden but said with a friendly voice that he was the Sun god himself and that he saw and heard everything I did. Although he was kind and polite, I awoke frightened.

5
School on the Reservation

I GREW UP BELIEVING that Whites are wicked, deceitful people. It seemed that most of them were soldiers, government agents, or missionaries, and that quite a few were Two-Hearts. The old people said that the Whites were tough, possessed dangerous weapons, and were better protected than we were from evil spirits and poison arrows. They were known to be big liars too. They sent Negro soldiers against us with cannons, tricked our war chiefs to surrender without fighting, and then broke their promises. Like Navahos, they were proud and domineering—and needed to be reminded daily to tell the truth. I was taught to mistrust them and to give warning whenever I saw one coming.

Our chief had to show respect to them and pretend to obey their orders, but we knew that he did it halfheartedly and that he put his trust in our Hopi gods. Our ancestors had predicted the coming of these Whites and said that they would cause us much trouble. But it was understood that we had to put up with them until our gods saw fit to recall our Great White Brother from the East to deliver us.[1] Most people in Oraibi argued that we should have nothing to do with them, accept none of their gifts, and make no use of their building materials,

---

1. See Appendix, pp. 434.

medicine, food, tools, or clothing—but we did want their guns. Those who would have nothing to do with Whites were called "Hostiles" and those who would coöperate a little were called "Friendlies." These two groups were quarreling over the subject from my earliest memories and sometimes their arguments spoiled the ceremonies and offended the Six-Point-Cloud-People,[2] our ancestral spirits, who held back the rain and sent droughts and disease. Finally the old chief, with my grandfather and a few others, became friendly with the Whites and accepted gifts, but warned that we would never give up our ceremonies or forsake our gods. But it seemed that fear of Whites, especially of what the United States Government could do, was one of the strongest powers that controlled us, and one of our greatest worries.

A few years before my birth the United States Government had built a boarding school at the Keams Canyon Agency. At first our chief, Lolulomai, had not wanted to send Oraibi children, but chiefs from other villages came and persuaded him to accept clothes, tools, and other supplies, and to let them go. Most of the people disliked this and refused to coöperate. Troops came to Oraibi several times to take the children by force and carry them off in wagons. The people said that it was a terrible sight to see Negro soldiers come and tear children from their parents. Some boys later escaped from Keams Canyon and returned home on foot, a distance of forty miles.

Some years later a day school was opened at the foot of the mesa in New Oraibi, where there were a trading post, a post office, and a few government buildings. Some parents were permitted to send their children to this school. When my sister started, the teacher cut her hair, burned all her clothes, and gave her a new outfit and a new name, Nellie. She did not like school, stopped going after a few weeks, and tried to keep out of sight of the Whites who might force her to return. About a year later she was sent to the New Oraibi spring to fetch water in a ceremonial gourd for the Ooqol society and was captured by the school principal who permitted her to take the water up to the village, but compelled her to return to school after the ceremony was over. The teachers had then forgotten her old name, Nellie, and called

2. See Appendix, pp. 446–450.

her Gladys. Although my brother was two years older than I, he had managed to keep out of school until about a year after I started, but he had to be careful not to be seen by Whites. When finally he did enter the day school at New Oraibi, they cut his hair, burned his clothes, and named him Ira.

In 1899 it was decided that I should go to school. I was willing to try it but I did not want a policeman to come for me and I did not want my shirt taken from my back and burned. So one morning in September I left it off, wrapped myself in my Navaho blanket, the one my grandfather had given me, and went down the mesa barefoot and bareheaded.

I reached the school late and entered a room where boys had bathed in tubs of dirty water. Laying aside my blanket, I stepped into a tub and began scrubbing myself. Suddenly a white woman entered the room, threw up her hands, and exclaimed, "On my life!" I jumped out of the tub, grabbed my blanket, darted through the door, and started back up the mesa at full speed. But I was never a swift runner. Boys were sent to catch me and take me back. They told me that the woman was not angry and that "On my life!" meant that she was surprised. They returned with me to the building, where the same woman met me with kind words which I could not understand. Sam Poweka, the Hopi cook, came and explained that the woman was praising me for coming to school without a policeman. She scrubbed my back with soap and water, patted me on the shoulder, and said, "Bright boy." She dried me and dressed me in a shirt, underwear, and very baggy overalls. Then she cut my hair, measured me for a better-fitting suit, called me Max, and told me through an interpreter to leave my blanket and go out to play with the other boys.

The first thing I learned in school was "nail," a hard word to remember. Every day when we entered the classroom a nail lay on the desk. The teacher would take it up and say, "What is this?" Finally I answered "nail" ahead of the other boys and was called "bright."

At first I went to school every day, not knowing that Saturday and Sunday were rest days. I often cut wood in order to get candy and to be called a "smart boy." I was also praised again and again for coming to school without a policeman.

At Christmas we had two celebrations, one in the school and another in the Mission Church. Ralph of the Masau'u Clan and I each received a little painted wagon as a reward for good attendance. Mine was about fifteen inches long with two shafts and a beautiful little gray horse.

I learned little at school the first year, except "bright boy," "smart boy," "yes" and "no," "nail," and "candy." Just before Christmas we heard that a disease, smallpox, was coming west from First Mesa. Within a few weeks news came to us that on Second Mesa the people were dying so fast that the Hopi did not have time to bury them, but just pitched their bodies over the cliff. The government employees and some of the schoolteachers fled from Oraibi, leaving only the principal and missionaries, who said that they would stay. About this time my mother had a new baby, named Perry much later.

During the month of January I danced for the first time as a real Katcina. One evening I entered the Howeove kiva, to which both my father and grandfather belonged, and found the men painting for a dance. Even though I had not practiced I decided to paint myself and dance with them. When my father and grandfather arrived, they discouraged me, but the kind old man who had promised to protect me from the Giant Katcinas in the same kiva about a year before was an important man and insisted that I could dance. When I finished painting, my grandfather gave me a small black blanket to use as a sash, and, since there were not enough gourd rattles, someone gave me an inflated and dried bull scrotum which contained a few small stones and made a good rattle. We left the kiva for the women to enter and then one of the Katcinas carried me down the ladder on his back which made the people laugh. I was at the end of the line and danced well enough for an old woman to pull me over by the stove so that all could see me. Then I went with the Katcinas to the other kivas. The people praised me and said that my reward might be a nice girl for a wife.

One day when I was playing with the boys in the plaza in Oraibi, the school principal and the missionary came to vaccinate us. My mother brought me in to the principal who was holding a knife in his hand. Trembling, I took hold of his arm which caused him to laugh.

They had a small bottle of soapylike liquid which they opened, and placed a little on my arm. After it had dried, they rubbed my arm with a cloth and the missionary took a sharp instrument and stuck it into my skin three times. I proved myself brave enough to take it and set a good example for the rest of the family who were vaccinated in their turn. It was spring when the disease disappeared. We were lucky. The old people said that the vaccinations were all nonsense but probably harmless, and that by our prayers we had persuaded the spirits to banish the disease—that it was Masau'u, who guards the village with his firebrand, who had protected us.

One night some of us boys decided to sleep out on Oraibi Rock by the shrine. While we were lying on our blankets, I happened to look southeast and saw a blaze of fire moving along about a foot above the ground. I knew it was the torch of Masau'u and watched it run along the edge of the mesa and jump down into a large crack between the stones at the place where the people said Masau'u lived. We gathered up our blankets and hurried back to our houses. Our parents said it was good that we came quickly.

One morning we were playing in front of our house, shooting arrows through a cornhusk hoop. I had the bow and arrows which my ceremonial father had given me. Looking up at Naquima, who sat in the door of our summer house, I said, "I am going to shoot you." He laughed, thrust out his chest, and replied, "All right, shoot." I shot and hit him squarely on the chest. He fell over, and my brother Ira laughed and rolled in the dust; but I was worried and quickly climbed to the third story. Naquima was sitting up again holding the arrow and smiling. Opening his shirt he showed me a red spot, saying, "I don't think you meant to hurt me," and then praised my marksmanship. I begged him never to tell my mother or father, and we kept the matter secret. If I had used an arrow with a metal tip I might have killed him.

During the summer I caught my first jack rabbit. On the hunt the girls were instructed to follow the men and run up to any man making a kill, take the game, and say "Askwali" (Thanks). The dogs chased and caught a big jack rabbit and we all ran up. I got hold of the animal first, but did not know how to kill it. One man on a burro shouted to me, "Cut open his stomach and rip out his intestines." Another said, "Put some rabbit blood in his anus." They were all laughing and teasing me. A girl named Margaret ran up and seized the rabbit, which was still struggling. Her brother Herman hit it behind its ears with the edge of his hand, and killed it easily.

In October I returned to day school and continued until the following spring, but I did not learn much. I was more interested in the stories told by the old people and especially in the Katcina dances held in the kivas at night. I was ten, had been given a Katcina outfit, and could now dance and sing very well. My father told me to listen to the advice of my uncles in the kiva and to do whatever they said. I was taught that dancing was not for my pleasure but to persuade the Six-Point-Cloud-People to bring rain so that we would have a good harvest.

During the summer I again helped with the herding and worked with my father in the fields. He taught me to chop weeds, even when I was tired and thirsty, and insisted that when I got used to it work would be easy. The summer was very dry and our crops began to fail. So after the Niman dance—a home-going dance for the Katcinas—in July, we assembled our burros and went to Moenkopi in order to conserve our food supplies. My father's brother also went with his family and his little boy, Luther, and we all stayed at the house of Iswuhti, my father's mother's sister, making a big family.

It was in Moenkopi that I quarreled with my mother and nearly committed suicide. One day I complained to her that Luther was a cry baby. "Well, Chuka," she responded crossly, "you should not tease him so much." I made some reply which angered her, and she seized a small stick and hit me three or four times. Feeling that I had done no wrong, I began to feel sorry for myself but did not cry. "Don't look for me after I leave," I said, "I may go back to Oraibi." I went out to the foothills, sat down, and cried. I pitied myself more and more and began to think of plans for ending my life. Finally I remembered an accident in which a man was buried by a cave-in while digging for gophers, and decided to dig a hole in the sand, lie down, and wait for it to fall in on me. Using my hands and a stick, I dug a hole about three feet wide and four feet deep and hollowed out a cave at the bottom. Then

I lay down and waited. I fell asleep and slept most of the afternoon. When I awoke I saw that nothing had happened and climbed out to defecate. Feeling a little better, I walked back to the hole, wondering whether to enter it again or go home and get some food. As I came up to my deathtrap, it caved in before my eyes.

I was frightened. My heart began to pound, and I thought bells were ringing in my ears. It dawned upon me that if I had been killed nobody would have found me until my body had rotted enough to attract the dogs. I went home. When I reached the village the people were looking for me and my mother was crying. I reminded her that she had struck me with a stick and told her what I had done. My relatives did not believe me until they went out and found the hole.

One day while we were in Moenkopi ten or twelve other boys and I went to a low place where cattails grow. There we found muddy water about a foot deep. In some places we swam on our bellies to keep from sinking into the mud. We caught a few small fishes and brought them home, where we borrowed a pan, got some piki, and had a feast on the white, tender flesh. We were warned that the fish might make us swell up and die but we liked them and asked our parents if they had ever seen anyone die from eating fish. They were unable to answer, and as nothing happened we went back fishing for several days. I hated to leave Moenkopi because we were having so much fun.

That autumn some of the people took their children to Keams Canyon to attend the boarding school. Partly because I was tired of working and herding sheep and partly because my father was poor and I could not dress like some of the other boys, I was persuaded to go to the Agency school to learn to read and cipher—and to get clothes. My mother and father took three burros and accompanied me to Keams Canyon. When we arrived at the end of two days, the matron, Mrs. Weans, took me into the building and gave me a bath, clipped my hair, and dressed me in clean clothes.

I ate my supper in the dining room with the other children. My father and mother ate outside in a camp. That night I slept in the dormitory on a bed. This was something new for me and felt pretty good. I was eleven, and the biggest boy in that dormitory; I did not cry. The next morning I had breakfast with the other children. My father and mother went to the kitchen, where the cook fed them. For breakfast we had coffee, oatmeal, fried bacon, fried potatoes, and syrup. The bacon was too salty and the oatmeal too sloppy.

After breakfast we were all told to go to the office and see the superintendent of the Reservation, Mr. Burton, for whom my parents would have to sign their names, or make their marks, before going home. There were a great many of us and we had to stand in line. The agent shook hands with us and patted us on the head, telling us through an interpreter that we had come to be educated. Then he told us to pass into another room where we would receive some gifts. They gave my mother fifteen yards of dress cloth and presented an axe, a claw hammer, and a small brass lamp to my father. Then they asked him to choose between a shovel and a grubbing hoe. He took the hoe.

We did not go to school that day. We returned to the kitchen, where the cook gave my parents two loaves of bread and some bacon, syrup, and meat. Then we went to the camp, where my father saddled a burro and told my mother to mount. "Well, son," they advised me, "don't ever try to run away from here. You are not a good runner, and you might get lost and starve to death. We would not know where to find you, and the coyotes would eat you." I promised. My father climbed on a burro and they started off. I kept my eyes upon them until finally they disappeared in the direction of Oraibi. I moaned and began to cry, fearing that I should never see them again. A Hopi boy named Nash, whom I did not know, spoke to me and told me to stop crying. My parents would come back again, he reassured me, and they might bring me some good Hopi food. He took me through the Canyon to the other end, where the school building stood. There we gathered some wild roseberries and began eating them until I discovered that they were full of worms.

At noon we all lined up, with the smallest boys in the lead. I was the tallest and the last boy for our dining room. At the table somebody spoke a few words to God, but failed to offer him any of the food. It was very good.

After lunch we smaller boys were given a job cleaning up trash in the yard. When we had finished, Nash and I took a walk up the southeast mesa to the highest point. As we reached the top, Nash turned and said, "Look over to the west." I looked and saw the top of Mount Beautiful, just beyond Oraibi. It seemed far away and I cried a little, wondering whether I would ever get home again. Nash told me not to worry, because I was put there to learn the white people's way of life. He said that when he first came he was homesick, too, but that now he was in the third grade and satisfied. He promised me that when his relatives brought some good Hopi food he would share it with me. His talk encouraged me. As we climbed down the mesa, we heard the supper bell ringing and ran but arrived late. The disciplinarian stepped up to us and struck Nash twice on the buttocks saying, "You are late." Since I was a new boy, he did not put his hands on me—I was lucky.

We went to the dining room and ate bread and a thing called hash, which I did not like. It contained different kinds of food mixed together; some were good and some were bad, but the bad outdid the good. We also had prunes, rice, and tea. I had never tasted tea. The smell of it made me feel so sick that I thought I would vomit. We ate our supper but it did not satisfy me. I thought I would never like hash.

I had trouble defecating, too. A person had to be very careful where he sat. Little houses called privies were provided—one for boys and another for girls. I went into one of them but was afraid to sit down. I thought something might seize me or push me from below and was uneasy about this for several days.

After supper we played a little. Some of the older boys, who had been in school before, wrestled with me. I had been a big, brave lad at home, but now I was timid and afraid. It seemed that I was a little nobody and that any boy could beat me. When it came time for bed the matron took us to the small boys' dormitory, where she made us undress except for our underwear, kneel, and put our elbows on the bed. She taught us to ask Jesus to watch over us while we slept. I had tried praying to Jesus for oranges and candy without success, but I tried it again anyway.

The next day we had to go to school. The little boys went both morning and afternoon. I had to commence at the very bottom in the kindergarten class. When we had entered the classroom and taken our seats, the teacher asked me my name. I did not like my name, Max, so I kept quiet. "Well," said the teacher, "your name shall be Don," and wrote it down in a little book.

The teacher used to pick up a stick, turn the leaves of a chart, and tell us to read. Some of the little boys from First Mesa, who had been there before, could read right along. Although I was the biggest boy in the class, I could not read at all. I felt uncomfortable, especially since they had dressed me in little brown knee pants which I did not like. The first things to learn were "A hat," "A cat," "A horse," "A cow," "An eagle," etc. Then came such things as "A cow has four feet," and "The man had two feet." Another step was, "Put a ball on the box," "Count up to ten." After several days I finally began to understand the words. Soon we were reading long sentences like "'A rat, a rat,' cried Mae."

I grew tired of school and thought of running away. But one of my father's nephews, Harry Kopi, was watching me and noticed that my face was growing sorrowful. One afternoon, as I was sitting still and sad in the building, he came to me and said, "Come out with me to the place where the pigs live." As we walked along he asked me if I were lonesome, and I almost cried. "I have brought you out here to see the pigs," he said. "When I used to get homesick I would come here and look at them; they made me laugh and feel better." There were about twenty pigs in the pen, all of different sizes. They were funny animals—like dogs with hooves. They looked horrible with their little eyes, sharp mouths, and dirty faces. "Let's go into the pen and ride a pig," said Harry. He caught one by the tail and I clambered on its back and rode it about the pen. It was great fun. I felt better when I got off, and thought to myself that if my homesickness returned I would ride a pig again.

Every Sunday we were taken to the chapel, where we sang, prayed, and had a lesson about Jesus Christ. On those days we were supposed to wear clean clothes and have our faces washed and our hair combed. At Christmas we had parties and a tree and received many gifts.

In February they promoted me to the first grade. I had begun to feel better and sent a message by a man who was going to Oraibi, asking my father to come and bring me some Hopi food. One day he came, bringing some watermelons. I shared them with Nash, who had been generous with his food. In the afternoon I went for a walk on the mesa with Harry, Nash, and my father. We stayed there talking for a long time. We also roasted some piñon nuts and picked some juniper berries. When my father left for home on the following day, I sent with him the Christmas gifts that I had received—a piece of cloth, some of the juniper berries, and a little candy that I had saved.

A few weeks later we had some excitement at school. The assistant disciplinarian, an Oraibi man named Edwin, who had been educated at Grand Junction, climbed through a window into the girls' dormitory one night to sleep with his sweetheart. Soon some of the larger boys tried this with other girls. One night the matron caught Jerry, a Second Mesa boy, in a girl's room. She locked him in another room and kept him there all night without any clothes except his underwear. The next morning she questioned him as to whether he was the only boy involved. Finally he broke down and gave her a long list of names, which she turned over to Mr. Burton, the superintendent.

As we lined up to go to breakfast on the following day, which was the Sabbath, Mr. Burton came with a paper in his hand. "Well, boys," he said, "when I read off your names please step out of line." He started with Edwin and called names slowly until there were thirty boys out of line. Of the larger boys only one was left—Louis, the older clan brother of Nash. When the list was completed the superintendent said, "Will the boys who are left please close up the line and march in to breakfast?" Looking very angry, he led the guilty boys to a large room where he locked them up without any food.

We small boys went into the dining room, where we found that two of the kitchen boys had been summoned to remove their aprons and join the party to be punished. We noticed that many of the girls were absent too. We felt like a flock of sheep huddled together in a corner of a big corral after the wolves have been among them. Mr. Boss, the disciplinarian, said grace quickly and announced, "Eat all you want, children; there will be plenty today." After breakfast, Sunday School was called off. People seemed worried and unfit for prayer.

We stood around in the yard waiting to see what would happen. Mr. Burton and Mr. Boss unlocked the closed room, lined up the boys, and marched them to the girls' dormitory. When they arrived, they were seated in a large room where the girls had already assembled. Mr. Burton gave the culprits a long, stiff talk. Then they were taken to a room upstairs, while we remained in the yard and listened. Soon we heard strapping. Each boy received from fifteen to thirty lashes with a rawhide, the number depending on his age. They were whipped in the presence of the girls, but no boy cried out. Then the girls were taken to another room and paddled, but not before the boys. Some of them cried. After giving the boys another lecture, Mr. Burton marched them through the yard to the toilet, where every boy seemed anxious to go. They were then taken back to the room and locked in again.

At noon we formed a short line and marched back to eat. Later in the day a small boy named Hicks, of the Tewa tribe at First Mesa, went up to a window of the locked room, and the prisoners asked him to bring them some food. He ran to the small boys' building and returned with several rolls of piki. As he was pushing these through a broken pane in the window, the disciplinarian slipped up behind him and caught him. He scolded the boy, laughed and told him to beat it or he would put him in with the prisoners. I stood around all afternoon and watched. For supper the boys were given bread and water and were then released.

In May we had a Decoration Day celebration. We stuck little flags in our caps, took bunches of flowers, and marched out to the graves of two soldiers who had come out here to fight the Hopi and had died.

On June the fourteenth my father came for me and we returned home, riding burros and bringing presents of calico, lamps, shovels, axes, and other tools. It was a joy to get home again, to see all my folks, and to tell about my experiences at school. I had learned many English words and could recite part of the Ten Commandments. I knew how to sleep on a bed, pray to Jesus, comb my hair, eat with a knife and fork, and use a toilet. I had learned that the world is round instead of flat, that it is indecent to go naked in the presence of girls, and to eat the testes of sheep or goats. I had also learned that a person thinks with his head instead of his heart.

At home I found two disappointments. Old blind Tuvenga had died and my dog, Yucca, was dead too. The news made me very sad.

When they told me that my dog was dead I worried about it until late into the night.

During the summer another dog took Yucca's place. A stray bitch had had puppies out on the mesa under a rock. One day I planned with seven other boys to kill the dog and catch her pups. When we approached the den the mother rushed out at us growling. We shot her with arrows until she died. The puppies ran in every direction. I chased one, calling out, "I will take the yellow pup with the white neck," but another boy caught it. I wanted it very much and said, "Will you give me the dog for my five arrows?" "What else?" asked the boy. I began to think, remembering that I still had two small cats at home. I said, "I will give you five arrows and a cat." He did not answer me at first, but rubbed his head over the dog and put its nose up close to us to tame it. On the way home he said I could have the dog. I walked straight to my house, tied the puppy to a stone, and took down the five arrows that were fastened to the bow which my ceremonial father had given me. My mother saw me and asked, "What did the boy give you for those arrows?" I smiled but said nothing. I hoped that the boy would choose the white cat, but he took the black one. When he had left I told my mother the whole story. She laughed until she almost cried. The dog grew fast and became a good hunter. He was strong and could dig rabbits and prairie dogs out of their holes like a badger. I named him Muitala (Moonlight) because he was yellow.

While I was at home that summer I traded the good bow that my ceremonial father had given me to the Rev. Mr. Voth for a piece of calico, a few sticks of candy, and some crackers. I hated to part with the bow. At that time, however, my father was very poor. He made a shirt for me out of a flour sack and pants out of unbleached muslin. The same summer I noticed that the arrow with my placenta cord upon it was no longer in the ceiling of our house. I don't know what became of it.

By the end of summer I had had enough of hoeing weeds and tending sheep. Helping my father was hard work and I thought it was better to be educated. My grandfather agreed that it was useful to know something of the white man's ways, but said that he feared I might neglect the Hopi rules which were more important. He cautioned me that if I had bad dreams while at school, I should spit four times in order to drive them from my mind and counteract their evil influences.

Before sunrise on the tenth of September the police came to Oraibi and surrounded the village, with the intention of capturing the children of the Hostile families and taking them to school by force. They herded us all together at the east edge of the mesa. Although I had planned to go later, they put me with the others. The people were excited, the children and the mothers were crying, and the men wanted to fight. I was not much afraid because I had learned a little about education and knew that the police had not come without orders. One of the captured boys was Dick, the son of "Uncle Joe" who had stirred up most of the trouble among the Hostiles. I was glad. Clara, the granddaughter of Chief Lolulomai, was also taken. The Chief went up to Mr. Burton, who was writing our names down on a piece of paper, and said, "This girl must be left here until she is older." She was allowed to return to her mother. They also captured my clan brother Archie, the son of my mother's sister, Nuvahunka.

When Mr. Burton saw me in the group, he said, "Well, well, what are you doing here? I thought you were back in school at the Agency." I told him that I was glad to go with him. This seemed to please him, and he let me go to my house to get my things. When I returned with a bag of fresh peaches, I discovered that they had marched the children to New Oraibi to be placed in the wagons. I followed and found my grandfather in a group near the wagons. When I noticed how crowded the wagons were, I asked Mr. Burton if I might ride a horse. He sent me with Archie, Dick, and my grandfather to ask the police. Two of them were my clan uncles, Adam from First Mesa and Secavaima from Shipaulovi. I walked up to Adam, smiling, shook hands with him, and introduced my clan brother Archie. "You don't need to fear us," said my uncle, "we are policemen." I asked him whether Archie and I might ride double on horseback to the Agency. They laughed and said that I had a brave heart. They warned me that the Hostiles might follow us on the road and give battle, but they were only teasing.

When we were ready to leave the police took us three boys behind their saddles. Near the foothill of First Mesa we made a short cut through the gap to the mission house, where we stopped and waited for the wagons to bring our lunch. After eating, Adam told me that his week's term as policeman was up and that this was as far as he was going. He took me to Mr. Burton, who told me that I might ride with him in his buckboard. When we were ready to start, I climbed on the buckboard back of the seat. Rex Moona, an educated Hopi who worked in the office at Keams Canyon, was riding in the seat with the superintendent. We drove on ahead of the procession and reached Keams Canyon about sunset.

The children already at the school were eating their supper when we arrived. Rex and I went to the kitchen and asked for food. We each got a loaf of bread and ate it with some syrup. The cook asked me if I would like some hash. I said, "No." We ate our food at the door and told the people in the kitchen that the children were coming in wagons. Then we went to the dormitory and rested. The next morning we took a bath, had our hair clipped, put on new clothes, and were schoolboys again.

That day we were badly scared when a Navaho policeman shot at his uncle in the office. They were having a trial, and our disciplinarian told us to stay away because there might be gunplay. We boys were out in the yard picking up rubbish when we heard a bang. I seized Archie's hand and we ran into the dining room. Archie cried and cried. The boys said that when the Navaho aimed at his uncle someone knocked his arm up, causing the bullet to hit the ceiling.

The next day I had three surprises. They put me in the dormitory with the big boys, gave me some long khaki pants, and promoted me to the second grade. I was twelve and felt like a man. After a few weeks I was taken off the yard work and given a job with four other boys cleaning the dormitory, making beds, and tidying up the sitting room.

The teacher for the second grade was late in coming from Chicago. Mr. Boss, the disciplinarian, taught us until she arrived in the middle of October. She was a good-looking blond about forty-five, named Mrs. DeVee. She taught us the sounds of the letters, showing us how to hold our mouths to pronounce them correctly. I had to work hard to keep up with the class.

I was punished twice within a short time. One day I struck a boy who hit me first; but the teacher looked up only in time to see my blow and made me stand in a corner with my left arm raised high above my head for a full half-hour. This was hard to do. On another occasion I talked too much with a deskmate and Mrs. DeVee made each of us chew a piece of laundry soap until foam came out of our mouths. She said our mouths were dirty. The soap was strong and made our mouths so sore that it pained us to eat for two or three days. When the teacher got sick and had to leave the school I was glad.

I kept close watch on Archie, who was not getting along very well and showed sorrow in his face. It made me remember my first days at school. At last I thought of the pigs and took him over to the pen. He looked at them and laughed. I helped him get on a pig and take a ride. When he became interested, I slipped off my pig and climbed to the edge of the mesa where I sat down and watched. I felt grown up as I sat there in my long pants, looking down at him. We returned to the building before the bell rang.

I got along very well at school that year and heard my name praised highly. In May my father came for me. I returned home and spent the summer working in the fields and herding.

One day in July, when the avatsie flower was in bloom, I went to my father's field southwest of the village to thin melon plants. I noticed the clouds gathering and took refuge from the rain in a little shelter that my father had built. After the rain there was a great deal of water standing in the field, and I began pouring it down prairie-dog holes. When the animals scampered out, I struck them with my hoe. In this way I killed seven of them and had lots of fun. I took the carcasses home, knowing that my folks were fond of prairie dogs when they were fat.

When I reached home I climbed to the housetop and looked southward at the dam. It was full of water, and four girls were swimming about in it, naked except for a small cloth around the waist. They asked me to join them, but I declined because I had learned at school that boys should not swim with girls. I stood at the edge of the pond and watched them until about sunset. Three of the girls went home, but Mae, one of my ceremonial aunts of the Greasewood and Road-

Runner Clan, waited near the pond. Finally I said to her, "Let's go." We walked together toward the village near the place where the people throw afterbirths. There was a chicken house close by. Mae motioned to me and walked in. I followed and closed the door. We sat down on the floor of the chicken house and became interested in each other's bodies. She was about thirteen, and at first I thought she was a virgin, but I quickly changed my mind because she knew so much about what to do. We had little difficulty getting together but I don't think I had an ejaculation. I peeped out and saw her mother, Kamaoyousie, passing along the path. When she had gone, I slipped out and ran home. I came nearer to having intercourse this time than ever before, and liked it. I was almost thirteen and had already begun to feel restless at night and to dream about girls, but when people teased me about them I said I did not care for them and did not want ever to marry.

When we returned to school in September, I had occasion to see some of the boys masturbate until they ejaculated. Sometimes we played a little with each other. One boy wanted me to pretend that I was a girl with him, but I did not want to do it.

I discovered that some of the boys were playing sick so that they could stay in bed and cut classes. The doctor sent out a warning that this practice had to be stopped. I thought about what kind of sickness I could have and chose sore eyes because one can get that from studying. One day at recess I threw a handful of sand in my eyes and went to the doctor with tears rolling down. He was in his office mixing medicine on a marble slab, stirring it with a knife to make a salve for a Navaho boy. He looked up and said, "What is the matter, Don?" "Sore eyes," I replied. He took a tool shaped like a butter knife, lifted the lid of my eye, and had me roll the ball about. "Well, Don," he said, "when did you put sand in your eyes?" I did not answer. He took a small hatlike cup from the top of a bottle, poured some medicine in it, and made me lie on my back with this medicine hat on my eye. He held his watch and waited about two minutes, telling me to roll my eyeball. Then he repeated the same procedure on the other eye, washing out the sand. He laughed and said, "Now, Don, don't put sand in your eyes again and pretend to be sick or you will really have sore eyes. Your parents put you here to learn something." I told him that I was tired of school and that I wished the teachers would get sick. He laughed, wrote something on a piece of paper, and told me to take it to my teacher. When I came out of the office I thought of destroying the note, but I was afraid that he might ask the teacher about it. When I handed it to her, she read it, then laughed and laughed until tears ran from her eyes. She said, "So you want me to get sick? Do you see this paddle? I am in good health and can use it."

I had lots of fun at school that year. Sometimes I played jokes on the teachers, but only on days when they seemed happy. They never whipped me, although the disciplinarian paddled me once. One evening after roll call we had gone upstairs to bed. Taps had not yet sounded and the oil lamps were still lighted. Draping a white sheet around my body, I climbed up on the head of the bed, extended my hands, lifted up my face, and said, "Boys, I am Jesus Christ the Second, the Son of God. I am the resurrection and the life. Suffer little children to come unto me and forbid them not——." Just then the disciplinarian walked in and said, "What is this?" I told him that I had done no harm, that I was only preaching, but he looked stern and started to paddle me. "These other fellows were in it, too," I protested. "Well," he replied, "since you are Jesus I will let you suffer for their sins." He paddled me pretty hard. Next day the boys laughed and teased me, saying, "Hello, Second Jesus!"

The following summer I returned to Oraibi and worked as usual. During my absence old Honwuhti had died. I loved that old woman and missed her very much.

It had been arranged that different groups of boys and girls should return to the Agency for two or three weeks to care for the buildings and grounds. They were building a new school plant and it was necessary to move the equipment. One day in June the Hopi judge, Koyonainiwa, sent word to Oraibi that I was to report to the principal at the day school in New Oraibi. I started down to New Oraibi after dark, walking along the footpath to the edge of the mesa where people repeat their morning prayers to the sun. As I glanced eastward down the side of the mesa, I saw a light, apparently in the hands of an unseen human form, moving along two or three feet above the ground. I stood there watching and wondering what to do. I wanted to go back to the village but I knew that the principal was a stern old man and I had been told to report immediately. When I started down the path the light moved along ahead of me a little to the west. I turned to the east. The flame hovered over a big rock and flared out in all directions. I was frightened but braced myself and walked a few steps toward it, thinking that it might be the fire of Masau'u or of an evil spirit. I could find no tracks, however, so I returned to the road and ran as fast as I could to the principal's office. He looked up and said, "Hello, boy." It was arranged that I should start for the Agency the next day (Sunday) with three other boys from Old Oraibi. I ran most of the way home, avoiding the place where the flame had appeared. My mother said that it was probably the fire of Masau'u.

Early the next morning my father saddled two burros and we started for the Agency. In the afternoon we passed a store belonging to Tom Pavatea from First Mesa, who had been adopted by an old woman of my father's linked-clans, the Sand-Lizard-Snake clans. Tom took us into his house and told his wife to feed us. We had a good meal and thanked them for it. His wife gave us two loaves of bread and two pieces of dried meat to eat on the way. Passing the new school that the government was building, we reached the old school building at about six in the evening. I took my father to the place where the boss worked. When I had unsaddled and hobbled the burros, the other boys arrived on foot. There were nine of us altogether, some from the other mesas. I was the youngest in the group—too young to have walked such a long distance.

Mr. Commons, the disciplinarian, welcomed us back and took us to the dining room, where there were nine girls who had come to help us. We ate a good supper—with no hash. After singing a few Hopi songs we went to bed. The next morning my father started for home. We hitched horses to a wagon and went to the new school plant, where we worked all day painting beds.

That night I was sick. Every few minutes I had to vomit or defecate. The doctor came the next morning and had me swallow three tablets that looked like white buttons. I was kept in bed all day. Nannie and Maud, two girls from First Mesa, not of my kin, waited on me and even gave me a bath. I ate nothing until supper, when I took some milk and toast. My head was aching. I remembered seeing the fire on the mesa at Oraibi and concluded that Masau'u had caused my sickness. David, a boy from Second Mesa, said that I should have looked straight ahead and paid no attention to the fire. When I told him that the fire was in front of me, he said, "Well, you did not have to follow it, even one step." I knew that was right. I was better next day.

On the fourth of July our time was up, and after breakfast I started for home on foot. The girls were to follow in a wagon. On the way I passed an old Tewa shepherd who was related to my father. He told me that there was to be a celebration at Tom Pavatea's store and for me to stay there until I found someone from Oraibi. When I had crossed Keams Canyon Wash I heard a horseman coming fast. The rider, a Navaho, stopped and motioned for me to get up behind him. I got on, well pleased, and we galloped along.

Many Navahos and Hopis had gathered at Tom's store for races and broncho-busting. There was also a chicken-pulling contest. They dug a hole and buried a live cock up to its neck. Then they mounted their horses and galloped past, trying to grasp the fowl's head. When a Navaho yanked it out of the ground the others chased him, tearing the chicken to pieces. Finally the winner brought in the head and got his reward. I pitied the poor rooster.

Tom had killed two cows for a feast. As we ate, my father's brothers, Kayahongva and Talashungnewa, came up with five burros loaded with sacks of flour. While they ate I said, "Will you take me home with you?" They agreed, and that afternoon we left on the burros.

I spent the rest of the summer helping on the farm, planting, hoeing, thinning, herding sheep, looking for burros, hauling water, and sometimes going for wood. We did not own horses or a wagon but only some sheep and goats, five burros, two dogs, and a couple of cats.

In September I returned to school in the new plant. It was there that I first sat on a modern toilet which was like a spring, and flushed. I was uneasy at first and expected the bowl to overflow; but I caught on quickly and liked it—although it was a waste of water.

That year I really had sore eyes. No medicine seemed to do me any good. I would close my eyes to ease the pain, but they got worse.

One day Sam from Second Mesa, a clan uncle, took me to First Mesa. I could not see well with my one good eye and stumbled over a stone halfway up the mesa. In falling my eye was cut and black dirty blood ran out. My clan uncle pressed the flesh, forcing out more blood. Finally the black blood stopped and yellow came. Then the eye stopped paining and seemed to be cured. I asked him to get a piece of obsidian glass and open a place near my left eye. He refused to do it, so I took my knife and made a hole. After that I felt better.

I got into mischief with a Navaho boy. We Hopi hated Navahos and decided to make this fellow miserable. As he climbed the stairs from the basement one day, I overtook him, seized an ear, and jerked it. On the next floor I caught the other and jerked that. He yelled just as Mr. Haffner, the disciplinarian, turned the corner. He scolded and slapped me right and left. I ran but he overtook me and slapped again. I escaped as soon as possible and said nothing, fearing that I would make matters worse. And from then on I stayed out of his way—at least ten steps.

One day Mr. Haffner caught me. "Now," said he, "I am going to put a saddle on you and tame you like a burro." He took me into his office and said, "Don, you are getting wild. I am not going to strike you. Treat that Navaho right. His father sent him here to learn." Then he gave me a quarter, which made me feel better. After that he treated me like a son and at Christmas bought me a shirt, collar, and necktie. He was a German and at first he was the carpenter of the school; but the boys liked him and voted to make him disciplinarian in place of Mr. Commons, who was terribly strict and had once nearly killed a boy. Mr. Haffner had military manners and made us exercise and drill even on cold mornings. He married our matron, a civilized halfblood California Indian. I got a kitchen job through their influence and I liked it better, for the meals were slim and the job gave me a chance to eat more.

When I returned home in the summer, the people joked about my voice, which was changing. Hair was growing on my body; although I pulled it out at first, it kept coming over a wider space. So finally I let it alone. I plucked out the few hairs which grew on my face; but I did not bother with that under my arms. I thought and dreamed more and more about girls. Sometimes I dreamed of making love to one; but when I examined her closely I would discover that she was a boy. Then I would wake up and spit four times, feeling that an evil spirit had played a bad joke on me.

One day I had my first opportunity to get even with the "grandfather" who had pretended to castrate me when I was a child. I was walking down to New Oraibi with a manila rope in my hand when I met the old man coming up the mesa trail with a big jug of water on his back. "Well, my grandson," he greeted me, "where are you going? When did you get back from school?" Without saying a word I lassoed him like a steer and dragged him all the way down the mesa. When he started up again he acted a little mad. I heard later that he told his wife about it. She clapped her hands and reminded him that he had it coming to him.

In the late summer I started with two burros to Moenkopi to fetch some wheat which my relatives were gleaning from the Mormon fields. I tied a jug of water on the back of one burro and rode the other. On the way my burro kicked at the other and broke the jar on its back. I soon grew very thirsty. I cut down a cedar tree and chewed the inside bark, but in the evening I was unable to eat because I could not swallow my food without moisture. After I had lain down to sleep, a couple of men passed with their wives on their return from the wheat fields. They had water, which was lucky for me.

When I returned to school in September, 1905, I was assigned to stable duty for a time. I cleaned out the manure and spread it over the fields. One morning a Navaho teamster failed to show up, and I was sent out with Nash to feed the horses and milk the cows. I tried to milk but could not get a drop into the pail. Nash laughed and said that although I was fifteen I was fit only to curry horses and spread manure. The Navaho died that evening and his funeral was held the following afternoon. This was the first time I had ever seen a dead person. He lay in a box with his eyes wide open and bloodshot, as if he had suffered much pain. We sang "Nearer My God to Thee" and other hymns, but I left before they buried him.

Some time after this I was transferred from stable work to the blacksmith shop, where I learned to weld iron. Then they needed a boy in the bakery and sent me there. Later I was made a kitchen boy again and helped a little with the cooking. I also paid more attention to the girls, attended the socials, and practiced the square dances.

In May, 1906, I went to Rockyford, Colorado, with a large group of boys to work on sugar-beet plantations. We were divided into groups of eight boys each and moved from farm to farm, thinning beets during the day and sleeping in tents at night. We worked eleven or twelve hours a day at 15¢ an hour.

One Sunday another boy and I went for a long walk and found three or four small turtles. We sat down under a tree and butchered them, taking out the meat so that we could use the shells for rattles in the Katcina dances. I made a speech to the turtles before killing them, telling them that we had nothing to give them now but that when we got home we would make pahos for them.

By the fourth of July we had finished the work and were ready to come home. I had earned $45.80, of which $10 was paid in cash. Our superior officer said, "I don't want to give you all you have earned now because last year some of you spent your money before you reached home. I will send it to the Agency." I bought a secondhand pistol, for I thought a man with a gun in his holster looked important.

When we returned to Oraibi the people were still divided between Hostiles and Friendlies and the quarreling was getting worse. Our old Chief, Lololomai, had died about a year before, and his nephew, Tewaquaptewa, was Chief in his place. Because of the factions we had to hold two Katcina home-coming (Niman) dances—an awful thing to do. Arguments continued and reached a climax on September 8. Early that morning, as I returned from hobbling the burros, I saw dust rising from the plaza. I ran home and found my mother crying with Ira, who was sick. She said that the Friendlies were driving the Hostiles out of the village. The Hostiles were trying to persuade my parents to join them. Most of my father's relatives were Hostile and many of my mother's people, too. My great uncle, Talasquaptewa, told the Hostiles to get out. Since he was a high officer they had to obey him; otherwise we might have had to go with them. I went to the housetop and saw the men taking sides for a fight in the plaza. Loading my six-shooter, I went over to the Friendly side; and some of the

Hostiles were surprised that I did not join with them. The Friendlies, though fewer in number, fought like demons. They struggled with the Hostile men and drove some of them out of the village.

The government officials came and confiscated some of our weapons. I kept my gun concealed. In the afternoon there was a long argument out on the mesa ledge. Yokeoma, who was leader of the Hostiles and thus opposed to Tewaquaptewa, finally made a line on the rock and said, "Let it be this way. If you push us over this mark the matter will be settled." In short, he was challenging us to a contest like a tug of war, except that we would push instead of pull, with the condition that the losing side would leave Oraibi. We lined up with Whites as judges and pushed with all our might. In about fifteen minutes we had shoved the Hostiles over the line.

By sunset all the Hostiles left the village with their women, children, burros, and equipment. Some were angry and others were crying. This meant that we would have no more dealings with them. Most of my kinfolk went with the Hostiles. My sister Gladys stayed in Oraibi for a while, although her husband, Tuvaletztewa, left; but soon she got lonesome and followed him. Later he became interested in other women and made Gladys so unhappy that our uncle, Dan Coochongva, told her to come back where she belonged. Then she returned to Oraibi. The village seemed deserted. The Hostiles had moved about six miles away to a place called Hotavila and started to build houses there. Two divisions of troops came and carried away most of the men, who were either put to work on the road or sent to school. Some were imprisoned in Fort Wingate, and a few young men were sent to Carlisle. The women and children in Hotavila had a very hard time that winter.

In September we returned to the Agency school. Soon we received our checks for the summer's work. I had never had so much money and felt like a millionaire with my $35.80.

One Friday night at a social with games I was talking to Louise of the Tobacco and Rabbit Clan. She said she was leading a hard life, that neither her father nor her stepfather seemed to care for her. Some days she did not get enough to eat and, what was worse, she had few clothes. She cried a little and said, "My fathers bring me no food and

I often am hungry. What shall I do? If any man should care for me, I would be his wife." The tears in her eyes touched my heart and made me want to save her from hunger. I sat by the table, holding her hand and talking softly until she brightened up. Then I squeezed her hand, laughed gently, and said, "I never go hungry. I am a kitchen boy." I told her softly that if she could like me I would help her. I said, "I love you and I will get food from the kitchen. I will tell my head boss. She is a good woman and will help us." I also told her that I had $35.80 in my pocket and that I was not a spendthrift. From then on I began to look after her. When I did not get enough from the kitchen I took my money and bought jelly and bread for her at the store. She was a good, smart girl, and worked hard.

One Saturday afternoon, as I worked alone in the kitchen, I spied Louise on the porch of her dormitory and beckoned through the window for her to come over. After feeding her, I hugged her warmly for the first time, told her that she was a sweet little thing, and that I wanted her for my wife. Then I moved with her gently into the pantry, and locked the door. The little room was crowded and we had to stand and be quick; but she knew what to expect and seemed experienced. It was the first time that I had found and given real pleasure in love-making. After that I cared more for her than ever.

One day Louise told me, to my surprise, that she was the daughter of my clan brother, and therefore my clan daughter. She said that her father was Talasveyma of the Gray Hawk Clan, which is linked with the Sun and Eagle clans. This was bad news for me. Her real father had lived with her mother, Kelmaisie, only a short time. Then her stepfather, Kalmanimptewa, had married her mother and raised several children. I had not known that Louise was the daughter of my linked-clan brother and therefore my daughter. I knew that our relatives would not like for us to be in love, and wondered what we could do. After we had talked the matter over for a long time, I said, "Well, we have our agreement; and I don't care what our relatives say. Your father is not supporting you, and I will look out for you as long as my money lasts." But we were both worried about it all.

The next day Louise told the matron the whole story and I discussed it with the head cook, a half-breed Cherokee Indian. They talked together and called us into the office. The matron left us to make our decision. We were determined to stick to each other. I called the matron and told her that I had decided to marry Louise the next fall. The matron took me with her to the office of the new superintendent, Mr. Lemmon, a kind and wise old man with a white beard that reached to his belly button. I stood outside while she went in and told him the story. He called me in and asked me a number of questions. One of them was, "Don, maybe you want to have a good time with this girl and then forget her, do you?" "No, I think we can have a good life together," I replied. He finally approved of our plan; and it seemed that I had put my name on the girl's back, and that she was mine.

I told the superintendent something else while we were talking. Looking straight into his eyes, I said that he ought to feed us better. I pointed out that the supplies and the clothes in the warehouse were put there for us and asked, "Why not give us more? We work hard; we need more." From that day on they did give us a little more to eat, but the other children never knew that I was responsible.

In November, before Thanksgiving, our superior officer told forty or fifty of us that we were to go to school at Sherman, the nonreservation school in Riverside, California. Our Chief, Tewaquaptewa, was also to go and learn the white man's ways. Louise and I planned to go together.

Before we departed I had another talk with the superintendent. I told him that Louise and I had an agreement to marry, that I was helping to support her, and that it was my right to have intercourse with her. I was not afraid to say this because I knew that for Hopi lovers who are engaged this is the proper thing. The superintendent agreed partly, but he insisted that "education is more important," and said that Louise would have to leave Sherman if she became pregnant.

We were to go first to Oraibi and from there to the railway station at Winslow. Some of the larger boys and I set out on foot for Oraibi, while the girls followed in a covered wagon. When we were overtaken in the late afternoon, I got on the wagon; and the girls smiled and moved over so that I could sit by Louise. Since she had no mittens, I offered her my gloves, but she said they were too large and returned them. When it grew a little darker I held her hands in mine to keep them warm. We reached New Oraibi after dark and separated into small groups to climb the mesa to the old village. Louise and I walked together and I carried both suitcases. On the way we dropped behind, then stopped by the side of the road in a quiet place out of sight and had intercourse. We walked up to Oraibi, and before we separated I gave her $5. The next day, before we left for Winslow and Sherman, I gave about half of my remaining money to my parents, keeping only $10 for myself. I also left my pistol at home and never saw it again.

6

School off the Reservation

LOUISE AND I WERE together on the train part of the time until we reached Riverside, California, at about noon on Thanksgiving day. We were taken immediately to the dining room for lunch and served large yellow sweet potatoes which I had never seen before. I peeled mine, and put gravy, pepper, and salt upon them. But I could not eat them and noticed that others were laughing at me. The Indian waitress came, laughed, and gave me another plate. After that I ate my sweet potatoes "straight," and also learned to eat tomatoes raw. When we had placed our baggage in the Sherman School for Indians, where we were to remain for three years, the assistant disciplinarian told us that there would be a football game in the park at three o'clock. Riverside High School was playing Pomona College with admission free. We decided to go.

Now Susie, the wife of Frank Siemptewa and the younger sister of Louise's mother, had gone to Sherman with Chief Tewaquaptewa's party a few weeks before. She came over with a sharp look on her face and took Louise away. I felt uneasy and feared that she might learn about our courtship and complain to our relatives that I was making love to my clan daughter.

During the afternoon I grew tired of the rough football game and walked over to the skating rink with Louis Hoye from Moenkopi. There I saw my older clan sister Hattie from Moenkopi, with a good-looking girl friend. Adolph Hoye, who was in his third year at Sherman, had stopped his roller skating to talk with them. I went over and shook hands with Adolph. As we talked I exchanged glances with the pretty girl and thought that she must be a Hopi from another village because she smiled at some of my remarks in the Hopi language. When I spoke to Hattie, this girl was introduced to me in English as Dezba Johnson, a Navaho from Crystal, New Mexico. In shaking hands with me she smiled and squeezed my fingers, giving me a thrill.

When Adolph resumed skating with his girl friend, we three decided to go to the zoo. Dezba whispered something to Hattie about me. Hattie told me in Hopi that she had informed the girl that I was her clan brother. We passed the wildcats' cage and came to the monkeys. I inspected them closely and thought that they must be human. One was as tall as I and looked intelligent. After we had fed them some peanuts, two of them sat down and picked lice off each other carefully and in a very human manner. By and by a male monkey mounted a female. I laughed and said, "Well, girls, how do you like that?" Dezba said, "Shame on you." "Well," I replied, "I don't think it is so bad. It is the way to increase." She smiled, pulled my arm, and said, "Let's go."

We went to the cage of bears and fed them some peanuts until Adolph came and took Hattie away to see the bantams. Dezba and I went together to the grocery store and bought two bottles of strawberry pop, a loaf of bread, and some jam. When I started to pay, Dezba took a little roll of greenbacks from her purse and said, "Never mind." She seemed well off. We took the food to the park and sat down on the grass under a tree. As we ate she asked many questions about my life and the climate. When we had finished she said, "Well, honey, what do you think about us? Could we fall in love?" This was the first time I had ever heard "honey" used in courtship. I liked it and replied, "If you have no other lover, I feel sure we can."

While we talked on the subject of love, Esau, Jacob, and Saul came up. Esau and Jacob, my clan brothers, introduced me to Saul, a fourth-year man at Sherman. He extended his hand and said in Hopi, "Stay with that girl, brother." When Dezba offered the boys some food, they started to sit down with us. I spoke in Hopi, "Say, brothers, take your food to some other place." They laughed and left; and Dezba asked me what I had said to them. When I told her, she took hold of my hand and pulled me over close to her, causing me to wonder if I might kiss her. I did a little later as we lay together on the grass. When I tried to kiss her several times, she said, "No, this is your first day at school, and I don't want to spoil your name too soon." Then we got up and went back to watch the monkeys.

While we were standing by the cage of monkeys, Louise and her clan mother, Susie, came up and looked sharply at us. I saw sorrow in my clan daughter's face and wondered how she felt at seeing me with a strange girl. Susie appeared crosser than ever. This made me think I had better drop Louise, because her mother's sister might get me into trouble. These thoughts began drawing me away from my first love. I whispered to Dezba, "Let's get away from these girls." "I don't give a damn," she replied. That was the first time I had ever heard a girl cuss; and it caused me to admire her more.

We walked over to the bear cage and heard the whistle blow at the school plant. I asked my new girl friend how I could get back to the boys' building. She put her hand in my arm and we walked together along the sidewalk until some Indian girls ahead of us turned and said, "Dezba, where did you get that good looking boy?" "I found him in the park," she replied. The girls said, "We wish we could find such a boy there. Did you know him before?" "Of course," she answered, "I would not be with him if I had not known him." "Well, you are lucky," they said. I parted from her at the superintendent's office and entered the boys' building to wash and comb my hair for supper. I knew I was forgetting Louise and falling in love with Dezba—and felt lucky.

Within a few days the teachers gave us a test on the multiplication tables and sent me back from the sixth into the fourth grade. Ira, my brother, was put in the second grade and we were given part-time jobs in the bakery. Besides going regularly to classes, we joined athletic clubs and debating societies, and attended many socials, including square dances. I was also taken into the Y.M.C.A. by two Hopi boys, Adolph Hoye and Harry McClain, who led me into a room and had me sign my name before I knew what I was getting into. I had no idea that I was committing myself to Christianity. They had me attend the meetings every Thursday evening and gave me a prize for learning the names of all the books of the Bible. They also urged me to memorize Scripture verses, which I did during the week ends, and won a Bible.

At the Y.M.C.A. meetings we were expected to stand on our feet and testify for Jesus Christ. I prepared a little sermon which I could get up and repeat: "Well, my partners, I am asked to speak a few words for Jesus. I am glad that I came to Sherman and learned to read and cipher. Now I discover that Jesus was a good writer. So I am thankful that Uncle Sam taught me to read in order that I may understand the Scriptures and take my steps along God's road. When I get a clear understanding of the Gospel I shall return home and preach it to my people in darkness. I will teach them all I know about Jesus Christ, the Heavenly Father, and the Holy Ghost. So I advise you boys to do your best and pray to God to give us a good understanding. Then we will be ready for Jesus to come and take us up to heaven. I don't want any of my friends to be thrown into the lake of hell fire where there is suffering and sorrow forever. Amen." At that time I was half-Christian and half-heathen and often wished that there were some magic that could change my skin into that of a white man.

I learned to preach pretty well, and to cuss too. The Hopi language has no curse words in it. But at Sherman even the Y.M.C.A. and the Catholic boys cussed like hell. At first so much of it made me tired; but when I got into the habit myself it was all right. When I wanted anything I would say, "Give me that God-damn thing." But I soon learned when and where it was appropriate to curse.

We got a book from the Y.M.C.A. on masturbation. It said that the practice ruined a boy's health and caused him to go insane. But I saw the boys doing it right along. They did not mind being watched by other fellows. I never masturbated much myself because I did not want to lose my strength. I had wet dreams, however, and continued to dream occasionally of a girl in bed with me who always turned out to be a boy. I would ask her, "How long have you been this way?" She would say, "From my birth." I would stop caressing her and say, "I don't think I can have intercourse with you." I always felt disappointed in making this discovery, and when I awoke I wondered if I would be as unlucky in getting a girl. I was not.

I kept seeing Dezba at the socials and sometimes in the kitchen. One evening in May, 1907, I made a date to meet her upstairs in the pantry above the kitchen after the evening meal, when the other girls had gone back to their building. When she came, we lay down on the floor and had intercourse quickly, fearing that someone might catch us. Within a few weeks she went home and I never saw her again. I missed her sorely, and although I later learned that she was already married, I still thought that she was one of the sweetest girls I ever knew.

In the summer I was sent from Sherman to Fontana, a farm a few miles away, where I worked pitching hay for $2 a day. I soon formed a friendship with the cook, Olive, a Mexican girl one-eighth Klamath Indian and rather high-toned. I don't think I would have dared start an affair with her if she had not invited me. One evening after supper she asked me to drive her to Riverside on a buckboard to get groceries. She drove the mules because she was a forward girl and could do almost anything. When we returned to the farm we put our supplies in the kitchen and took the buckboard to the barn. Discovering that the overseer was away, Olive hinted that we might rest together in the loft on the hay. We had intercourse two or three times and made plans to meet there on other nights. One evening the boss caught us in the barn but did not say anything, perhaps because he was having a good time with her too. I had seen him playing with her in the kitchen and had tried to catch them doing something more, but never did. I did not pay this girl; but whenever we went to town I bought her nice gifts and took her to the movies. She was about a year younger than I, and seemed to enjoy the meetings in the barn as much as I did, sometimes having an orgasm ahead of me. I trained her so that whenever we were washing dishes I only had to make a motion with my lips toward the barn to let her know that I expected to meet her there.

One night Olive and I made a mistake by coming out of the barn together. I heard someone whistle in the dark and began to look around while she hurried to the house. I did not find anyone, but next morning when we started pitching hay the old Dutchman who worked with us said, "Well, Don, did you get your reward last night?" "Jesus Christ," said I, "was that you who whistled?" He laughed and said, "I wish I were young again." "Well," I remarked, "you better go out northwest to the fountain of youth and get yourself fixed up." He replied, "No, the best part of my body is sleeping and will never wake up again." Then he hit me on the buttocks and said, "Let's get to work." After that I often teased him and asked him if he were awake yet. He told me many stories which he called "dirty" and which I stored in my mind to retell some day in Oraibi.

When I reëntered school in the fall I was well dressed in citizen's clothes. I bought a good suit and made myself look "sporty" in low-top patent-leather shoes, a fancy hat, a velvet shirt, and a silk necktie. I had my hair cut in the American style and parted it on the left side instead of in the center, because I was a twin with two whorls instead of one and my hair refused to part in the center. I plucked out the stray hairs on my face, and a few more on my pubes, and again wished that there was some way to turn myself into a white man. I attended the socials, enjoyed the square dances, and spent much money on the girls in gifts, tickets, and refreshments. Some of the socials cost as much as $100 for the whole group, but we encouraged each other to spend heavily out of our summer earnings, saying that we were helping Uncle Sam.

One evening in November I made a great mistake.[1] We had an ice-cream and cake party in the Department of Domestic Science. After the refreshments and while we were having a good time with the girls, Hattie came to me looking sad and said, "I have bad news from home. Our older sister, Viola, passed away about a week ago." When I asked her how this happened she said, "Viola had a baby after three days' labor but retained the afterbirth. During the night my father stepped outside and saw a woman fleeing with a cotton mask on her face like a person dressed for burial. He overtook her and told her that she must

---

1. Don regards the following experience as the most significant event in his life. For an earlier account and analysis of it as reported by Don in 1932, see Mischa Titiev, *A Hopi Visit to the Afterworld*, "Papers of the Michigan Academy of Science, Arts, and Letters," Vol. XXVI (1940), pp. 495–504.

be the witch who had cast a spell on our sister. At first she denied it, then begged him to keep her secret and offered him a string of beads and sexual favors as rewards; but warned him that if he reported her to the people he would live only four more years. He returned to the house and tried to shake the afterbirth out of our sister—until she died in his arms!" I hung my head in grief and anger at this news and cried, "These Two-Hearts want to kill us so they may live. That witch might as well kill us all and be done with it. I don't care if she does kill me. I am a single man and have no children." Hattie was frightened and said, "Don't say that. She may kill you. Those are careless words that may cause you to get sick." They did.

I asked the disciplinarian if I might be excused from the party because I had heard of the death of a clan sister. As I left the disciplinarian said, "Don, don't make yourself too sad." "I will not," I replied, "we all have to die." I had caught a cold and could not sleep. I tried to work next day but had to give up and go to bed, feeling first hot and then cold. Our assistant disciplinarian arranged for me to enter the hospital.

They took me upstairs, put me to bed, felt my pulse, examined my chest, and took my temperature. My head ached and I got worse from hour to hour. At the end of a week they moved me to the second floor near the office of the head nurse where I stayed for a month. In late December they put me on a ward with very sick boys who were not expected to live, said that I had pneumonia, and placed my name on the danger list. The head nurse said to the doctor, "Don is very sick; nothing helps him. If you agree, we will give him some whiskey in orange juice." I did not want to take liquor, but with my life in despair they propped me up in bed, held a cup to my lips, and said, "Don, you are getting cold; this will warm you." It did. I got drunk, acted crazy, cursed freely, and said shameful things to the nurses. When I awoke in the morning Ollie Queen was watching over me. She was a pretty Hupa Indian from California whom I had courted several weeks.

I grew steadily worse and could barely speak. Boys and girls came to cheer me up. The pain in my chest was dreadful. I spat blood and could take no food, except a little milk through a glass tube. I refused to eat and told the nurses to leave me alone, for I wanted to die and get out of pain. They cried and begged me to live, praising my name highly. But my feet were already getting cold.

I began to think of the Two-Hearts and to review all that I had heard about them. I knew that they were very unfortunate but powerful people, members of every race and nation, organized into a worldwide society in which they spoke a common language, and that they were able to postpone their own death by taking the lives of their relatives. I understood that Hopi Two-Hearts were leaders of this terrible society, that they held their underworld convention at Red Cliff Mesa northeast of Oraibi, and that Two-Hearts in Oraibi were probably the worst of the lot. I realized that they were mean, fussy, easily offended, and forever up to mischief. I knew I had been careless, had spoken rashly, and had probably offended some of them.

On Christmas Eve Lily Frazer, an Indian girl of some other tribe, stayed away from the entertainment to watch over me. She was not my sweetheart but my best friend—a sort of big sister—who seemed to look out for me. We had exchanged gifts and done other favors for each other. She spoke tender words and begged me to get well. I was very restless, and at about nine o'clock in the evening I looked at the door transom and saw movements. Four Hopi boys peered through the glass and made funny faces at me. A fifth face appeared, looked at me strangely, and drove the others away. The four faces were those of my schoolmates and the fifth was that of Frank Siemptewa, the husband of Susie and the Chief's lieutenant at Moenkopi. I felt angry but helpless.

Then I saw a tall human being standing by my bed in Katcina costume.[2] He was well dressed in a dancing kilt and a sash, was barefoot, and wore long black hair hanging down his back. He had a soft prayer feather (*nakwakwosi*) in his hair and carried a blue one in his left hand—blue being the color which signifies the west and the home of the dead. He wore beads and looked wonderful as he watched me. When the nurses brought food, he said, "My son, you had better eat. Your time is up. You shall travel to the place where the dead live and

2. See Appendix, pp. 444.

see what it is like." I saw the door swing slowly back and forth on its hinges and stop just a little open. A cold numbness crept up my body; my eyes closed; and I knew I was dying.

The strange human being said, "Now, my boy, you are to learn a lesson. I have been guarding you all your life, but you have been careless. You shall travel to the House of the Dead and learn that life is important.[3] The path is already made for you. You had better hurry; and perhaps you will get back before they bury your body. I am your Guardian Spirit (*dumalaitaka*). I will wait here and watch over your body; but I shall also protect you on your journey."

The pain disappeared and I felt well and strong. I arose from my bed and started to walk, when something lifted me and pushed me along through the air, causing me to move through the door, down the hall, and out upon the campus in broad daylight. I was swept along northeastward by a gust of wind, like flying, and soon reached the San Bernardino Mountains. There I climbed a corn-meal path about halfway up a mountain and came upon a hole like a tunnel, dimly lighted. I heard a voice on the right saying, "Don't be afraid, walk right in." Stepping in through a fog and past the little lights, I moved along swiftly, finally came out upon a flat mesa, and discovered that I was walking near the old water holes out on the ledge at Oraibi! Very much surprised, I thought, "I will go home and get some good Hopi food."

As I entered the door, I saw my mother sitting on the floor combing my father's hair. They just stared at the door for a moment and then turned back to their interests. They didn't say a word, causing me to wonder sadly. I walked about the room for a minute and then sat down on a sheep pelt by the stove to think. I said to myself, "Well, perhaps my grandfather will come and give me food." After about an hour of silence, my grandfather did come in, stared at me for a moment, and said nothing; but he sat down opposite me and dropped his head as though worried. Then I thought to myself, "They don't care for me. I had better go and leave them alone." When I arose to leave they didn't even look up or say good-by.

3. See Appendix, pp. 448–450.

I walked out by the dry basin near the Oraibi Rock. There was a little stone wall on the rim of the dam. A large lizard ran along the ground and into the wall. As I drew near I saw peeping out from the rocks an ugly, naked woman with drawn face and dry lips. She looked tired, half-starved, and very thirsty. It was my old grandmother, Bakabi, my mother's mother's sister. Since she was still living, I didn't know how her spirit could be on its way to Skeleton House; but I think my Guardian Angel[4] placed her there to teach me a lesson and to show me that she was a Two-Heart. She said, "My grandson, will you please give me a drink?" "No, I have no water," I replied. "Well, please spit in my mouth to quench my thirst?" she pleaded. I said, "No, I have nothing for you. Are you the one I saw as a lizard?" "Yes, my father is a lizard and I have two hearts." "Then I will have nothing to do with you, for you killed our sister!" I said. "I am one of those who are killing your people"; she answered, "but I am not the one who killed you. From here to the House of the Dead you will see people like me who can take only one step a year over a path of sorrow. Please let me go along with you. You have only one heart and will arrive safely." "Never mind," I said, and hurried along, for I had no time to monkey with a witch.

I moved along quickly, touching the ground only in spots until I came to the west point of the mesa. Along this way I saw many faces of Two-Hearts who called out to me for food and drink; but I had no time for them. When I reached the foot of Mount Beautiful, the Judgment Seat, I looked up and saw nice regular steps about twelve feet wide and twelve feet high, of a red color, and reaching like a mighty stairway to the highest point. I started to climb but seemed to float up on air, just touching my feet lightly on the top step. There a bell rang from the west side so clearly that I heard echoes out among the mesa walls.

As the ringing grew louder, I looked and saw a man climbing up the mountain from the west, dressed in a white buckskin, wearing a horn, and holding a spear and a bell. It was a Kwanitaka, a member of

4. Don very often calls the Spirit his "Guardian Angel," due no doubt to Christian influence.

the Kwan or Warrior society, who watches the kivas during prayers and guards the village to keep out strangers and let in the dead during the Wowochim ceremonies. He came up to me but did not shake hands,[5] because he was now a spirit god and doing police duty directing good people over the smooth highway and bad people over the rough road to the House of the Dead. He said, "My boy, you are just in time, hurry! Look to the west and you will see two roads. You take the broad one, the narrow one is crooked and full of rocks, thorns, and thistles; those who take it have a hard journey. I have prepared this broad road for you. Now hurry and you will find someone to guide you."

I looked to the left and saw a wide road sprinkled with corn meal and pollen. On the right was a narrow path about a foot wide and very rough. Strewn along the side were Hopi clothes that had been dropped by Two-Heart women who had received them from men with whom they had slept. I saw naked, suffering people struggling along the path with heavy burdens and other handicaps such as thorny cactus plants fastened to their bodies in tender places. Snakes raised their heads along the edge of the path, sticking out their tongues in a threatening manner. When they saw me looking at them they dropped their heads; but I knew they could bite anyone that they did not like.

I chose the broad road to the left and went along swiftly, almost flying, until I came to a large mesa, which I shot up like an arrow and landed on top. There I saw on my left summer birds singing and flowers in full bloom. Moving rapidly, I passed along the edge of Cole canyon with its steep white walls which I had seen before on my way to Moenkopi. In the distance were twelve queer-looking striped animals chasing one another. As I drew nearer I saw that they were clowns (*tcuka*) who had painted their bodies with black and white stripes and were joking and teasing one another. The leader—who was of the Eagle Clan which is linked to my Sun Clan—said, "My nephew, we have been expecting you. It is late and you must hurry.

5. For the Kwanitaka to touch Don would have signified that he would not return to life.

We think you will return, so we will wait here for you. Your Guardian Spirit is protecting you; but you must hurry back to your body. You may live a long time yet if you get back."

Somewhat frightened, I sped along to the left, reached the top of a steep mesa, and sort of floated down. Before me were the two trails passing westward through the gap of the mountains. On the right was the rough narrow path, with the cactus and the coiled snakes, and filled with miserable Two-Hearts making very slow and painful progress. On the left was the fine, smooth highway with no person in sight, since everyone had sped along so swiftly. I took it, passed many ruins and deserted houses, reached the mountain, entered a narrow valley, and crossed through a gap to the other side. Soon I came to a great canyon where my journey seemed to end; and I stood there on the rim wondering what to do. Peering deep into the canyon, I saw something shiny winding its way like a silver thread on the bottom; and I thought that it must be the Little Colorado River. On the walls across the canyon were the houses of our ancestors with smoke rising from the chimneys and people sitting out on the roofs.

Within a short time I heard a bell on the west side at the bottom of the canyon and another one somewhat behind me. The same Kwanitaka who had directed me on Mount Beautiful came rushing up the cliff carrying a blanket and dressed in a cloak and buckskin moccasins as white as snow. Another Kwanitaka came rapidly from the rear, ringing his bell. The first one said, "We have been expecting you all morning. This partner and I have raced here for you. I won and you are mine. You have been careless and don't believe in the Skeleton House where your people go when they die. You think that people, dogs, burros, and other animals just die and that's all there is to it. Come with us. We shall teach you a lesson on life." I followed the first Kwanitaka to the southwest and was trailed by the second who kept off evil spirits. We came to a house where we saw a Kwanitaka in red buckskin moccasins making red yucca suds in a big earthen pot. Near by was another Kwanitaka from the west in white moccasins making white suds. Each one stirred the suds with a stick, causing a vapor to rise like a cloud. Then one of them said, "Now we are ready, take your choice. From which pot will you be washed?" I chose the white suds.[6] "All right, you are lucky," said the Kwanitaka. "It means that you may journey back along the Hopi trail and return to life." I knelt down so that he could wash my hair and rinse it with fresh water. Finally he said, "Get up and come along. We must hurry because the time is going fast."

The Kwanitakas led me southwest toward the smoke rising in the distance. As we drew near I saw a great crowd of people watching a fire which came out of the ground. On the very edge of the flaming pit stood four naked people, each of them in front of another individual who wore clothing. On the north and south sides stood a naked man in front of a clothed woman, on the east and west sides a naked woman in front of a clothed man. I could see these people as plain as day, even their private parts, but I did not know a single one of them. They had been traveling for a long, long time at the rate of one step a year, and had just reached this place. I noticed on the ground paths leading from four directions to the hole. Near by I saw another Kwanitaka tending the fire in a deeply tunneled pit like that in which sweet corn is baked.

"Look closely," said a Kwanitaka. "Those in front are Two-Hearts. They killed the people standing behind them and now it is their turn to suffer. The crowds of people have come from the House of the Dead to see the Two-Hearts get their punishment. Look!" Then he called out, "Ready, push!" The woman on the north pushed her Two-Heart into the pit, and I could see the flames lap him up, sending out rolls of black smoke. Then the man on the west pushed over his naked woman, and the woman on the south shoved in her man, causing great volumes of smoke to rise out of the pit. Finally the man on the east pushed in his girl and the work was done. No Two-Heart said a word; it seemed they had no feelings. The Kwanitaka said to the people, "Now go back where you belong."

"Now, my boy," said the Kwanitaka to me, "come and look into the pit." I stepped up close to the rim and saw an empty hole with a network of two-inch cracks broken into the walls through which

6. See Appendix, pp. 448–450.

flames of fire were leaping. In the center at the bottom were four black beetles crawling about, two carrying the other two on their backs. The Kwanitaka asked me, "What do you see?" "Beetles," I replied. "That's the end of these Two-Hearts," said he, "and the fate of all their kind." They will stay there as beetles forever, except to make occasional visits to Oraibi and move about the village doing mischief on hazy days."

The Kwanitakas then took me back over the course that we had traveled until we came to the steep ledge where the road had ended. I had stood there before, looking across the canyon to the opposite wall where the people sat on their housetops. Now the canyon was full of smoke, and when I peered down I saw a gruesome creature in the shape of a man climbing the cliff. He was taking long strides with his shining black legs and big feet; an old tattered rag of a blanket was flying from his shoulder as he approached swiftly with a club in his hand. It was big, black, bloody-headed Masau'u, the god of Death, coming to catch me. One of the Kwanitakas pushed me and cried, "Flee for your life and don't look back, for if Masau'u catches you, he will make you a prisoner in the House of the Dead!" I turned and ran eastward, while they pushed me along with their wands or spears so that I rose about six inches from the ground and flew faster than I had ever traveled before.

When I reached Cole Canyon the clowns were waiting for me, standing in a straight line facing west with their arms about each other, as children do in playing London Bridge. As I approached them at full speed, they cried, "Jump, Masau'u is gaining!" I jumped and landed on the chest of the leader, knocking him down. They all laughed and yelled, seeming not to mind, for clowns are always happy. They said, "You just reached here in time, now you belong to us, turn around and look!" I looked west and saw Masau'u going back, looking over his shoulder as he ran. Then the leader of the clowns said, "Now, my nephew, you have learned your lesson. Be careful, wise, and good, and treat everybody fairly. If you do, they will respect you and help you out of trouble. Your Guardian Spirit has punished you so that you may see and understand. Lots of people love you. We are your uncles and will see that no harm comes to you. You have a long time to live yet. Go back to the hospital and to your bed. You will see an ugly person lying there; but don't be afraid. Put your arms around his neck and warm yourself, and you'll soon come to life. But hurry, before the people put your body in a coffin and nail down the lid, for then it will be too late."

I turned and ran quickly, circling back to the mountains through the tunnel and over the foothills to the hospital. I entered quickly and saw my Guardian Spirit and a nurse at the bedside. He greeted me kindly and said, "Well, you are lucky, and just in time. Slip quickly under the cover at the foot, move up alongside your body, put your arms around its neck, and be still." My body was cold and little more than bones, but I obeyed the command and lay there clinging to its neck. Soon I became warm, opened my eyes, and looked up to the ceiling and at the door transom. Nurses were about the bed, and a head nurse was holding my hand. I heard her say, "The pulse beats."

I thought I heard bees buzzing, but it was the music of a band, for it was Christmas morning and students were marching from building to building singing carols. I said, "Father, mother." A nurse said, "Here we are." The head nurse said, "Sonny, you passed away last night, but did not cool off quite like a dead person. Your heart kept on beating slowly and your pulse moved a little, so we did not bury you. Now we will get the credit for saving your life." All the nurses shook hands as if I had been away for a long time, and said, "We worked on you because your parents did not know that you were sick and we wanted you to be able to return to them. We love you more than the other boys and girls because you are kind-hearted and act like a brother."

Ollie Queen—my best girl—took hold of my hand and with tears in her eyes said, "Well, you have had a hard time, but you have come back to life. Now I shall keep you always." The head nurse said, "We ordered your coffin and perhaps it is now on its way, but you won't need it. Look what Santa Claus brought you." At the foot of the bed were lying gifts of candy and fruit, a uniform suit, and a bouquet of flowers. I found that my face had been washed and my hair combed in readiness for the coffin, and that the new suit was to have been my burial shroud. I felt grateful but took pity on myself and cried, saying in my heart, "I have learned a lesson and from now on I shall be careful to do what is right." When the nurses had given me a good massage to warm and limber up my body, I begged for food and received a little milk and toast. I grew dizzy and pleaded for more food even in small quantities, but the nurses patted me on my shoulder and told me to wait. At noon they gave me a good square meal, which made me feel perfectly well.

After lunch my Guardian Angel appeared to me and said in a soft voice: "Well, my boy, you were careless, but you have learned a lesson. Now if you don't obey me I shall punish you again, but for only four trials—then let you die. I love you, and that is why I watch over you. Eat and regain your strength. Some day you will be an important man in the ceremonies. Then make a paho for me before all others, for I am your Guardian Spirit that directs and protects you. Many people never see their Guide, but I have shown myself to you to teach you this lesson. Now I shall leave you. Be good, be wise, think before you act, and you will live a long time. But I shall hold you lightly, as between two fingers, and if you disobey me I will drop you. Good-by and good luck." He made one step and disappeared.

Then I saw a soft eagle prayer feather rise up from the floor, float through the door into the hall, and vanish. I spoke out loud, "Now my Guide is gone and I shall not see him again." "What guide?" asked the nurse sitting by the bedside. "The Guide who protects me and brought me back to life," I answered. "You act crazy," she replied. "We protected you and brought you back to life." I didn't argue about it but just asked for more food.

That night Ollie Queen sat in a rocker by the bed and watched. She said she was afraid I might die again, and waked me ever so often to see if I were all right. Next morning I felt better. Chief Tewaquaptewa visited me in the hospital, and when I told him about my death journey he said it was true, for those were the same things that the old people said they saw when they visited the House of the Dead.

After nearly a month in the hospital I was able to go from ward to ward and walk over to the Department of Domestic Science for my meals. One Saturday afternoon, when most of the nurses were off duty, Ollie Queen made her rounds and invited me up to her bedroom to play flinch. Placing me in a rocking chair, she talked about home life for a while, taught me some new tricks in flinch, and finally won a game. Then laughing softly and breathing faster, she drew me to her for a moment, stepped over, and locked the door. We had our pleasure, played several more games of flinch, and made love once more before returning to the wards. I had the good fortune to see her once again before my discharge from the hospital. Later I returned on a Saturday afternoon for a checkup on my health and managed to visit her room. But she soon found another friend, and I saw no more of her in private. She had a fair complexion and was a lovely girl.

I stayed in school until the early spring of 1908, when a number of us boys were sent to Imperial Valley to help harvest cantaloupes. In June we came back to Sherman for the Commencement exercises, and then returned to work in the cantaloupe fields until July. Our skins turned dark brown, almost like Negroes'. When we finished with the cantaloupes our disciplinarian, Mr. Singleton, sent us to work on a dairy farm near San Bernardino. I did not like this place and stayed only two weeks. We had to get up too early in the morning; I did not like to milk cows; the boss was too strict and seemed to pick on me because I was the slowest milker. I could not stand his nagging. One day after breakfast I went up to him and said, "Here, Boss, I want to quit. I don't like your treatment. I was never treated this way by my parents. I am getting to be a man and I won't stand for it." He appeared angry, but wrote out a check for $19.50.

I walked to Colton, took a streetcar to Riverside, and reached the school at suppertime. The disciplinarian came up to me and said, "Hello, Don, why have you come back so soon?" I told him I would make a report after supper. Later in the evening I went to the cottage on the campus where he lived with his family, and knocked on his door. He invited me in and placed a chair at the table, so that I could drink a cup of coffee with him. I conducted myself like a gentleman and told him the whole story. We went together that evening to Arlington and cashed the check, and I let him keep $10 for me.

I felt more and more like a prosperous man. I dressed well, treated the girls at the socials, and carried my money in the concealed pocket of a fancy belt. I possessed a good knife, owned a decent suitcase, carried a five-dollar watch, and had recently purchased a secondhand bicycle. Although I was a poor milker, I could pitch hay with anyone and I had shown courage enough to tell one white man that I would not stand for unfair treatment.

In about a week I was sent back to the farm at Fontana where Olive worked. She was in the kitchen washing dishes and seemed happy to see me again. I spent the rest of the summer there chopping weeds, ploughing with a team of mules, cutting alfalfa hay with a mowing machine, and meeting with Olive in the barn. She seemed to be on the lookout, and whenever she saw me stroll out that way in the twilight she usually appeared after dark. I had nothing to do with the other two girls, for they had white lovers.

When we returned to school in the fall we were taken on a trip to Los Angeles, California, and out to Long Beach to see the Pacific Ocean. It was there that I had my first boatride, and I liked it.

In school I was promoted to the sixth grade and took an active part in the debating society in our classroom. I found it hard work to stand on my feet and think, giving proof for everything I said. At first I got excited but later liked it.

Finally the evil day came when I was selected to debate in the auditorium before six or eight hundred students. I felt this was too much for me and refused to do it. The assistant disciplinarian was called and offered me a choice between debating and getting a thrashing. I stood my ground and chose the thrashing. He led me into the basement. Two strong boys let down my pants and held me. After about fifteen blows with a rawhide in a heavy hand, I broke down and cried. I slept very little that night and was sore for several days but was never again asked to debate in the auditorium.

Ira and I had worked in the bakeshop for more than a year. I grew tired of it and asked to be transferred to the tailor shop, where I stayed eight weeks and made two pairs of pants. Then my eyes got bad, and they made me janitor in the principal's office with two boys under me.

I also played baseball some and enjoyed it very much. In this game we used nicknames and "razzed" each other. They called one boy "Rooster," and others "Snipe Shooter," "Holy Ghost," and "Happy Hooligan." They called me "Don Chicken," which made me mad at first but I got used to it. I did not like football because it was too rough, and I never played it. At the socials I began going with a girl named Mettie from Moenkopi, which caused everybody to call her my girl.

In May, 1909, Ira and I were sent with others to Hazel Ranch, where we worked pitching hay for board and $2 a day. On the second day our superintendent came and told us to go back to Sherman and prepare to return to Oraibi. In the evening of the third day our boss wrote our checks, hitched his team to the buckboard, and took us back to school. We had a bath and packed our things to start for Oraibi.

Early next morning, instead of waiting for breakfast, Ira and I went down to Arlington about a mile from the school to cash our checks, and we went to a Chinese restaurant to get our breakfast. Returning to the school, we changed from our government clothes to citizens' clothes and got ready to leave. I could not take my bicycle, so I gave it to a chum in the bakeshop. We boys walked to Arlington station, while the girls came in wagons. I went into the packing house and bought a gunnysack full of oranges for ten cents.

When the train came we got on board with all our possessions. There was a crowd of us, enough to fill twelve or fifteen wagons. My girl Mettie got in a seat with Philip from Second Mesa. I sat in my seat alone and ate oranges. Later, when I went to the toilet and returned, I found Irene of the Masau'u Clan in my seat. She was the granddaughter of old Chief Lolulomai and a pretty girl. I had paid no attention to her in school. But I knew, of course, that Sun Clan boys often married Fire Clan women. Ira was already going with a Fire Clan girl. I sat down beside her and treated her to some oranges from my gunnysack. While we were eating I joked with her a little and asked her if she would think of becoming my wife some time. She laughed and said, "Well, if Mettie doesn't get you I may, but you will have to drop her first." I liked Mettie far better.

We stopped at Needles, California, for lunch. Some Mohave Indians came among us trading necklaces, beads, and other jewelry. I bought two strings of beads, one for myself and one for Irene, which she accepted shyly. Mettie came and asked me to buy a string for her. I told her that I would be glad to do it but I was afraid that her friend Philip would get mad, for he had no money. When she begged, I pitied her and bought her some beads. I went back to sit with Irene, and we ate oranges and talked all afternoon. Since I could not have Mettie as a seat partner, I made the best of Irene and enjoyed her company. When night came on the conductor called all the girls into the forward car to sleep. The next morning they came back, and as we were riding along a peddler came through calling, "Fruit for sale." Mettie came to me and said that she was hungry. I bought some canned fruit and we had our breakfast together. Mettie was eating my food as we passed Williams and came to Flagstaff. We reached Winslow at about nine o'clock in the morning.

As we got off the train in Winslow we found our relatives with their wagons to meet us. A man who looked like a Navaho and was dressed "sporty" came along asking for Chuka. Coming up to me, he said, "I am Frank, the new husband of your sister Gladys. I have come to take you to Shipaulovi." I hated to go with him because I had planned to travel in the wagon with Mettie. He took our two grips, and Ira and I carried my gunnysack of oranges to his camp with other Second Mesa people out east of the town. There we built a fire and had some coffee. Frank was worried because his sister Sophie, who had returned from Sherman, wanted to go with the other girls to Oraibi. She had her way, too, as most Hopi girls do. Frank said that my mother had asked him to take Ira and me in his wagon to save expenses. After lunch I asked, "Well, brother-in-law, when are we leaving?" "Tomorrow," he answered. "I will have a white man in the morning to take to Hopiland." I asked him to go in to the town with me to buy a rifle. We walked to William Daggs's store and looked at a twenty-two caliber rifle for $3.50. Frank said, "Brother-in-law, that rifle is not a good one. Buy the $5 one and I will give you $2." We bought it. I told him that I would walk over to the Oraibi camp and see what I could learn. At this camp an Oraibi man came to me with some blankets that my mother had sent for us to use on our way home. I told him to keep my blankets there because I might spend the night in that camp.

I walked over to the campfire, where Mettie was eating with her uncle and some other people. While the uncle was talking Mettie whispered to me, "Don, where are you going with the gun?" I told her I was going out toward the railroad roundhouse to hunt for game.

She whispered back that she would follow. Pretty soon I left with my rifle and hunted around until I saw her coming. We walked together toward the railroad and sat down among some bushes, where we stayed most of the afternoon. It was here that I had Mettie for the first time. I was not afraid to do it, because we were back among our own people. We walked about among the bushes and killed three rabbits. When we returned to the camp I handed the rabbits to Mettie and told her to cook them, but she seemed bashful and timid because of the blood. Mettie's uncle dressed and cooked them, and we had an early supper. Then I told Mettie that I was going to take one blanket over to the Shipaulovi camp for Ira but that I would leave my blanket with her.

I returned to Frank's wagon and gave Ira his blanket. After supper some of us walked back to town, went through the stores that were still open, and then went to a movie. When we came out I told them that I was going to the Oraibi camp, and followed along behind a bunch of girls who were returning from the show. At the camp the men had a big bonfire and were dancing their Katcina dances. I had been out of this for three years and did not know the tunes. We stayed up until after midnight. When it was time for bed I took my blanket and lay down beside Mettie. Her uncle saw me but said nothing. I had Mettie twice more during the night. We could hear others doing the same thing, for we were sleeping close together. All the fellows were with their girls, for we were now free from the school officials and back with our uncles and fathers.

Before daylight I whispered to Mettie that I would meet her in Oraibi, and slipped away with my blanket to the Second Mesa group. Frank was missing, so I lay down on his bed until it was time to build a fire and get breakfast. Then I left Ira to tend the fire and went into town to get six loaves of bread, some wieners, potatoes, corn, and onions. I also bought two pounds of ground beef and one pound of bacon. When I reached camp Frank had come in with his horses. I said, "Well, we have an education, but we don't know how to cook at camp." He laughed, took out his knife, and peeled the potatoes. After breakfast we hitched up and drove to the depot to meet our white passenger, Mr. Kirkland, who was a carpenter on his way to Hopiland. I did most of the talking with him because I could speak better English. We loaded our wagon and started along the old trail. Frank had a good trotting team, and by noon we reached the foothills of the mesa south of the Hopi Buttes where we stopped for lunch. After eating we started again and drove up on the shelf of the mesa, and crossed on the east side near the spring, where we camped for the night.

After supper I talked with the white man about my schooling and how we played football and beat most of the schools in southern California. I talked until he seemed tired. Then we lay down and Frank began teaching Ira and me the Long Hair Katcina song.

As I lay on my blanket I thought about my school days and all that I had learned. I could talk like a gentleman, read, write, and cipher. I could name all the states in the Union with their capitals, repeat the names of all the books in the Bible, quote a hundred verses of Scripture, sing more than two dozen Christian hymns and patriotic songs, debate, shout football yells, swing my partners in square dances, bake bread, sew well enough to make a pair of trousers, and tell "dirty" Dutchman stories by the hour. It was important that I had learned how to get along with white men and earn money by helping them. But my death experience had taught me that I had a Hopi Spirit Guide whom I must follow if I wished to live. I wanted to become a real Hopi again, to sing the good old Katcina songs, and to feel free to make love without fear of sin or a rawhide. I wondered where Mettie and the Oraibi party were camping that night and made up my mind to see more of her among our own people.

7

The Return to Hopiland

WE AWOKE IN THE DESERT, washed our faces in the spring, had a quick breakfast, and started along the cliff toward Second Mesa. Our white passenger stopped at Toreva Day School just before sunset and offered to pay his fare. Frank put up the fingers of one hand twice, indicating $10 but later told me in Hopi to ask for $5 more. I urged him to be quiet, explaining that among Whites the only polite way is to state the full price at first.

We reached Shipaulovi by dark and found my sister Gladys and her baby, Delia, waiting for us with a good Hopi supper of fried bread, piki, and stew. After talking about school and singing Katcina songs until midnight, I went to sleep on the housetop. Early in the morning we took Gladys and her baby in the wagon and started for Oraibi in a fast trot.

Our mother nearly cried when we shook hands, but she did not kiss me, for that is not the old Hopi way. My grandfather and old Naquima greeted us fondly, but my father was out at his field at Batowe. The folks fed us the finest food they had—white piki, stewed mutton, and boiled dried peaches. Then I looked out southwest over the desert and saw twelve covered wagons approaching like a caravan—with Mettie in one of them.

Ira and I filled a flour sack with my oranges and took them to our "mother" Nuvahunka (mother's sister) who ran to meet us, and said,

"My sons, I am glad to see you. Where are the others?" We sat down with her on the floor and ate piki, parched corn, dried mutton, and onions, telling her that we were glad to be back home to eat the good old Hopi food. We were still talking with her when the wagons entered the village and stopped at the house of the Chief where there was to be a feast. My Uncle Talasquaptewa, who had been acting chief in the absence of Tewaquaptewa, shook hands with us and invited us to eat. We stayed around all day, talking about school and listening to stories of herding, farming, and fuel gathering. Everybody was so friendly that we thought quarreling and strife had ended in Oraibi. Our people had no dealings with the Hostiles at Hotavila and we were told not to go there. In the evening I went over to Claude James's house where Mettie was stopping, and shook hands with his family. We talked until after midnight, but I had no chance to speak to my girl in private. So I slept out on the roof with Claude, while Mettie slept below.

I awoke at dawn and sat on the roof watching the sunrise—as my father had taught me in my boyhood. Soon Perry, my ten-year-old brother, called me to eat. Teasing Naquima, I reminded him of the time when I shot him with an arrow. We sat on the floor of my mother's house and talked until my father came with fresh mutton on his burro. At noon I was still telling about school. I also told my parents of my sickness and death, how I came back to Oraibi, and where I sat on a sheepskin before their very eyes. Then I described how I had gone away disappointed, journeyed to the House of the Dead, and discovered that I had a Spirit Guide to protect me. My mother and father wept and said that they never saw me, nor even dreamed of my death; and my mother reminded me of her own death and long journey. My grandfather prophesied again that I would become an important man in the ceremonies.

In the afternoon Louis Hoye and I hunted rabbits with my new rifle and killed nine, which I gave to my mother to make a stew for the Katcina dance which was to be held the next day. At supper I kept thinking of Mettie, went over to Claude's home, and joined his family who were eating out on the first roof. While Claude told stories of school life and of his work with Whites, Mettie caught my eye and winked. At bedtime I marked the place where she spread her blanket and climbed with Claude to the second roof. When everyone seemed asleep, I crept down, touched Mettie's foot, and whispered, "Follow me to a safe place." We went quietly to the second roof, lay down on my sheepskin and enjoyed each other twice while Claude snored. When Mettie returned to her place I fell asleep; but I awoke with the crowing of the cocks and moved quickly to the roof of our own house—not caring to be teased by anyone who might have heard us. At the appearance of the yellow dawn, I sat up, prayed, and watched the Katcinas come into the plaza.

We Oraibi people were together all day watching the dance and inviting friends to eat with us. At noon Frank came from Shipaulovi with his sisters, Sophie and Jane. Hopis from other villages, Navahos, and government agents came to Oraibi on foot, in wagons, and on horseback. As I watched the dances, I wanted to be a Katcina again and to sing the old songs. The clowns played tricks to please the people, and at about sundown I expected the Whipper Katcina to come and flog them in order to purify their hearts and bring rain. But instead, a woman spoke to the Father of the Katcinas and asked for a second day of dancing. The head Katcina rattled his gourd to say "Yes," and the Father sprinkled corn meal upon them and led them to the Mongwi kiva to spend the night apart from their wives and sweethearts. That evening I saw Mettie again but did not care to sleep with her because she was menstruating. After a talk with Sophie and Jane, I slept alone on my mother's housetop while the girls slept inside to be safe from prowling fellows who might want to make love in the night.

Frank hitched up next morning to take his family home, and asked Ira or me to go along and help him herd. Ira was slow in answering as usual, so I went, missing the dance. Sophie and Jane were very friendly all the way, but I slept alone that night, for I was not very well acquainted with the Shipaulovi people and had to be careful lest I get a bad name.

In a day or so I mounted a burro, went to herd with Howard, Frank's nephew, and became very tired, sore, and sunburned. We slept at the ranch house, and on the fifth morning Frank relieved us and sent us home with our burros loaded with mutton. I was so weary from herding that I slept the rest of the day and night. Next morning

I went with Howard to hoe watermelon plants and place little brush screens around them for protection from the sun and the sand drifts. And the following day was spent in spraying corn plants with Howard and Frank. We collected about ten pounds of dried dog dung and a few roots of a special plant. Mixing the dung and roots with water at Burro spring, we used a broom and sprinkled the solution on the five- and six-inch plants to protect them from rabbits and other animals. After another night in the field house, I began another four days' herding with Howard.

When we returned to Shipaulovi, the men were practicing in the kiva for the Niman dance and invited me to join them. As the date for the Niman drew near, I walked to Oraibi to get a dancing outfit, had lunch with my mother, and rode back in a buckboard with Mr. Miller, the agent at Keams Canyon. He asked me many questions about my home, school training, and trade. I braced myself, looked straight into his eyes, and answered with the truth without boasting, for now I could talk with Whites like a gentleman. He seemed to like me and said that I might get a job at the Agency.

That evening we practiced for the Niman in the kiva until midnight. Then I went out to the south edge of the mesa and lay down in my blanket on the ledge, quickly falling asleep. Suddenly I felt something wet and cold on my face, and, jumping up, discovered Jane pouring water on me, for it was long after sunrise. Laughing and drying my face, I threatened to douse her sometime.

There was to be a Niman dance at Oraibi within a week. On that day Sam, a clan uncle about my age, and I saddled our burros and reached Oraibi at noon. We quickly corralled the burros, climbed upon the roof of a house, and watched the Katcinas dancing in the plaza. I spied Elsie and Mettie from Moenkopi on another housetop. Nudging Sam, I said, "Look, there is my girl and Elsie. We will have them tonight." We stepped over and shook hands. I made a date with Mettie and, leaning over, whispered to Elsie, "May we go to your house after dark?" She answered, "Sam might not want me." "I will take care of that," I replied.

In the evening after supper Sam and I walked out by the Coyote Clan cistern and saw our girls on the mesa edge watching the sunset with other young people. We walked over and sat down by Mettie and Elsie, Sam being a little bashful. After dark most everyone went into the village, but Mettie and I walked to the very edge of the mesa, stepped down upon a cozy little ledge, and found a seat. After brief kissing and petting, I took the blanket from her shoulder and made a little bed for love-making. I later found Sam, and we took our girls into the village. During the night we slipped into the girls' room and slept with them until nearly dawn. But at sunrise we were asleep on our own roof. I took Sam among my kinsfolk where we ate seven or eight times before we saddled our burros and set out for Shongopavi. On the way we felt so tired and weak from loss of sleep and strength that we decided to hobble our burros and take a nap in an old field house. We awoke in the late afternoon, rode on to Shongopavi after sunset, and went straight to bed.

The Niman at Shipaulovi was getting near. The men took their masks to the kiva to decorate them and asked Sam, Jacob, and me to take five burros and go for juniper boughs. We took along prayer feathers, sacred corn meal, some mountain tobacco, and a pipe. Upon reaching the junipers, we broke a bough, sat down by it, smoked, exchanged kinship terms,[1] and prayed to the Six-Point-Cloud-People for rain. Then we filled the bags with boughs and returned to Shipaulovi by noon. The Katcina Father, who is always a member of the Powamu society, met us in the plaza, took us into the kiva, and had us smoke again, while the head man praised our work and said that it would bring rain. After supper we returned for another smoke and were told to stay away from the girls for we had gathered the sacred juniper.

We slept that night but stayed awake in the kiva on the following night to practice fourteen songs, smoke, and pray. At four o'clock in the morning we took our outfits to the Katcina shrine and resting place at the edge of the village, sprinkled corn meal in the six directions, and returned to the plaza where we formed in a line at the north end and danced while the people still slept. The Special Officers came

1. Addressing one another by proper kinship terms is an important ritual in prayer.

out of a kiva and placed prayer offerings on the shrine in the plaza. When we had finished this dance, the Father of the Katcinas said, "Well, I am glad that you have come here and that I am the only one who has seen you. Go back to your resting place till morning. Then bring gifts so that we may have a good time." We returned to the resting place, dressed as Katcinas, and at dawn the leader made a corn-meal path toward the village and placed a soft downy prayer feather upon it. We were dancing at this shrine when the sun arose. Then we put on our masks, formed into a long line, and were led into the village. After dancing in the plaza, we were taken to the Powamu kiva to dance and to be sprinkled with corn meal by the women members of the Powamu society. Then we returned to the plaza with presents for the children—bows, arrows, dolls, sweet-corn plants, etc. When these were distributed, we went back to our resting place and waited for our female relatives to bring us breakfast. We entered the plaza to dance and returned to rest many times during the day.

It is a rule that Katcinas may drink no water until midday unless it rains; and my throat and lips were parched from singing and dancing in the heat and dust. At noon the women brought food and water to our resting place. While dancing in the afternoon, I peeped through my mask and saw Jane and Sophie on the housetop with their friends, Esther and Lillian, from Oraibi. I noticed that they were talking, and saw Jane point her finger at me. Before sunset the Powamu members came from the kiva, sprinkled corn meal upon us, and gave us prayer sticks and soft prayer feathers which we tied to our belts. Then at the end of the last dance the Father of the Katcinas told us to depart for the season and take our prayer feathers to the Six-Point-Cloud-People, praying for rain. Before we left the plaza, all the men and boys rushed up to us and broke off the spruce boughs that were suspended from our waists in order to plant them in their fields with prayers for a good harvest.

Frank saddled his horse next morning, taking with him a spruce bough and the prayer feathers that I had received from the Powamu members and which he would plant in his field. Before he left, he reminded me that I should not sleep with any girl for four days. I went to Sophie's house and invited Esther and Lillian to eat with us. They would look at me, glance at each other, and laugh; and this alarmed me. They admitted that they knew something about me, but said they would not tell me until we went to Oraibi for the Flute dance.

The Crier at Shipaulovi announced a rabbit hunt. Four days later we rounded up the horses and gathered in the afternoon at Burro spring, where we made a bonfire. Jay, the leader of the hunt, sprinkled corn meal in a circle and placed some rabbit dung in the center to represent the animals. He threw in some grass for their food, struck a match—in former times it would have been a flint—and built another fire, signifying that the women could expect fresh meat. We hunters held our rabbit sticks in the smoke for good luck. Then we formed a circle more than a mile across and closed in, beating the bushes and yelling. Rabbits were running toward the center, and whenever one broke through the line, a horseman chased it. I could not hit rabbits from horseback with a curved stick so I rode a burro; but later I became so excited that I ran on foot after rabbits—and some of them had very narrow escapes. When the killing was over, many hunters held rabbits in their hands, some as many as ten. I killed three, besides one which a dog caught. We made six more roundups during the day. My burro was loaded with rabbits because Frank, who was a good hunter, helped me from horseback. When we reached home the women rejoiced, gave thanks to us, and set to work dressing rabbits. Frank, Sam, and I helped my sister Gladys.

The next day we had a big rabbit feast, cooked in an old-fashioned outside oven. Sophie and Jane ate with us and wanted to tease and play with me roughly, but I kept a close eye on Frank and showed reserve. In the evening Sam and I went to bed out on the ledge and sang the Katcina songs we had used in the Niman dance. I was anxious to learn them perfectly, but my mind was troubled about the secret which Esther and Lillian had promised to tell me in Oraibi.

I was getting tired of living in Shipaulovi and working so hard for Frank. He was hot-tempered and sometimes he scolded me worse than if I had been his own nephew. I liked Jane and wanted to sleep with her, but I feared that her folks might want me to marry her and live there in Shipaulovi under Frank's thumb. He was an influential man because he was of the Bear Clan and his uncle was Chief. I also wanted to go to Moenkopi to earn some money and to see Mettie.

On the day of the Flute dance in Oraibi, Frank was away. I told Gladys that I was going to the dance but would return before leaving for Moenkopi. Jane saw me as I passed through the plaza and guessed that I was bound for Oraibi. With a broad smile she said, "Give my best regards to Esther and Lillian." I was embarrassed and wondered what secret they knew about me.

I set out on foot, but made such poor progress that I took off my shoes, hung them around my neck, and ran as much as I could, reaching Oraibi before noon. Many of the people had gone to Loloma spring with the members of the Gray Flute society to deposit prayer offerings for our dear ones who had passed away. I ate lunch with my mother, who told me that Esther and Lillian had spread the news in Oraibi that Jane and I were lovers. That worried me and I was glad that Mettie was not in Oraibi. I remained in the house wondering what to do about this rumor until the children reported that the Flute members were at the Oraibi spring. Then I went out and watched the foot race up the mesa to bring rain. After seeing the Gray Flute members dance near the Marau kiva and go to their shrine to deposit prayer offerings, I went into my mother's house and ate supper almost in silence.

At sunset I went out to the Antelope shrine and saw Esther and Lillian beckoning to me from the rocks at the edge of the mesa. When I joined them they teased me and said, "Jane claims you for her lover, and she told us much more, too." I denied that we were lovers, begged them to keep this news from Mettie, returned to the house, and made my bed on my mother's roof—very worried.

The next day I walked back to Shipaulovi and went to Jane's house after supper. I sat with her on the roof in the twilight and questioned her about the girls' report. She hung her head and came so near to tears that I took her hand, drew her to me, and told her to forget it, saying softly that I never dreamed she would have me as a lover. After midnight I made an effort to go, but she held my hand so tightly that I lay down and slept with her. Her folks knew that we were together, so, although I kissed her many times and caressed her freely, I was careful not to have intercourse with her for I knew that I was a suitable person for her to marry and might get trapped. I wanted to remain free to have Mettie and I was afraid of Frank. We finally fell asleep under separate blankets. I knew now that her family wanted me, but I was not afraid to be caught with her for we had not had intercourse. I felt that I could stand on my feet and tell the truth whenever it was necessary to defend myself against marriage.

Next morning Jane's folks found us together, teased us, brought us water to wash our faces in the same basin, and had us sit beside each other at breakfast—like a young married couple. When I told them that I was going to Moenkopi, they asked me many questions about when I would return. I finally managed to say good-by and went to my sister's house for a square meal, for I had been too timid to eat much. Gladys watched me while I ate and noticed that something had happened. When I told her, she said, "Well, it is up to you to decide for yourself, and then if she treats you badly you do not have to blame me." She also said that the girl was known to entertain married men, and that she did not prefer that kind of a sister-in-law. She cried a little and said that she did not want me to leave Shipaulovi, for I was a great help to Frank.

I packed up my things and stopped at Jane's house on the way out of the village. When I told her good-by, she squeezed my hand and, with a few tears in her eyes, pulled me to her and kissed me on the right cheek, in public. I stood gentle and quiet and urged her to take good care of herself. Then as I walked down the mesa it seemed that I had stepped from a very narrow path on to a wide road. I felt free from prison and, smiling to myself, thought, "Now I have two girls. Maybe they had better divide me into halves, the lucky girl getting the lower part." I felt a little sorry for the unlucky one; but I was afraid that on one side or the other the people would call me kahopi. I walked all the way and reached Oraibi in the afternoon, so hungry and tired that my mother fried me an egg.

I spent the night on my mother's roof, feeling like a bird who had just escaped a trap. The crickets seemed to be telling me to drop Jane and take Mettie, and I thought the stars were smiling their encouragement for a honeymoon in Moenkopi. I was restless to be on my way, and learned in the morning that Masawyestewa, my mother's sister's husband, planned to leave for Moenkopi the next day with four burros. After a long day and another night, we set out, riding two burros and driving two with packs. I had rolled my clothes in a flour sack and discarded my awkward suitcase. I thought of my girl step by step and mile after mile, wondering if she would be standing in the door, shading her eyes with her hand, and looking for my appearance over the last hill—or would she have another lover and hate to see me?

We reached Moenkopi after sunset and drove our burros to the house of my grandmother Iswuhti, and my Aunt Frances. My ceremonial father, Sekahongeoma, was living there too. He did not recognize me at first but then ran to me, threw his arms around me, and held me to himself a long time, saying, "My son, my son, I did not know you because of your long absence at school." The family questioned me about my school life until late bedtime, so that I did not have a chance to see my girl; but my grandfather Roger, my aunt's husband, who was also the brother of my ceremonial father, teased me about her, and my aunt said that she was going to take me for her own lover and drive her old husband out of the house. Finally I climbed to the roof with my ceremonial father and we slept together.

Jackson, a Sherman schoolmate, took me next morning to the Navaho Agency at Tuba City to look for a job in the bakery. When we were told to return on the following day for an appointment with the superintendent, we walked about the village and entered the store. I was dead broke until Jackson loaned me $5 so that I could buy a can of tobacco and have some spending money. We returned to Moenkopi, looked up Louis Hoye, and spent the day with his family, telling tales about our school life.

After supper I saw my girl standing in the back door of her house. Passing near her, I spoke softly, "Hello, Mettie." She smiled and replied, "Where are you going?" "Out this way," I whispered, "but I'll be back." Returning soon, I said, "It is not nice for me to be seen standing here with you; is there some place we may meet after dark?" She promised to sleep just outside the door. I returned to the house and ate a melon with Louis and his family. At bedtime Louis and I climbed on the housetop and lay down. I told him that I had seen my girl and had a late date with her. He said that we would go together because he had a date with his girl Elsie, who lived next door to Mettie and often slept with her. When the lights were out and the people were all quiet, we took our blankets, crept down, stole to the edge of the yard, lay flat on the ground, and rolled ourselves over to where the girls were lying. My head came close to Elsie who whispered that Mettie was on the other side. Moving over, I pulled myself under her cover and lay still and quiet for a while. Then we began to whisper softly, kiss each other, and use our hands to get acquainted, paying no attention to Louis and Elsie. We had intercourse three times and were still enjoying each other when the moon arose. Then I became uneasy, reached over to Louis, and whispered, "Let's go."

We had a good nap on our roof before sunrise, rolled our blankets, went down to breakfast, and then set out for Tuba City, stepping lively with a lunch under our arms and comparing notes on the affairs of the night.

The superintendent put us to work picking peaches with two other boys at $1 a day. Within a few weeks I was made foreman of the peach-picking outfit and did not have to work so hard myself. Mettie also worked at Tuba City part of the time, washing clothes and doing housework for Whites. I began picking fruit at the Agency in the middle of August and continued until the third week in October, living with my aunt until she left for Oraibi in September to attend the Marau ceremony. I then moved to the house of my mother's sister Tuwanungsie, but began to sleep in the kiva with the unmarried men and boys because the nights were getting colder. Louis and I remained partners and met together with our girls once or twice a week, usually in the corn-grinding room where they often slept. It became public knowledge that Mettie and I were lovers. This pleased her uncles but worried her mother. At first I tried to be careful and safeguard Mettie from pregnancy—because she wanted to return to school—by avoiding too frequent intercourse, especially near the time of her monthlies. Later when I found that her mother was so opposed to her marriage, I hoped that Mettie would become pregnant, because that gives a man some advantage over his sweetheart's mother. For when a girl has a baby, the mother usually wants her daughter to marry the child's father.

Other girls came into my life even while I was planning to marry Mettie. They seemed to trust me because I built up a good reputation in Moenkopi by keeping myself in hand and never taking a girl by force as was the custom among some youths. When the girls returned from a walk together in the evening the fellows would waylay them and the lucky boys would catch their girls and take them to one side, insisting upon favors. This was especially true after the occasion of the Snake dance at Oraibi, but was not infrequent at other times, and made it necessary for parents to guard their girls closely, if they wished to protect them.

We were at home one evening when two or three girls came to grind corn with my clan sister Meggie. One was Eva of the Bamboo Clan, who was well-built with nice, smooth arms and legs, broad, shapely hips, and a pretty face with rosy cheeks and sparkling eyes. Many fellows sought her eagerly and some of them told me that she never cried out when a boy laid his hands upon her. While she ground corn with Meggie, the boys stood outside at the window and teased her. When she was ready to go home, she called me inside and said, "I am afraid of those fellows, will you please take me home?" I consented and whispered to Meggie, "Tell the boys that we are going to have a melon in the back yard. When they are eating, I will slip out with Eva." As they were feasting on the melon, I wrapped a quilt about me to resemble a girl and slipped out the front door with Eva, saying to her, "Let me put my head under your shawl and my arm around you so that we will look like two girls." Then as we walked along, I whispered, "You are sweet." "But not so sweet as Mettie," she replied.

The fellows discovered that Eva was gone and rushed after us, pulling the shawl off our heads, grabbing the girl, and causing her to scream. I held on to her wrist until the people rushed out of the houses and ordered the fellows to leave her alone. We went to the door of her house, where I asked her whether there was any way for us to meet again that night. She whispered, "Lie down near the door in the dark when all are asleep, and I will slip out to you."

I departed promptly, but returned and waited until finally, when the village was very quiet, I felt a hand touch my shoulder and heard Eva whisper, "Let's go to the roof of the second story and into the corn-grinding room." She led me to the upper room with a sheep pelt under her arm. There I found her so loving and coöperative that I made a date for another night, and could persuade myself to steal away only after the cocks crew.

Mettie and Elsie ground corn in another house. Louis and I frequently crept there to sleep with them. But one day Louis was sent by the Agency to Flagstaff for freight. That evening I sang Katcina songs in the kiva for a while, then went to the corn-grinding room and found Elsie alone. She said that Mettie was at home sick with her monthly and suffering some pain. I expressed disappointment and sighed that I, too, would have to go home in discomfort. Elsie laughed softly and said, "Wait a while." I lay down on a sheep pelt with my head close to the grinding bin, and told her some stories while she worked, occasionally letting my hand find her arm playfully.

She would say, "Don't tease me, I am working." Finally I asked her if she really meant for me to go and leave her alone. She said, "No, it is up to you, but I hate to cheat on Mettie." A little later she put the corn meal in a bowl and said that it was bedtime. I got up and pretended to go, but she beat me to the door and locked it, saying, "I had an argument with Louis, and he quit me two days ago."

I stepped over to her blanket and lay down. To my surprise she undressed completely, helped get off my clothes, and then lay down close to me. No girl had ever done this before, and I had never felt so much soft, warm flesh joined with mine. She had even plucked out the pubic hair, as it is said that Hopi women used to do. I thought I could love her forever, and asked her then and there to marry me. She kissed me thoroughly and asked me to put my tongue into her mouth, which was another new experience for me. When I did it, she sucked and bit upon it hard in orgasm, while I struggled in pain to free myself. Finally I lay over on my back, groaning a little with a bleeding tongue, while Elsie laughed. On the next trial I took her tongue in my mouth which was better for me. In spite of the pain, I liked her and still wanted her to be my wife. I was fast asleep when she called me at cock-crowing and said that I had better go.

Within a few days Louis and I were talking about women and I asked him whether he had ever had a girl undress completely for him. He answered, "No," and asked me the same question. "Yes," said I, but mentioned no names, smiling in my heart and congratulating myself for knowing more about his girl than he did. Later, I gave Elsie a $5 ring.

Around the first of October Louis and I decided to put on a Paiute dance, for that would make us popular in the village. We went to the Crier Chief and asked him to call the men and boys to the kiva. Then we lighted our lanterns, built a fire, and waited. The Crier Chief invited me to tell the people what was on my mind. I spoke, saying that Louis and I wished to put on a dance to make the people happy and bring rain, before the boys and girls returned to school. They agreed and I picked out two boys, Clarence and Walter, to watch over the girls so that there would be no love-making during practice. Everyone said that he would do his best and would have no arguments to spoil the dance and cause droughts. Frank Siemptewa, the Governor of Moenkopi, asked me what kind of dance we would have, and I said, "A Paiute dance." Everybody jumped up and yelled to show that they were well pleased. Then most of the fellows went out, but Frank and the other officers remained to smoke and pray. Louis and I slept in the kiva that night because we were responsible for the dance. The next day we went back to Tuba City and worked.

In the evening Clarence and Walter gathered the girls and brought them into the kiva, telling them each to select a dancing partner from among the boys. They whispered the names of their choices into the ears of Clarence and Walter. Elsie picked Walter as her partner, and all shouted their approval. Sadie picked Louis. According to custom, every boy was chosen by a real, clan, or ceremonial aunt. Euella, my father's clan sister's daughter, chose me.

We asked the men to compose songs for the dance, and lined up to practice with the tallest couples in the lead. Many laughed and said that I danced like a Mexican, because I had been away so long. When it came Mettie's turn to stand by me, the boys laughed and teased her—knowing that she was my lover. We practiced every night and worked during the day at Tuba City.

In about a week Louis, Walter, Clarence, and I pooled our money to buy two sheep, coffee, and sugar for the feast. We had already hired two silversmiths to make large buttons for the girls to wear. We bought velvet cloth to make waists for the girls, and red cloth for skirts. Louis' sister made his girl's outfit and I hired an aunt to make mine. Two different girls would wear these outfits for each dance. Louis, Walter, Clarence, and I agreed to watch one another and see that we kept pure during this period. If any one of us had broken the rule of continence, fierce winds, cold weather, and droughts might have come upon us all.

During practice at midnight before the day of the dance, I stepped out of line and said, "Attention, please! Louis and I will select four boys to come with us and fetch food to the kiva." Our families were waiting with stew and coffee. We took this food into the kiva in five large bowls and placed it in the center of the kiva on a wagon cover. The girls ate first and then sang while the boys ate. Since Louis and I were the leaders, we ate last with the Special Officers.

When the kiva was in order again, all the dancing boys went to their homes and brought gifts for the girls, such as candy, peanuts, dishes, and anything they had been able to purchase. They also gave gifts to the brothers and fathers of their partners. I bought ten dollars' worth for Euella and her closest kin.

Then some of the boys left the kiva, dressed in costume, and returned to give us a special dance, a Buffalo dance, with two little girls. The singers entered the kiva first, shooting revolvers in the air and yelling like enemy warriors. They gave us such a good surprise dance that we wondered if we would be able to do as well next day. I arose and thanked them, inviting them to return and repeat it.

Finally I climbed out of the kiva to watch for the coming of dawn, and when the sky turned yellow, I reëntered the kiva and said, "Let's go into the plaza and dance." The first set of four dancers were like very old Paiutes. After our dances we returned to the kiva, changed to our regular clothes, and went to our houses for breakfast.

I returned to the kiva first and Louis followed soon after. "Well, partner," I said, "let's watch ourselves, act nice and quiet, and say nothing to displease anyone." "That's right," he replied. "Today we will treat the people politely." I was afraid Louis might slip and say almost anything, for I knew his record.

Two old men had been selected to prepare the headdress for the dancing girls. They had gathered eagle feathers for war bonnets and dressed the two girls who were to dance first, painted their cheeks red, braided their hair, adorned it with silver buttons, and placed silver belts around their waist. Each girl wore a war bonnet and held an arrow in her hand to use in dancing. The boys dressed as Paiute warriors and carried revolvers and war shields decorated with red fringes and eagle feathers. All the other men came from the kiva, beating the drums and singing. The girls climbed to the roof of the kiva and we sang Comanche songs. The two leading dancers led their partners into the plaza and danced in the four directions, singing and stepping slowly at first, but later very fast. It was wonderful. Navahos and Whites came into the village to watch.

In the first dance I took part with the singers and was not dressed for my special performance. When we returned to the kiva it was Tewanimptewa's turn and mine to take the leading parts. The same two men dressed our girls in the costumes of the previous dancers. I dressed to resemble a very old Paiute man, painting my face black and red from the tip of my nose to the top of my forehead. I took off my pants and went barelegged, except for an old-fashioned G-string. Below my knees I wore leggings made out of an old saddle blanket, tied at the top and bottom with a buckskin string. I placed an old Paiute moccasin on one foot and tied another to my belt. I wore a wig, placed a string of shell beads around my neck, put on an old-fashioned hat, and carried a forty-five-caliber revolver like a cowboy. Tewanimptewa dressed like a young "sporty" Paiute. We led the way into the plaza with our girl partners and danced to the singing of the men and the beating of the drums. The people laughed and laughed, pleasing me greatly.

While we were dancing, my aunt, Talayesnim, rushed into the plaza and stepped in front of her daughter Euella, telling her that she wanted me for herself. Euella's older sister Pole also rushed in, pulled her mother out, and danced with me. The old mother returned, threw her arms around my neck, and kissed me repeatedly on the mouth to show that she was jealous of her daughter, which is the way a good aunt should act. I was pleased to have the people see how much my aunts loved me, but of course I was expected to buy something for each of them after the dance. We finally danced out of the plaza and back into the kiva. After my special dance, I dressed again as a Comanche warrior and took my part with the other boys and girls at the side of the leading couples. We had nine dances by sunset when we returned to the kiva and undressed. The day was fair and calm, with no bad wind or cold weather, which showed that Louis' heart and mine were both right.

Before we disbanded I said, "Well, my partners, will it be all right for me to take Euella to her house dressed in the special outfit?" They all agreed and helped me to dress her again in all the finery. I led her to her house before the eyes of the people and presented the entire outfit to her as a reward for choosing me as a dancing partner. All the things were then removed from the kiva and we were dismissed by the Special Officers, but Louis and I were advised to sleep in the kiva and keep ourselves pure for four nights.

A public harvest for the Governor of Moenkopi was announced from the housetop next morning. The Crier Chief urged all who had participated in the dance to go to the Governor's field and gather his corn. The men and boys went for their horses. I chose a gentle horse, because each dancer was to return from the field with his girl partner riding back of him in the saddle, with her hair done up in the squash-blossom design. Horses were hitched to the wagon to take the girls five miles to the old Mormon field. The Special Officers led us on foot. We boys raced each other back and forth on our horses. At the edge of the field the special men sat down to smoke mountain tobacco and pray. Then we let out a big war whoop and rushed our horses all over the field before we got down to work. I carried a white sack for gathering the corn, Euella working with me.

When the harvest was completed, the head man advised us before we broke up, saying, "We are glad you have done this fine work for your mother and father, our Governor and his wife. Let us return home with happy hearts." We fellows, on our horses, made a big circle around the girls who had assembled by a great pile of corn. The Governor said, "Now, ladies, since the wagons are all laden with corn, each of you may choose a boy to take you home on horseback." I tightened the saddle belt of my horse and placed Euella behind me. The boys without girls were to chase a leader, Robert Talas, who carried a white tanned buckskin. Just after we started, the boys fired their revolvers in the chase and frightened my horse. I jumped off, put Euella in the saddle, and got up behind her, guiding my prancing horse to one side so that the racers could pass. We tried to trot, but Euella could not hold her seat very well, which caused us to fall far in the rear of the party.

As we rode along, Euella told me what a good time she had in the dance and how happy her folks were to receive so many gifts. She said they teased her and told her that she might pick me as her husband, and gleefully reminded me that since she was my aunt I had no right to refuse. When the officers were out of sight, leading the people toward the village, Euella became coy, laughed a lot, and led me on to love play. Holding my arms about her waist to keep her from falling, I let my hands play around in front of her and kissed her repeatedly on the neck as we jogged along. Suddenly, when there was no one in sight, she pressed hard against me, breathed short and fast, and began to quiver with excitement. I held her firmly, smiled to myself, and said nothing, remembering that I had to keep myself pure for four days.

We were the last to enter the village, while the women were preparing the feast at the Governor's place and spreading food out on the floor in long rows. The people laughed and teased us, saying, "Here comes a couple who are very late."

After the feast I went with Euella to her house and then mounted my horse to join the riders, who were still chasing Robert Talas with the buckskin. They were charging downhill toward the village like Navahos about to attack. Robert's father advised me to go to the house and wait. Robert rushed up on horseback and threw the buckskin to me. I ran into the house with it and the race was won.

For four nights I slept faithfully in the kiva. On the fifth day, the Crier called from a housetop for the people to go to the kiva. We assembled and the Governor announced, "Now, my brothers, there is to be a Butterfly dance at Oraibi and I would like to take the Paiute dancers there to entertain the people on the night that they stay awake in prayer and practice. Shall we go?" We all cried, "Yes." We were to leave Moenkopi in two days. I stopped working at Tuba City and spent my time preparing a war bonnet and a fancy costume. I borrowed a pair of Indian moccasins and a string of beads from the trader. He also loaned me a quiver for holding arrows which was made of the skin of a mountain lion with the tail attached.

That night, the fifth after the dance, when I was free for love-making again, I slipped out of the kiva and met Mettie in a vacant room where she and Elsie were accustomed to grind corn. There I had my reward for the long ceremonial restraint and made plans to accompany my girl to Oraibi. She told me that her mother had objected to our meeting together in private and had warned her not to marry me. To spite her mother, she had definitely made up her mind to return to Sherman, which was bad news for me.

When I returned to the kiva, I found the Governor smoking his mountain tobacco in prayer. I smoked with him, but used my store tobacco, because I had already spoiled myself for prayers by love-making. After the Governor went out, I made my bed and was asleep when Louis came in, caught hold of my nose, and gave it a twist. I awoke frightened, thinking that an evil spirit had captured me, until I heard a laugh. When I scolded him, he laughed again and said, "This is the fifth and free night after the dance. I have just come from my girl." "Which one?" I asked. "Sadie," said he. "How many times?" I inquired. "Seven, and I am weak," he boasted.

Louis soon began to snore, but the twisting of my nose had so thoroughly aroused me that I was still awake when the chickens crowed. I reached my hand over and twisted his nose, but he slept on. Then I pushed back the foreskin of his penis, tied a string to it, and fastened the other end to the rung of the ladder. I also took soot from the stove and painted large black circles around his eyes to show the people how he had spent the night. Soon I heard him yell and say, "Ouch."

I appeared innocent and asked, "What is it?" I had tied the string in such a hard knot that he had to use a knife to free himself, after which we had a little tussle. At sunrise we dressed and went to his house where everyone laughed at him, until he looked in the mirror and saw his big, black eyes. He turned to me and said, "You damned fool." His folks were laughing, but he did not tell how he had been tied.

After breakfast we took our bedding from the kiva and bridled our horses for the journey to Oraibi. The Governor sprinkled sacred corn meal on the ground, making a "road" for us to step upon before departing. He said, "My children, go to Oraibi, dance for our Chief, and make his people happy." Then we departed on horseback in a double row. I placed my horse near Mettie, who was riding with her uncle. We seemed like a gang of warriors on the warpath as we trotted along in costumes and war bonnets, each man carrying a load of watermelons. Henry and I were riding back of Mettie and her uncle, Billy. During lunch Billy whispered to me, "When we start I will ride off to one side, and you may take my place with Mettie."

When I rode my horse up beside Mettie, Henry punched me in the ribs and said, "Stay with it, boy." Mettie looked embarrassed and the fellows laughed, causing everybody to look at us and cheer. At the top of Bow Mesa Mettie whispered, "Don, I need to urinate." I passed the word back to her uncle who said, "You may go with her." We rode our horses off to one side and waited for the others to pass. The fellows laughed and said, "See the young couple." I dismounted, helped Mettie down, and kissed her as soon as she was ready to ride again. Before we overtook the crowd, we made a date to meet in Oraibi after dark. As we rode along she cried a little and told me that she was worried about her mother who opposed our marriage. I pitied her and promised that I would watch myself faithfully while she was at school. She said, "If you should marry another girl while I am away, I will return and cut her out, for you were mine first. Whoever marries you must share you with me, no matter what the Hopis say." Finally we galloped along, overtook the other riders, and entered Oraibi after dusk.

After supper with my mother, I borrowed some little brass bells from Ira, strung them on twine, and attached them to the border of my fancy pants. Then I ate a melon and went to the place where we left our equipment, while the Moenkopi men were smoking and praying with the Oraibi men in the kiva.

Before the dance practice began, I went to Claude's house where Mettie was staying. Claude, who had not seen me for a long time, squeezed my hand and whispered, "Your wife, Mettie?" I answered, "Yes," and we laughed. He promised to tell me where Mettie made her bed.

After we had arranged our costumes we went into the kiva and enjoyed a feast. Then we watched the boys bring their gifts to the girls and their brothers and uncles. The Oraibi people had borrowed the outfits which our girls had used in the Paiute dance, one of which I had given to Euella. When it was nearing midnight, we dressed in our costumes—I in my fancy pants with bells jingling, a white vest, and an eagle war bonnet. My buckskin hung in front from the silver belt to the middle of my thighs, and I gripped a forty-five-caliber revolver. When we were ready, the drummer began and we filed over to the kiva, singing Comanche songs and firing blanks into the air. I led, entering the kiva as quickly as a bird, uttering a big war whoop, and prancing about. During the dancing I saw Claude standing back of the ladder. He said, "Mettie made her bed in the second room at the back."

Finally we finished our singing, placed our costumes in their bags, and stored them for the night. I ate a melon, walked over to Claude's house, and listened at the door. Then removing my shoes, I entered, sneaked across the room like a cat, and put my hand down along the floor until I touched Mettie's shoulder. She lifted the cover. While we were together, Claude came into the house, drank some water, slipped over near where we lay, and whispered, "Don," with a smothered snicker. Finally I sneaked out. I had broken no ceremonial rule because I was not to be in the dance next day.

While we ate breakfast at my mother's house, my father told me that my uncles had decided that Ira and I should be initiated into the Wowochim in November. He said that when I returned to Moenkopi I should go hunting and kill ten jack rabbits or twenty cottontails for this ceremony. I knew that it was a Hopi rule for boys to take this important step into manhood. Some of my uncles had told me that if I were not initiated, the people would call me a boy all my life. They said that my childish name, Chuka, would stick to me forever and that the girls would not regard me as a man. I was not sure that I wanted to be initiated now, but feared that if I refused all my uncles and relatives would be against me.

I returned to Moenkopi ahead of the others so that I could paint the missionary's barn, which was a new job for which I had just been hired. Euella came over that evening to get our young clan sister, Meggie, to help her grind corn. Now Meggie had teased me about Euella in public, and I had warned her to stop it or I would keep a close watch on her and neither of us would have any fun. I soon went over where the girls were grinding and stood around chatting until I got a chance to ask Euella to slip out to a secret place with me. She said, "You go first and I will follow." Meggie overheard Euella, but I gave her a sign to mind her own business. I slipped down the hill in the dark and lay on a sand pile in a protected place, waiting. Soon I heard Euella coming and whistled softly. After a little petting, we hurried our pleasures in order to return before her family missed her. This was love-making with my little "aunt" and was the safest kind of all because I could not be expected to marry her, of course. When I returned to my house, Meggie was there with a knowing look on her face. She laughed, ready to burst with her secret. But I whispered, "Now it is your turn, and I won't tell."

When I returned to Moenkopi in the evening after a day of painting on the missionary barn, Robert Talas had just come back from Oraibi. He slapped me on the back, saying, "What do you mean running away? You were to have been married to Mettie. Her Uncle Billy had planned to marry you and Mettie that night. He had planned to have your heads washed together on the third day." "Well, I am glad it did not happen," said I. "Her mother would be my enemy." This news from Robert made me wonder whether I should ever marry. I studied this problem several days as I painted on the barn. Some thoughts favored marriage, but others canceled them out.

On the fourth night Elsie told me that they had planned to leave for school next day and that Mettie wanted me to meet her in the old corn-grinding room. That night Mettie said, "You know I have a stepfather whom my mother took away from your clan mother. She must think that if we marry her husband will see much of his old wife at the wedding feasts and want to go back to her." Mettie wanted me to promise that I would wait for her. We talked and talked and cried some between love-making. Finally we fell into a deep sleep, and when I awoke the sun was shining into the room. I jumped up, put on my clothes, took my shoes under my arm, and sneaked out the back door where old Billy saw me and smiled; but I moved right along.

After breakfast I went back to work on the mission barn, keeping a close eye on the road. I was painting the roof when I saw the girls leave the village, walking ahead of the wagons. Climbing down, I went to the edge of the road and shook hands with the girls, telling them that I was sorry to see them go. Mettie and Elsie, who were behind, urged me to go with them. But I told them that I must obey my uncles and be initiated. I warned them to take good care of themselves and to have no other lovers. Then I reached into my pocket and gave Elsie $3 and Mettie $5—squeezing her hand. Tears came into her eyes and a lump rose in my throat so that I could barely speak. I told her good-by, turned back to the barn with a heavy step, and said to myself, "Alas, what a hard time I shall have for the rest of my life."

8

The Making of a Man

I COULD NOT PUT OFF initiation into the Wowochim. My father, grandfather, and two great-uncles urged me to forget about school and become a man. They said it would please the gods, prepare me for ceremonial work, put me in line to become Chief of the Sun Clan, and fit me for a higher place in life after death. Talasvuyauoma, the big War Chief, advised me to join the men's society without delay. My ceremonial father, clan fathers, mother, godmother, clan mothers, and other relatives encouraged me; and they implied that any boy who did not seek membership in the Wowochim proved himself to be either incompetent or kahopi. They said that only hopeless cripples like Naquima or young men who had been spoiled by Christianity failed to take this important step into manhood.

Soon after my companions left for Sherman, I borrowed an old rifle and hunted rabbits two days with no success. On the third day Tewanietewa, the ceremonial son of my father, patted me on the back while we ate breakfast and said, "My brother, I hear you have failed to get your rabbits for the ceremony. Come to my corral and my brother and I will help you." We saddled a mule and set out, killing ten rabbits in a few hours. The older brother boasted of his marksmanship, but we warned him to be careful lest we lose our luck. We killed thirty more, some for other boys, tied them behind the saddle and came home, where my clan mother, Tuwanungsie, skinned and cooked them to keep for the ceremony. I felt cheered by our success, and visited Euella that night for a little love-making.

We soon started for Oraibi in four wagons. And the first night at camp old Yuyaheova joked me about the new name I would receive at the Wowochim ceremony. He said I might be called Massaki, which means the ladder stick of a grave, because my ceremonial father was of the Greasewood Clan, and grave sticks are made of greasewood. Everybody laughed at the idea of calling me "Grave Ladder." He then said that if I were not called Massaki I might be named Mashyie, which means dead greasewood hanging down, and explained that this would signify that my penis was dead, dry, and droopy. Everybody laughed, but the old man's daughter scolded him.

When we reached Oraibi, I went straight to my mother's house with my load of rabbit meat and a bag of apples. After breakfast on the second day we candidates were sent to the spring to bathe for the ceremony. I returned to the house a little worried until my father assured me that I would not be hurt—as in the Katcina whipping—and told me to remain in the house until I was called. Soon my ceremonial father peeped in and said, "Is my son here? We fathers have to see that our boys are ready."

My mother had me undress, put on a dancing kilt, wrap myself in a blanket, and wait. My ceremonial father soon came and led me toward the Mongwi kiva, which worried me, for it meant that I might become a Special Officer. I preferred to be initiated as a common man into the Kwan, Tao, or Ah1 societies and held back a little until he urged me to step lively. My mother had given me some corn meal to sprinkle on the society emblem (*natsi*) resting on the hatchway and also to cast on the new ceremonial fire which had been kindled by friction in the kiva. The officers seated me with eight other boys and told us that we were now young sparrow hawks (*Keles*) and should cry "Kele, Kele," like young hawks begging for food, whenever a ceremonial father came to the mouth of the kiva. Knowing everything would be unsalted, we made a secret agreement to help one another eat whatever was brought. About dusk my ceremonial father brought a dish of Hopi dumplings and several rolls of white piki, promising that if I ate it all he would bring something better. We ate a great deal but did not feel satisfied or strong, which proves that it takes salt to get strength.

We were kept awake and members of the Wowochim society taught us the special songs. My grandfather Poleyestewa beat a drum, sang softly, and repeated until we caught the tune. His song touched my heart and became firmly fixed in my mind. Other members took turns teaching us all night long. At gray dawn an Ah1 member called us out of the kiva and led us, with initiates of the other societies, to the foothills just off the southeast edge of the mesa. There we threw corn meal to the rising sun and prayed for a long, happy life. Returning to the kiva, we watched our ceremonial fathers weave our new outfits, practiced songs and dance steps, ate unsalted food, and took part in some special songs and rituals which cannot be revealed. Four days were spent in this manner and it proved to be a long, tiresome experience. We were under supervision continuously and even when a boy had to go outside, we all went together with a guide. For four nights I had to sleep under a blanket with my ceremonial father, just as I slept with my mother as a baby, in order that he might "raise me to manhood."

Early in the morning of the fifth day our ceremonial fathers washed our heads in yucca suds. Then our clan brothers, uncles, and nephews repeated the operation. Members of the linked Greasewood, Road-Runner, and Bamboo clans also washed my head, because my ceremonial father was of that group. We were placed in a line outside the kiva to receive new names. Each Bear Clan member proposed a name for Louis, who was first in line, and the most appropriate name was selected for him. When my turn came, Sekahongeoma held a mother-corn ear before me and said: "Now I adopt you so that you may live long and be strong and happy. You shall be called Talayesva. I belong to the Greasewood and the Bamboo clans. The Greasewood has a tassel and so does the Bamboo. The name means Sitting Tassel, for these two plants." Everybody cheered and began calling me Talayesva immediately, seeming to forget my old name Chuka, which surprised me, for this change was very sudden.

We returned to the kiva and were dressed by our ceremonial fathers in the new Kele outfits—two white capes and a belt arranged in such manner that the tails of the capes were left loose like the wings of the sparrow hawk. A soft prayer feather was fastened to our heads. The older members also dressed in their costumes, let down their hair, and tied decorations on their heads which resembled wild spinach. The drummer led us outside the kiva, where we nine Keles were placed in a horseshoe line, east of the kiva. We were told that our wing feathers were almost grown and that we were ready to fly from the nest (childhood). Holding hands and dancing to the drum and the singing, we shuffled sidewise into the plaza and circled all the kivas, making believe that we were tracing the boundary of Hopiland. Then we returned to our kiva, rehearsed more songs, and made a smaller dancing encirclement to represent the valley where our fields are located. In the songs we prayed for rain to awaken our crops and renew our lives.

On the sixth day before sunrise we were led to the east edge of the mesa to pray and report our new names to the Sun god, for we were no longer boys. The officers said this established our manhood and fixed our names forever; and that for anyone to use our childish names again would be like a slap in the face. Only my "grandfathers" would dare call me Chuka after this—and then as a joke.

We made the dancing encirclements for four days. Then on the eighth day of the ceremony we dressed in the Kele costume, bedecked ourselves with jewelry, and went at night to each of the other kivas to smoke, pray, and dance. Our ears had been pierced in infancy so that we could wear the valuable earrings on this occasion. We danced all night long.

At sunrise we prayed at the east edge of the mesa and returned to our kiva. My ceremonial father took my blanket and new mother-corn ear, which he had given me in the ceremony, and led me to my mother's house along a path of sacred corn meal which he sprinkled before me. He made four corn-meal marks on the ground by the door and said to my mother, "I have brought our son home. Now he is a man and is called Talayesva." She thanked him and received from him the corn ear and the blanket. Then Sekahongeoma returned to the kiva for a final ceremonial smoke. I later removed my Kele costume, dressed in regular clothes, went to the house of my ceremonial father, and invited him to our place for the feast of rabbit meat which I had brought all the way from Moenkopi. I was nearly twenty and proud to be treated like a man.

The first Katcina of the season came into the plaza in the afternoon to open the Mongwi kiva for the great Soyal ceremony. He came over the cliff from the southeast, groping and hobbling like a very old man. He was dressed in a worn cotton shirt, a dancing kilt and belt, and a tattered old blanket. His mask was green-blue, marked with black lines at the eyes and topped with a bunch of red horsehair. He circled the Mongwi kiva, sidestepped to the right, sprinkled meal on each side, and stopped in front of the hatchway to shake his gourd rattle twice. A man came out of the kiva with a flat basket and a paho over which he sprinkled corn meal. The old Katcina took the paho, entered the plaza, sprinkled meal on the shrine, crossed the village to the southwest, and disappeared.

We Keles were told to set old-fashioned stone traps for mice and rats to be used in a feast four days later. We also went hunting twice, crying "Kele, Kele" as we chased the game, and gave the catch to our ceremonial fathers. We strung the rabbits in the kiva, letting them hang on a line from the ceiling. Some strings of game reached to the floor and along the ground for four or five feet. Mine barely touched the floor because I was a poor runner, but I caught many mice and rats in my traps.

On the fourth day we had a mock fight with our fathers, and a feast. Our relatives cooked the rabbits, but we had to take our mouse and rat meat to the Chief's house and cook it ourselves, making gravy without salt. We entered the kiva with a dish, and sat down by our ceremonial fathers. Mine took out a piece of mouse meat and ate it warily, with a little gravy. When I was not looking, he struck me a hard blow on the back, which was a signal for all the ceremonial fathers to fight their sons. One father grabbed the dish and threw its contents all over us. We struggled, rushed out of the kiva, and placed a wagon box over the entrance to imprison the fathers. Finally they escaped and rushed at us, but we were waiting for them with handfuls of mud made ready in pails. I plastered my father's face and neck, grabbed a large watermelon rind, and placed it over his head, making him look like bloody-headed Masau'u. We wrestled until I threw him and then he whispered, "Fill my mouth with dirt so that the people will laugh." While I did this, other fellows were fighting their ceremonial fathers all about me, and the people were laughing and cheering. When the fight was over, we all raced out west to some water holes in the rocks and took a bath, boasting about our feats. Some of us had even stripped the loincloths off our ceremonial fathers. We took our rabbit stew and piki to the kiva for a feast with our fathers; and then we were free for love-making, but I had to go without, for I had no special girl friend in Oraibi.

When the Soyal was about to begin—sixteen days after the appearance of the old Katcina—my uncle Talasquaptewa asked me to herd in his place so that he could perform his special duties as Chief Priest. He went to the kiva with the Special Officers to smoke in prayer and spend the night. In the morning they ate breakfast in the kiva and began the preliminary ceremony of making pahos to place on the shrines. When I returned from herding, the priests were preparing to spend another night in the kiva.

In the morning, the first day of the Soyal,[1] my grandfather Poleyestewa took a tray with meal and pahos, deposited them in the shrine on the housetop where announcements were made by the Crier Chief, and informed the people that Soyal had begun. Before I went to herd again, I saw my uncle go to the kiva with his paho-making outfit—feather box, sticks, corn meal, cotton string, and herbs. The Special Officers spent the day carding and spinning cotton and preparing equipment for the altar.

On the second day of the Soyal I took a pinch of corn meal, sprinkled the ceremonial emblem on the hatchway, and entered the kiva to eat with the other Keles. Little happened all day, or the next, except that a few men carded and spun cotton for pahos. We were careful to have no arguments and do nothing to upset the minds of the Special Officers and thus spoil the ceremony.

1. For very elaborate details of the ceremony, see G. A. Dorsey and H. R. Voth. *The Oraibi Soyal Ceremony* (Anthrop. Series, Field Mus. Nat. Hist., 1901), Vol. III, No. 1, pp. 1–59.

On the fourth day after breakfast in the kiva, Talasvuyauoma, the War Chief (Kaletaka), said to us, "Go bathe in the spring and have your heads washed in yucca suds, so that you will be ready for the Medicine Making ceremony." The heads of all Soyal members were washed in purification for this solemn rite. I knew that the charm medicine must be made exactly right in order to be safe and effective. There could be no careless conduct with so much at stake.

When I returned to the kiva in the afternoon, there were bags containing roots, herbs, stones, bones, and shells on the floor near an old medicine tray. The War god's equipment of shield, bow, and tomahawk hung from a peg in the wall. The officers were spinning cotton, smoking, and making prayer offerings of eagle, hawk, and turkey feathers. After we had stripped, except for loincloths, Talasvuyauoma, the War Chief, took five prayer feathers, some corn meal, and an old gourd, and went to the Flute spring to make sacrifice and fetch water for the medicine. When he returned, he smoked the pipe, chewed a piece of root, and rubbed it over his body for protection. He then wet an old basket, so that it would become water-tight, for use as a medicine bowl, and smoked over some eagle feathers, which he wrapped in cornhusks and placed on a tray.

The Soyal Chief made other pahos, prepared four cornhusk packets containing meal and honey, smoked over them, and put them on an old tray. He divided the prayer feathers into three piles, smoked, prayed, and spat honey over them. Then he squatted with the Assistant Chief on opposite sides of a tray of pahos, and both sprinkled corn meal and spat honey on the tray and in the air about them. After a period of smoking they rubbed their hands in corn meal and waved the tray up and down, whispering a prayer. The pahos were then taken out and buried at a place where a priest obtained white clay to be used in the ceremony. Another priest consecrated other pahos, and went to deposit them on the shrine of the Spider Woman.

The War Chief sprinkled meal in the northeast corner of the kiva from six directions and set the medicine bowl in the center on the cornhusk ring. He threw small stones, bones, and spear and arrow points into the bowl and also on the six corn-meal lines. He then placed a black eagle wing feather on each line and poured water from the gourd into the bowl six times, once from each direction. I saw him chew some roots and spit into the bowl and, it was said, he also sprinkled into the medicine a little of the powdered brains of former enemies slain in battle.

The War Chief then took his natsi (twelve arrows or spearheads tied to a stick) and sat down at the southeast side of the kiva to be decorated and equipped as the great War god, Pookon. His forehead was painted red, and white marks were drawn on his cheeks, chest, back, arms, and legs. He was handed a white corn ear, moccasins, knee and ankle bands, stone tomahawk, shield, bow and arrows, two caps, the natsi, and a bandoleer said to contain the dried entrails of enemies slain in former battles.

Thus dressed, the War god sat down at the north side of the medicine bowl and motioned for the Chief Assistant to sit east of it. He then placed the extra cap on the Assistant's head, sprinkled meal in the medicine bowl, and handed his natsi to the Assistant. This man then stood the natsi in the bowl, with the arrow and spearheads up, and held it with both hands. A few of the Special Officers squatted near the bowl, and we, still almost naked, sat down west and south of the group and prepared to sing the nine powerful charm songs, which must be kept secret lest misfortunes overtake the Hopi.

The War god, holding in his left hand the bow, arrows, and old corn ear, sprinkled meal and some coal dust—a little of which he rubbed on the face of the Chief Assistant—and then smoked with those about him, blowing the smoke upon the natsi. While we sang the first and second songs, he continued sprinkling meal and praying. During the third song he seized the six long black feathers, one at a time, and thrust them into the medicine bowl, saying "Pooh," withdrew them together, and handed them to the Soyal Chief to be tied in a bundle and returned to him. As we sang the fourth song, he poured extra water into the medicine bowl and beat time with the feathers, dipping them in the water and sprinkling about him. He then called loudly into the bowl, "Hai, aih, aih, hai, hai," stirred the stones and the medicine with his hand, and sprinkled it with his fingers. During the fifth song the Screen Priest wet a lump of clay in the medicine and smeared a little on the chest and back of everyone present. Before the sixth song ended, the War god blew smoke over the medicine bowl, sprinkled occasionally, went up the ladder, spat honey, and sprinkled outside the hatchway. During the seventh song the War god stood north of the medicine bowl with the corn ear tucked in his belt, the shield on his left arm, and the tomahawk in his right hand. The Screen Priest faced him, holding in his right hand an old stone spear point picked out of the medicine bowl, and in his left a bunch of feathers. The two swayed sidewise with the singing, and the priest feigned to stab the god as our song grew wilder and wilder. Suddenly the War god stopped and beat the edge of his shield on the floor, striking the shield at the same time with his tomahawk. The Screen Priest struck the shield of the god with his charmed spear point and we all yelled our war cry; this was repeated six times.

Some of the priests smoked through the eighth song, and in the ninth the war god smoked and placed the cornhusk cigarette into the mouth of the Chief Assistant, who was still holding the natsi in the medicine bowl. Some of the officers smoked four puffs toward the natsi, and the War god uttered a prayer. He removed the Assistant's cap, relieved him of the natsi, and rubbed it and the Assistant's arm and shoulder with medicine dipped from the bowl. He then removed his own cap, took a draught of the strong medicine, fished out a few stones, bones, and shells, sucked them, and held them to his heart. We all took a drink, dipping medicine from the bowl with our hands or a shell, and sucking stones or bones, then holding them to our hearts to make us strong.

We each retained the strong, bitter medicine in our mouths, took a lump of clay, and went to our houses, where we moistened the clay with the medicine and rubbed a little on the breast, back, and limbs of every member of our families in order to insure their lives for another year. I hoped that I would never be War Chief of the Soyal, because I realized how misfortune might befall us all if I made a mistake and spoiled the medicine. When in former times a man was going to become a warrior, he fasted four days, sat on the ground in a circle of sacred corn meal for four days, and later killed and scalped an enemy.

We returned to the kiva, dressed, and ate a big supper of stew, which was to be our last salted food for four days. We soon began our songs and dance practice, without masks or costumes, but wearing turtle-shell rattles on our right legs and holding gourd rattles in our right hands. The practice meant that we were calling upon our Katcina ancestors to return and dance for us on the ninth day.

After four or five dances Kwan and Ahl members came and stationed themselves outside the kiva to ward off intruders, while we prepared to perform the important Wing ceremony. A pair of wooden cones were produced, and two bunches of hawk feathers resembling wings. The Hawk-and-Bow Priest put on his ceremonial kilt and daubed his shoulders, forearms, feet, and hands with white clay. We crushed certain herbs between our teeth, spat into our hands, and rubbed our bodies to protect ourselves. Talasvuyauoma dressed again in the war costume to represent Pookon and sat by a pile of moist sand in the northeast portion of the southern elevated half of the kiva. We took seats on the floor at the east, north, and west sides of the northern, deeper portion. The Hawk Priest took the cones, a tray of meal, and an old weasel skin, stepped to the ladder, and prayed. He placed the skin on the sand pile, sprinkled a triangular path of meal in the lower portion of the kiva, and placed the cones at the two corners of the triangle about eight feet apart, east and west, and near the center of the kiva. After a smoke we began our secret prayer songs, accompanied by the rattling of gourds, which lasted two hours. Just after midnight we prayed. The Hawk Priest removed the weasel skin and the cone, picked up the hawk wings, stepped to the east side of the ladder, and waved them up and down while he sang softly. Then he moved from right to left along the line of singers, touching our feet with the wings; stepped to the west side of the ladder, waved the wings again, and passed along the line from left to right, drawing the wings across our knees; retraced his steps, touching our shoulders; and back again, stroking our faces and finally touching the tops of our heads. When he sat down in the northeast corner of the kiva, we all spat in our hands and rubbed our arms, legs, and bodies. This ended the Wing ceremony.

We awoke in the kiva at gray dawn on the fifth day of Soyal and were led, dressed only in loincloth and moccasins, by the War Chief and the Hawk Priest to the southeast foothill to sprinkle our sacred corn meal and pray to the Sun god. Then the War god held his natsi to the breast of each man and the Hawk Priest touched us with the wings. We returned shivering to the kiva, dressed, and sat down to a meatless and saltless breakfast. The Special Officers could eat nothing until nightfall, which caused me to pity them. I took some cotton to my grandfather Homikniwa and hired him to card and spin it for my pahos, because I had to herd for my old uncle Kayayeptewa, whose special services were needed in the kiva work.

The sun had set when I reached home, took my unsalted food to the kiva, and ate with the other Soyal members. We did not like this lifeless food but had to obey the rules so that the Six-Point-Cloud-People could hear our prayers and enrich our lives. My uncle, the Soyal Chief, had finished sixteen short single pahos and a number of longer ones made with thin sticks. Extra sand and ceremonial equipment were collected, much cotton spun, and four bunches of ten or a dozen cornhusk packets provided, which contained seeds, herbs, and grasses. After we Keles and the common members had finished eating, we sang our Katcina songs, while the Special Officers broke the long day's fast. We then practiced the Katcina dances in the lower portion of the kiva until the Big Dipper stars were almost overhead and the time had come for the Hawk ceremony.

The Screen Priest and his Assistant put on their kilts and concealed bone whistles in their mouths, while the War Chief dressed and took his place by the sand pile to guard the kiva. We all chewed a sprig of spruce bough, spat on our hands, and rubbed our bodies. Four women were led into the kiva—Punnamousi, the wife of the Soyal Chief; Nasinonsi, the wife of Chief Tewaquaptewa; Sadie, his adopted daughter; and Ada, the daughter of his brother. They carried white corn ears, sprinkled the sand pile with meal, chewed a piece of spruce bough, and sat down on a stone bench along the east side of the kiva wall. The wooden cones and weasel skin were placed in their former positions, and the officers smoked native cigarettes made of cornhusks and mountain tobacco. The Assistant Hawk Priest left the kiva with four corn-meal balls about two inches across. We waited in silence and suddenly heard a screeching sound like that of a hawk. It was answered by the Hawk Priest in the kiva, while the women called out, "Yunyaa" (Come in). The Assistant Hawk Priest entered, holding the two wings; he squatted on the elevated portion of the kiva east of the ladder, faced north, and screeched several times. When our singing and rattling commenced, he flapped his wings rapidly and screeched, facing west, south, and east, until our song ended and the women said, "Askwali" (Thanks). At the beginning of the second song he stepped to the lower portion of the kiva, encircled the east cone, followed the corn-meal line to the northwest corner, placed the wings on the floor, and left the kiva, but was soon heard screeching. The Hawk Priest again answered and the women said "Yunyaa." The Assistant reëntered and was sprinkled with meal by the women. He pranced over to the northeast corner, where he screeched with bells jingling from his legs, seized the wings, and slowly lifted them above his head in a quivering motion. He advanced crouching, jumped twice over each cone, returned to the northeast corner, and laid down the wings, as the singing ceased and the women said, "Askwali."

Presently the Hawk Priest screeched again, faced north, and stamped his feet in time with the singing, turned about screeching, grabbed a wing in each hand, thrust them behind his belt, raised and lowered both arms as a bird flaps its wings, swooped down several times, picked up a bow in his right hand and an arrow in his left, turned north and screeched, holding the drawn bow upward at various angles from north to west, then repeated the performance south and east. Shifting the bow to his left hand and the arrow to his right, he danced about, swooped down, and passed the bow from behind between his feet, placed it on the floor, returned the wings to the northeast corner, and left the kiva, while the women cried, "Askwali."

During a short interval the wooden cones were removed from their places and the Hawk Priest returned, took up the wings and used them as a bird flying, while he stamped and screeched. Sadie, the Soyalmana (Soyal maiden), dressed in a white ceremonial robe, followed close at his heels, imitating his motions but holding a white corn ear instead of wings. She finally sat down as if exhausted while he danced around the circuit once more and placed the wings on the floor. At the beginning of another song he seized the wings again. Waving them vigorously in a squatting position, he worked his way to the sand pile, screeched, and thrust the wings into the sand. He drew them out almost immediately, and moved in a crouching position over to the Soyalmana. With quivering up-and-down motions, he touched the wings on each side of the Mana, stroking her feet, knees, shoulders, and head, and then touching his own in reverse order, a performance which he repeated three times.

As we commenced another song, he went back to the sand pile, waving the wings rapidly and screeching, seized with his teeth the old weasel skin which the War Chief was waving over the sand pile, and worked his way to the northeast corner of the kiva, where another priest took the skin and the women repeated "Askwali."

In a few minutes the Hawk Priest squatted in the north end of the kiva, faced the wall, and held the wings in his hands with points on the floor until smoke was blown over him. He then screeched and worked his way in a crouching position to the east side of the ladder, followed by the Soyalmana who mimicked him. They both left the kiva, but soon returned without the wings.

The Assistant Chief entered the kiva with the wings, squatted east of the ladder, screeched, waved the wings up and down with a quivering motion, and glided forward, followed by the Mana stamping her feet. They both sat down by the fireplace, where he smoked and uttered a prayer. He then stepped to the east of the ladder, waved the wings up and down with his left hand as he hummed a song, and moved back and forth four times along the line of men, touching our feet, knees, shoulders, and heads. We spat in our hands, rubbed ourselves, and concluded the ceremony for the night. We then made our beds and lay down, feeling confident that our prayers had reached the Six-Point-Cloud-People.

On the sixth day, after we prayed at the edge of the mesa as usual and ate unsalted food in the kiva, I set out on foot to my uncle Kayayeptewa's corral nine miles away. After a tiresome day of herding I walked back, took my food to the kiva, and ate with the others. They had made further preparations for the altar, carved out of soft wood some artificial flowers for the headdress of the Star Priest, smoked, and prayed. All conversation had been in a low tone or a whisper. We practiced the Katcina songs and dances and then went through the same two-hour Hawk ceremony of prayer to our ancestral spirits.

The seventh day was spent in paho making. After prayers to the Sun god and breakfast, the men let down their long hair. We all undressed except for the loincloth or, in some cases kilt, arranged ourselves in rows in the lower section of the kiva, and began making pahos with feathers, native string, herbs, and willow sticks. I had never done this work before, and had to be instructed by my ceremonial father, who spoke in a whisper because of the presence of ancestral spirits. I made first the prayer arrow, then soft prayer feathers for my Guardian Spirit, the Spider Woman, Masau'u, the Twin War gods, the sun, moon, stars, and all the springs, oceans, and rivers about which I had heard. Then I made prayer offerings for the Six-Point-Cloud-People, for our dear ones who had recently departed, and for all the other spirits that I could remember. I also made them for all the members of my family, my special friends, the livestock, dogs, cats, houses, trees, and other objects of value. I thought about each god, spirit, person, or object while I made a paho for him. I learned that this is the most important work in the world, that the gods and the spirits are holding out their hands for pahos, and that if the Soyal should fail, life for the Hopi might end. We were instructed to keep our minds pure and filled with these thoughts while we worked and wished strongly for rain, good crops, and long life. If a sexual thought had come into my mind, I would have tried to free myself of it and would not have mentioned the subject to a fellow member even to relieve him of hiccoughs—an excellent remedy on other occasions.

When the pahos and the prayer feathers were finished, they were placed on the floor, where a little honey was spat on them and the makers smoked over them before tying them into little bundles and hanging them on the kiva wall. When our work was over at sunset— for it is a rule that paho making must cease at that hour—we swept the floor, gathered up the trash carefully, sprinkled it with corn meal, and threw it into a gully, where the rains could take it into the valley over our farms. We had worked all day without eating, and the Special Officers had eaten nothing since the night before. When we had finished our lifeless meal, food was brought for the priests, and we sang, as on other nights, while they ate. Then we practiced our Katcina songs and dances, keeping an eye on the Great Dipper stars.

Some Soyal members set to work making *hihikwispi* (something to breathe upon), consisting of four cornhusks tied at tip and stub on a string, about twelve inches apart. At the point of every husk was fastened an eagle prayer feather, together with a feather of six other birds. The four husks were placed one within another, the long string folded into the upper one, and the packages put away for use the next day.

When the Great Dipper stars reached the appointed position, we sang our prayer songs again for two hours as on the preceding night, with the women participating. I was so tired and drowsy that they called me sleepyhead and poured water on me to keep me awake until the ceremony was completed.

The eighth day of the Soyal was a long tiresome task. Early in the morning the Soyal Chief took the black pahos to the other kivas, and each person who had prepared a hihikwispi put corn meal and pollen upon it and held it to the rising sun, saying, "Breathe on this." He then carried it to the house of his relatives, letting them breathe on it for protection against sore throats and coughs. After prayers at the edge of the mesa and breakfast in the kiva, we were sent to the spring to bathe and then home for head washing. As soon as my mother had washed my head, I collected corn ears and meal from neighbors and took them to the kiva, where the officers were smoking and drying their hair. The large altar frame was set up in the north end of the kiva, back of a sand field forty inches wide and thirty-two deep. A priest made holes in the moist sand, blew a puff of smoke into each hole, and closed it. Semicircles and lines were drawn on the sand to represent rain. Many sacred objects, including a quartz crystal *tiponi* (sacred emblem of authority), were placed about the altar. Corn ears of various colors were piled back of the altar frame, and the Special Officers took a little corn pollen, held it solemnly to their lips, and sprinkled it over the altar and the sacred emblems.

About noon we dressed in our Kele costumes and prepared to begin our prayer songs. The Soyalmana entered, dressed in a red, white, and blue blanket, an embroidered ceremonial robe, and turquoise ear pendants. After she sat down on the east bench four young men began to dress in fancy Katcina costumes with sash, kilt, and beads, and put bright feathers on their heads. White clay was daubed on their feet, hands, shoulders, and hair. The Soyal Chief and other priests sat down before the altar near a tray of pahos, smoked, and then spat honey on the altar and sacred objects and into their hands to rub their bodies. Two priests shook gourd rattles for half an hour, while a third sprinkled corn meal and pollen. Then one blew a bone whistle, facing the altar, several smoked, and we all sat in silence until the four costumed men leaned against the ladder in succession, went through vigorous motions as in sexual copulation with the ladder, and departed to collect more colored corn ears for the altar.

The Chief Assistant was erecting a small altar in the southwest corner of the deeper part of the kiva, while many Soyal members went to their homes and returned with meal, some of which was placed in four large trays in a row between the fireplace and the large altar. On the trays were placed thin black pahos, and, between them, the bundles of hihikwispi. A few priests were singing around the smaller altar. Special Officers from the other kivas entered with their initiates, and two Kwan members in costume sprinkled meal upon the altars and sat down opposite the ladder, where they smoked native cigarettes, each resting an arm around the nearest ladder pole. The War Chief, with shield, bow, and tomahawk, sat southeast of the ladder, smoking and guarding the kiva entrance. We Keles sat on the elevated portion of the kiva. Three special women, who had attended the previous ceremonies, entered and took their seats, while the Soyalmana retained her position on the east bench. When the singing and rattling had commenced again at the small altar, the four messengers who had collected the corn took up the large trays of meal and pahos, hung the bunches of hihikwispi over their left shoulders, circled inside the kiva four times, ascended the ladder and circled outside four times, and then started in file to the Oraibi spring to deposit the offerings. While they were on this errand, two masked Katcinas (Mastops) appeared from the Kwan kiva with their bodies painted black and covered with white handprints. They wore old skin kilts, had dry grass wreaths around their necks, and wore large black masks decorated with white dots, hooked marks, cornhusk pendants for ears, two white drawings of frogs on the back, and a bunch of eagle feathers and red horsehair on top. From their belts dangled bunches of cow hoofs, which rattled when they ran among the spectators, seizing women from behind and going through vigorous motions of copulation. After each conquest a Katcina would run to the kiva, jabber in a disguised voice, and set out to catch another woman. They finally entered the kiva and sat down east of the ladder, where many Soyal members sprinkled them with corn meal and gave them prayer feathers asking for rain. The Katcinas put their prayer offerings in a sack and departed. Singing and rattling continued at the small altar, and a man kept whistling into a bowl of water in the southeast corner. The War Chief handed us a crystal to suck four times and hold to our hearts, while he bit off pieces of root, chewed them, and spat on his shield, seeming to paint it. He held in one hand a white corn ear and the six old eagle feathers used in the Medicine Making ceremony. The four messengers returned from the spring and received our thanks.

Near sunset the priests from other kivas brought in their plaques of pahos and placed them near the large altar. After having smoked, the Chief Assistant rubbed his hands with corn meal, took up his tiponi, rubbed meal on it, stepped north of the four empty trays which had been returned by the messengers, sprinkled meal on the pahos, waved his tiponi to the southeast, and prayed. We all responded with "*Kwaikwai*,"[2] spat on our hands, rubbed our bodies, and ended a long ceremony which had been necessary in order that we Hopi might not disappear from the earth.

The leaders of the Kwan, Ahl, and Tao societies took their initiates back to their kivas. We removed our Kele costumes, dressed, and went to our houses for food—salted stew this time, for the fast was broken. The stew was excellent and made our eyes shine with health. The officers ate after us on the lower floor and then invited us down to eat some more, signifying that at the next harvest we would have food enough and to spare. The food which remained was carefully saved

2. The men's word for thanks.

to symbolize our frugality. In the evening we again performed our Medicine Making ceremony of the fourth day and followed it with the Hawk ceremony of the fifth day, with some elaborations.

Just after midnight the Chief Assistant and the Soyalmana left the kiva. Soon the Screen Priest and his Assistant brought in a large buckskin stretched on a frame. Painted on the screen was the picture of Muyingwu, the god of germination. He held in his right hand a growing cornstalk and in his left an emblem of authority (*Monwikuru*). On his head were symbols of clouds, with falling rain and rays of lightning. Under the cornstalk was a symbol of the moon and on the other side of Muyingwu was a symbol of the sun. To both sides of the screen were attached artificial flowers, and to the lower part were fastened watermelon, muskmelon, squash, cotton, pumpkin, corn, and other seeds. Eagle feathers below and red horsehair on the sides and base represented rays of the sun.

Screeching was heard outside and the Chief Assistant entered with the Soyalmana, dressed in elaborate costume consisting of a ceremonial blanket held in place by a knotted belt, a man's Katcina kilt tied over her left shoulder, and numerous strands of beads around her neck and yarn around her wrists. The Chief Assistant sat down east of the ladder, then moved forward, squatted, screeched, and waved the wings, while the Mana followed in an upright position as both worked their way around the screen. A tray with two corn ears, some corn meal, and pahos was handed to the Soyal Chief, who prayed over it. The officers smoked and one priest blew smoke back of the screen. The Soyal Chief received the tray, after four other priests had prayed over it, stooped down, and scraped with a corn ear all the seeds from the screen into the tray together with the artificial flowers on the edge. When he stood up and prayed, the Assistant Chief led the Mana from the kiva, the screen was removed, and the tray placed near the altar.

The War Chief took the medicine bowl and left the kiva, but soon returned with the Star and Sun Priest. We all stood up as they entered, and the War Chief sprinkled medicine from the bowl, while someone beat a drum in muffled tone. Men from other kivas entered in costumes. The Star Priest, representing the Sun god that I had seen in my dream as a boy, was barefoot and dressed in a Katcina kilt and sash, ankle bands, and turtle-shell rattles on each leg, green arm bands, a buckskin, and numerous strands of beads. His body was unpainted except for lines of white dots running from the point of the big toe up and around the front of the leg, from the heel over the calves, from the thumb along the front of his arms to the shoulder and down to the nipples; and from the hands along the outside of the arms to the shoulder and down each side of the back. His headdress consisted of a frame of leather bands, to the front of which was attached a four-pointed star and to the sides artificial flowers. In his right hand was a long crook, in the middle of which was fastened a black corn ear; in his left were seven corn ears. He danced backward and forward to the beating of the drum, talking rapidly and incoherently. The Soyal Chief stood west of the fireplace, holding a paho and meal tray from which he occasionally sprinkled meal upon the Sun god. To his left stood the Assistant Chief in a white blanket and with face painted white. All at once the Sun god leaped toward the Soyal Chief, handed him the crook and the corn ear, and received from the Assistant Chief a rawhide sun symbol fastened to a stick which had been concealed under the white blanket. The god took hold of the stick with both hands, shook it, and danced north of the fireplace, sideways from east to west and back, twirling the sun symbol rapidly, clockwise. Someone screamed and a song was intoned. The beating of the drum became louder and louder, as the Sun god danced and leaped about in a marvelous manner. As the song ended he leaped toward the Soyal Chief and ascended the ladder. The Special Officers began to smoke over the corn ear and the crook which the god had left with the Soyal Chief.

In a short time officers from the other societies came for their pahos which had been consecrated on the altar and in the ceremony. Lomavuyaoma of the Fire Clan prepared to take a special offering to the shrine of Masau'u, a journey which required a brave heart. He sat by the fireplace and smoked, while every member of the Soyal, including us Keles, placed a paho on an old plaque for Masau'u. Special piki made by members of the Fire Clan was placed on the plaque, together with a piece of raw rabbit meat, some mountain tobacco, and corn meal. When Lomavuyaoma lifted the plaque to go, we all said in unison, "With your brave, happy heart take our pahos over there and deliver our message to Masau'u." When he returned from his mission, we said, "Kwaikwai." He sat down and smoked, relating how when he deposited the plaque and prayed, he heard a strong breath coming from the shrine, which signified that Masau'u who guards our village had heard our petition and received our offerings.

In a short time Katcinas (Quoqulum) in yellow masks and red horsehair came from the Ahl kiva and danced for us. A priest was sent with offerings to the Sun shrine (Tawaki) on top of a high mesa about three miles southeast of Oraibi. It was to be a hard journey for him, because he had to run fast, present the offering just as the Sun god peeped over the horizon, and return swiftly. This prayer offering was very important because the Sun god is chief over all, and gives heat and light, without which there would be no life.

I was taken by my ceremonial father to the house of his sister Solemana to have my head washed again and to receive another name. She held the mother-corn ear before me and said, "My sweetheart, now I name you Tanackmainewa, which means the shining feathers of the Road-Runner. Take this name, look up to our Sun god, and call it loudly to him who is your uncle." This name did not stick like the Wowochim name, which seemed to be glued to me.

Before dawn we took our prayer offerings to our relatives who had washed their heads and were ready with happy hearts for the Paho Planting ceremony. At sunrise the entire village, including babies on their mothers' backs, assembled at the east edge of the mesa, thrust many hundreds of pahos into the ground, and sprinkled them with meal. The people who belonged to my father's clan placed their pahos at a spot called Bow Height (*Awatobi*), because the Sand Clan came from Awatobi, a village now in ruins. Many men and boys, including myself, placed pahos on the Antelope shrine in order to have success in hunting. As we returned to the village, one could see hundreds of willow switches standing three or four feet high with seven or eight turkey, hawk, eagle, or other soft feathers attached to them three or four inches apart. No chicken or crow feathers were ever used. Fathers who had sons less than a year old planted little crooked pahos for them in order that they might thrive, be happy, and live long. Most of the prayer feathers were fastened to the long sticks for our departed dear ones. The short double pahos were made for all the dead and for the Six-Point-Cloud-People who send rain. It is our belief that the spirit gods and our ancestors come with outstretched hands, seeking pahos in exchange for the blessings of health and long life, and that if they find none they turn away sorrowful. We know that they take with them only the souls of the pahos.

We ate breakfast in our own houses, distributed our prayer feathers among our friends, and attached them to animals, and other objects of value. I gave pahos to several people, tied them to the Katcina masks, to the ceiling of our house, to the necks of our dogs and burrows, and to branches of the fruit trees. During the forenoon Katcina masks were painted, the altar taken down and stored, and the sand in the kiva sprinkled with meal and thrown in a gully to wash down over the fields.

In early afternoon fifteen or twenty Quoqulum Katcina and five or six "females" entered the village from the south. They went to every kiva, where one of them made four lines of corn meal and meal paths leading out in four directions. This was to "open the kiva" and arouse the Spirit Katcinas from their long rest in order that they might visit us again. The Quoqulum Katcinas sang and danced several times, and then made corn-meal paths leading southeast from the village as far as their meal lasted. When the paths were completed they returned, and the Father of the Katcina (a Powamu member) took the rattles from their legs, sprinkled the Katcinas with meal, and gave each a soft prayer feather to take to the Six-Point-Cloud-People. They departed southward over the cliff to the Katcina shrine, where they deposited the feathers, prayed, undressed, and returned to the Ahl kiva with their masks concealed from the children.

We Soyal members returned to the kiva, where the Special Officers smoked and made prayer feathers to use in a rabbit hunt. They made them for the divine mothers of rabbits and chicken hawks because these deities are good hunters. The ceremonial father of the Soyal-mana was Hunter Chief. He went through the kivas announcing the place to build the ceremonial fire and begin the hunt. We smoked and went to our houses for supper, but returned to the kiva to sleep, because love-making was taboo for four days more.

We hunted rabbits for three days, leaving the catch in the house of the Soyalmana. On the fourth we arose and went to the east edge of the mesa to pray, returned to the kiva, dressed, and went to our houses to get our heads washed before sunrise, according to Hopi rule. It is our belief that whoever washes his or her head on this day will be among the first to taste the ripe melons in summer. The Sun god had reached his winter home four days before—when we planted the pahos—and was now turning back to his summer house, leading us along his trail.

In mid-afternoon we prepared for a shower bath and a feast. Our folks made unsalted gravy which we took with our dancing outfits to the kiva. There we painted our bodies with whitewash in stripes, dressed in Katcina costumes, and formed a line, taking the gravy in little plaques. The ceremonial father of Sadie (the Soyalmana) took a pot—with two cooked rabbits partly exposed—and led about forty of us into the house of the Soyalmana. On each side of the door were two tubs of water, with a woman standing behind each holding a plaque. We undressed quickly and ran out between the tubs, where the women dashed cold water over us, washing off the white paint. After our bath we reëntered the house and threw out great quantities of food to the scrambling spectators. The bath signified rains, and the distribution of food a good harvest. We returned to the kiva, dried and dressed ourselves, and had a feast of rabbit stew. After the meal my old uncle, Kayayeptewa, told a long story of our history to which we were supposed to pay close attention. But some of the men seemed restless for love-making and joked in undertones—for they were free of the ceremony and could return to their wives and sweethearts.

I had learned a great lesson and now knew that the ceremonies handed down by our fathers mean life and security, both now and hereafter. I regretted that I had ever joined the Y.M.C.A. and decided to set myself against Christianity once and for all. I could see that the old people were right when they insisted that Jesus Christ might do for modern Whites in a good climate, but that the Hopi gods had brought success to us in the desert ever since the world began.

9

Clowning and the Bean Ceremony

SINCE I SEEMED TO FIND no girl in Oraibi—and was dead broke, too—I welcomed the opportunity to return to Moenkopi with relatives. So after the first Katcina dance in January we departed with four wagons in a light snowstorm. I rode muleback and was teased about my new name and the name that I might have received—Hanging Greasewood. As we unhitched the horses in Moenkopi at the end of the second day, I was pleased to spy Euella standing at the corner of the house in the twilight. She entered our house while we ate and shook hands with me warmly. Meggie smiled, but I winked a warning to her and later signaled slyly to Euella to leave by the back door while I stepped out the front. We met at the corner, and I whispered, "Will your door be locked tonight?" "Certainly not," she answered, and hurried on. I took my blanket and went straight to the kiva, but crept out during the night and knocked lightly on her door. Euella opened it, took my hand, and led me to her bed, where we lost no time in preliminaries after weeks of restraint. When we were relaxed, she questioned me closely about the Wowochim and the Soyal. I told her the news between our love-making, but skipped all the secrets that were sacred. I was happy now to be a Hopi, and would never again feel ashamed to be an Indian with red skin. When the first cock crowed I sighed, "Well, auntie, I must return to my kiva." We had kissed each other so much that I jokingly said, "This will last me a

187

lifetime." But I was wrong, and from then on the remark became a pet phrase with me. When I awoke in the kiva an old man said, "Young fellow, I saw you sneak out last night; did you get what you went after?" I admitted the truth—without naming the girl—and told him how an old Dutchman once had caught me with Olive at the barn. I also told some of the Dutchman's "dirty" jokes, which caused everybody in the kiva to laugh. The old man repeated the best phrases as though memorizing them.

As I was on my way to Tuba City to seek work, a man slipped up behind me and held his hands over my eyes. He proved to be Adolph, the Christian fellow who had tricked me into joining the Y.M.C.A. at Sherman. He was a backslider now, but had also stayed out of the Wowochim, being neither hot nor cold, White nor Hopi. We went to the office of the Navaho Agency and were advised to see the construction foreman at the dam. I returned some borrowed sandals and the fancy quiver to the trader and told him that I was now a member of the Wowochim and the Soyal, and a full-fledged Hopi man. He congratulated me and gave us cigars—the white man's sign that he likes an Indian. He said he thought we could get work at the dam, but suggested that, if I failed, he would give me a job dishwashing.

At noon Robert, Ira, and I went to the dam. Mr. Sears, the foreman, was eating his lunch apart from the Navahos. I shook hands and told him my business. He seemed interested and said that seven of his Navaho workers came late to work and stayed out to gamble so often that he was giving them their walking papers. I thought that meant to give them a vacation, but he fired them. I liked the expression "walking papers" and later used it in my conversations. He told us to find three extra men and return the next day. We watched the Navahos working in a ditch. They moved slowly as though they were exhausted, and stopped work whenever the boss was out of sight. Robert asked me in Hopi, "Is this the way a Navaho works?" "Yes," I replied, "and we can work ourselves into their jobs." The next morning we found three other fellows, went to the dam ahead of the foreman, and sat waiting for him. I said, "Partners, let's work hard and surprise the boss today, then tomorrow we can take it easy." We got into the ditch and found it hard work to pitch the frozen dirt up ten feet. The foreman watched us closely at first, as people watch Katcina dancers. I told funny stories to make him smile now and then, but kept pitching dirt. At the end of the day he said, "You fellows did a good job. Tomorrow don't work so hard."

A Katcina dance was planned for Saturday night. In the practice I was asked, because of my height, to dress in the Giant Katcina costume and frighten the children. I hesitated, explaining that I did not belong in Moenkopi, but finally consented. During the practice nights I stayed away from love-making because I wanted to keep a good name and never start a rumor, "Talayesva sleeps with the girls while he practices for the dance." I asked my ceremonial brother, Tewani-etewa, to paint the Giant Katcina mask for me. One morning I went to the house of Frank Siemptewa, the Governor, and selected a mask, wrapped it in my coat, and took it to the kiva before going to work. As I entered the kiva in the evening, all laughed and said, "Here comes Talayesva, the giant!" My mask was ready—a massive head with long black hair, big yellow eyes, a long bill, red mouth, and sawlike teeth. I examined it and said, "It seems that my giant friend is hungry." The leader of the dance replied, "Yes, I am going to feed him." He put some food in its mouth and smeared honey on its lips. I smoked, collected my dancing equipment, and made ready to practice. Talasvuy-auoma, the War Chief of Soyal, instructed me how I should behave as a Giant Katcina. He also warned me not to touch any child, because that might frighten him too severely and would make him a prisoner of the terrible Giant Katcina Spirits.

When it was time to dress for the night dance, I daubed my chest with whitewash, painted my hands and arms blood-red to the elbows, put on moccasins and a pair of buckskin breeches, and fastened a buckskin under one arm and over the other shoulder. Then I put on the Giant mask and took a basket on my arm and a hatchet in my right hand. We left the kiva, went to the west end of the village, and sprinkled corn meal, notifying the Six-Point-Cloud-People of the dance and requesting that their spirits come and enter our bodies. We thus believed that we were turning ourselves into real Katcinas, like those who used to visit the village and help the people. Then we made Katcina noises to notify the people of our arrival, and walked to the kiva, following the leader who rattled a gourd. We circled the kiva four times, and the leader called down the hatchway, "We have come to make you happy. Shall we enter?" The Father of the Katcinas replied, "Come in." The Katcinas, who were mixed dancers, entered, making various noises.

Standing on the hatchway, I peeped in and said sternly, "I see you are keeping naughty children down there!" The leader who had put on the dance replied, "Katcina Giant, we were not expecting you. We want to keep our children, even though some of them are very bad." "I have a record of their naughty ways," I replied. "I can see that they are fat, and I have come to take them away for a feast." "Please let us keep our children," pleaded the leader; "they will behave better when they grow up." I argued boldly, and said, "I was asked to come here tonight; so now you must let me in." Climbing down the ladder, I made a rattling noise and growled, alarming the children, who cried and hid themselves under their mothers' blankets.

The leader begged me to wait until the dance was over. The Father of the Katcinas sprinkled the dancers with meal and gave them the signal to start. I danced too, taking long steps and peering about. I would jump this way and that, pull my long hair back from my forehead, leap forward and stare at any child who dared peep from his mother's blanket. When the dance ended I attempted to step to the upper floor where the people sat, but the Father of the Katcinas asked me to wait, and, sprinkling the Katcinas with meal, invited them to dance again. When they left the kiva, I said in a loud, gruff voice, "Well, naughty children, I was asked to come here and get you. Now I will take you away and eat you. Parents, hand over your children." The Governor's wife arose and said, "I will not let you take them. Since they have seen you they will behave better and grow up to be good and useful." Another old lady stood up and said, "Giant, if you want to take somebody home with you for a feast, I have an old husband who is not much use to me now and who won't work. You may take him." "He has done no wrong," I replied, "and he is old and tough, too tough to eat." "I think not," she answered. "I have seen your sharp teeth and I am sure you could chew him." I looked the old man over and said sternly, "I want tender meat."

The mothers arose and went to their houses, leaving the children with friends, but still upset and crying. They soon returned and filled my basket with food, saying, "Here, Giant, take this and leave our children alone." I examined the food, picked out a loaf of bread, looked at it critically, and said, "What is this, a stone?" They replied, "No, it is food made out of wheat and called bread." I examined the meat and remarked, "This is dog, that is cat, and here is a piece of tough old burro steak." They denied all this and assured me that the meat was venison, saying, "Don't you see the horns?" My basket was piled high, and the children were uncovering their heads to look.

I climbed out of the kiva and joined the other Katcinas who were waiting outside, peeping in. They slapped me on the back, laughed, and said that I made a dreadful noise, and that they were a little frightened themselves. A group of Coyemsie Katcinas entered the kiva to dance. They sang funny songs which amused the people, and had gifts in their bags for the children, the adults, and even for Navahos who were present. I took the food to my Clan mother's house, returned to the kiva, and waited outside. Finally the Hehelele Katcinas came with a great noise. They danced and then all joined in a mixed Katcina dance. I entered again, causing the children to cry. The Father of the Katcinas said, "Well, Giant, we sent you away with meat, why have you returned?" I insisted that I wanted more food and would take the children if they refused me. When my basket was filled, I warned the children that if they did not obey their parents I would return from the San Francisco Mountains, capture them, and take them away for a feast.

I saw some girls in the audience dressed for the Buffalo dance. Looking at them closely, I warned them that the fancy dances were spoiling young women and making them unfit for wives. The mothers took the small children out, and two boys and girls danced. I watched them closely, stepping around in a stooping position and pulling my hair back from my face. Then I showed that their dancing had touched my heart, and, placing myself between a boy and a girl, danced with them. The people laughed and said, "Now, Giant, we have caught you in a trap." They took away my food, hatchet, and dress; but they did not touch my mask which was sacred. They said, "We have stripped you of your possessions; now we will send you home. Tell your Cloud-People that our land is dry and our stock is poor. Ask them to send rain quickly in order that we may live." I nodded my head and said, "The journey is too far overland. I will travel underground to the San Francisco Mountains." I walked over to the sipapu (a hole in the floor of the kiva representing the entrance to the underworld) and sat down by it with a prayer feather and corn meal. I prayed silently but earnestly for rain and for a good life for the Hopi. Placing the prayer feather in the hole, I sprinkled it with meal and removed my mask, which signified that the Giant Katcina Spirit had departed for his home in the mountains.

The food in my basket was spread on the floor, and a boy was sent for the first basket of meat which the women returned hot from the ovens. The people thanked me for the feast and praised my performance, saying that my head reached almost to the beams of the kiva and that my voice frightened everyone and would certainly improve the conduct of the children.

When the feast was over, we made our beds to sleep. I was tired and restless, and dreamed that I was still a Giant Katcina arguing for the children. I reached out my hand to grab a child and touched him! The little one held up his hands to me, crying and begging to be set free. Filled with pity, I urged him to be a good child in order to free himself from the Giant Spirit. I awoke worried, with a lump in my throat, and bells ringing in my ears. Then I spat four times and decided that if I were ever the Giant again I would have a better-looking mask and speak in a softer voice.

We spent most of the next day resting and loafing. In the evening I stopped at Euella's house for supper. Their praise of the Giant performance pleased me greatly. Euella's father, Naseyouaoma, who was my "grandfather," jokingly called me sleepyhead, lazybones, and a poor hunter who never would get a wife. Euella and her mother took my part, telling him that I was a smart young man and that if they had me for a husband they would be better off. I smiled before him, but laughed up my sleeve, for he did not know that I had been sleeping with his daughter.

On the fourth day the Crier called the men to the kiva to plan another dance. We sang the songs that evening, but did not practice the steps. During the night I crept to Euella's door and knocked lightly. I had her only once, when she informed me that she felt pain under my pressure. We decided that she was about to menstruate and stopped. I was afraid that more loving might make her pregnant. I had to be very careful about that, for she was still in the day school.

Every evening until Saturday we practiced for the White Duck Katcina dance. During this performance I was very tired. When the dance was over, I lay on my bed in the kiva and traced my conduct to discover what caused me to be so weary. I recalled that I had been with Euella on the fourth night after the first dance and the first night of practice for the second dance, and when she was about to menstruate! No good had come to my life out of that. I apologized to the spirits, and promised myself that I would never make love again until I was completely free of my ceremonial duties.

One evening the Crier Chief announced a meeting in the kiva to arrange for another dance. I went but did not take part in the practice. Adolph, Logan, and I had agreed among ourselves that we wanted to be clowns in a day dance. We stood about in the kiva joking; and I remarked that I had a strange dream the night before in which Adolph, Logan, and I were clowns. I said that in the dream I felt that I was doing very important work sprinkling the sacred corn meal. It was a lie. My partners looked at me in surprise, and some of the officers smiled. After the practice we got together and discussed what we could do in case we were called for clown work. Adolph, the former Y.M.C.A. promoter, suggested that we could capture an old Katcina "lady" and give the people a demonstration of love-making in new positions, or, said he, "We might use a tame burro." I agreed that the idea was fine, unless the school principal happened to be present. I told them I had heard that once a clown made such use of a dog in the plaza, and that the Whites jailed him. We discussed this subject every evening on our way home from work and had fun making our plans.

The people decided to have an extra dance on Saturday night. This proved to be a fine one, with songs that touched my heart and made me wish I were in it. Kewalecheoma was the side dancer and did a good job. He would fly in and out of the kiva, making funny postures to fit the words of the song. He could compose more songs than any man I knew and was full of jokes and vivid words which the Whites called "vulgar." He always wore a smile on his face, and I never saw him unhappy.

After the night dance Logan, Adolph, Harry, and I went to the place where we slept, and found Ira and Robert had not been in the dance either because there were not enough masks. We smoked together, wishing for a good dance day, and then went to bed about midnight. A man came in with a lantern and said, "Get up, it is sunup." We saw that it was still night and sensed a ruse. He said, "Well, fellows, I have been sent here for you because we have some extra masks. Talayesva, you, Adolph, Logan, and Harry are requested to come to the kiva."

He led us into the kiva, seated us around the fire, lit a pipe of mountain tobacco, smoked four puffs, and handed it to me. I smoked and passed it on, noticing that the men in the kiva were smiling. When we finished, the leader smiled, hung his head, and said, "Well, we are glad that you are here. Tomorrow you will go to the plaza and eat." Harry arose and said, "I did not realize this. I beg to be excused from the clown work." Adolph leaned over and whispered, "Don, what shall we do?" "Shut up," I answered. "Whenever I speak you support me." When my turn came, I said, "Well, my fathers, uncles, and older brothers, we feel honored to be called; we will put our hearts together and pray to the Six-Point-Cloud-People, and cheerfully look forward to the coming day."

We returned to our sleeping place, smoked, and made plans for clowning before going back to bed. When I awoke, I twitched Adolph's nose, then pulled the cover from Logan and reached for his penis. When he awoke and protested I said, "Well, we must get used to this play because now we are clowns."

At breakfast my "mother" (mother's sister) said to me: "Son, I am worried about you, because you do not belong here and are not yet married. I am afraid that you will clown too roughly and offend or frighten the girls. Please be careful not to expose your penis to the people." "I don't think that is serious," I replied. "They looked into my heart and decided that I was a goodnatured man before they chose me for the clown work. Now I have no right to botch it. If I prove unsatisfactory they will not choose me again." Meggie ground some corn meal for me, and sewed a little bag in which I could carry it. She also made a stronger G-string to hold my loincloth, saying, "I do not want it to break in the plaza."

I entered the kiva with Adolph and Logan and found the Katcinas in line, waiting for the Father to sprinkle them with meal. The man responsible for the dance stood at the foot of the ladder and said, "Now with our happy hearts we will go to the Governor's house." The Katcina Father sprinkled his meal and led them into the plaza. The Powamu members (Fathers and Mothers of the Katcina) sprinkled them with corn meal. After three dances in different places, the sponsor of the dance said, "Well, my friends, I am glad you are here to dance for our people and make us happy." The Father of the Katcinas spoke, "My friends, I have led you to the plaza, and you are invited to bring food for the people and dance until sunset. Now you will go to your resting place and return." He led them to the Katcina shrine, and we clowns returned to the kiva. We painted our bodies in stripes and tied our hair above our ears to resemble horns. The Katcinas danced four times during the morning, but we did not join them.

When the Katcinas returned to the plaza at about noon, I stepped to the foot of the ladder and said, "My partners, let us go over there with happy hearts. If we are lucky some of the people will smile upon us. We will put our hearts together, praying to the Six-Point-Cloud-People for rain." We ran westward around the village, climbed on the roof, and sneaked along on hands and knees. When we reached the edge next to the plaza we sprang up, yelled, and dropped again four times, to represent clouds rising from the four directions. On the fourth time we stood looking around and making short speeches. I said, "See the beautiful valley and the lovely flowers; what a wonderful sight to behold!" We were lucky, for the people yelled and laughed. I hoped they would laugh all day, for I knew that sometimes there was little laughter at the clowning, and this was considered unlucky.

Someone handed me a rope, and I slid down headfirst and was followed by the other clowns. We walked over to the west end of the plaza to sing and dance. Yuyaheova, who had joked me about my new name, composed some funny songs for us. One of them recounted how we were grasshoppers going to the pond for water. As we poured water in our jars we heard a maiden's voice crying that she had a baby in her womb and that we were its fathers. We said in our songs, "It's good news that the lady will have a baby for us. Thanks, thanks."

Finally we saw a Katcina dancing near us and said, "Well, this is a good-looking boy, what is he doing?" He nodded his head and stamped his foot to show that he was dancing. He also made motions to indicate that there were others. We ran toward the Katcinas, trying to encircle as many as possible with our arms, each of us saying, "I have this many." We saw a side dancer and finally caught him. He trembled with fear while we praised and petted him, rubbing our hands over his body to make him gentle. I ran over to the Head Katcina and said, "Well, at last we are here. We spent the night with our private wives and are late, but it is not yet noon. Are you Chief of the Katcinas?" He nodded his head, and I said that I was Chief of the Clowns. "We will dance and be happy until the sun sets," said I, "bring your good food for us." Then we mentioned some fancy American foods to which we Hopi have attached double meanings, such as "monkey food" for candy kisses, and "pies" for sexual favors. The people laughed when we called for these. As the Katcinas left the plaza, we sprinkled them with corn meal, urging them, "Bring food! We have come to eat."

While the Katcinas were away, I reminded my partners that I was Chief of the Clowns and that they must obey me. I announced that we would build a house, and ordered them to bring beams from the San Francisco Mountains. They ran to a woodpile and brought logs. I said, "That won't do. Those are not beams but ashes; now bring logs," and I whispered to them to bring the opposite, ashes. They ran to the dump pile and brought ashes. I sang a magic song, imitating those used in housebuilding, and made the outline of a house, sprinkling the ashes to indicate logs and stones. Then I took a rag doll out of my belt, put it in the room, and said, "Now, sister, we have built a house for you, be diligent and cook food so that we may eat. If anyone comes, be sure to treat him kindly." We unwrapped the blankets from our waists and placed them in the "house." Our aunts came, bringing loads of food. In addition to real aunts, I had many ceremonial aunts in Moenkopi belonging to the Greasewood and Bamboo clans.

Euella and her mother came with loads of food. I thanked them, kissed the mother, and started to kiss Euella, but she seemed so embarrassed that I let her go. The Navahos laughed at me, but this was good clown practice. Sometimes we just patted an aunt on the back and said, "You are my good private wife." When I saw the Katcinas returning to the plaza, I said, "I feel ashamed, because I notice that the people keep laughing at us." Logan replied: "That is what we are here for, to keep the people happy and laughing." "Then excuse me," I responded, causing more laughter.

When the Katcinas danced, we ate. I picked up a colored egg and we all examined it curiously. Suddenly I hit Adolph on the head with it to crack it. Adolph cracked one on my head and Logan cracked his egg on the head of the Katcina Father, which caused much laughter. Finally, the Katcinas distributed choice foods among the people. We clowns held out our hands, and I received a piece of boiled sweet corn on the cob. Now the Hopi used to call sweet corn from the Katcinas a pet horse. I stuck the corn ear between my legs and pranced about, imitating a horse. The other clowns received ears and did likewise. I saw Euella laughing at me and felt happy.

As the clowns returned to their resting place, I spied two comic Katcinas in a harness drawing a wagon. A third old Katcina sat on the seat holding the reins. When the "horses" became balky, the driver struck them with his whip and used strong language like a First Mesa man. One of the "horses" whispered to us to unhitch them. We did so and struck them on the rumps, telling them to go. The driver tried to whip us but we drove him from the plaza. This old man called me to the kiva and said, "I am going to dress as a female Katcina and play checkers with you. I will win and have you take off your right shoe, then your left, your corn-meal bag, your clothes, and finally your hair, unless your aunts object." When I returned to the plaza, Adolph said, "Where have you been, with your private wife, an underworld woman? You must be a witch! Something bad will happen on account of your love of women." The people laughed.

The Katcinas returned to their resting place and our aunts brought more food. We ate and ate, like young worms, but were not satisfied. It is a mystery that clowns can eat so much and so long and remain hungry. While we were eating, we saw the old Katcina "lady" coming with a flat rock on her shoulder. Upon it was carved an old-fashioned Hopi checker game. She challenged us to play, and promised that in case we won she would reward us with her favors. The game started and she beat us again and again. We played until we had lost everything except our hair and loincloths. Then the old Katcina won our hair; but when she drew shears from her bosom to clip it, our aunts rushed into the plaza, took them from her, and saved us. The old lady warned us that if she won again, she would take our loincloths. We played and lost. She grabbed my G-string to snatch it off. I looked around for government employees and saw the school principal watching us with a frown on his face. I whispered, "Stop, there is the principal, and he looks cross." The old Katcina replied in an undertone, "That doggone white man should stay away if he can't stand it." "She" let go my G-string and said, "Well, we will have a race. If you win, you may do what you please with me; but if I win, I surely shall have your loincloth."

We agreed to race, but were afraid that the white man would spoil that too. We were to run in laps. I started because I was the poorest runner, although the tallest clown. When we counted four, the race began. The old Katcina could run like a horse. She passed me with her braids sticking out behind and her skirts flying like a whirlwind. Adolph overtook her in his lap, and they ran neck and neck. Logan came out about one step ahead. The old woman fell on the ground wailing, "Oh, what shall I do to save my life? Abuse me as you please, but let me live." The principal was still watching, but we decided to take our reward in spite of him. We dragged the "lady" around the corner out of his sight and placed her on a sheepskin. I claimed first turn as Chief of the Clowns. I made ready, then glanced around and saw the white man had moved to a better view and was leaning forward, looking. The people laughed, but I was angry.

We called off the demonstration, led the old Katcina to our "house," gave her some corn meal, and told her to take our prayers to the Six-Point-Cloud-People. She seemed very pleased and said, "All right, your reward shall be rain."

Then I turned to my partners and said, "I'm going to fix that white man." I walked up to him, shook hands, and said in Hopi, "Well, white man, you want to see what goes on, don't you? You have spoiled our prayers, and it may not rain. You think this business is vulgar, but it means something sacred to us. This old Katcina is impersonating the Corn Maiden; therefore we must have intercourse with her so that our corn will increase and our people will live in plenty. If this were evil we would not be doing it. You are supposed to be an educated man, but you had better go back to school and learn something more about Hopi life." He seemed embarrassed, reached into his pocket, drew out a half-dollar, and said, "Here, take this and get some tobacco." I thanked him and sent a man after the tobacco.

The Katcinas had returned to the plaza and were dancing again. I hurried over and sprinkled them with corn meal; then looked around for someone to whip and purify us before the dance closed. I went to the kiva and found the old Katcina there alone. He said there was no one to do the whipping. It was getting late, and the Katcinas were giving out their strings of boiled sweet corn to signify that we would have plenty at harvest time. After the dance the Father of the Katcinas gave them the prayer feathers and made the farewell speech: "Go to your homes and send us rain so that hunger and sickness may not overtake us and we may live in peace and plenty." We sprinkled them with sacred corn meal and they walked away toward the north. I tucked the doll in my belt, picked up my food, took the drum, and beat it softly as we walked to the kiva to smoke prayerfully with the Father of the Katcinas and conclude the ceremonial dance.

We had been eating all day, but at supper I was still hungry. The people talked about our clowning and praised it for many days. My Clan mother was pleased and said she would not be afraid for me to do clown work again. The Navahos who had seen the dance called me "The Clown." On the fifth night I saw Euella and received her praise and rewards in private.

I worked for the Agency at $2 a day until early in February, when my uncle, Talasquaptewa, sent word for me to return home and help with the Powamu ceremony.[1] When I reached Oraibi on horse-back—with a gift of dried apples and onions for my mother—I was served a late lunch and told to go to my uncle in Mongwi kiva. He welcomed me and said, "My nephew, I am glad you are here. The Chief Priest of the Powamu society brought his prayer offerings this morning, smoked, and informed us that it is time to plant beans in the kiva and pray for rain, good crops, and a rich harvest. You will plant your beans today." He told me that Herbert and I had been selected to assist the Bean Maidens in carrying the fresh plants into the plaza. My father advised me to plant lima beans because they looked better and grew taller. I put some adobe in an eight-quart can, almost filled it with sand, and planted my beans, placing the pan on a bench in the north end of the kiva. Then I sat down and smoked with the officers, exchanging kinship terms and praying.

The next day we went with five wagons to collect greasewood to fuel the kiva stove, which had to be fired night and day to make the beans grow. I had planned to return to Moenkopi and work until the beans were ready for harvest, but my uncle asked me to remain and watch the crops as a Kele whose duty is to water the plants and fire the stove. It was hard work bringing water up the mesa from the spring and firing the stove at night. There were many special ceremonies in the Powamu kiva which were unknown to me.

The children were initiated into the Powamu and Katcina societies. In the evening of the fifth day the young candidates were taken into the Powamu kiva with their ceremonial sponsors and each was given a white mother-corn ear. They witnessed the prayer songs, saw the altars and the sand mosaic, and were instructed in the secrets of the Powamu society, with warnings that they must never tell what had been revealed to them. During the evening the Katcina Mother sang at the Rock, and Katcinas ran through the village shouting. On the sixth day I watered beans in the Mongwi kiva, while men sat about the stove carving dolls, bows, arrows, and rattles as presents to their children. In the evening the young boys and girls chosen for initiation

1. For elaborate details, see H. R. Voth, *The Oraibi Powamu Ceremony* (Anthrop. Series, Field Mus. Nat. Hist., 1901), Vol. III, No. 2, pp. 67–158.

into the Katcina society were taken by their sponsors to the Marau kiva, where they were permitted to see the sacred emblems, were instructed in the secrets of the society, met face to face with Muyingwa, the god of germination, were held on the sacred sand mosaic, and thrashed by the Katcinas. My seven-year-old sister Mabel was in the group. I was sorry for her, remembering my own great ordeal, but I realized that it would do her good in the long run. I had no part in this ceremony because I was a young man who had not yet proven myself to be of sterling character; for only such worthy persons are selected as ceremonial fathers to children in the Katcina society.

The usual prayer ceremonies took place in the Powamu kiva on the seventh day, but little happened in our kiva except care of the beans and the preparation of presents for the children. We again practiced the Katcina dances in the evening and were not permitted to eat salted food or break the rules of continence. Only routine duties were performed in our kiva on the eighth day, but the prayer ceremonies were concluded in the Powamu kiva and the officers underwent purification rites, which are secret.

The ninth day was of great importance to the children. About three o'clock in the morning we cut the beanstalks to take to our houses or to tie on the presents for the children. The earth from the pails was buried out of their sight, for they were told that the Katcinas brought the beanstalks to the village from the mountains—as they actually did in former times. Before sunrise a sound, "Hu—hu-hu-hu-hu," was heard north of the village. A Hahai-i Katcina dressed as a woman approached, blowing a bone whistle and uttering a noise every few steps. "She" entered the plaza, where women and children sprinkled "her" with corn meal and took from "her" tray some corn sprouts and pine twigs. Walking to the Powamu kiva, "she" was joined by an Aototo and an Aholi Katcina from the Mongwi kiva. The Aototo wore a mask of native cloth daubed with white clay, with a fox skin tied around the lower edge and a few feathers on top. He was dressed in sash and kilt, over which he wore an old white shirt of native cloth embroidered with designs of clouds, plants, and flowers. He held a bag of sacred corn meal in his right hand and a small bunch of green corn in his left. The Aholi Katcina was dressed in kilt, sash, and moccasins.

Over his shoulder was an old blanket of native cloth on which were designs of clouds. In the center of the blanket was a drawing of a human head on the body of a large bird. His mask was of yucca leaves covered with native cloth, with feathers at the top and a fox skin at the bottom. He held a stick, a symbol of authority, in his right hand, and a brass bell, a bag of corn meal, and some green corn in his left.

The Aototo made a cloud symbol on the ground and the Aholi set the end of his stick upon it, circling the upper part from right to left and uttering a high-pitched sound. The two then went to an opening in the ground (*batni*), deposited a paho and some corn meal, made corn-meal lines, and poured water into the hole from the cardinal points. They then rejoined the Hahai-i at the kiva and repeated the meal-sprinkling and water-pouring performance into the opening of the kiva. Powamu officers came out of the kiva, blew smoke upon the three Katcinas, sprinkled them with meal, received the tray, and gave them a paho and some meal to deposit on the Katcina shrine. Katcinas came from the other kivas and ran through the streets giving presents to the children. During the day many Katcinas appeared, among them the Haa Katcina (Mother Katcina) dressed like a woman, with cornhusk stars fastened to her dress, her hair arranged like a squash blossom on one side and hanging down on the other. At the back of her head was a disc representing a scalp, to which some crow feathers were attached. She joked with the other Katcinas. I also ran about dressed in Katcina costume and presented gifts to children. In the afternoon the Giant Katcinas (*Cooyoktu*) came into the village and frightened some of the children.

About sunset the Special Officers of the Powamu society went to a shrine northeast of the village, called *Pohki* (doghouse), where it is said that the dogs lived before they moved into the village with the people. Dressed as old Katcinas, they led into the village five masked Bean Maidens, who had their hair in whorls and were robed in red, white, and blue ceremonial shawls. They had come to harvest the bean crop and bring it into the plaza next day. The Katcinas sang their songs and the Father of the Katcinas gave prayer feathers to the males and sent them away. The Mother Katcina took the Bean Maidens to a house for the night.

The initiates were kept in the homes of their ceremonial aunts until the kivas were made ready for the night-long dance. We were practicing our songs and preparing our costumes when Seletzwa, the Powamu Chief, came to the kiva and told us to paint our bodies. Later he returned and said, "Now dress without masks." He kept going from kiva to kiva, until nearly midnight, telling the Katcinas what to do next. At last he came and said, "Now, come out." We took our rattles and went to the Katcina shrine to pray, while the ceremonial mothers led the children into the kiva. We Katcinas, in five or six groups, went from kiva to kiva dancing. The Katcinas of the Powamu society were impressively dressed in embroidered kilts and sashes, green ear pendants, numerous strings of beads, artificial squash blossoms on their heads, green moccasins on their feet, tortoise-shell rattles in their right hands and pine saplings in their left. There were youths dressed as maidens, with sashes, moccasins, and the ceremonial blankets. Their hair was done up in whorls, when possible, and they were arrayed in jewelry, with sunflowers fastened to their foreheads. Corn meal was rubbed over their faces, their hands and arms were painted with white clay, and they carried twigs of pine in their left hands. Some Katcinas were dressed as old, decrepit women, wearing deeply wrinkled masks. They carried male and female dolls partly hidden in pine branches. Women in the audience who wanted babies threw pinches of corn meal at the dolls, to a female doll for a girl and to a male for a boy.

As I danced in the Howeove kiva where Mabel was sitting, I remembered my own distress when I discovered that the Katcinas were only people and my relatives. I turned my face from her stare and feared she would be unhappy for a long time. When we returned to the Mongwi kiva, Poleyestewa, dressed as an old woman, was teasing the other Katcinas, telling the males that they were lazy, poor hunters, and total failures as lovers. He called the "female" Katcinas cross-eyed and hopeless cooks, ladies who are fond of strange men, but who never bathe. He boasted in a lady's voice, "I am a Christian and never do anything wrong."

When the performance was over, Talasvuyauoma, the War Chief, stood up and said to the initiates, "You boys and girls have seen that your uncles and fathers are the Katcinas. I warn you never to tell this to others; don't even talk of it among yourselves. If you do tell, Whipper Katcinas will come and punish you, and perhaps kill you." Then the ceremonial aunts took the sleepy children to their homes, washed their heads before sunrise, and named them.

After breakfast on the tenth day Herbert and I dressed in the Mongwi kiva to assist the Bean Maidens with their loads. The Mother Katcina sang songs and had the rest of us line up, climb outside, and circle the kiva four times. Then the Special Officer of the Powamu society came with a notice that it was time for the Katcinas to get angry and drive the people into their houses, so that the men could harvest the bean crop. The Mother Katcina climbed on a housetop, waved her quiver and arrows, and warned everyone to flee to his house and close the windows. Katcinas from all the kivas rushed around in an angry manner and placed themselves on guard so that no young child would see what was going on. They would have flogged any person who made his appearance on the street. Workers in the kivas cut the plants and placed them on large wicker baskets equipped with four rod handles. We were told that the tender stalks must be handled with great care, and that once long ago the Katcinas found many stalks broken and thrashed all the members of the kiva, nearly killing some of them. The baskets were taken to the Special Katcina shrine, where we all met with the five Bean Maidens. Herbert and I were masked and had dressed ourselves in the Snow Katcina costume and looked impressive. The Bean Maidens tried to lift the baskets, and one maiden had to pray for strength. I followed one of them to relieve her. As we approached the village, the other Katcinas flocked around, continually saying to Herbert or me, "Ask the Maiden if she is tired." I would say, "Are you tired?" When a maiden grew weary she would nod her head for us to take her place.

The people were crowded at the edge of the plaza, watching. At the head of the procession were the Soyal and Powamu Officers, including the Village Chief, Chief of Soyal, Chief of Powamu, Crier Chief, and War Chief. They led us to the Powamu kiva, which we circled four times. The Bean Maiden whom I followed was very strong and needed little assistance. It is considered lucky for a young woman to be able to take her load into the plaza without help, but it is a rule for the Katcina to receive it in the plaza. At the end of the journey the maiden turned and motioned for me to take it. The officers took the bean stems from the five baskets. The Crier Chief called for the women to hide the small children under their shawls. Then we Katcinas all fled to the kivas, taking the baskets along. When the children were uncovered, there were to be only two old Katcinas left in the plaza, who would receive a paho from the Powamu Chief and depart leisurely toward the west. Chief Tewaquaptewa and Frank Siemptewa, who were taking these parts for the first time, forgot and fled with the rest of us. When the children were uncovered, their mothers told them that the Katcinas flew away. They would say, "Look up into the sky and you will see them flying around."

After a smoke in the kiva, the great Powamu ceremony was completed and we had secured ourselves against crop failure. We Katcinas undressed, stored our costumes in bags, and hid our masks. I was told that my Kele quills were now full-grown and that—as a hawk—I could fly any place in safety. I saw the importance of the Powamu ceremony for successful farming. The old people praised my work and said that when this ceremony was not performed correctly famines occurred. They also cautioned that people who perform their parts carelessly often either die soon after or lose a relative. I resolved never to neglect the ceremony or to fail in its proper performance.

Magic and Marriage

I RETURNED TO MOENKOPI on foot—forty miles in seven hours. My father's uncle used to rise with the chickens, run there before break- fast, cultivate his farm, and race back in the evening. Now everybody said that white ways were weakening the Hopi; and I felt in my feet that it must be true. Since there was a large family at my clan mother's house which would make it necessary for me to help with the grocer- ies, I decided to stay with my Aunt Frances, save my money, and buy a horse.

On Saturday Secaletscheoma put on a dance hoping to please the gods and get help for his sore eyes. I watched the Katcinas all day and slept with Euella that night. The next morning Secaletscheoma asked me to do clown work; but I told him frankly that I was unfit for it. I did not wish to spoil the ceremony by bringing a bad wind, or to have it said that his eyes were no better on my account. My aunt was surprised until I told her the reason. Then she said, "I'm going to beat Euella for cutting me out. But you are getting your punishment by missing the good food that we would have brought you." We often joked about love-making, but I never tried it with her. She was much older than I, the niece of my father, and the wife of my ceremonial father's brother, Roger. Even if she had been younger and unmar- ried, I would not have touched her because she was of the Sand Clan, like my father. It was all right to make love with a niece of either of my grandfathers—like Euella of the Lizard Clan for example—but not with my father's close relatives. These aunts had teased me about love-making a great deal; but I had never tried to make a Sand Clan woman, and knew that I never would for that would not be right.

Freddie and Pierce, the two clowns, left the village with Secaletscheoma, tracked the Katcinas to the shrine, and led them back to the plaza, a necessary ceremony, because the Father had sent them home the night before. As the Katcinas danced, I sat on a housetop watching, quietly humming the songs with them and thinking about Euella. The clowns did good work and there was no bad wind—proof that their hearts were pure.

I worked on the dam next day and visited Euella again that night. While we lay together, I felt a sneeze coming and rubbed my nose hard to check it. But I lost control, had to duck under the cover, and sneezed twice. Euella's mother came to the door and asked, "Who is there?" "Nobody," said Euella. "The voice is yours," replied the mother, "but not the sneeze!" She came with a light, uncovered my face, smiled, and asked, "How did you get in here?" Encouraged by her manner, I said, "Auntie, you have always teased me and called me your lover. I thought this was a good time to come." She laughed, scolded me a little, and said, "When I was a girl, my parents were too strict with me. I don't think I shall deny Euella this pleasure. You may stay, but don't let her father catch you." Since he was at the sheep camp for the night, we had nothing to fear.

I got into the habit of seeing Euella every other night, until we became fearful that she was pregnant and might have to stop school. I knew that would get me into trouble with the government and might even land me in jail. So we decided to be on the safe side and have each other only about once a week.

There came word from Oraibi in May that we Keles should go home for the Spinach Gathering ceremony. I borrowed a horse from Harry Kopi and returned with some green onions, peppermint plants, and other vegetables to share with my mother, and to give to the girls in the Spinach ceremony. But I did not realize what was in store for me. As I entered the village, Claude's father, a quiet old man, said: "Well, Polehongsie's boy friend, I am glad to see you." Inquiring what he meant, I was surprised to hear that I was the private lover of this girl, and that I was to be married to her within a short time. I jokingly admitted that I had a girl friend in Moenkopi, but denied any affair with Polehongsie, the old-maid clan sister of my friend Louis. As I passed the Snake kiva, Nashingemptewa of the Masau'u Clan called out, "Polehongsie, have you just arrived from Moenkopi?" "Yes, I am here," I replied and rode on, wondering who had started this lie.

I had stopped at my mother's house and was talking with Robert Talas when Chief Tewaquaptewa walked over, shook hands, and patted me on the back. My ceremonial father came up and said: "Talayesva, my son, I have an unpleasant matter to discuss with you. Billy tells us that you are going to marry Polehongsie. He says that she is coming to Oraibi for the wedding just after the Spinach ceremony." I replied jestingly, "Well, I have my buckskin and cotton. Let her come if she wants to; it will be a good chance for me." He put his hand on my shoulder and said, "That girl is much older than you and she has had many other men. She is still fine-looking; but she is too promiscuous to make a good housewife. She will tire of you and turn to others. So listen to me, my boy, and leave her alone." Robert came to my defense: "A boy's partner is supposed to know all about his love affairs. Don and I go together all the time. He has a girl all right, but she is not that wrinkleface."

I tried to take the matter lightly, but felt quite upset when my mother called us to lunch. She noticed my silence and said, "Son, eat your food. The news has worried me, too, but if you want this girl, I have nothing to say. On the other hand, if you tell me that the story is false, I shall believe it." The Chief was eating with us and kept up a line of jokes. He was always working to keep the people happy.

After lunch the Crier Chief announced that we should go to the spring and prepare to gather wild spinach. I passed along a narrow alley and saw Irene of the Fire Clan on a housetop. She leaned way over and whispered, "Polehongsie, Polehongsie." I tried to smile and kept walking. She was one of the few suitable girls in Oraibi for me to marry but I had seen almost nothing of her since she ate my oranges and accepted a string of beads from me on the train from Sherman. Irene had been ill and could not join us to collect wild spinach because she had lost most of her hair and could not put it up in the customary squash-blossom style. Ira was still going steady with her clan sister, but I claimed no girl in Oraibi.

On my way to the spring people on every side were calling me Polehongsie. Robert overtook me near the Rock, hit me on the buttocks, and said, "Why don't you wait for me, Polehongsie?" I struck him a strong blow on the back and said, "Cut it out, you darn rascal, don't you join that gossip gang." He laughed and replied, "Well, you have nothing to lose. You can have a good time, and then leave her." When we joined the girls at the spring, they looked at me, smiled, and called me the same name until both ears were full of it.

We followed the officers to collect wild spinach. When we reached the sand hills, the Crier Chief announced a rest and told us to give the girls the spinach that we had gathered. I would say to a girl, "Here is my spinach." Accepting it with thanks, she would place it in her shawl and give me some food in exchange. We collected spinach, rested, and exchanged it with the girls four times. I also took bunches of fresh, green onions from my bag and gave them to the girls in the place of spinach, a very modern practice. At the fourth and last resting place I had emptied my bag of green onions and received so much food that my load was heavier than when we started. It is customary at the last stop for a girl to select a lover and present to him a cake of baked sweet corn in token of engagement. It is embarrassing for a boy to receive the sweet-corn cake before the crowd; but I had no fear on that score, for the false rumors would discourage any Oraibi girl from choosing me, and Irene was not with us anyway. Claude received a sweet-corn cake from Alice, and later married her. The Crier Chief announced, "Let us return to the village with our happy hearts." But my heart was not happy.

We returned to our homes, ate supper, and heard that the Katcinas were entering the village. They danced near the kivas and the Father sent them home. There was no one to act the part of Masau'u because the old man who used to take that part had gone to Hotavila with the Hostiles. I tried to be cheerful and told my family that, since fake rumors had spoiled my chance of getting a girl in Oraibi, I had decided to go back to Moenkopi right away. They urged me to forget the gossip and stay until the next day. As I lay on the roof that night, I felt trapped. I worried and wondered whether I might not have to marry Polehongsie after all, especially if other girls took it for granted that we were lovers and avoided me. I did not like the idea of rolling that wrinkle-face on my sheepskin for the rest of my life.

I mounted my horse next morning, said good-by, and started off. But my ceremonial father beckoned to me from his housetop and told me to wait for him at the Rock. There he advised me in private; "Take my word, my boy, and watch out for Polehongsie." I took his hand, assured him that I had never slept with her, and promised not to hang around her house after dark.

I saw Logan and Jackson on their horses near Masau'u's shrine and quickly galloped past them. They called out, "Polehongsie, why are you in such haste?" "Cut it out," I replied. "I am full up to my neck with that name!" They wanted the true story. I told them it was a frameup. Later as we rode along, I saw a man chasing us on muleback and recognized Billy, the windbag who had spread the false rumor. I said, "Boys, here comes that rascal, and it's a good chance to have it out with him." He rode up and exclaimed, "I had a hard time overtaking you." "And I have had a hard time on your account," I replied sharply. "I have many questions to ask you. Why did you spread the lie about Polehongsie and me?" He laughed in a silly manner—which made me want to smash his face—and said: "I never made up that story. I merely listened to the neighbors and passed on the news without getting the details. Is it true?"

This explanation calmed me a little, but I reminded him that he should have asked me whether I had ever had intercourse with Polehongsie before spreading such a report. I told him that he had spoiled my chance of getting a lover in Oraibi. He apologized and said that he had to stop by the roadside. I whispered to my pals, "Let's leave this liar." We whipped our horses into a gallop and left him.

When we reached Moenkopi, I returned Harry's horse and offered to pay him. He said, with a wink, "Keep your money for Polehongsie." I learned that the rumor had spread all over Moenkopi, but that most of the people were on my side. My aunts questioned me closely and were very angry with Polehongsie's family for starting the report. Every time I saw Polehongsie she looked at me and smiled in a familiar and possessive manner. But I took pains to keep out of her company. I was still thinking of Mettie and received a letter from her every week; but some of the girls had written me that she had a Navaho lover, besides two Hopi boys. Mettie's mother had heard of the Navaho and told my relatives that if I waited until Mettie returned, we could marry. She did not want to lose her daughter to a Navaho. I did not want to wait.

I returned to the dam for work, and one day a man offered four of us $1.50 each to dig a grave for a Mormon. Ira, Robert, Adolph, and I agreed to do it, but Pierce excused himself on the grounds that he was too short to pitch dirt out of a grave. He was the best ditcher in the gang, and I knew he was afraid. The Mormon and his wife came to the cemetery in a wagon loaded with a coffin, which was covered with expensive velvet. They cried and cried because this seventeen-year-old boy was their only child, and had come with them from Salt Lake City. Some of the government employees sang "Nearer My God to Thee" and "Shall We Gather at the River?" I was sorry for the parents and joined in the singing. We filled the grave with earth and placed stones at the head and foot. I did not care to be buried in a coffin, even a fancy velvet-covered one, because it was sealed tightly with no way of escape.

In about three weeks I returned to Oraibi to help my father with his farming. I had purchased a small horse from Harry Kopi for $17.50, but I left it at Moenkopi to eat alfalfa hay and rode on a wagon with Mark, an uncle of Mettie, who was bringing apples to trade. He questioned me about Polehongsie and advised me against marrying her because of her age and her numerous love affairs. He also suggested that if I waited until Mettie returned from school I might marry her. "I hear Mettie has a Navaho friend," I replied; "and it is hard to wait. If I can find another lover, I may have to marry her."

When I reached Oraibi, I greeted my mother and asked her whether she had much food in the house. Of the white man's groceries she had only a little flour and coffee. I went to New Oraibi and bought 8 24-pound bags of flour, 5 pounds of coffee, 5 pounds of sugar, and several cans of baking powder. My mother was well pleased, for Ira was never so generous.

When my father caught up with his work, I tried to find another job in Moenkopi, but without success. So I helped the Hopis cultivate their crops at $1 a day for about a week. I took my money out of savings at the Navaho Agency and bought a new $35 saddle. But I found only odd jobs until I became ill.

One morning when I was combing my hair, I glanced into the mirror and saw a dead lizard attached to my shirttail. Picking it off, I showed it to my Aunt Frances who seemed worried and urged me to take off my shirt and burn it immediately. She explained that it was the only way to check the spread of poison through my body. I did this, placed the dead lizard in a baking-powder can, and buried it under a stone back of the kiva. In the evening when I had returned from work, I washed for supper and went to the place where I had left the lizard. Glancing around to see that no one was looking, I removed the stone and peeped into the can. The lizard was gone, and there were no tracks to be found. Suddenly I heard the voice of Ponyangetewa, the husband of my clan mother: "What are you looking for?" When I told him about the lizard, he said, "It must be Polehongsie."

In a few days I felt sleepy and sick and discovered that I was losing my memory. A good Hopi doctor, Arpa of the Badger Clan, from First Mesa, who happened to be in Moenkopi, was called in to examine me. When he had finished his meal, he had me lie on a sheep pelt before him. He looked at me closely, smiled, put his ear to my heart, and listened. Finally he said, "Are you having pleasure with the girls?" "Not much," I answered. He pondered for a moment and remarked, "There are two girls who are interested in you. One is all right, but the other is not. She has trapped you like a bird and has filled your clothes with the loco pollen to make you crazy over her." He examined me further and said, "My boy, your heart is out of order. Sometime when you were asleep, a whirlwind came and twisted it into a knot. I will straighten it out." He massaged my chest, had me remove my shoes and socks, placed his fingers on the bottom of my foot, and rubbed it lightly. It felt as if a tiny animal were chasing around under the skin. He took two fingers, moved them rapidly, and said, "I can't catch this thing."

Finally he extracted something, placed it in his left hand, and showed it to me. There was the tiny tail of a lizard, wriggling and jumping about. He caught a second one in my left foot, looked at me sharply, and said in a sober tone, "My boy, you may die. You have been poisoned with the terrible tails of the lizard, which is one of the worst diseases. But the power has not yet reached to your heart. It is now in your thighs." I became nervous and felt as if I were losing my mind. I thought immediately of Polehongsie and knew that she possessed some magic power; otherwise she could not do this to me. I was sure that I would never marry her, but feared that when she lost hope, she would get angry at me and do something even worse.

Finally the doctor asked, "What do you know about lizards?" I described the dead lizard on my shirt and told him about Polehongsie. He hung his head, looked very worried, and said, "I am sorry to hear this. Polehongsie must have put the lizard in your bed while you slept. Let me examine your eyes." He told me that my eyeballs were rolling about in an awkward manner, and picked out something from each eye which he said were poison arrows. They may have been the eyes of the lizard. Finally he said, "Well, I have saved you from death, but Moenkopi is not the place for you. You had better start for Oraibi in the morning. As you go, you may see lizards with tails like these. Be careful to avoid them. If you get sleepy, do not lie down, for something may be trailing you. I will follow in a day or so and see you at your home."

I mounted my horse early next day, set out in a slow trot, and galloped into Oraibi before I got sleepy. I was glad to be safe from the evil woman, and felt then that I never wanted to return to Moenkopi. I told my mother the whole story. She cried at thoughts of my narrow escape. I looked straight into her eyes and told her that I had never touched Polehongsie, and that she had no claim on me.

In two days the doctor stopped at Oraibi and ate supper at our house. When he had finished, he examined me and said that I was almost well, but that he would sing a special song to purify me. He made up a medicine in an abalone shell, sang over it, and had me drink the bitter drug to the last drop. Then he turned to my mother and said, "You remember the birthplace of your boy. Go there, gather up some dust from the spot where he first lay when he dropped from your womb, mix it with water, and let him drink it. It will free him from the power of the whirlwind that has settled in his clothes and his body." When I drank this medicine, the doctor said, "Now you are well, but you must rest until you regain your strength." My mother thanked him many times, wept a little, and said, "If you had not been in Moenkopi, I fear my boy would not be alive today. I shall give him to you as a real son." The doctor took my hand and said, "Now you are mine, and no one shall draw you away from me. Be good and be strong." He was about to rise when I said, "Wait," drew a $5 bill from my pocket, and handed it to him, for I cared more for my life than for my money.

When I was strong again, I helped my father herd, haul wood, and farm, and was in Oraibi for the Niman dance in July but did not take part because of my recent illness. I was on the roof watching the dance when Chief Tewaquaptewa came up to me with a star on his coat and a pistol in his belt, for he had been made a government policeman. He held a paper in his hand and said, "Don, I have some news for you. See if you can find your name on this." It was there with the name of Louis and others who had joined the Y.M.C.A. at Sherman. The missionary at New Oraibi had received this list from Sherman and had instructed the Chief to tell all Christian boys to stay away from the Katcina dances. The Chief said, "The missionary told me to have you boys leave the dance and assemble at the Sunshine Mission." I asked him, "Did you get this order from the government agent too, or just from the missionary?" "The missionary only," he replied. "Then you can use this paper for your toilet," said I. The old people and my Guardian Spirit had led me into the Wowochim and the Soyal, and I knew that I was spoiled for the Holy Ghost. I had forgotten the Sabbath Day to keep it holy, and had worshiped the Hopi "idols"; but I still honored my father and mother, had not stolen anything, killed any person, nor yet committed adultery.

One day, while I was working in the field, it rained. Since it was nearly noon, I went to my father's field house and lay down to eat my lunch. Glancing to my left, I saw a snake coiled with raised head. He looked straight into my eyes and stuck out his tongue several times. I remained very still, thinking hard and prayerfully. When it stopped raining, the snake crawled to me, touched the toe of my shoe, and drew back. He returned, touched my ankle, came up to my knee, and drew back again. He seemed to think for a moment, came a third time, crawled up along my side to my chin, and licked my face and nose. I was frightened and sweating, but tried not to tremble. I spoke to the snake very quietly and in a pleasant voice: "My Father, I am the son of the snake and the lizard. You have come to examine my heart and learn what kind of man I am. I am only a common man and not very good or wise. Please do me no harm." Then the snake coiled partly around my neck and lay still for a moment. I thought to myself, "If this sacred snake wants to harm me, what can I do?" Finally he moved away as if satisfied with me. I was glad that he had come to me, for if my heart had been evil, he never would have been so gentle. I felt that this was the work of my Guardian Spirit, and that I was safe in his hands. I remembered how I had once raised a stone to kill a snake that almost choked me, and now I knew that it was my Spirit Guide that changed my mind just in time. I could also remember how when I dug a hole to die in, I was saved at the very edge of my grave. And, of course, I could never forget how the snakes dropped their heads when they saw me on the death journey and how my Guardian Spirit restored me to life and promised to protect me. All these things were proof to me that the ancestral spirits approved of my conduct and wanted me to stay on the Hopi Sun Trail.

The time came when I wanted to go back to Moenkopi, at least for a visit. My parents warned me that, if I must go, I should return shortly and be very careful not to fall asleep near a spring where an evil lizard could get upon me. When I arrived, my Aunt Frances welcomed me joyfully, questioned me closely, and cried in pity when I told her the complete story of my sickness and narrow escape. She advised me to stop seeing Euella in private; but I assured her that my little aunt was not against me and that I wished very much to visit her. While I ate, Roger, the husband of Frances, came in, shook hands with me warmly, and inquired about my health. When I told him that

I could stay only ten days, he replied, "You have had enough punishment, and I don't think you will be afflicted again. Keep happy and treat the people right, and they will love you. Then, if anyone turns against you, there will be plenty of friends on your side." He was a good, wise, patient man who seldom showed anger, and who always spoke soft, smooth words that helped the people. He told me the good news that in five days the First Mesa people were coming to Moenkopi to dance. I offered to help him do his work so that he could watch the dance all day.

At bedtime I wrapped myself in a blanket and lay down in the back yard, singing Katcina songs to notify Euella that I had returned. When the village had been quiet for a long time, I sneaked to her room and pressed on the door. The peg was out of place and the door opened easily. I entered as softly as a cat, eased under the cover, and found Euella asleep. Placing my hand on her knee and moving it upward, I let it rest here and there, but finally rubbed her hard. She awoke startled, and was about to scream when I whispered, "Stop, it is your friend from Oraibi." She quieted down quickly and seemed well pleased. I inquired, "Have you had a lover in my absence?" "You have found me waiting for you," she answered. I knew she had one other lover, because Mark told me in Oraibi that my partner, Louis, was seen leaving her room. Louis was my best friend and Euella was my aunt whom I could never marry. Therefore this news did not make me unhappy. I did not expect Euella to admit it, however, because it would not have been right for her to name another fellow to me. I had slept with no girl since I left Moenkopi, and could not persuade myself to leave until the eastern sky was getting gray. I then returned to my bed in the yard and was sound asleep when the sun arose. Roger doused me with cold water, and we wrestled until the people came out to watch.

I helped my "grandfather" Roger cultivate beans and corn for two days and then got into trouble again with old Bakabi, the Two-Heart. I found her, in the evening, at the home of my clan mother, Singumsie. After eating with them, I lay on the floor, resting my sore back. The witch watched me closely, asked me if I were sick, and offered to rub me. Like a fool, I carelessly accepted her offer. She rubbed me and pounded my back with her fist from shoulder to waist, assuring me that I would feel better. But, instead of improving, I got worse. The next day I went with Roger to patch leaks in the irrigation dam, but felt so miserable that I had to lie down and rest. As we returned to the village, Roger said, "My boy, what is wrong with you? Did you commit the unhealthy love act?"[1] "'No," I replied, "I have never done that."

I spent the afternoon lying on the floor in the house of my Aunt Frances. Euella came in and sat on a sheepskin near me. Frances said, "Euella, you are a lazy, useless girl. You have cut me out with my boy friend." Euella blushed, laughed, and replied, "Well, you keep him here at your house and have him whenever you want him. Now it is my turn to enjoy him." When Frances went on an errand, I asked Euella to rub my back and then told her about old Bakabi. She said, "The old lady looks like a bad woman. I am not a doctor, but I think she has disjointed your ribs." She lay down beside me, caressed me a little, and finally went to sleep. My aunt returned, looked at us, smiled and said, "Why don't you pet her?" "I did," I replied, lying, for I was too sick to be much interested. Euella's mother also came in, laughed, and said, "My daughter is sleeping with her boy friend again. She does not give me a chance." I invited her to lie on the other side. To my surprise, she came, lay down, and placed her arm and fat leg upon me, showing great interest. We fondled each other until she held me tightly and kissed me excitedly. I was a little embarrassed. When Euella awoke, her mother told her to go home and prepare supper.

After my aunts had departed, I stepped out of the house and saw people from First Mesa entering the village in wagons. My doctor, Arpa, was with them. At supper Euella and her mother brought me some food, because they had lain with me. Roger, who had returned from work, joked me and said, "Euella is a sweet little auntie. If I were you, I would marry her." Frances looked sharply at her husband and said, "You are too old for that."

Roger went to meet the First Mesa people and told the doctor that I was sick again. He came to the house immediately and asked, "Where

1. Cunnilingus.

is my son?" He reminded me that I had disobeyed his orders in returning to Moenkopi. I explained that I had a different disease now, trouble with my back instead of my heart. He examined me and inquired who had disturbed my ribs. I hesitated to answer, but finally named old Bakabi. He hung his head and said, "That is too bad. Your ribs are out of joint, and two of them are bent down into your stomach." He warned that the operation would be painful and told Roger to hold me down while he reset the ribs. The pain was severe, causing me to yell and struggle. When the treatment was over, he said, "My son, the old Two-Heart is killing people right along. Masau'u has called her, and she ought to die, but she wants to live and has destroyed many of your relatives in order to prolong her own life."

I told him how I had seen old Bakabi with my own eyes, naked on the Death Trail, and described how she asked me for a drink, even begging me to spit into her mouth. He nodded his head in an understanding manner and said: "I will tell you something. Your 'grandmother' was a Two-Heart when she was young and pretty, and she often let men sleep with her. I did myself. That is why you saw her naked on the Death Trail." I was angry and foolishly said, "When I am well, I shall thrash that old fool for killing my people and causing me so much trouble." But the doctor warned me to let her alone, and reminded me that no ordinary person can cope with magic power.

While watching the dance next day, I spied Nash, an old schoolmate, called him over, and asked him if he were married. When he complained that he had failed to find a wife, I warned him to make haste, for all the pretty girls were marrying off. I said, "I know a girl with one eye who is still single. You may try her." That was a common joke that we fellows often repeated to each other. We reviewed our early school days and the occasion when we slept together in one bed. I told my aunt that we used to be good pals with just one heart between us. While going among my relatives for food, we came upon old Bakabi, and I kept a close eye on her. Finally she said to me, "Would you like to have your back rubbed again?" "I should say not," I replied. She looked surprised, and I added, "You will find out why some day." She dropped her head in silence. We came out quickly, returned to the plaza, and sat down against a house wall in the shade.

Soon the clowns came, ten or twelve of them from First Mesa. I recognized Edwin—the former assistant disciplinarian at the Agency School—who had received thirty lashes for climbing through a window to his sweetheart in the dormitory. After a dance, the comic Katcinas came into the plaza—two boys and their "mother." The Mother Katcina scolded her sons and reminded them that they were getting old enough to stop chasing after girls, and should choose a wife and settle down. They protested, stating that to know different girls was the only life worth living. One of them got up and danced around saying, "Ho, ho, ho," which meant that he was happy with his girl friends and did not intend to give them up. The Mother Katcina scolded him soundly. I punched Louis, who was standing near by, and said, "Now, Louis, listen to the Mother and leave the girls alone." He replied in an undertone, "I will never do that, for it is the happiest part of my life." The comic Katcinas sat down to eat, and the clowns gathered around them. Clown Edwin informed the Mother that she had advised her sons wrongly because, next to eating, love-making is the greatest joy of life. She struck him on the head and said: "You are as wicked as my sons. I know your record. You were whipped by a white man for climbing through a window to see a girl." The people laughed and laughed.

The Mother Katcina informed the clowns that she had always been popular with the men, but had managed to keep her virtue. Finally she said, "Well, it is getting late, we will go to bed." Before lying down on her sheep pelt she took a cowbell from her ceremonial shawl and tied it to her ankle for an alarm in case a sneaker came to make love. We watched closely. Soon another Katcina joker crept around the corner, crawled nearer, lay flat on the ground, and rolled himself toward the "lady." He spied the alarm, silenced its clapper, removed the bell with great caution, handed it to a clown, proceeded to make love to the "sleeping beauty," and then escaped. When the Katcina awoke and missed her bell, she excitedly aroused her sons and sent them and the clowns to find the offender. The clowns came upon the sneaker outside the plaza and asked him how they might find the guilty party. He innocently suggested that they get an accurate measure of the footprints of the intruder and fit it to the feet of different men in the plaza until they found the culprit. The clowns came among us, measuring feet, each of us fearing that he would be trapped. Then they measured their own feet, but none was a perfect fit. Finally they caught the Katcina sneaker himself and measured his foot, which was the exact length. Then the clowns and the Katcina Mother's sons gave him a sound thrashing.

The First Mesa Katcinas danced three days in the plaza and departed for home on the fourth. They were well treated by the Moenkopi people. Before the old doctor left, he examined me again, advised me to go home, but said that I might return to Moenkopi for short visits. He warned me never to marry a Moenkopi girl. "For," said he, "the Moenkopi people prefer to marry their daughters to their own men." I stayed two or three days longer, gave Euella a few gifts and some money, and returned to Oraibi.

I went back and forth from Oraibi to Moenkopi for short visits, and one night in Moenkopi decided to try window peeping just as other Hopi men do. A young woman undressed in such manner as to provide a good show, and made me want her badly. I stepped toward the door, but stopped short when something in my mind quickly said, "No,"—the voice must have been my Guardian Spirit. Later I saw this girl, told her about the night that I had passed her window, and asked her whether it would have been safe for me to enter. She blushed, but I assured her that she had no reason to be ashamed of such a beautiful figure. She hung her head shyly and protested that she was not very good-looking. I gave her $5, and later found her door unlocked.

I was in Oraibi in September and helped build a new mission house and drill a well. The missionaries tried to get me to accept Christianity and be baptized. They praised my strong character and said that I would make a fine Christian. I told them that if my Guardian Spirit led me into Christianity, I would accept it, but otherwise never, because I already had a good road to travel, the Hopi Sun Trail. I was willing to be friends with them so long as they did not tire me with their talk about the Holy Ghost, or speak against the Hopi gods. I told them in polite language that nobody could force me into Christianity.

The government surveyors were completing their work and we were to receive our allotment of land in late September. Eight or nine men came from Moenkopi to attend the allotment meetings. We followed the allotment officer around like dogs, each of us trying to get good farming and grazing land. I was not a Special Officer in Oraibi and did not have first choice in land allotment, but I was selected to represent my father, mother, brothers, and sisters in their dealings with the government. Robert Selema, the Hopi interpreter, decided to quit his job and offered it to me. He earned $3 a day, plus $1 extra on certain days for carrying the surveyors' mail. That was a good job, and I took it.

One evening when I had returned from the surveyors' camp and was eating supper, my old pal Louis came from Moenkopi. We welcomed each other heartily, and he said that he had missed me sorely and was determined to find me, even though I hid myself in the ground like a prairie dog. That evening he was as eager to go out among the girls as ever and asked me to suggest one. I told him that I was not familiar with any girls in Oraibi and did not like it so well for that reason. Louis said, "I have made love with Iola of the Fire Clan before, but now she does not like me very well." I knew that she was staying with her clan sister, Irene, whose parents had gone to the field house at Loloma Spring. Since we could think of no other available lovers, Louis said, "Let's take these girls by force." I discouraged it and told him that I had never used force on any girl, that I had never been familiar with Irene, and that I might get into trouble. I knew that Irene was marriageable for me but I did not know whether she wanted me or not. I argued that since Louis had had Iola before, he could get away with it, but that it was too risky for me to try forcing Irene. But Louis urged until I finally agreed.

We found the girls grinding corn and decided to sneak into Irene's house and wait in the dark. Finally, as the two entered, Louis grabbed Iola and blew out the light. I caught hold of Irene and quickly assured her that she had nothing to fear. She remained still and quiet;

but Iola struggled with Louis for a while, then stopped, and became very friendly. They went off into a corner. I put my arms around Irene, drew her to me, and said, "What is in your mind?" "Have you asked your parents about this?" she inquired. "No, but I will shortly," I answered. We talked softly for a while and when we heard Louis and Iola at love-making, I begged Irene urgently with words of love and promises of marriage. Finally she said, "It is up to you." Then I led her, with a sheepskin, to another corner of the room where she remained passive but very sweet. After some time she said, "Now you must ask your parents about our marrying. Let's go and leave this terrible man, Louis." I told her to be a good girl, gave her a nice bracelet, slipped out, went to the roof of my mother's house, and lay down to sleep out under the stars.

The next day was Sunday. And since I was working for the government, I went down to the store at New Oraibi, hung around, and "kept the Sabbath Day holy." I had a good job now, and I thought some of marriage. When I returned from the surveyors' camp Monday evening, Irene's parents were home. After supper I went to their house. They offered me food, and the father later asked if there was anything he could do for me. Then I asked for the hand of Irene. He replied: "My daughter is not a good-looking girl. If your relatives are willing, you may have her." I told him that I had my parents' consent and that they were well pleased. This was a lie, but a necessary one in order to spend the night with Irene. They agreed and arranged for us to have the next room. We had a very good time. I reminded her of our train ride and how she later teased me about Polehongsie and asked her whether she wanted me as a lover then. She laughed and said that she did, but that I had another girl and, after all, it was my business to ask her first. She asked, "What would you have done if I had proposed to you?" I told her that I would have clapped my hands for joy. Then we kissed without limit. All our talk was sweet and I thought there could never be an argument between us. At cockcrow I went home for a nap on the old roof.

At breakfast I raised the subject of marriage. "I spent the night at Huminquima's," I said. "And now I want to marry his daughter, Irene." "What did they say?" asked my mother. I assured her that

Irene's parents had already agreed. My brother Ira smiled. He was engaged to Blanche, Irene's clan sister, and expected to be married in the fall. My father spoke: "Well, I won't object, for then you would think I am against you. You are not a good-looking man, and she is not a beautiful woman, so I think you will stay together and treat each other fairly. A good-looking woman neglects her husband, because it is so easy to get another." My spirit was high when I left for work. Riding down the mesa, I waved to Irene, let out a war whoop, beat my horse into a gallop, and thought that I would always be happy.

We worked all day surveying and allotting land. I stood around and interpreted, saying mostly, "Yes," "No," and "All right." We stopped early, but I received a full day's pay. It seemed wonderful to earn a good living without using my full strength. I could see that knowledge of language was very important for an easy life and began memorizing new English words. In the late afternoon I rode to the post office for mail, went home for supper, took my blanket, and called upon Irene. She listened to the full story of my parents' consent, and seemed satisfied. The night went very fast.

We worked day after day allotting the farm and grass lands. I tried to put my relatives on the best land, even getting a piece for Naquima. I kept the job through October, and when the allotments were completed, I helped my father harvest his crops and herded a little. Dennis, Iola's brother, and I became close friends and slept together, while his girl, Ada, chummed with Irene. It was a good arrangement, making it possible for us to see much of our girls—so much that I wondered whether Irene was pregnant.

One day the news circulated that Ira was getting married in November, and that my turn would follow four days later, making a double wedding. Both our girls belonged to the Masau'u or Fire Clan, and their people made this plan. My brother was worried and complained, "Our father is poor and cannot afford a double wedding. What shall we do?" Then he remembered that our great-uncle, Talasquaptewa, had approved of our marriages and said, "Perhaps he will buy a buckskin for one of us or give us some sheep for the wedding feast." I replied, "If he doesn't, we will refuse to herd for him." My father took $30 or $40 of my money to help buy the buckskins.

One evening after the crops were harvested, Ira's girl, Blanche, was brought to our house by her mother. She ground corn meal on her knees for three days, remaining in the house most of the time, but Ira was not permitted to sleep with her. I herded, and was told to keep away from Irene because she was grinding white corn meal at her house for our family.

On the evening of the third day the female relatives of Blanche's clan came to our house and spent the night. I stayed away, sleeping with Dennis. Early in the morning these women washed Ira's head, and our female relatives washed the bride's head, placed the bride's and groom's hair together in one bowl of yucca suds, and twisted it into one strand, believing that this would cause them to cleave to each other like the meat on a clingstone peach. Our women bathed the girl's arms and legs, and her female relatives removed all Ira's clothes except his loincloth, and bathed him thoroughly. Then Ira and Blanche went to the east edge of the mesa to pray at sunrise. The new bride spent the day grinding corn and baking piki. That night Ira slept with her in our house.

On the following morning Iola, the sister of Dennis, called to me, "Get up and go see what is in your house. I hear you have a pet eagle." I found Irene grinding corn with all her might. She had been brought there by her mother the night before. As I stood in the door and watched her, I felt as though I were dreaming and scratched my head, seeking for words. My mother smiled and said, "Talayesva, don't be foolish." I went out sheepishly, returned to my sleeping place, yanked the cover from Dennis, who was still asleep, and said, "Get up, lazy-bones, it is your turn next. I am now a man with a wife." Iola teased me, claiming that I ran around with other women so much that my relatives had to marry me off. I did not show up again at my mother's house all day. Later Irene told me that she was worried about this.

The aunts of my father's clan, and of my ceremonial and doctor fathers' clans, ganged up and staged a big mud fight with the men of my family. They caught my grandfather, Homikniwa, and plastered him with mud from head to foot. They also poured mud and water all over my father and tried to cut his hair for letting me marry into the Fire Clan. They made all manner of fun of Irene, calling her cross-eyed, lazy, dirty, and a poor cook, and praised me highly, asserting that they would like to have me for a husband. Dear old Masenimka, my god-mother, threw mud on my father and uncles and said that she wanted me for her lover. This mud fight was to show that they were very fond of me, and that they thought Irene was making a good choice.

On the third day I began worrying about my coming bath, for I was very ticklish and did not know whether I could stand still under the hands of so many women. A little after sundown my mother told Irene to stop grinding the blue corn and sit by the fire on a soft seat. I had not seen much of her since she came to our house, and when we had spoken it was usually in a whisper. Soon her relatives came to spend the night—the same women who had stripped and bathed Ira. I thought I had never seen so many women, and even those whom I had known all my life seemed a little strange to me. I had little to say all evening, and at bedtime I took my blanket and started out. My father said, "Wait a minute, Talayesva. Where are you sleeping? I want to be able to find you in the morning." When I told him that I was sleeping with Dennis, he replied, "Be sure to leave the door un-locked so that I can wake you early." I was worried. When I reached my sleeping place, Iola looked at me and laughed. Dennis offered en-couragement by telling me that he was in the same trap and had to get married soon. We discussed this problem until midnight. I reconciled myself by saying, "Well, we have to stand and take it. If we run off, the people will call us kahopi."

My father struck a match and said, "Get up, son, and come quickly. They are preparing the yucca suds." Then he woke Dennis and asked him to see that I started. As I dressed to go, Dennis said, "You are now on your way to the happy life, you old married man." When I entered the house, I saw many eyes staring at me. There were Irene's mother and her sisters, Blanche's mother and her relatives, in fact all the women of the Fire Clan, also the women of the Coyote and Water-Coyote clans, and most of my real and ceremonial aunts. They had assembled to give me a bath. My mother was assisting Irene's mother with the yucca suds. I was so timid that I took steps not more than an inch long. My mother said, "Hurry up." I laid back my shirt collar and knelt with Irene before a bowl of yucca suds. My relatives washed

Irene's head and her relatives washed mine. Then they poured all the suds into one bowl, put our heads together, mixed our hair and twisted it into one strand to unite us for life. Many women rinsed our hair by pouring cold water over it. When that was completed, Irene's mother told me to take off my clothes. I felt so uncertain about my loincloth that I made an excuse to go out, ran behind the house, and checked it carefully. When I had returned and undressed, Irene's mother led me outside. My real aunts tried to bathe me first in fun, and scuffled with Irene's relatives. Then Irene's mother bathed me from tip to toe. All the women took their turn bathing me, while I stood shivering in the cold. I had to appear gentle and kindhearted and say to each of them, "I thank you very much." They assured me that they had washed away all remaining traces of youth and had prepared my flesh for married manhood.

I hurried into the house, wrapped myself in a blanket, and stood until Irene's relatives told me to sit down near the fire. Irene's hair was arranged in the married women's style, and her mother advised her to be a good housewife. Irene and I took a pinch of sacred corn meal, went to the east edge of the mesa, held the meal to our lips, prayed silently, and sprinkled it toward the rising sun. We returned to the house in silence and my mother and sister prepared our breakfast. Before Irene's mother left, she built a fire under the piki stone. After breakfast Irene made batter and began baking piki.

I returned to Dennis' house for a few minutes. He shouted our football yell, felt my wet head, and said, "Now you are a married man, stay on your side." "Yes," I replied, "all our pleasures are over."

My father distributed staple cotton among all our relatives and friends, asking them to pick out the seeds and return it. In a few days we butchered a couple of sheep, and it was announced from the housetop that there would be carding of cotton and spinning in the kiva for my father's new daughters-in-law. The invitation was made that "Whoever does not have much work to do may assist."

I herded sheep for my uncle, Talasquaptewa, so that he could supervise the spinning for Irene in the Mongwi kiva, while my father had charge of the spinning for Blanche in the Howeove kiva. I returned from the sheep camp in the evening, ate supper with Irene and my family, and went to the kiva to card cotton. I had never learned to spin very well, or to weave at all. Many men were helping us. My grandfather was a top-rank Hopi doctor, and the people whom he had healed were glad to help us in order to please him and repay him for their treatments. My ceremonial father helped with the spinning, but did not know how to weave. Crippled old Naquima was there too, picking seeds out of the cotton. Finally I was teased and reminded that it was bedtime and that I had better go. We slept together in a separate room in my mother's house. I thought I would never tire of sleeping with Irene, and she agreed that it was a good life.

The brides remained in our house for the rest of November and all the next month, for it was considered bad luck for them to go home in December. The people were surprised that the spinning was completed so early. The women fetched water and we hauled several wagonloads of wood in preparation for the wedding feast just before the Soyal. Irene and Blanche ground corn almost daily. On the day before the feast we cut much wood and butchered 16 sheep, 10 from my father's flock, 4 from my uncle Talasquaptewa's, and 2 from my uncle Kayayeptewa's. Kalnimptewa, my father's brother, gave us 2, which we decided to keep until the brides were ready to go home. The mutton was cut up in small pieces for cooking. Many people came to our house during the day, and Frank and my sister from Shipaulovi arrived in the afternoon; but no one came from Hotavila, and only Solemana's daughter from Bakabi, because we were having no dealings with these people. Some of my clan mothers came from Shongopavi. The women cooked piki all day, and the men finished the spinning. Many jokes and stories were told until late at night. Ira and I slept in separate rooms with our brides, while Frank and Gladys slept with my mother and father.

In the morning, long before daylight, we arose, built fires under the pots outside, and cooked the mutton stew. Pots were boiling all around our place, and almost all the people in Oraibi were present at the breakfast feast. Then the men assembled in the different kivas to weave. Two of our uncles from Shipaulovi took back cotton string with them to weave the belts. There was work under way in all five kivas in Oraibi. Ira and I went out to herd for our uncles. The weaving continued day by day, and the progress appeared almost miraculous.

One day I went to the post office with Chief Tewaquaptewa and received five letters, which caused him to open his eyes in surprise. We started back to Oraibi, sat down by the roadside, and read them. There was a letter from the school principal in Sherman, and another from the head baker, both urging me to return and graduate. They promised to get a baker's job for me in Riverside when I got my diploma. The Chief said he hoped he had not made a mistake in taking us out of school too early. The third letter was from my clan sister Meggie, who had recently gone to Sherman, and stated that when Mettie heard the news of my marriage, she cried all day, even though she had three lovers at school and had practically ruined herself in the eyes of the Whites. There was also a letter from my little ceremonial aunt, Eva, whom I had loved in the upper room at Moenkopi. The fifth letter was from my old girl Mettie, which said:

My dear Friend:
I am heartbroken to hear of your marriage. I cry myself to sleep every night and wish that I could leave school. You were my lover first, and when I return home, I shall have you again in spite of your wife and all the gossip in the village. You will never get away from me.

Your loving friend,
Mettie.

When I read that, I raised my head for a long breath. The Chief asked, "What is the matter, Don?" "In this letter," I replied, "Mettie says that I will always be hers." I read it to him. He smiled and said, "I think she means just that. When she comes home, I would go to see her and cheer her up." I think I would have been more excited over my wedding if she had been the bride.

I reminded the Chief that Louis and Robert had returned to school a few weeks before, and asked him whether he thought I was making a mistake by staying home. He replied, "I can see that school is important. If you want to return, do so. I won't try to persuade you either way." "Chief," I replied, "I am caught in a trap. Now I have a squaw. I will try her out, and if she treats me unfairly, I may escape and go back to school."

I destroyed Mettie's letter because I knew it would not be good news to Irene. When I sat down near where she was grinding corn, she whispered, "Did you get a letter from Mettie?" "No," said I, and showed her the other four. Finally she said, "I am sure Mettie wrote, because these letters mention her." I denied it, but she kept asking me for several weeks until finally I admitted the truth. She cried, said that I was hers, and that I should stop writing to Mettie. I told Mettie to stop writing, but that I would look forward to seeing her sometime.

The wedding costumes were completed in January. For each bride there were two blankets whitened with kaolin, a finely woven belt, and an expensive pair of white buckskin moccasins. Soft prayer feathers were attached to the corners of the blankets. Each bride was to wear the large blanket and carry the small one rolled in a reed case when she returned to her house. The small blanket was to be carefully preserved and draped about her at death—as wings to speed her to dear ones in the House of the Dead. The beautiful belt was to serve as tail to a bird, guiding the bride in her spiritual flight.

There was a feast for our close relatives on the day that the men completed the wedding outfits. The brides made puddings, and we butchered and cooked the two sheep that Kalnimptewa had given to us. We gathered at sunset, and the brides took special pains to be good hostesses and to see that everyone was happy and well fed. After the meal they cleared the food away, and our great-uncles, Talasquaptewa and Kayayeptewa, made speeches to them: "We Sun Clan people are very thankful that you brides have come to our household and have taken such good care of us. You have proven yourselves to be good housewives by feeding us well. The wedding outfits are completed, and tomorrow you will return to your homes. We are now the same people, sisters, brothers, uncles, and aunts to each other. Look on the bright side of each day, treat your husbands right, and enjoy your lives. Visit us often so that we will be happy." The brides were expected to say: "Thanks very much for your work on the wedding outfits." Kayayeptewa turned and said, "Well, it is now time to advise our nephews." But Talasquaptewa reminded him to wait and advise us when the brides were gone.

Early in the morning our mother, assisted by her sister, Nuvahunka, awoke the brides before daylight, washed their heads, and dressed them in the wedding outfits. They led them to the door, sprinkled a corn-meal path toward the rising sun, and placed a prayer feather upon it. The brides stepped out upon this path, followed it to the end, turned and went to their homes, carrying before them the small blanket rolled in a reed mat. There they were received by their mothers and other female relatives, who removed the wedding garments and tried them on themselves. I remained in bed for another nap and did not see my bride depart.

The brides and their relatives prepared food to bring to our house in the evening. About sunset they came with their mothers, bringing a large tub filled with food. When they returned to their houses, our own relatives were invited to come and eat. That was the occasion for giving us advice. Our great-uncle, Talasquaptewa, spoke first: "Thank you, my nephews. You are not very good-looking, and I thought you were never going to marry. I am glad that you have chosen such fine wives. You know every woman hates a lazy man, so you must work hard and assist your new fathers in the field and with the herding. When they find that you are good helpers, they will be pleased and treat you like real sons. When you kill game, or find spinach or other food plants in the fields, bring them to your wives. They will receive them gladly. Make believe that your wife is your real mother. Take good care of her, treat her fairly, and never scold her. If you love your wife, she will love you, give you joy, and feed you well. Even when you are worried and unhappy, it will pay you to show a shining face to her. If your married life is a failure, it will be your own fault. Please prove yourselves to be men worthy of your clan."

The next day my parents killed two more sheep, made a stew, and took a large tub of food to our wives' homes. Irene and Blanche invited all their relatives to come and eat, and it was then that their uncles advised them on their family duties.

After the feast in the brides' houses, it was time for them and their relatives to prepare corn-meal gifts in exchange for the wedding costumes. The brides and their relatives ground corn for many days. Little girls seven and eight years old helped with the grinding. Many heaping plaques of fine corn meal were taken to our house—perhaps twenty bushels—to be distributed among the relatives who had assisted us. This completed the wedding obligations.

It is customary for the groom to decide when he will move into his wife's house. I remained at my house for about two weeks, visiting Irene every night. Ira stayed three weeks longer. It was necessary for me to go live with Irene early, because her father, Huminquima, was not a very good worker. Before I went, I hauled wood for them like a dutiful son-in-law. I also took part in the Soyal ceremony, observing the rules of continence. After the Soyal I borrowed Frank's team and wagon and went for an extra large load of wood without telling Irene. I returned late in the afternoon, stopped the wagon at my wife's door, and unhitched. Irene's mother shelled corn for my horses while I unloaded the wood. Irene came to the door and asked me how I liked my eggs. I thought of sneaking home, but, knowing that would never do, I timidly entered the house and ate a little of the scrambled eggs. I soon remarked that I was not very hungry, and hurried out with the shelled corn, feeling that the Fire Clan were very high-tone people. Taking the wagon to my home, I asked my mother for a square meal, which caused her to laugh. About sunset, as I returned from hobbling the horses, Irene came to our house calling, "Come and eat." She invited all my family—according to custom—but they properly declined. I meekly followed my wife to her home and sat down with the family to a dish of hot tamales wrapped in cornhusks and tied with yucca stems. But I ate so slowly that Irene's mother unwrapped tamales and placed them in a row before me. I thought, "This old lady is very kindhearted, perhaps she will do this for me always." But I was mistaken; at breakfast I had to unwrap my own tamales, and was put to work for my wife's people.

I I

Subsistence in the Desert

WITH MARRIAGE I BEGAN a life of toil and discovered that education had spoiled me for making a living in the desert. I was not hardened to heavy work in the heat and dust and I did not know how to get rain, control winds, or even predict good and bad weather. I could not grow young plants in dry, wind-beaten, and worm-infested sand drifts; nor could I shepherd a flock of sheep through storm, drought, and disease. I might even lead my family into starvation and be known as the poorest man in Oraibi—able-bodied but unable to support a wife.

I turned to my uncles and fathers and asked them how to make a living. In substance they said, "Talayesva, you must stay home and work hard like the rest of us. Modern ways help a little; but the Whites come and go, while we Hopi stay on forever. Corn is our mother— the main support of our lives—and only the Cloud People can send rain to make it grow. Put your trust in them. They come from the six directions to examine our hearts. If we are good, they gather above us in cotton masks and white robes and drop rain to quench our thirst and nourish our plants. Rain is what we need most, and when the gods see fit they can pour it on us. Keep bad thoughts behind you and face the rising sun with a cheerful spirit, as did our ancestors in the days of plenty. Then rain fell on all the land; but in these evil days it falls only on the fields of the faithful. Work hard, keep the ceremonies, live peaceably, and unite your heart with ours so that our messages will reach the Cloud People. Then maybe they will pity us and drop the rains on our own fields."

We talked about Hopi practice day after day as we herded, hauled wood, and cultivated our crops. I thought I would be willing to go back to the very beginning of Hopi life, wear native clothes, and hunt wild deer. I let my hair grow long, tied it in a knot at the nape of my neck, and stored my citizens' clothes in a gunnysack. I ate old Hopi foods, practiced the Katcina and Wowochim songs, and brought sand up the mesa in my blanket to start a bean crop in the kiva.

During the Powamu ceremony I observed the rules of continence, watered the beans, performed my ceremonial duties, and tried to do or say nothing that would disturb the minds of the Special Officers and thus spoil the ceremony and our chances for a good crop. We took crippled old Naquima into the kiva and had him smoke and pray with us, for we thought that his prayers were better, since he had a strong mind and was single, handicapped, and less likely to be spoiled by love-making. The men said, "Naquima, although you are a crippled and weak old man, your prayers are stronger than ours."

My uncle, Talasquaptewa, gave me twenty sheep, and his brother, Kayayeptewa, gave me four. I was glad to start a herd, for my uncles and fathers encouraged me and my grandfather predicted that the price of wool would be high. Everyone seemed to think that life was easier for a sheepherder than a farmer. Herding for others in fair weather was all right, but a family dependent upon a flock of my own was something different. I joined herds with Talasquaptewa, Kayayeptewa, and Saknimptewa—three old men—and had to go out and herd in the worst weather—in sleet, snow, and rain, on days when it was too cold to ride a horse, and when shepherd and flock had to run to keep warm. Strong winds drove sand into my face and eyes, filled my ears and nose, and made it difficult to eat my lunch without catching mouthfuls of grit. My clothes were often heavy with sand and chafed me as I walked; and my hair was caked with earth so that I could hardly reach the scalp with my fingernails. I built fires in the gullies, or lay on the ground behind windbreaks—sometimes falling asleep and losing all trace of my sheep.

Dust and snowstorms scattered my flock and forced me to search days for stray animals. I found some half-eaten by coyotes and plucked a little wool from the decayed carcasses. Hailstorms—called up by Two-Hearts—were the most frightful. Black clouds rushed forth from the mountains—like warriors on a warpath—and joined with lightning, thunder, and bad winds which hurled hailstones at my herd and scattered sheep and goats into small huddles under sage bushes, causing them to cry for their lives. All I could do in a hailstorm was to crouch with my head under a blanket until the fury passed. Storms frequently caught sheep in labor or drove them from new-borne lambs. These young things were beaten about and often killed by hail, water, and wind. I would gather wet, shivering lambs in my arms and bury them up to their eyes in warm, dry sand from a sheltered bank. I studied clouds and paid close attention to my dreams in order to escape being trapped by storms too far from shelter.

I sorely needed an education in sheepherding, and quickly learned birth control by tying denim or burlap aprons to rams and billy goats in order to curtain off contacts out of season. I tried to castrate my males, but did not have the heart for that; for I loved my sheep and knew the face of every one. They seemed to know and trust me, too. I hired others to castrate, sprinkled salt in the wounds to keep out the flies, and threw the testes to dogs—like any white man. I clipped the tails of lambs myself and cut my property mark on each animal's ears—three half-circles in the upper edge of the left and a horizontal "V" in the tip of the right. I also learned to put salt in the sore eyes of my sheep and to cut a vein below the eye to examine their blood and test their health. If the blood were yellow or dirty black, I cut a gash below each eye and drained it off. I learned that whenever a sheep opened its mouth and breathed short, it needed to be bled. I also pounded roots of certain plants, soaked them in urine, and sprinkled the sheep to dispel diseases.

The lambing season was a critical time. A shepherd had to watch his flock closely, keep off dogs and coyotes, wait on mothers in labor, assist them with the afterbirth sometimes, and carry the new lambs until they could keep up with the flock. I became skillful in riding past, reaching from my saddle, and picking up lambs. It was a happy feeling to lead my flock to the corral in the evening with my arms full of new-borne lambs and kids. Sometimes I placed them in a gunny-sack with their heads sticking out of holes, and carried them back of my saddle. Whenever a sheep bore twins, I took the weaker one home and butchered it for a feast, because twins are too great a drain on their mother. I found that it was a good plan to mark mother and lamb with paint, axle grease, or a colored string, so that I could match them correctly when they were mixed in the corral, and especially when a mother refused to recognize or suckle her offspring.

The nursing lambs were problems. Often the mother had to be hobbled, and the lamb held to the udder. I squirted milk on its body and sprinkled its back with salt to induce the mother to lick her lamb and learn to love it. All the lambs needed a fill of milk daily, before I placed them in the lambs' pit for the night and kindled a fire of dried sheep dung to frighten away coyotes.

Lambs born overnight in the corral often froze or were crippled or crushed. Once I found a lamb in the field with a broken leg, cut splints, and tried to reset it. When I placed the poor thing in the corral, it stepped around lively and pleased me greatly. When lambs followed the flock on warm days, it was hard work circling the herd to keep it together, and helping little ones out of gullies and over rough places. It was not unusual for grown sheep to get stuck in the mud. I had to be especially careful to clear out straw and caked mud from between the hooves of both sheep and goats.

I became skillful in butchering—a bimonthly task. I bound all four legs of the animal with a short rope—or with my headband—squatted behind it with my knees against its body, drew back its head to stretch its throat, cut its neck with my knife, and caught the blood in a basin for my dog. Splitting the hide down the belly, I jerked it off, opened the stomach, rolled out the intestines, pulled out liver, lungs, and heart, and hung the mutton on a post to dry. Then I stripped the intestines and twisted them into a roll like a married woman's braid.

I got so I could butcher in thirty minutes or less. I could not castrate a dumb animal, but I did not mind cutting its throat, for I knew it was placed here for our food.

I watched my herd closely, and whenever I found a very sick sheep, I cut its throat and let out the warm blood before it hardened in the body and spoiled the meat. I learned to examine the liver, lungs, heart, and gall bladder and discard any diseased parts. One day I found a poor goat dying. I quickly cut its throat and opened its belly to save the meat. It had a heart larger than that of a cow and full of yellowish water, but the meat was fine.

To make the herding day seem short, I often lay down for a nap, collected dry bushes for firewood, looked for the honey of wild bees in rat holes, chased coyotes on horseback, or hunted rabbits. It was common practice to go home with four or five cottontails tied to my saddle or slung over my shoulder. This was a pleasure, for any woman in Oraibi thanked me joyously for a rabbit. I taught my dog to hunt and to bring the game to me by praising him, and by squirting rabbit urine on his nose to improve his smell. While I herded, there was usually a stick in my hand or a grubbing hoe on my shoulder to dig out rabbits from prairie dog or rat holes. I also became skillful at twisting out rabbits with forked sticks. If the rabbit kicked and cried, I politely reminded it that the Hopi gods had placed it here for our food. Whenever I caught game, I trained myself to say, "Thanks to my Hopi gods."

My best friends in rabbit hunts were hawks. I watched for them and asked for their help. Whenever I saw a hawk dive and stay down, I ran to the spot, expecting to find a rabbit in its claws. Catching up the rabbit, I would say, "Thanks, Mr. Hawk; you have answered my prayer. I will make a paho for you at Soyal." If the same hawk killed three rabbits for me in one day, I let it keep the third; for I knew that they were placed here to feed our hawk relatives as well as ourselves. Once when my dog chased a cottontail, a hawk sat on a sage bush and paid no attention. As I drew near, the bird flew a short distance. There lay a jack rabbit, half eaten! "No wonder you won't help me," I exclaimed. "You have a feast already. I shall make a prayer feather for you, and it is my wish that you prove yourself a better friend next time."

Sheepshearing came in April. Irene and her mother went in a wagon to the sheep corral, where we butchered a goat and spent the night in a temporary shelter. Early next morning we placed dry earth on the corral floor to keep the wool clean, tied the legs of my animals, and clipped them. Irene helped with the shearing, but never did any other work in sheepherding, although a few Hopi women herd when their husbands are disabled. We had to be careful to see that the wool was dry, clear of sand, and kept under a blanket so that the wind would not blow it away. We took it to the trading post and exchanged it for groceries, cloth, and other supplies. I had clipped my longhaired dog and mixed his wool with that of the herd, which the trader did not discover.

Farming was hardest for me. In March and April, on days that I did not herd, I cleared a field of stubble and bushes, secured some posts, and worked several days at road building for the Agency in exchange for barbed wire. I wanted a strong fence so that I would not hear it cried from a housetop that a certain man's burro was in my cornfield. Neither did I want to cut off the ear or tail of any animal in punishment for trespass. I decided that if I found a horse or burro in another man's field, I would drive it out and notify the owner, so that my name would be praised. I also took part in nearly all Katcina dances, and helped collect wild spinach to show that my heart was right. I knew that I was not dancing for pleasure, but to help with the crops. "Think of rain while you dance," the old men advised.

I had planted a patch of early sweet corn in April. We had to dig holes four inches deep and cover the grains two inches, leaving a shallow pit above the seeds which served as a pocket to catch the sun's rays. Mice and kangaroo rats scratched out much of the grain. We had many little brown mice which were newcomers to the desert, and the old people said the Christian devil brought them. I fitted little grass and twig windbreaks around each plant, or collected old tin cans, opened both ends, and set them over the seedlings. The cans were better, for they also protected the plants from mice and worms. I wanted this corn ripe for the Niman dance in July.

At the end of April we were told that the sun had risen at the right point on the horizon for the planting of melons, squash, and early beans. During May I planted muskmelons, more watermelons, and lima beans. By the twentieth of June we planted the main corn crop, hoping that it would be late enough to miss the hard winds and the worst sand drifts. Several men helped me for work in exchange. We planted 12 to 15 grains of corn in holes 6 to 9 inches deep and 15 feet apart, using greasewood planting sticks, for the old farmers warned that iron sticks were harmful to the ground. We planted the white, blue, and mixed corn in different sections of the field, and with wind blowing so that we had to set stakes to keep track of the rows. I became so hot, tired, and sore that I planted on my knees. When the plants were up, we packed the dirt around them with our feet to make it too hard for worms to enter. It was a good practice to run races by cornfields to encourage young plants to grow rapidly. And, of course, no farmer would have intercourse with a woman in a cornfield, for this would offend the Corn Maiden Spirits who protect the crop. We did not throw anything from one person to another, which would cause hail. Neither did any person who had touched a corpse work in a cornfield for four days. Many farmers had shrines in their fields, but I did not. Old men stood at the edge of their fields, scolded the clouds, and ordered them to bring rain, but I was not very successful at this.

Soon after corn planting, I rode my horse to my father's field at Batowe northeast of Oraibi, hoping to find some wild spinach. I failed to find any, and rode northward looking for young hawks. I found a nest in a big juniper tree, climbed it, and caught one hawk. Farther on I found two hawks in another tree and caught one. Later I spied three hawks in a tree, frightened two out, caught them, and lassoed the third on a limb. Making cradles out of juniper boughs, I wrapped my hawks in gunnysacks and tied them to the cradles with yucca stems. Each hawk looked like a little papoose hanging from my saddle. Mounting, I rode homeward very gently, trying not to jolt my young birds. In my excitement I had left my rope at the last tree, and never thought of it until I had gone too far to return without discomfort to the hawks. I finally reached the field house of Masahongneoma, the son of my uncle. He was called Nice Man by everyone now, because a prostitute in Winslow had praised him highly for his very long penis and had called him a "nice man." He helped me unbind the birds from their cradles, tied them on the roof of his house to rest them, and kept me and my horse for the night.

I took the hawks to my mother next day so that she could wash their heads in yucca suds—like new-borne babes—and name them. I gave one hawk to my young brother Perry, one to Ira, and kept three. We tied them on the roof of our Sun Clan house and caught rats, mice, and grasshoppers for them.

In a few days my uncle, Talasquaptewa, killed a sheep, took his paho equipment, and went to the Sun Clan house to make prayer sticks for the summer solstice. This was an important ceremony of our Sun Clan to insure good crops. We had a feast, the men smoked in prayer, and my uncle made pahos which were placed on the Sun shrine early next morning.

When the crops began to grow, I borrowed Frank's mules from Shipaulovi to cultivate my field once, and then chopped weeds day after day, alternating with herding to rest my arms and back. On very hot days I sang or whistled to revive my spirit, danced a little, or took a nap in the shade of a bush. I remembered my easy life at school and the money I had wasted on girls; but I worked on, for we needed food. I wanted a good-looking cornfield, and wished to buy a fancy shawl for my wife and some horses and ornaments for myself. Then, too, I needed to build up my reputation as a hard worker, so that my wife could hold her head high.

With plenty of rain and no wind, worms, or rats to destroy our crops, and no weeds to choke them, we would never need to work so hard. But whenever friendly clouds gathered overhead, hostile winds scattered them. The men looked tired and worried and passed each other on the road without comment, each knowing what was in the other's mind—discouragement and a wish for rain. I probably made twenty-five trips to my cornfield to replant, chop weeds, poison rats, set traps for rabbits, and spray my plants with a mixture of powdered rabbit intestines, dried roots, dog dung, and water. It took so much strength in herding and field work that I had to cut down on love-making from every other night to only once a week.

My melon patch was a trial. When the sun lifted itself from the "melon-planting point" in May, I had taken seeds to a sandy field, planted them five steps apart, and covered each hill with a thick sheet of paper to protect it from kangaroo rats. The paper was pegged down with tall sticks so that I could find it again under sand drifts, and remove it when the plants came up. In spite of this common precaution, the rats destroyed half the seeds. When I had replanted, an evil wind blew for four days, destroying many more hills. I uncovered a few seedlings and replanted a second time, but there came another windstorm. After I had dug out the plants and built twig windbreaks to protect them, a third wind beat many to threads and parched others. In five days there came a fourth sandstorm which made it necessary for me to scratch out the seedlings again. About ten days later I chopped the weeds and set deadfalls to trap rats which were eating the tender sprouts. A whirlwind upset most of the traps and spoiled more plants. Sand covered them twice more, and a jack rabbit made harmful visits. Finally, an east wind tangled the vines thoroughly before young melons appeared.

In July I was happy to bring a few sweet-corn stalks into the village for the Niman dance. I made dolls and tied them to cattail stems while my mother prepared little plaques three inches across. We took these things up on the roof, and presented them to the hawks on the day of Niman. We feasted and danced all day and presented sweet corn, dolls, and other gifts to the children. The Katcinas were sent away at sunset with urgent prayers for rain upon our drooping crops. Nearly every man and boy broke off a spruce bough to plant in his cornfield. Next morning we choked the hawks to send them home, plucked their feathers, tied pahos to their necks, wings, and feet, took them out in the direction whence they came, and buried them with corn meal. We told them to hasten home and send us rain. I then took a spruce bough to my cornfield, set it in the sand, held meal in my right hand, and prayed silently to the sun, moon, and stars for a good crop. I also sprinkled a path of corn meal and wished for rain, taking care not to step upon the meal. When it did rain, the ceremonial officer said that it was proof that our prayers had reached the Six-Point-Cloud-People.

One day I had an accident, but did not know it at the time. Ira found a dead horse in the field, struck down by lightning, and came upon the carcass before he realized the cause of its death, thus getting the lightning disease which makes a person timid, nervous, and excitable, especially in stormy weather. A member of the Ahl society should have gone to the spot and purified the ground, but he failed to do it. Some weeks later I passed the place without knowing it. I felt no harmful effects at the time, except a headache, but the strange power had gotten into my body.

In the last week of August, my father prepared to go on a long journey for salt.[1] He was a Wowochim member, of course, and had made pahos and placed them on the shrine of the Twin War gods last Soyal, which qualified him for the trip to the Grand Canyon and the Home of our dear ones. The salt lies in dangerous territory, and long ago the War Twins had set up shrines and established rules to make the journey safe for the Hopi. My father had the Crier Chief announce from the housetop that the salt expedition was planned, and that all who wished to go should patch up their moccasins, prepare salt sacks, and gather in their burros. I decided to go along as far as Moenkopi. Loading three burros with supplies, we mounted two others and set out. To insure a good journey and to prevent weariness, my father stopped near the Masau'u shrine, made a corn-meal path leading westward, and placed on it a prayer feather with its breath line pointing in that direction. As we trotted our burros toward Moenkopi, we occasionally looked back to see if others would follow, but none came.

We reached Moenkopi after dusk, stopped at the house of my Aunt Frances, and learned of a Butterfly dance in the village next day. I went to the kiva to watch the practice, help with the songs, and share in the feed. Euella and her partner, Mark, were leaders in the dance. During the night feast I shook Euella's hand, but was careful not to squeeze it, for I did not want to spoil her before the ceremony. They danced all the next day, singing songs which touched my heart.

At noon I was invited to Hattie's house and saw her sister, Polehongsie. While eating, I became conscious of her eyes glued on me, and once I winked. She beamed at this, which pleased me. When I had finished the meal, instead of stepping straight to the door, I circled the

1. For additional details on the salt journey, see Mischa Titiev, *A Hopi Salt Expedition* (Amer. Anthrop. n.s., 1937), XXXIX, 244–258.

room casually, passed Polehongsie in the corner, shook hands with her, and gave her a chance to squeeze my hand, which she did. We talked together a few minutes until I noticed people smiling, and then passed out the door. We spent the afternoon in the plaza, where most everyone watched the dancers; but Polehongsie and I watched each other from separate housetops. After dark I wanted to visit her, but feared that her relatives were still angry at me, so I spent the night with my ceremonial father.

On the next day there was a horse race with the Havasupai and Navaho Indians. I went with Mark to eat breakfast among his relatives and stopped with Mettie's mother, who was very nice to me. From there we went to the horse race, where the Havasupai had fine buckskins to bet on their horses against those of the Navahos. I had $1 in my pocket, made a bet on a Navaho horse, and won. I won bet after bet and by midafternoon I had $16. Every time I took a step, silver dollars jingled, making me feel like a millionaire. By late afternoon my pockets were so heavy that I went alone to a horse corral, sat down, and counted $38.85. A small fortune had grown up around $1. I tied up my cash in a rag, stuck it in my hip pocket, went to Frances' house and learned that my grandfather Roger had won $83 and was now a rich man.

While we were eating and talking about the horse races, my clan mother, Tuwanungsie, the wife of Talasvuyauoma the War Chief, came and said, "Son, your father wants you to come to our house. If you wish to go on the salt expedition, you had better come now." I found him with the War Chief and some Shipaulovi men. They were making prayer feathers so that they could fetch yellow clay from the canyon—a special clay always used in paho making. While Talasvuyauoma busied himself with a prayer feather, he said that no one seemed willing to join them, and asked me. I agreed to go. The War Chief showed me how to prepare my prayer feathers and told me how many. Each of us wrapped our feathers in separate paper bags and smoked the mountain tobacco, exchanging kinship terms. When I arose to go, my clan mother said, "Son, you have already made your prayer feathers for the salt expedition, so you must stay away from the girls tonight." That disappointed me, for I had a pocket full of money and wanted to see Polehongsie.

We saddled the burros in the early morning, packed the food, took some baked sweet corn meal with our prayer feathers, and departed, reminding our relatives to keep happy hearts and insure our safe return. Outside the village the War Chief sprinkled a corn-meal path, placed a prayer feather upon it with the breath line pointing westward, and said, "Let us travel with happy hearts." Each of us stepped upon the "road-marker," and the expedition was under way.

We came abreast a sacred spring, deposited a prayer feather opposite the spot, passed another spring with similar sacrifices, and arrived at the shrine of Mountain Sheep nine or ten miles from Moenkopi where our ancestors used to hunt. There were antelope tracks set in soft mud which the War Twins had turned to stone. We placed prayer feathers upon these, prayed to the Mountain Sheep for success in hunting, and asked them to come back so that we could hunt them again.

Traveling a mile farther, we arrived at the shrine where Hopi salt gatherers carve their clan emblems on the rocks. Our ancestors had gathered salt for many generations, and there were hundreds of clan emblems cut into the rocky base of the shrine. Every traveler, on each successive trip, had carved another symbol to the left of his original one. My father had carved eleven sand dunes in the course of his life, and Talasvuyauoma had carved ten coyote heads. I selected a smooth surface near by and carved my Sun symbol, also tracing my initials on the emblem; but I kept this secret, fearing that my companions would object to it as something modern. When I had finished, I placed the breath line of a prayer feather at the mouth of my Sun symbol, pounded it with a stone until it stuck, sprinkled corn meal upon the face of the emblem, and prayed: "My uncle, the Sun god, please notice that I have carved my clan emblem upon the stone. Direct our steps to the Salt Canyon, and watch over us until we return safely. Make our path smooth and renew our strength, so that our burden may be light." I prayed earnestly, realizing that we were entering the land of spirits and would have to cope with strange powers.

We journeyed to a sacred spring, placed prayer offerings by it, and prayed to the spirits who live there to send rain upon our crops and gladness to the hearts of our relatives. From there we climbed a hill and came to the shrine where the Twin War gods played Hopi checkers. After a sacrifice of prayer feathers, we each played checkers with the invisible Twins, arranged the games to our advantage, and then prayed: "Well, War Twins, we have won. Our reward shall be rain, health, and long life. Watch over us, that no harm may befall us."

We followed an old river bed northwest through a gap, passed over a hill, and entered a narrow gorge. When we had climbed to the opposite shelf, the War Chief said, "My saddle is not right, I will tighten the band." But instead of tightening the cinch, to my surprise, he loosened it and took out a white wedding blanket. Glancing at me, he smiled and said, "This is the shrine of the Salt Woman. We will have intercourse with her." He stepped to a white, slightly elevated sandstone about two feet wide and six feet long, and covered it with the wedding garment. Removing his trousers and loincloth, he took a prayer feather and some corn meal in his hand, crawled under the cover, and went through motions of copulation. At the same time he named a woman whom we all knew. Then he arose, expressed thanks for the pleasure, and dressed. After my father had gone through the same performance, I was told to do likewise. I felt embarrassed, but undressed, except for my shirt. The War Chief told me that, since I was a Kele on my first trip, I must strip entirely naked; and my father added, "If you don't do as you are told, our journey may be very difficult." I obeyed, stepped to the stone, raised the cover, and looked. Embedded in the center of the smooth, white surface was a small, black stone shaped like a vulva, with a hole about two inches in diameter and the depth of a pencil. At the bottom lay the prayer feathers and the sacred corn meal of the War Chief and my father. I added my own prayer feather and corn meal, named my Aunt Frances as my sexual partner, inserted my penis, and pressed hard four times—but without an erection. Except for the "vulva," the stone looked more like a shrouded corpse than a naked woman.

I arose, thanked the Salt Woman, dressed, and said, "Well, fathers, I would like to know the meaning of this." The War Chief replied:

"When the Spider Woman, who owns the salt, was making a trail for the Hopi to Salt Canyon, she grew tired, stopped here, told her grandsons the War Twins to complete the trail to the canyon, and then turned herself into this stone so that she could guide the Hopi to salt. Whenever we have intercourse with her, we are doing it to increase our children and improve our health. This is not a 'dirty trick,' as the Christians have called it, neither is it the worship of a stone image, for we know that the Salt Woman is a living goddess, and that intercourse with her means life."

As we traveled on four or five miles, I recognized some of the scenery which I had seen on my death journey and surprised my companions with a detailed description of future points along the way. When I minutely described a particular bush (*mongpivi*) from which the Hopi made arrows in the old days, my companions opened their eyes and said that it was full proof of my death and visit to the House of the Dead.

At sunset we stopped in a hollow at an old camp site, hobbled our burros, and sat down to smoke, exchanging kinship terms and hoping to get our messages through to the spirits. Since I was a Kele, I prepared the supper of coffee, fried potatoes, piki, and mutton. In the evening the old men told me the story of the Salt Woman and the War Twins and gave me a history of our ancestors journeying for salt. My father said that several years ago he went with a party on a salt expedition and all lay with the Salt Woman, but on their return something went wrong. When the party had gone a short distance past the shrine, someone looked back and saw a great, white form creeping upon them. Even the burros were frightened, fled in great disorder, and scattered the precious salt for miles. It was a difficult task to track them down and pick up the small lumps of salt. When the party was together again, the Special Officer said, "This never could have happened if everyone had obeyed the rules. We must have the truth; who has broken them?" One man confessed, "I am the guilty party. I brought a big chunk of salt for the Salt Woman, but I kept it for myself and gave her a small lump." The men replied, "No wonder we have had all this trouble. You doubted the Hopi beliefs and thought you were dealing with a piece of stone. You ought to have known better. The Salt Woman is a living spirit, and she won't stand for cheating." When my father told me the guilty man's name, I was surprised and pitied him. I knew him well, for he was a clan brother of my ceremonial father. I resolved to observe all rules carefully. We ate a melon, smoked again, and went to bed; but I could not sleep for thinking of the careless man who tried to cheat the deity and wrecked the salt expedition.

We resumed our journey in the early morning and passed through the flat country with the large cactus plants where I had seen the coiled snakes by the rough road of the Two-Hearts. At a rounded slope I discovered broken bits of pottery and old ruins where, in my death journey, I had seen houses inhabited by people dressed in the costumes of the Kwan society. We climbed an elevation and, when we looked west along the rim of Salt Canyon, it seemed that I could see houses with windows through which people threw their ashes into the canyon. Blue smoke seemed to rise over the canyon, and my father said that it was from the Houses of the Dead along the rocky rim. I felt self-conscious and uncomfortable, wondering whether our ancestors were watching us and making comments.

The War Chief said, "Here we will unpack; and we must hurry." While I hobbled the burros, the Warrior made dough of sweet corn meal and kneaded it into the size and shape of baseballs. We hid our saddles and equipment and laid rocks on the canvas cover so that evil winds could not strip it off. Placing food in our blankets and taking along our prayer feathers and a ball of corn-meal dough for each man, we proceeded to the southwest edge of the mesa and came to a jagged rock, the shrine of the War gods. Talasvuyauoma explained to me that the War Twins were making a path to the salt and that here the younger brother grew tired and changed himself into a stone to mark the way. I looked into the canyon, which seemed miles deep, and saw the Little Colorado River shining from the bottom. I was frightened and wondered if we would ever return in safety. The War Chief said, "Line up for prayers." Standing in front, he cried loudly, "War gods, at last we are here. We have come for salt. With pure hearts and happy thoughts we pass into the canyon. Receive our offerings, lead us on, and let no evil cross our path. May we return safely and without sorrow." I could hear echoes of his prayer ringing along the canyon walls. He sat down, sprinkled meal eastward, placed a prayer feather before the image of the god with the breath line pointing east, stuck a piece of sweet corn meal on the face of the god, and invited him to eat. My father and I prayed and did likewise.

We descended to a lower shelf and followed a zigzag course. Whenever our feet upset a small stone, causing it to roll downhill, we threw a pinch of sacred meal after it to appease the spirits. At a place called Spreading Buttocks steps were cut in the rock which required wide strides to pass over. Occasionally I saw a stone placed upon a big rock, marking our path. We came to a second shelf and momentarily lost our way. I chided the War Chief and my father, reminding them that they had made the trip many times. My father cautioned, "You better keep quiet, you may get lost on the return journey." I placed a small rock upon a stone to guide us back, but the Warrior warned, "You must not do that; it is against the Hopi law. Only Kwan members or a War Chief can safely set up markers." When I had taken just four steps more, I received my punishment. I fell flat on the rocks and bruised my left arm so that it bled. My father said, "Now you have learned your lesson; obey the rules." We came to a thorny tree near the edge of a cliff. The War Chief said, "I will fix this," and bent a branch out of the path. He stumbled in the act and had nearly rolled off the cliff when my father grabbed his foot, turned to me, and said, "You see, even a War Chief gets his lesson."

Entering a gorge, we climbed a narrow path and came to a shelf where I was advised to pay close attention to directions, since I would be in the lead when we returned. My father said, "There are three shelves that look alike. On your return take the middle shelf, because the top one ends with a sheer drop." We continued and passed a broad cliff, the special home for ancestors of the Reed Clan. Here we sprinkled corn meal and passed on to a red stone upon which were the carvings of an old-fashioned fur quilt pattern, with stitches and seams used in ancient times for sewing wildcat skins into robes. We placed a prayer offering upon it and expressed a wish that if we ever had occasion to make blankets of this type, our workmanship would be equal to that of the War Twins.

Passing the home of the Mountain Sheep and the place where the Havasupai used to gather agave to make bread, we coated our faces with red paint and came to a gap called the Nose-Scraping place. The Hopi rule requires that each man stand astride this gap with his nose placed against a flat stone wall on a spot of red paint scraped from the noses of former salt gatherers.

We soon reached a slab of rock leaning against a huge upright stone. Upon the stone were tracings of chickens carved by the War Twins, a rooster daubed with red ocher, and drawings of hens and baby chicks. The War Chief said, "Here is a Chicken shrine. If you wish to have success with chickens, make an offering and pray for good luck." He took a piece of dough, stuck it upon the carving of a chick, and fastened a prayer feather to it. Then he sprinkled meal, crowed loudly, and set up an echo along the rim of the canyon. My father made his offering and crowed with a low, harsh voice, followed with a cough, which caused us to laugh. I made my offering, stuck dough on the rooster, fastened my prayer feather, crowed loudly, and heard many roosters answer along the rim.

When I looked around, my father and the Warrior had reached the edge of the shelf and disappeared. I hastened along and overtook them near a cave below a huge yellowish rock. The War Chief said, "At last we have come to the shrine of Masau'u. Here lives the god of Fire and Death." With some excitement I said, "Ah, this is the home of the bloody spirit that chased me on my death journey." The War Chief replied, "It is my duty to crawl into the cave and make an offering to Masau'u. Give me your prayer feathers and meal." We presented our offerings and prayed: "Great Masau'u, accept our gifts and grant us a smooth path and an easy journey. Send rain so that our people may live in plenty without sickness, and sleep in old age." The Warrior said he would deliver our message to Masau'u and crawled into the cave, while my father and I hastened on. We understood that the Warrior would see a milling stone like those in our homes, and that if he found something very new in the cave, like green corn or a fresh piece of watermelon rind, it would be a bad omen, indicating poor crops; but if he found something very old in the cave, like an old corncob or faded cornhusk, it would be a favorable sign. We walked around the mesa point and waited. We were shortly relieved of our suspense, for the War Chief came with a smile on his face.

We continued to the house of the Coyemsie, or Muddy Head Katcinas. There we deposited prayer feathers and corn meal and prayed: "We have come at last, bringing these offerings. Give us rain, good crops, and strong lives." Placing the prayer offerings within a cleft in the wall, we went down a sandy slope to the Little Colorado River, drank some water which tasted salty, deposited a prayer feather here and there, and followed down the right bank. I was impatient to hear more about the shrine of Masau'u and asked the War Chief, "What news have you for us?" "Good news," he replied. "I saw four old corncobs and some dried beans. The grinding stone had some very old meal upon it."

We followed down the stream and reached the place of blue salt. There we deposited prayer feathers and climbed on to a little hillock surrounded with bushes. This was the original kiva and the hole through which all mankind emerged.[2] We stepped over the soft, damp earth and worked our way through the bushes of hard wood, such as is used in making drills to kindle new fires in the kiva for the Wowochim ceremony. Beyond the ring of bushes we came to a central mound of yellowish earth and stepped to the north side to remove our moccasins before entering the sacred place. The War Chief took four prayer sticks and four feathers, one with a breath line upon it, and stepped with us upon the hillock to a flat area about ten feet in diameter. At the very center was the original *sipapu*, the opening leading to the underworld. There was some yellowish water about two feet down which served as a lid to the sipapu so that no ordinary human could see the marvels of the underworld. This may be the fountain of youth which white men have sought in vain. Some ignorant, foolhardy Whites had plunged two poles into the sacred sipapu and left them

2. See Appendix, pp. 432–434.

standing against the west wall. Those profane fellows had desecrated the sacred spot where our ancestors—and theirs—emerged from the underworld. It was a great disgrace.

The War Chief stood erect and shouted, "At last we are here." And sure enough, the spirits answered, for the yellowish water bubbled up as if it were boiling. The Warrior stuck the prayer sticks at the edge of the hole and sprinkled corn meal eastward, making a path upon which he placed the blue prayer stick and a prayer feather. He placed a second set of offerings a little farther out on the path, for this is the main road that the Six-Point-Cloud-People travel when they emerge from the sipapu to bring rain to the Hopi. They ascend into the air at this spot, look eastward, and go to the farms of the most worthy people. Each of us placed prayer feathers by the entrance to the underworld and prayed silently to the Cloud People to accept our offerings and send rain.

When we went to get our moccasins, the War Chief said to me, "Remove your shirt, there is another place we must pray." We walked southwest of the yellow mound about fifteen feet and looked about for a hole that is connected to the kiva like the draft funnel of a sweet-corn oven. Finally he found a little hollow space about the size of a saucer and covered with white salt-like sand. He scraped this out and found dark brown clay below. When he had removed this and piled it on his shirt, he came to an empty cavity which was connected, no doubt, with the great kiva below. He said, "My boy, you are a Kele and must reach down for the yellow clay which you will receive from the spirits in exchange for feathers." He told me that I was supposed to be entirely naked, but since I had behaved so well on the journey, I could keep on my pants. I was advised to keep my mind and heart full of good wishes for myself and my people. He said that I could concentrate far better than he, because of my youth. The War Chief and my father placed in my right hand a prayer feather and sprinkled it with meal on behalf of its maker. Then they seized my left wrist and held me securely. I reached down into the hole as far as I could, let go the feather, and caught a handful of clay. I could feel the presence of the spirits below, who accepted the feather and gave me clay. I was not very much frightened; I trusted my fathers to hold me and did not expect the spirits to draw me in, for my time had not yet come. I first disposed of the prayer feathers for the War Chief and my father and then used those of the Shipaulovi men. Finally I put another prayer feather in the hole and drew out very poor clay. My father remarked that the spirits had decided that we had enough for this time. Since we had four feathers left, I placed them into the hole together and drew out a final handful of the same poor grade of clay.

Having placed the clay on stones to dry, we dressed and hurried along to the junction of the Colorado and the Little Colorado rivers. There we prayed, deposited prayer feathers on the water so that the waves could take them away, dipped our hands into the river, and threw water toward our villages four times, encouraging the Cloud People to hasten to our homes with rain. But we felt weary. This worried the War Chief and caused him to wonder whether he did right in letting me keep on my pants when I gathered the clay.

After a hasty lunch and a drink from the sacred river, we hurried on for three or four miles to a precipitous ledge overlooking the salt deposits. Projecting from the ledge was a stone like a man's chest, the image of Pookonghoya, the elder War Twin, who had changed himself into stone at this spot to help Hopi descend the steep cliff. In former times our ancestors fashioned ropes of rawhide which they looped over the War god's chest and used as ladders for descent. We threw down our blankets and salt bags, and the War Chief fastened a rope to the stone image and prepared to descend. I noticed that his hands and knees were trembling and asked if we were in danger. My father answered, "We are getting old and may not be able to climb the ladder with our salt." I saw his chin quiver as he talked and knew that he was afraid. The War Chief wiped his sweaty hands on his pants and stepped to the rope with a prayer feather. Trembling, he fastened the prayer feather to the chest of the image with a piece of dough, and prayed, "Great War god, please hold me securely as I descend." I watched him disappear over the cliff with a strained expression on his face. A few steps away there was an old ladder made out of timbers by Whites, but we dared not use it and break the old Hopi rules. When I deposited my prayer feather and prepared to descend, my father cautioned me to be careful. I replied that I felt sure my Guardian

Spirit was with me and that I had learned rope climbing at the Agency school. My father followed, scratching his back on the rocks as he descended.

We took our blankets and prayer feathers and proceeded to a cave which was partially filled with sand. The War Chief said, "Here is where the Kwan society members live. When I die I shall live in this house. Until a short time ago the cave was empty and we could see suspended from the ceiling two huge horns of salt, like those worn by our members; but the river washed out the salt horns and filled the cave with sand—a sign which foretells the end of the Kwan society at Oraibi." Having deposited prayer feathers and prayed, we proceeded to a small fountain, in the center of which was a solid rock about three feet high and with a cupped top. High above this stone basin was an inverted cone of salt suspended from a ledge like an icicle. Salty medicine was dripping from the cone into the cup. My father said that this cup was always filled to overflowing with medicine. I looked in and saw three pieces of rock, one white and two gray, about the size of my thumb, resembling mountain lions. I learned in amazement that whoever wishes to do so may take a piece of dough, knead it into the shape of an animal, and deposit it in the medicine bowl. At the end of a year this dough will turn into a stone mountain lion such as is used in the ceremonies and by the medicine men—a wonderful work of the spirit gods for the people. I removed one of the little animals and inspected it, asking my companions whether it would be all right for me to keep it. They said, "That would not be right, because you did not place the dough in the medicine bowl yourself." I thought of leaving some dough, but gave up the idea, since the journey was hard and dangerous, and I was not sure that I would return. We placed our prayer feathers in the cup, sprinkled sacred meal, and prayed. Then we stepped to the clinging salt by the rock wall and deposited our last prayer feather. The old men had known exactly how many feathers to bring.

At the conclusion of another prayer we gathered salt. I wished to gather the white shining salt hanging from above, but was told that the old salt chunks grubbed up out of the sand were better. Each of us filled a bag holding about sixty pounds and a smaller bag with a chunk for the Salt Woman. I remarked that I would like to stay longer and explore the surroundings, but the War Chief warned, "Don't say that or the spirits may get you." As I carried my bag to the foot of the ledge, I said, "This is not very heavy." My father cautioned, "Stop that kind of talk, or you may not be able to get it up." The War Chief climbed the rope and drew up our load. Then I ascended and my father followed, doing very well for an old man.

We hurried along with our salt and reached the junction of the rivers by dark. When we lay upon our bellies to drink the sacred water, the waves rushed out and ran back quickly, filling our nostrils and teasing us. We kindled a fire and prepared supper, being careful to use only the old Hopi foods. While we ate, I kept looking around. The War Chief said, "If you look around too much you may see an evil spirit." They described a dreadful spirit that other salt gatherers had seen on the walls of the canyon, and informed me that on one occasion a man looked southwest to the wall of the canyon and saw a girl with a squash-blossom hairdress. When he reached home, he found his sister dead. After that I took only fleeting glances. Soon we smoked, prayed, and went to sleep in our blankets.

We made an early start next morning and stopped to gather up the yellow clay near the sipapu. I wanted to examine this sacred spot more carefully, but the old men would not permit it. The War Chief led the procession with his load of salt; I followed, and my father brought up the rear in order to protect us from evil spirits. As we passed Masau'u's shrine, the Warrior warned me not to look back, for I might see the terrible god of Death on our trail, a sign that I or one of my relatives would die shortly. I strictly obeyed that rule, remembering how bloody Masau'u had chased me in my death flight.

As we passed the Chicken shrine, I saw my prayer feather still clinging to the rooster, indicating that it had been favorably received. At the three shelves I forgot my father's counsel and took the upper ledge which led to a steep drop. I sat down to rest and saw my father pass below. When I hollered, he put his load down and threw me a rope. I lowered my sack of salt and walked back a quarter of a mile or more to get onto the middle shelf, where I had difficulty in overtaking my companions. The War Chief teased me for missing the trail, and said that this error on my part gave him the right to sleep with my wife. We were growing very tired, but my father lightened our load by telling us stories about his love-making with different women.

At last we reached our camping outfit, and I went with the War Chief to gather the burros. After a feast of melons and piki, we loaded our packs and started. My father inquired, "Well, my son, what do you think of the salt expedition?" "Pretty tough," I replied. "'This salt won't last a year. I don't think I will come again." The old men laughed and said, "That is the way most young men think now." We rode on to the next camp, ate supper, smoked, and rolled ourselves in our blankets. While we lay under the stars, we reviewed all our experiences on the journey, and my father repeated the old story of how the War Twins established the salt expeditions long ago.[3]

After a good rest and an early breakfast we came to the shrine of the Salt Woman and stopped. The War Chief took a large lump of salt, stepped up to the image, and said, "My Mother god, I have brought you a fine piece of salt. It will last you a long time." We all prayed and placed our salt on the "vulva" of the goddess.

We journeyed on without looking back, and soon reached the gap. As we rode along I again related parts of my death story and told how I felt at this gap on that first trip. We lunched near the checkerboard of the War Twins and reached Moenkopi in midafternoon. Our relatives rejoiced to see us, and while we ate a big meal, my father told the story of our journey with all its details. He concluded, "Now we have returned to you, and I think our reward will be rain." The people responded, "That is right. You will get your reward."

Early next morning, while we were still in bed, the women came bringing chilis, onions, and other vegetables for us to take to our wives in Oraibi. The mother of Polehongsie came with a basket of onions for my father. I spoke too quickly, thanking her for them. She replied, "I have nothing for you. You did not like my daughter. You were looking for a pretty girl, but you were not lucky. Now you have to sleep with a skinny girl and roll a skeleton on your sheepskin."

3. See Appendix, pp. 447–448.

My Aunt Frances was offended and talked for me. When the old lady left, my ceremonial father laughed and said, "My son, don't feel badly over this. I was one of the people who opposed your marriage to Polehongsie. Her mother was foolish. She could have married her off to the first man who slept with her."

As we approached Oraibi next day, clouds gathered overhead. And when we reached Masau'u's shrine northwest of the village, rain was dropping. We found the corn-meal path which we had made on our departure and picked up the feathers, turning the breath line eastward. We sprinkled more meal, and my father said, "Well, at last we are back, bringing the Cloud god with us. With happy hearts we will enter our homes." Then the Cloud People, who had trailed us from the sacred river, poured rain upon our crops—a true miracle.

At Irene's house the people seemed glad to see us, but began to cry. Irene said, "Three days ago my youngest brother passed away. I know you loved that little three-year-old boy." I was very sad and went to my mother's place for food and a nap. I carefully reviewed my salt journey and found no fault with myself. I had no bad dreams, saw no evil spirits, and did not look back to see if Masau'u followed us. I did carve my initials on my Sun emblem, but certainly that would not have caused the death of the little boy. I returned to Irene's house for supper, and her father asked me to tell the complete story of the salt expedition. I began and talked until midnight, but I did not mention the fact that I had carved initials on my Sun emblem. The women put a ceremonial shawl upon the salt for a time and then divided it among our relatives. I did not sleep with Irene for four days.

I borrowed a wagon in September and took Irene and other relatives to assist me in a sweet-corn bake.[4] We hauled wood, dug a pit, built a roaring fire, and gathered the corn. When the oven was very hot on the second day, I fastened a cotton string to an eagle feather to send prayers to the Sky gods. Then I attached the feather of a small

4. For additional details on a sweet-corn bake see Mischa Titiev, *The Hopi Method of Baking Sweet Corn*, "Papers of the Michigan Academy of Science, Arts, and Letters, 1937," XXIII, 87–94.

yellow bird so that the corn would bake the right color and my wife would have no cause to leave me—an idea which friends usually mentioned in fun.

Irene handed me one of the largest and best ears of the crop, which is called the "mother." I stripped the husk from one side and fastened the prayer feather and string to the middle part of the corn ear, running the breath line up to the tip. Replacing the husk, I attached to it the sprig of a little yellow plant (*ma'ove*) and a piece of the gray sage bush, and bound them with a yucca stem. Four "mother ears" were prepared as well as some special pahos. Irene selected an over-ripe ear, bit off some kernels, chewed them, and spat the mixture over the heap of corn to make it sweet and insure rain. I sprinkled corn-meal paths in the four cardinal directions and placed a corn ear and paho on each path. My father, Ira, Irene, and I each stood over an ear ready to push it into the oven. Irene pushed in hers from the north and we followed serially, west, south, and east. Then we tossed in the crop while Irene vigorously chewed and spurted fresh corn and saliva over everything. The connecting tunnel was stopped and several slabs of stone placed over the oven and covered with about a foot of earth. The corn was left to bake overnight, while we sat around and told stories until bedtime.

Early in the morning I removed the cover, faced the east, and called out to the Six-Point-Cloud-People: "Come, chiefs, uncles, fathers, and all; may you eat with happy hearts." We had to feed our ancestral spirits before we ate ourselves, to insure good luck. These are the teachings of our fathers, and I was now old enough to keep them in my mind.

After the invitation to eat, I jumped into the hot oven and threw out the corn as quickly as possible. Irene and the others came, stripped the husks from the hot ears, ate all they could, and selected a few choice ears as their personal possessions. Whoever was lucky enough to find the mother ears removed the prayer feathers and ate the corn. I later took the prayer offerings into the field and buried them with the breath line pointing east.

When the husking was completed, we loaded our possessions and returned to the village, where Irene took several trays of sweet corn to our relatives. The women came to our house, each bringing an awl fashioned from the front upper leg of a sheep. A hole was bored through the stems of the corn, which was then strung with yucca fiber and hung in bunches outside the house to dry. I was happy to provide sweet corn for my wife and her family, and was pleased to hear my name praised highly.

In October I harvested two wagonloads of corn, which my wife helped me gather and store in her house. I had worked hard all year and enjoyed very few holidays except the dance days. Most of my work had been in the fields and with the herd. I had brought a pail of water for Irene occasionally, but I rarely cooked or washed dishes. I did not know how to sew and weave like the other men, and I never thought of making baskets and pots.

About the first of November the women put on the Ooqol ceremony[5] in the Howeove kiva in order that something good might happen to the people. My grandfather was a high officer and one of the few men in the society. He assisted with the erection of the altar and for eight days he went to the kiva to make pahos, smoke, sing, and pray. On the ninth day he supervised the foot race, and the women put on an excellent dance in the plaza. We men watched the dancers and struggled for the gifts which they threw to the people. I was not as quick on my feet as the others, but I managed to secure three baskets, five plaques, a sifter, a coffee pot, and four pie plates, besides some Cracker Jacks and a package of Bull Durham tobacco. I needed these things very badly because there were four women in Irene's household who quarreled a great deal, and it had been suggested that Irene and I should move to another house. I did not enter into the women's arguments and got along very well with Irene's father. But one day Irene told me that the women had repaired a place next to the special Fire Clan house and that we were to move there. I was displeased, because I did not possess enough equipment and supplies to support a wife.

After we moved, I stored the corn in our new house, hauled wood on the burros, and continued to herd. In December I took part in

5. For a detailed account see H. R. Voth, *The Oraibi Oáqöl Ceremony* (Anthrop. Series, Field Mus. Nat. Hist., 1903), Vol. VI, No. 1, pp. 1–46.

Soyal, observed the rules of continence, and herded part of the time; but I was careful not to hunt rabbits during this period, because a Soyal member is not allowed to kill any game while he is attending the prayers and making strong wishes for all living creatures to multiply upon the earth.

On the day after Soyal I took my feathers and prayer sticks and went to the corral accompanied by my dog with a feather around his neck. I opened the gate, sprinkled a corn-meal path, placed my paho on the ground, and led my sheep over it toward the rising sun, silently praying for my herd to increase and prosper. When all had passed over the paho, I fastened it to the fence and followed my sheep through the snow. Behind me was a full year of married life, but I yet wondered whether I could support a family and how soon I would become a father.

Our life was hard the next year, 1912. The season was dry and the winds high; the worms and rats worked havoc with our crops; we did not raise much wool, and it sold cheaply. Frank, who was keeping my horse at Shipaulovi, let it wander off and fall into the hands of the Navahos. My clan uncle gave me a burro, but it was a poor substitute. Irene shelled our corn and took it to Hubbell's store on her back to trade for groceries. We had to kill our sheep to feed ourselves. As I braced myself for harder work, I thought again of all the money— perhaps $100—that I had spent on women before my marriage. I realized that I was supporting my wife very poorly, and wondered again whether I had made the mistake of my life in marrying instead of returning to school. I thought of going back to Sherman even then— for Mettie was still there.

When in midsummer I learned that Mettie had recently returned to Moenkopi, I regretted my marriage more than ever. And as I hoed corn in the hot sun and thought about my hard life, I decided to hire a horse to cultivate my crop and go to Moenkopi for a Katcina dance. Dennis came over for supper and was interested in my plan, but Irene talked strongly against it and actually implied that the chief attraction in Moenkopi was not the dance at all. Dennis laughed at the idea and promised to keep a close watch on me. During the night I dreamed that as I sat on a housetop in Moenkopi, a Katcina touched me on the shoulder to signify that I had been chosen for clown work. I felt embarrassed but heard the sweet voice of a girl from another housetop, saying, "My lover, I am glad that you are caught; be a good clown." The shouting of the people awakened me; and without disturbing Irene, I studied my dream and wondered if it could come true.

After breakfast Dennis and I borrowed two burros from my father-in-law and set out for Moenkopi, reaching there by sunset. I spent the night with my clan people, smoked and prayed with my ceremonial father in the kiva next morning, and went with two other men to gather juniper boughs for the ceremony. In the afternoon, as I walked out beyond the mesa point where once I had attempted suicide, I spied Mettie going out to toilet. She smiled and waved, but we had no chance for words. I passed her house in the evening and had just greeted her when her mother came out and talked so long that I left.

On the following day Mettie and I stood in crowds on different housetops, watching the Katcinas and smiling across to each other every time they did anything the least bit funny. I felt young and single again, but occasionally realized with a start that I was actually married. At noon Frank Siemptewa in Katcina costume crept up behind me and captured me for clown duty. The people laughed, and one of my aunts said that she was glad that I was caught. I went to the kiva with four others to prepare for clown work. All afternoon Mettie made me happy by watching closely and laughing at every little thing that I did. We took our food to the kiva at sunset and went to the stream for a bath; and as I returned by Mettie's house, she waved. I passed her house again after dark, and she must have been watching, for as I returned from toilet she met me in the path a short distance from the village. We stepped to one side, shook hands, and embraced without delay. She chided me for getting married and said, "But you are still mine." I agreed, but reminded her that I had just completed clown work and had to stay pure. Just then a woman came down the path, and I stepped into a chicken house out of sight. Mettie returned to the village with the intruder, and at first I was angry; but on second thought, I was glad, for—unless my Guardian Spirit had checked me on the spot—I might have been tempted to break an important Hopi rule. When Dennis and I returned to Oraibi, Irene seemed very glad to hear of my clown work, and at the end of four days she was quite nice to me.

After Niman, in which I danced as a Katcina in Oraibi, we looked forward to the Snake dance. When the members of the Snake society went toward Mount Beautiful, searching for serpents, I took the burros and went in the same direction for wood, hoping to be seen and captured. As I returned, I saw several Snake members talking together. One man raised a metal tool and hit it with a stick to notify his partners to assemble. I moved right along with my burros, thinking of an acceptance speech in case I was captured for membership. As I reached the crest of a little hill and looked back, one man started to follow, but returned to the group, greatly disappointing me.

Two days after the dance I noticed my clan brother Carl, who was a Snake member, rounding up his burros to go for wood. Saddling my own burro, I took a lunch and started with him. When we had gone about five miles, I said, "Brother, what did you fellows think of me on the day that you hunted snakes and found me going for wood? Did anyone want to catch me?" He replied, "I called them together and inquired if any man wished to catch my clan brother, but no one seemed willing. When I asked them why, they said that they had no buckskin to make moccasins for you. Later, my grandfather said he had an old pair of moccasins that he could spare, and started to catch you, but decided that you had gone too far." I thanked him for telling me and tried to show no disappointment. It would have been better for me to have become a member of the Snake society when I was a boy, because snakes never bite young boys whose minds are strong and pure and who have not slept with a woman. I had often noticed the good behavior of snakes held in the mouths of small boys, and now I wondered if I were pure enough for that work.

That same year a man was bitten by a snake in one of the dances and nearly lost his life. He must have had a very bad heart. When the dancers are not pure or do not pay close attention to their business, the snakes get angry. If a dancer has slept with a woman during the ceremony he will become sick or unable to perform, or the snake may bite him in the dance. Once a leader was bitten while hunting for snakes; and the old people tell of men who have died of snakebites when they have failed to do their duty. I decided that perhaps it was better for me to stay out.

The land was very dry, the crops suffered, and even the Snake dance failed to bring much rain. We tried to discover the reason for our plight, and remembered the Rev. Voth who had stolen so many of our ceremonial secrets and had even carried off sacred images and altars to equip a museum and become a rich man. When he had worked here in my boyhood, the Hopi were afraid of him and dared not lay their hands on him or any other missionary, lest they be jailed by the Whites. During the ceremonies this wicked man would force his way into the kiva and write down everything that he saw. He wore shoes with solid heels, and when the Hopi tried to put him out of the kiva he would kick them. He came back to Oraibi on a visit and took down many more names. Now I was grown, educated in the Whites' school, and had no fear of this man. When I heard that he was in my mother's house I went over and told him to get out. I said, "You break the commandments of your own God. He has ordered you never to steal or to have any other gods before him. He has told you to avoid all graven images; but you have stolen ours and set them up in your museum. This makes you a thief and an idolator who can never go to heaven." I knew the Hopi Cloud People despised this man, and even though he was now old and wore a long beard, I had a strong desire to seize him by the collar and kick him off the mesa.

Since our crops were poor, our food short, and salt scarce, my father and I decided to journey to Zuñi Lake for salt, and try to bring rain upon our drooping plants. The Crier Chief announced from the housetop: "In ten days the strong men will go for salt. Those who wish to join them will gather their burros and mend their sacks and moccasins." I made pahos, prayed for success in the expedition, and slept apart from Irene for four nights.

Early one morning we loaded ten burros with supplies, placed a road-marker on the trail with prayers, and set out, looking back now and then to see if others followed. At the spring near Second Mesa we made sacrifice, drank, scooped up water in our hands and threw it toward Oraibi, asking for rain. Following the old trail to Zuñi Lake, we camped the first night southwest of Awatobi ruins, the second night at Pussy Willow spring, and reached the railroad by noon. There we traded a blanket for groceries and about $12 in cash. I surprised the trader with my ability to speak English, and received a gift from him of soda crackers, canned beans, and tomatoes. We could eat modern food on the journey to Zuñi Lake, for this is not as dangerous territory as Salt Canyon near the House of the Dead.

Crossing the railroad, we proceeded to the Zuñi forests, where I killed a jack rabbit with my rifle, and we camped in the tall junipers. The next day we climbed a steep zigzag trail into deep woods, passed waterfalls, and came to an old corral, where the Zuñi used to catch antelopes by the power of secret charm songs which drew the animals to them and caused the corral walls to rise up by magic. My father reminded me that the Hopi knew magic songs strong enough to attract women as well as antelopes.

After breakfast on the following day my father poured water in a melon rind, wetted and kneaded some sweet corn meal, divided it in halves, and placed his part on a sack. While we were off guard, a burro ate it, which angered us, but we did not punish the dumb animal by cutting off its tail or an ear, as some Hopis might have done. We called that burro Chicken Hawk thereafter, because the beast had eaten sacred dough prepared for the spirit bird. I divided my dough with my father and smiled as I walked about a mile from camp to run a race with him. We began and I took my time like a rabbit racing a tortoise, knowing that I would win. We raced up a mesa with the dough and placed it with prayer feathers in a small hole for the Hawk deity. As we moved down the southern slope, my father said, "There is a long slab of stone; jump upon it and spring to the opposite side." As we completed the jump he said, "Well, we have performed the rites correctly, and our reward will be rain."

We proceeded with the burros through another juniper forest and came upon a pond fenced with barbed wire. A Mexican met us and said that he would sell us all the salt we wanted for $2 or $3. But since we had prayer offerings for the Hopi gods, we had to go on to the lake of course, make sacrifices, and gather salt in the prescribed manner; otherwise we would get no rain and run into a lot of bad luck.

We continued to the spring where some cowboys were camping and ate lunch with them. These Mexicans were fine, civilized fellows, and gave us a hunk of fresh beef. After lunch we placed prayer offerings in the spring and prayed for rain. The cowboys seemed to appreciate this, saying they needed rain as much as we, and showed that they were Whites with good sense, who could understand the rain-making business.

We traveled on and camped in open country where we had to keep a fire going all night because of coyotes. There we cooked the meat and ate as much as we could, for my father said we must get rid of it before we gathered salt. The next morning I killed a fat prairie dog, and we reached the great lake where we deposited our prayer offering at the shrine of the Twin War gods.

We went to the Mexican village near by and asked for a room where we could store our things. The women gave us some food for lunch, and we bought two loaves of bread. The Mexicans took all our piki and promised to bake bread in return. We cooked the dog over coals and had a good meal before we took our equipment and returned to the edge of the lake, accompanied by some Mexicans. There my father said, "Now we will have intercourse with the Salt Woman who lives in the lake." I felt embarrassed before the Mexicans, expecting them to laugh or show disgust like other Whites. But I removed my clothes, prayed, placed my prayer stick on the waves, got down on my belly in the water, and went through motions of copulation, repeating, "Now I am having intercourse with my godmother, Masenimka." Before I had left Oraibi I had chosen this old aunt to be my sexual partner in the ceremony. When I finished, I arose and informed my father that I had enjoyed making love with his mother's sister. He replied, "Thanks, I have lain with my aunt, your mother-in-law's sister." At the completion of this rite the Mexicans said, "Now we will soon have plenty of rain." I was surprised at their wisdom and respect.

The wind grew stronger as I waded out into the water and tried to gather salt. We had an unlucky day; the wind was so strong and cold and the water was so rough that we could gather only enough salt to fill two twenty-four-pound flour sacks. Therefore we decided to buy salt from the Mexicans and purchased enough to load the strong burros with two hundred pounds each and the weaker ones with one hundred. Then we tied a prayer feather to each burro's tail to increase his strength and traveled homeward as fast as we could walk, reaching Second Mesa at noon on the fifth day. The people were glad to see us, for it was already raining. We covered the salt with canvas, and that night my father told the complete story of the journey. When the rains had ceased on the second day in Shipaulovi, we packed our burros and set out for Oraibi, reaching the foot of the mesa in midafternoon. There we sprinkled meal, turned the road-marker, and prayed. Then we took some salt on our backs and carried it up the mesa just as the old timers used to do. My old godmother and my father's aunt, the women we had named in love-making, met us saying, "Thanks, thanks." We gave them our driving sticks, and Masenimka took my rifle and led me through the plaza to her house, where she fed me. My brother and others brought up our burros, placed the salt under shelter, and covered it with a woman's wedding blanket. After eating, I started to take my driving stick and gun, but Masenimka said, "Leave them here, and I will return them to you tomorrow after I have washed your head." I went to my house where Irene rejoiced at my safe return. And that night I told relatives and friends the complete story of our journey. I stayed away from my wife's bed for four days and rubbed my sore feet every night with a hot stone, thinking that I probably would never go for salt again.

At harvest I was disappointed with my corn crop, realized that I was a poor farmer, and wondered whether I would ever be able to support a family. Irene sold a black dress that my father wove for her and used the money to buy food. She also cut up her fine buckskin moccasins—her wedding gift—and sold them piece by piece. Later she sold her wedding robe for $15, the one that she should have saved for a burial shroud, and spent the money for food and a fancy Spanish shawl. We went all the way to Winslow with five burros to do this shopping. I had no right to say what should be done with Irene's wedding property; but I clearly felt that I was a poor provider and wondered if there could be some person against us. I entered a store in Winslow to shop and heard a Hopi man ask for rat poison and use such big English words that I knew he was a Two-Heart, for these wicked people have a mysterious command of language; and although of different races and nationalities, they are able to understand each other perfectly at their underworld conventions. I left the store quickly without trading.

Before very long Ira lost his wife. Blanche became very sick, and the Hopi doctors gave her up. I was fond of her and went over in the evening to advise her, the customary way to help a sick person. When I entered, her father, Joe, was on the floor holding her in his arms. Ira and others were eating. I tried to eat something but I felt too unhappy and told Joe to eat while I looked after Blanche. Sitting on the floor with my back to the wall, I held Blanche up against me and tried to talk to her, advising her to put bad thoughts out of her mind, face east again, and get well, for we all loved her. She would not answer; and when I noticed that her face was cold and her mouth numb, I wrapped her in a blanket. Joe finished eating, came over, and said, "Talayesva has come. It is his wish that you get well, and he is advising you to pull yourself through this sickness." Blanche failed to talk, so he scolded her, saying: "Well, we are doing our best to take care of you, going without sleep, watching you day and night, and begging you to brace up." With that he struck her once, but it did no good. I sat in the dimly lighted room and held her in my arms while the others waited, or tried to sleep. Finally I placed my hand in her bosom and discovered that she was getting cold. Then her family advised me to lay her on the earthen floor. When she died, we all cried. I said, "I will have nothing more to do with her. I tried to help her, but she would not listen. I think I will go." As I started out, her father said, "Wait, we are all tired and weak from watching; please help us bury the body." "I will be glad to help in the daylight," I replied, and sat down by the door.

When Blanche stopped breathing, we covered her with a blanket for a while; then the mother washed the girl's hair in yucca suds. We raised the body to a sitting position and Joe combed the hair, after which we put on a new dress, fastened prayer feathers to her hands and hair to take along to our dear ones, placed a cotton mask over her face to represent a cloud, wrapped her in her ceremonial wedding robe, and bound the bundle with a rope. In the early dawn Ira and Joe lifted the corpse to my back and told me to lead the way past the Oraibi Rock and down the mesa to the sandy slope of the burial grounds. They gathered up the bedding and followed, Ira helping to balance the load so that I might not fall over rough stones and bring bad luck upon us. Placing my burden on the ground, I took the shovel and pick from Joe and began digging the grave just as our Sun god appeared over the horizon. We dug down about seven feet, hollowed out a cave, placed the corpse in a sitting position facing east, filled the hole with stones and earth, placed some large stones on top, and set up the "grave ladder." Joe made a short speech to his daughter urging her to go to her loved ones. Returning to the house, we took a bath and purified our clothes and bodies in the smoke of juniper and piñon sap.

After four days Ira moved back into the Sun Clan house with our mother, father, grandfather, Naquima, Perry, my brother of thirteen, and Mabel, my sister of eight. The death of Blanche was very sad to me. She was a cheerful, quiet, industrious, good-natured girl, and I loved her like a sister. She had died in her youth, and we wondered again who could be against us.

One day as I gathered the burros, I spied Nathaniel,[6] Chief of the Ahl society, wandering in the field in an aimless manner and crying. When he saw me, he ran on ahead to the village, taking short cuts. Although he had acted strangely for some time and the Whites had said that he was insane, I wondered if he might be a Two-Heart and up to some mischief. Several old men agreed with me when I told them what I had seen. Sure enough, within a short time Nathaniel's wife died, which was clear proof that Masau'u had called him, and in his distress he had decided to kill his wife by magic in order to prolong his own life. Other people came to the same conclusion and began to look upon him with suspicion. We avoided all dealings with him except in the performance of ceremonial duties. I realized more than ever that the old people were right in their claims that the Two-

6. A fictitious name is substituted by request.

Hearts cause most of the trouble in the world, and that every person has someone against him. It may be a next-door neighbor, a very close relative, or a kiva brother. I had been told these things from my childhood, but they meant more to me year by year; and I began to suspect some of my neighbors.

12

Prosperity and Adversity:
1913–1927

MY MOTHER AND MY WIFE carried babies at the same time—but my mother was much bigger. One evening my young sister Mabel came running with news that our mother was in labor. I hurried over and found my father and grandfather with her. No midwife was called, for my grandfather was a good doctor. I was told to squat behind her, hold my right arm about her waist with my hand pressed to her belly, and place my left hand against the small of her back. Whenever she strained, I pressed down with my right, and in with my left hand, hoping soon to hear the cry of a baby. Sometimes I could feel the bones crack in the small of her back, but she bore up bravely.

When the baby's head appeared I ran to fetch Joe, the father of Ira's wife, who was expert in removing afterbirths. Without knocking I rushed in and said, "Father, my mother is having a baby, come and do your job." Returning quickly, I found the baby boy on the sandy floor, still attached to my mother. Joe entered, knelt behind her, put his knees against her back, pressed down on her belly with both hands, and then raised and shook her, telling her to gag herself with her fingers. We waited and watched, straining ourselves to expel the placenta. Finally it came, and in great relief I gathered up the waste and sand and took them out without letting any blood touch me. I was thankful to be a man, felt very sorry for all women, remembered how near I had come to being one, and wondered whether I could ever have stood so much pain.

From the placenta pile I hastened to fetch my aunt Kewanmainim, my father's sister who was the wife of Poleyestewa. Masenimka, my own godmother, was still alive, but too old and feeble now. Kewanmainim came through the dark with her two ears of corn, some cold water in a pail, and a small blanket. When she had finished her work and the baby was asleep, I went to tell Irene the news and to get a nap before daylight.

For many days thereafter I was sorry for my mother and anxious for my wife. I thought about babies and marveled at the manner in which they are made. I had known for a long time that they are produced from the semen of a man's spinal cord and the blood from a woman's heart; and that both parents must work faithfully to complete a good offspring. I paid close attention to Irene, made a doll for her at the Powamu ceremony, slept with her regularly until she was large and felt strong movements, and was careful to observe all pregnancy rules. I wanted to do my part toward making a good-sized baby. Since I was as fond of girls as of boys, I made no strong wishes for a son, neither did I ask my Sun god to do anything about it. Some noticed that Irene's cheeks were rosy, and said it would be a girl.

Although anxious for Irene, I was glad to have her pregnant; for she had been slow in getting a baby, and I knew that some women are barren. I had also heard that a few are half-men, having testicles inside their bodies. Once I had a sheep that was barren, butchered it, and found two hard balls the size of my thumb. I opened these, studied them, and was convinced that they were little testicles. When I told other men about it, they agreed that the sheep was like some barren women. My grandfather said there were other causes of barrenness and that he knew a few remedies for it, but did not tell me the special ones. He said that prayers helped, and that the gift of a doll to a woman at the Powamu ceremony, or at other ceremonial observances, might cause her to have a baby. He also spoke of a "penis plant," resembling the male organs which, when touched to the private parts of man or woman, greatly increases sexual vigor and insures fertility. I heard others say that some Hopi doctors used a "strong medicine" and then slept with the women themselves. I was glad that it was now plain to everyone that Irene could have a baby and that I could be a father.

I did not want twins. But I realized that if the Mother god wished to start two babies in one womb, there was no power on earth that could stop her. Therefore I advised Irene to see the same old doctor who had twisted me into one child so that, in case she carried twins, he could put them together before it was too late. The medicine man assured her that there was only one child, but said that it was coiled like a snake and needed to be straightened out, which he was able to do.

My anxiety for the baby continued. It was well known that an unborn child can be spoiled easily; or it may even feel offended about something and refuse to come out. Old Naquima reminded me of what had happened to him: Masatewa, an Oraibi man of the Lizard Clan, had visited my grandmother in his Katcina costume after a dance and had slept with her, thus spoiling the baby in her womb. Naquima had often said to me with tears rolling down his cheeks, "If I had had good hands and feet like yours, perhaps I would be a rich man now, with plenty of corn and a herd. Sometimes I am so angry that I want to shoot the man who got into my mother and ruined me." I also remembered our clan sister with a clubhand. Before her birth her father set traps for a porcupine and cut off its forefeet. A Hopi doctor examined the baby and asked the father, "Have you injured any animal?" When he heard of the porcupine, he said, "No wonder this baby is deformed. The child is lucky to have one good hand."

When I felt myself growing weak from the effects of Irene's bad breath on my body, I reminded her that a decent woman is careful about her breath when pregnant. I also encouraged her to work hard and pointed out that exercise makes for easy delivery. Yet I worried about childbirth, fearing that the baby would grow too large. As the time drew near, I went almost daily at sunrise to the mesa edge to pray. I was also careful not to flirt with another woman, hoping that by strict self-denial I might lighten the birth pangs and encourage the baby to come forth.

The birth was not bad. I was away, gathering wood with the burros, and my grandfather and Irene's mother helped with the delivery. My own mother bathed the baby and claimed it as a "child of the Sun Clan." When I returned, I was pleased to look upon my little daughter, thankful to know that my wife had been spared from death, and glad that I was away when it all happened. The men teased me, but I was proud of myself and Irene.

On the twentieth day my mother and her clan sister named the baby Tewahoyenim (Sun Movements); but the white field nurse, who made frequent visits and gave too much advice, called her Minnie. I stayed away from my wife's bed for twenty days longer, made love to no woman, and was careful to raise no arguments with Irene; for such conduct is known to worry a baby and injure its health.

The child was never very well. Food would not stay on its stomach, but came out both ways, sloppylike. I took her to the Hopi doctors, but their medicine would not stay down either, which was a sign that the baby would die; for as long as there is hope their medicine sticks. The field nurse wanted to try some new-fangled remedies, but I discouraged her.

Our baby died in four or five months. Irene cried pitifully while my grandfather helped me bathe the poor little thing and wrap it in a blanket. We placed no cotton on its face and did not bury it in the regular cemetery, for we wished the child to return shortly. Everyone knows that if a baby dies, a young mother may bear the same child again, but of opposite sex. I took the little bundle in my arms and went sadly with my grandfather to the cliff west of the village, where perhaps a thousand babies are buried. When I asked him where to bury my child, he replied, "Drop it in a rock crevice and cover it with stones." "A dog might get it," I replied. "I will go down to the sandy section and dig out a tomb." I found a large boulder with a cave below, dug out the sand, and made a hollow space with plenty of room. We placed my baby there, with head pointing west and feet east, closed up the tomb with rocks, and braced them with heavy stones. Then I set a digging stick upright in the pile of stones to make a ladder upon which the baby's spirit could climb out on the fourth day, return to our house, and wait in the ceiling for a chance to be born again. When we returned from the grave, my mother prepared a bath for us, and we smoked our bodies.

After two days I inspected the tomb to make sure that no animal had disturbed it, and on the third day I went again with food and pahos. I placed the pahos on the tomb, set the food on the stones by the grave ladder, and invited my little daughter to arise, eat, climb out, and fly back to our house early next day. I spoke only a few words and said nothing about her going to the House of the Dead, for I wanted my baby to stay around. I did not tell Irene where to find the tomb, fearing that she might feel sad or angry with me sometime, go out there, and wish to die.

After our baby's death some of the Fire Clan people made unfriendly remarks, implying that I was unlucky with children. I traced my conduct thoroughly to discover any mistake on my part that might have caused this sorrow. Finding nothing wrong with my record, I realized that someone was against me. When I asked a Hopi doctor about this, he agreed that a Two-Heart had killed my child, but insisted that it was better for me not to know who had committed the crime. He did tell me that the evil person was a close relative of Irene. To kill an innocent baby was an awful thing to do. The doctor said that this man had received a call from Masau'u, that the only way he could escape death was to kill a close relative, and that, since my baby was a girl, her death would probably give him four more years to live. No doubt this wretched man had cried alone in the field, wondering what to do; but before others he appeared bright and happy. I remembered the Two-Hearts on my death journey and how much I had already suffered on their account. I burned with anger, but I knew enough now to keep my mouth shut and tried to appear cheerful.

We soon discovered the murderer—Irene's uncle. Lomaleteotewa, a very old man, told Irene's mother, when he was dying, that she had two brothers who were Two-Hearts. "I am a witch too," he said. "I have been killing people to save my life but I did not kill Irene's baby. I am tired of taking lives and I'm going to die. Keep a close watch on Kewanventewa." When Irene told me this, I tried to keep the news to myself; and I watched the man who killed our baby. I avoided him as much as possible, but I was very polite whenever he was around, hoping thus to gain his pity and soften his spite.

In a short time my dear old godmother, Masenimka, died. She was very old and had been ailing for months. I was called to her house and found her on the floor. She said feebly, "My boy, I love you and want to follow your advice, but my strength is gone and I must die." With her bony hand in mine, she cried, looked into my face, and said, "Be good and be wise." My aunt, Poleyestewa's wife, told me to go before death came; and that same night she helped my father prepare the body for burial. My father took the corpse on his back and was followed by his sister with the bedding. I stayed out of sight. I loved Masenimka and resolved to make pahos for her at Soyal as long as I lived, trusting that she would return often to Oraibi with the clouds and drop a little rain.

We had a hard summer but rains came in August and there were many peaches in September. Masawyestewa, the husband of my mother's sister, loaded his wagon with my grandfather's peaches and asked my brother Perry and me to go with him to Winslow. We overtook other Hopis in a wagon at the Little Colorado River, and among them was Freddie, the man who had been with me in the clown work at Moenkopi, and who was now married. We camped outside the town and in the evening Freddie said, "Don, let's try a prostitute." "That suits me fine," I replied. I had long wanted to make love with a white woman, but had never dared to attempt it while at school. We stopped at a movie and bought Perry a ticket to the show, for he was only thirteen. Then we strolled along and spied some good-looking girls who smiled from a porch. "I want the fat one," Freddie whispered. "I'll choose one about my own size," I replied, "neither fat nor skinny." The girls beckoned and invited us inside where they lined up and seemed eager to be chosen. Freddie picked a big, round girl with black hair. I chose a tall one with a very fair skin.

My girl led me into another room and said, "Undress." When I did this, she pushed back my foreskin, examined me carefully, and said, "O.K., two dollars." The bed had a sunken place in the center which caused pain to my back. On account of this, I rested. "Say, boy, you've had your money's worth," said the girl. "Get up, or I'll call a police." As she got off the bed I protested, "This is not fair." "Give me another dollar and do whatever you like," she replied. I told her to put the mattress on the floor and I would do it. She took my dollar, but seemed slow about the mattress. I got impatient, jerked it off the bed, and grabbed her roughly. She became very friendly, complimented me on my powers, and invited me to "hurry back." I said, "You have charged me three dollars when your price is two; may I return for one?" She agreed. Freddie had heard our conversation from another room; and when we left the house we had a big laugh.

The next evening we went back to our girls. Freddie chose a different one; but I took advantage of my dollar bargain. When we were in the same room as before, my girl asked for two dollars again. But I reminded her that "honesty is the best policy," and she let me put the mattress on the floor. Before I left, she asked me to bring a Hopi blanket on my next trip to town, and as a special favor she let me kiss her.

In about two weeks Freddie and I went to Winslow again to get a load of freight for Hubbell's store. We went straight to the brothel and found that our old girls had been replaced by younger ones worth three dollars. I kept my blanket and paid cash to a fleshy girl of sixteen who inspected me, assured me that she was examined by a doctor every two weeks, and helped put the mattress on the floor.

Returning from Winslow, we camped at the Little Colorado River near a Navaho hogan, and spied a good-looking woman alone. Since Freddie could speak some Navaho, we walked over. The young squaw was friendly, said she was a widow, and laughed. Finally she told Freddie that we could pay her in flour, explaining that her small son was asleep, and the rest of her party had gone to a squaw dance. Freddie said, "I will be first." "I don't think so, Freddie," I replied. "You know I am a little older than you." He yielded to age and stepped outside. The young squaw was very coöperative and rocked back and forth so as to make the experience extremely short—leading me to wonder if it were a special Navaho way. Stepping outside, I told Freddie that it was his turn. A little later I eased back the edge of the blanket across the door and peeped in to see that Freddie was treated the same way. When they called me back in, I was surprised to hear this seventeen-year-old girl speaking good English. We talked and laughed about our school days for an hour or so; and then took turns again. As we rode over the desert next day, we compared Navaho and white women and agreed they were both fine in their own way.

When I had been home for a few days, different men asked me, "Don, have you ever heard of 'double pay'?" Then they would describe an experience like mine with the first white girl, smile, and ask, "Has anything like this ever happened to you?" I acted surprised at first. But someone mentioned this subject to me almost every day; and finally my wife asked me about it. I denied it as lightly as possible, looked up Freddie, and said: "I have been hearing something disgraceful. Have you not learned that when men are together they do not hide their private lives from each other; but that it is a rule for partners never to repeat such things to the women? I thought you were my friend and expected you to keep such things in your heart." He hung his head and acted sorry, but it was too late. Irene kept harping on the subject, cried a little, discouraged love-making for a time, and nearly drove me out of the house. Finally I had to admit the truth, act very sorry, and make a promise. After a few weeks she got over her anger, teased me about what happened, and actually joked me about it before other women; but I told her to cut that out, for I had heard enough of it. It was a long time before I could joke about "double pay."

I worked as hard as ever, but it seemed that I could not get ahead without horses. So during the winter I got some turquoise and shells and spent my spare time drilling and polishing two strings of beads. I traded them to a Navaho for a little studhorse named Blackie which I bound with ropes, and asked the Navaho to castrate. I hated to cut him, but I did not mind branding his hide with a hot iron.

I also purchased a mare for $20 which I earned hauling wood for Whites; but she was lazy and barren, so I traded her for a good-pulling bay horse. Then I purchased a secondhand wagon from my father-in-law for a set of earrings, a Hopi bridal belt which was made for my sister Gladys, and two black dresses woven by my father. A little later I used my team to draw the road scraper for the Agency, worked on the dam near Oraibi, and helped build a house in order to buy two more horses. Then I braided a fancy rawhide whip and became an expert driver of a four-horse team. I used these horses to herd, cultivate, and harvest my crops, haul wood and soft coal, draw the wood scraper for the government, and haul some freight for the trading post. Whenever I hitched them to the wagon to take Irene and our friends to Katcina dances, I wore what jewelry I possessed, put on a brightly colored headband, and drove in a fast trot, congratulating myself and feeling like a man who had climbed from the valley to the peak of a high mountain.

The horses made my work easier and led me to feel that I was a bigger businessman; but they also changed my daily routine. It became my habit when I arose in the morning to wash my face and hands, straighten and delouse my long, silky, black hair with a fine-tooth comb, and walk to the east edge of the mesa to defecate and to pray. Then I would climb a housetop and look for my horses. If they were in sight, I went for them before breakfast. Whenever I could not see them, I ate first and sometimes searched several hours or even a half-day to round them up, especially if a horse had lost its hobble. Water was a special problem, and during droughts I had to drive the horses long distances to springs. In winter I would break the ice and let them drink from pools on the rocky ledge. It took a great deal of my time caring for these horses. They had to be hobbled out on the mesa every evening to feed upon the scanty vegetation, for I had no money to buy hay. I was responsible for any damage they might do to a neighbor's crops and had to watch them closely through rain or shine, winter and summer. I had so much trouble keeping track of them that I tried fastening bells to their necks, but the Navahos stole all the bells.

Many people liked Blackie and wanted to buy him; but I would always say, "A fellow can't afford to sell his best horse." But one day in November my horse was frightened on the edge of the mesa south-west of the village and jumped to a lower shelf. I followed him and got hold of the rope, but he ran backward over the cliff and landed ten feet below on his tailbone. I hired three men with picks and shovels to open a path to level ground, but the horse was badly hurt. The wound became infected, and when I opened the flesh and found broken bones, I shot him out of pity. But we could not eat the meat because of the infection. Coyotes came to feast on the carcass, and I caught three in steel traps, and sold their hides for $15.

My father Kalnimptewa heard of my success, asked me to trap the wildcats that pilfered his herd, and offered a sheep for a cat. I took traps to his corral and found a dead lamb. Following the trail of blood, I came to a cave beneath a large rock, crawled in, found two eyes glaring in the dark, and heard a growl that sent me scrambling out to set traps at the opening. I caught this cat in a few days, killed it with my rifle, and saw where a coyote had dragged another trap. Two miles away I found it caught in a bush, and crept up to the tired coyote. Petting its tail, I gently moved up to its shoulders and said softly, "Well, coyote, I know you were sent by your Mother to be trapped in answer to my prayers." Then quickly seizing its neck, I dug a hole into the ground, pushed its mouth and nose in, and smothered it, for it is not right to club a coyote. I made pahos for it, tied one to each leg, placed one on its breast, and said, "Take these prayer feathers to your people and tell your Mother to send you back to us with other game." During the season I caught several more cats, coyotes, foxes, skunks, and badgers, traded their hides for cash or beads, and looked about for another horse.

I bought a little bay stallion and called him "Longtail" because he always carried a dangling penis. But when the government veterinarian was testing blood for a special disease, Longtail was condemned and ordered shot. I let a friend ride my horse to Moenkopi; but the doctor, a small, tough army man, ordered me to get it back in two days or furnish proof of its death—or else go to jail. I was angry and told him to shoot me and be done with it, knowing that the law would not let him do that, for I was neither a murderer nor a thief. Finally the doctor agreed to allow me four days to kill my horse. When I started to Moenkopi, my friend returned with word that my horse was sick on the road. I told him that I was in danger of losing my own head and set out to get the horse, thinking that if he had died I could skin off the brand and fetch it for proof. But I found him alive and led him back with a rope around his neck to save mine. The school principal said, "Well, Don, you just saved your life." We went together to the Oraibi Wash where he checked the brand and raised his rifle to fire. I turned away with a lump in my throat, and when I looked again, my horse was dying. So I stripped off the hide, dragged it to the trading post, and sold it for 75¢. But I collected $25 from the government in payment for the life of Longtail—and bought a fine black horse.

I loved my horses and learned to tell their age by their teeth, to treat their sores with bear grease, and to quiet their spirits with kind words. I never failed to tie prayer feathers to their tails at Soyal, and when a horse had the belly ache, I learned to put salt in its mouth, tie a piece of tobacco to its bridle bit, and hold a burning rag under its nose. If I did not see early improvement, I would pare my fingernails closely, rub my hand and arm with grease or vaseline, take a piece of raw onion, and push it into the horse's anus as far as I could reach. Usually there would be a bowel movement and return of the onion in about half an hour.

Dealing in horses and going long distances for wood brought me in closer touch with the Navahos. They were a pest that overran the land. A stray horse would tempt the best of them, and a tool left in the field was as good as lost. There were usually more of them than of Hopi on our own land and we had to make the best of their company with the help of Uncle Sam. I learned to keep a close watch on them, but it was a good rule to be friendly, to feed them occasionally, and to expect the same hospitality in return. Whenever Irene hesitated to feed a Navaho, I warned her, "That is not right, for the man needs to eat, and some day I may feel hunger in his hogan." Sometimes as many as seven or eight Navahos spent the night with us, but if they neglected to bring along fresh mutton now and then, they soon found "cold coffee." What I wanted most from the Navahos were wood, mutton, blankets, jewelry, medicine, and horses.

I soon formed a close friendship with Neschelles, a Navaho medicine man. We exchanged gifts; he stopped at my house when he came to trade; and whenever I went for wood I spent the night with him. We saw so much of each other that he taught me to speak Navaho.

One evening when I stopped at his hogan, he had gone away to treat a sick person, but his wife and sister-in-law fed me and made me feel at home. When the fire was low, I made my bed outside their hogan and tried to sleep. But before long, I felt a jerk on my blanket and a gentle hand on my shoulder. The sister-in-law had crept out alone, in a love-making mood. I finally sent her back into the hogan with a fine set of turquoise earrings and $3, for I hoped to see her again.

Like a true Hopi man, I realized more and more that a wife is not enough and that I enjoyed these squaws. Although Navaho men are generally unlucky with our women, we are fond of theirs and very successful with them. In fact, we like to boast of these affairs. At Katcina dances it is common for one Hopi to say to another, "Do you see that fine squaw with turquoise earrings and the fancy skirt? Well, I have had her five times." Or when we traveled together, we entertained one another with tales of our Navaho adventures. Now I had a third to add to the count of Dezba Johnson and the young widow on the road from Winslow.

From time to time I hired a man to herd and watch my horses so that I could go to Moenkopi for a few days and earn some money. I saw Polehongsie and had a good laugh when I learned that Robert Talas had followed his own advice—he had married the wrinkle face, rolled her on his sheepskin, and left her. I had nothing to do with the widow. Euella had married Jimmie, who ran a small store, and I had no more affairs with her, although I often stopped at her house. Mettie was also married, but I managed to see her in private—perhaps a dozen times—and paid her in cash.

Once, after a trip to Moenkopi, some old gossipers told my wife that I was seeing Mettie at night. Irene confronted me with this news and asked me point-blank if it were true. I had to tell an awful lie, which she believed at first. But the women kept on peddling their gossip, and Irene got after me again. I denied it once more and then kept quiet, knowing that to argue would make matters worse. As time passed, I kept seeing Mettie and told my wife more and bigger lies about her than about any other subject. It was clear that honesty is not the best policy here, for even if a woman commits adultery herself, she just can't stand the same truth about her husband. I was learning that the love-making business has two aspects, sometimes making a man very happy and sometimes worrying his life out.

For more than two years after the death of our baby, Irene never missed her monthlies. We wondered if she could have another child. I thought there must be something wrong with her, but her relatives blamed me and kept up rumors that I was seeing other women—but their stories were only partly true. Sometimes we quarreled over this and Irene was often cross and irritable.

Once I slapped my wife, and later in the field, I threw a stick, striking her on the leg. Then she would cry until she softened my spirit. In the evenings, when all was quiet, we could hear a little chirping noise in the ceiling—which sounded like a cricket—and knew that our baby was still waiting there, begging for a rebirth. So dismissing our quarrels, we made love frequently, hoping thereby to induce the little spirit to come down from its roost and be born again as a boy.

Finally a boy was born, probably in 1916. We named him Tawaquiva (Rising Sun), with Clyde for his English name. My son seemed healthy, grew fast, and could crawl within a year. I don't know what disease he had, but his body became very hot, his mouth would get dry in a few minutes, and even his eyeballs looked shriveled from heat. The same old doctor who had twisted me into one child in my mother's womb now came to treat my boy. We gave the baby all the water he would drink, put vaseline on his mouth, and fed him a few drops of milk to keep him alive. He did not seem very sick; he just dried up and died. My grandfather helped me bury him in the same tomb with his sister. I lifted out the rolled blanket containing the little girl, placed my son on the bottom, and laid her on top, feeling sad enough to cry.

Little Clyde was a wise baby and did many things to keep the people happy. He had kept up this funny behavior until he was very sick. Perhaps he knew that he was going to die and did this to be remembered. Oh, how I missed that little boy! We felt like crying whenever we recalled his cunning ways, and our misery was hard to overcome. We were very angry with the old uncle who caused his death, but we had no power to do anything about it, for the underworld people might kill us too. We again heard little chirping noises in the ceiling and did all we could to hasten the rebirth. But sometimes we felt discouraged, for Irene's relatives harped on the fact that I was unlucky with children.

When I went to look for my horses one day, I found two of the "penis plants" that my grandfather had told me about some years before. The root was a tuber with a pink surface resembling a scrotum from which grew a stem without leaves that looked like a hard penis. If one touches the plant when it is ripe or in "full-bloom," it discharges a fluid. I got an old pail, gathered these plants up with some soil, and took them home to my old Uncle Kayayeptewa, who explained to me that they were very powerful and that the Navahos used them in their sheep corrals at breeding seasons. He warned me to handle them with special care, stating that to touch them even to the thigh of a man or woman greatly increased love-making and often caused a wife to accept other men. He said that a man and his wife could use such a plant upon each other, with moderation, in order to pep life up a little and to get a baby. I took the plants to my house and showed them to Irene, telling her of their power. She laughed at first and did not seem to think much of them; but one night I persuaded her to try them with me. We made ready, and just as I was going to touch a plant to my body, something suddenly told me to let it alone. It was like being turned completely around in a single second. I am sure that it was my Guardian Spirit who saved me from this foolish act in the very last moment. A few days later I traded the plants to Neschelles, my Navaho friend, for four sheep.

I worked hard with my herd, cleared new land near my father's farm at Batowe, and for two or three years seemed to prosper in spite of droughts. Sometimes I raised seven or eight wagonloads of corn and sold $75 or $80 worth of wool. Although I lost several horses, I was able to buy others, continued in good health, dressed like a plain Hopi, and thought no more about education. Irene had sore eyes and rheumatism and was very cross at times, but in spring she went with me to the corral and the field house to cook during sheepshearing and corn planting; and in the fall she went out with me to sweet-corn bakes and to harvest the crop. When she was unable to stand on her feet any longer, she would sit by a corn pile and husk the ears.

At home Irene guarded the corn, kept it free from mold, mice, and bugs, shelled it for my horses, ground it for our food, and took bags of it on her back to the trading post to exchange for supplies. She also made baskets and pots, mended the earthen roof of our house, and kept the walls plastered inside and out. She brought water whenever she could, collected wild plants for food, and lugged heavy loads of melons and peaches up the mesa. She also worked at the school in New Oraibi to earn her clothes. I praised Irene for her housework and for the cheerful way in which she washed all the dishes alone, even when I sat by completely idle—for I disliked dishwashing.

There were times when I felt that I had been lucky to marry such an attractive, good-natured, Fire Clan woman who was respected as the granddaughter of the old chief. At the dances I was proud to see that she was nice and plump and in some ways better-looking than my old girl Mettie. It was plain that she tried to keep me happy too, for she usually let me sleep with her, was very coöperative when I had to be continent during dances or Soyal, and sometimes cried when her eyes were so sore and dim that she could not cook for me.

It was plain that I owed Irene something every day, whether we made love or not, and that there was no need for me to try to escape this obligation. It was my duty to keep plenty of food and fuel in her house, see that she was well clothed, and try to remain friendly and helpful to her relatives. I was responsible for the heavy work in house building, was expected to pay for a medicine man when he was needed, and was required to work hard and increase her wealth. I knew it was my duty to keep her happy.

I learned to respect Irene's rights, too. She owned the house and all the property that her relatives gave her, including orchards, stock, water holes, land, and personal possessions. She also owned any property she made with her hands, such as pots, baskets, milling stones, and clothes, or anything that she earned for work or purchased with our money. She owned the fuel and the foodstuffs that I brought into her house, as well as all household equipment and utensils. Whenever she received mutton, melons, fruit, corn, or any other produce from my hands and thanked me, it became hers. She was free to invite her relatives to eat our food whenever she wished. She could sell our corn even to buy fancy clothes, but I cautioned her about this. She kept our money in a suitcase or a baking-powder can most of the time, and was free to use it, but we usually agreed on the way it was to be spent. I would advise her on the use of our property as long as I lived with her.

Once I worked fifteen days on the walls of a store for a little buckskin horse which I traded for a pinto and named Milky Way. I broke this horse to the saddle myself and would not have parted with it for $100. But Irene wanted a new Spanish shawl and begged me to sell the horse and get it. She kept pleading, and sometimes nagging, until I finally sold my favorite for $25, hoping to buy it back later. It was in 1918 when shawls were expensive, and Irene paid $18.50 for hers. I never got my horse back.

Whenever I failed in my duties to Irene, she found ways to torment me. She scolded, cried, even before relatives and neighbors, wasted our property, gossiped about me, teased me in public, and called me "lazybones who sits in the shade." That was one of the sharpest taunts to bear. She drenched me for sleeping after sunrise, denied me sexual pleasure by coldness, or by acting like a dead sheep, and sometimes threatened to drive me out of her house. She had the power and the means to make me so unhappy that my health might be endangered. A wife may even wish for her husband's death, fill his mind and system with bad thoughts, and then do nothing to save him. On the other hand, she may wish for her own death in order to punish her husband and thus cause neighbors and even the poor man himself to believe that he is killing her.

It was better for Irene to persuade than to compel me, and she learned to do this very well. She trained herself in nice quiet manners, occasionally wore her hair in the married woman's style, always thanked me for wood, water, and food, and was willing to feed friends and Navahos who came to visit me. She complained very little when we had no meat. I suggested once that I would go to the corral and butcher a goat, remarking that I was getting tired of meatless meals.

"All right," she replied. "I feel the same way, but I'm not the one to say it, for it might hurt your feelings." She often waited meals until I had returned home to eat with her and frequently got up first to build the fires on cold mornings. She washed my head in yucca suds for the ceremonies, cooked unsalted food for me to eat in the kiva, and prepared special gifts for me to distribute as a Katcina. She put vaseline on my fingers when they were sore from shelling corn and often picked lice off my head. She rubbed my back and belly when I felt sick, made my bed soft, and held my head over a basin when I needed to vomit. Sometimes she even let me sleep during the day and awakened me to eat without calling me lazybones. Occasionally she praised my name highly as a hard worker, a good provider, and a kind husband; and once in a while she refused to believe gossip about me, and even found excuses for my shortcomings. As long as she was peaceable, worked hard, saved our property, avoided arguments, paid no attention to gossip, and kept me well fed and sexually satisfied, I had few complaints and was not hard to manage.

Some of Irene's relatives also helped to make our marriage a success. The women praised me, and her brothers and clan brothers might take my side in arguments, talk for me in trades, and compliment me highly in jokes. For example, whenever a man meets his brother-in-law on the road it is a good practice to praise his farm, even beyond its due, compliment his herd, and perhaps say, "I also note that you are a good hunter, for I see a mountain sheep in your wagon. I shall stop at your house very soon, for I am sure that you have some fine venison." It pays to flatter a brother-in-law as a powerful hunter or even a mighty war god who is able to produce thunder and lightning, control the weather, freeze water into ice, or change a man into stone. When I was praised like that, it made me feel better and caused me to work harder, although I knew that the compliments were jokes.

Whenever Irene's uncles visited us, some of them complimented me and advised Irene to be a good wife. Once, after we had repaired the house, Irene's uncles came from Moenkopi for one of the ceremonies. We fed four men for breakfast, and while we were eating they kept looking around like goats in a new corral. I suggested that they eat first and look later, and we all laughed. They praised the house highly. When all had gone out but one old man, he turned to Irene and said to her in front of me: "I am your uncle and I'm very glad to see that Talayesva supports you so well. Always remember that it is not the best-looking man who makes a good husband. I see that you are contented, and well fed, so I want you to keep him happy and spend no time with other men. Your husband is all right, and your house looks nice." Irene answered, "I will try to do what you say, but you know it is hard to always be good. Sometimes I get angry." "That is the way the world goes," he replied, "but try to get over your anger quickly and treat your husband and your neighbors fairly. That is all I have to say to you." I appreciated the remarks of this old man, and when he was ready to go, I gave him a fine basket of peaches. A wife's uncles can be a big help, or they can wreck a man.

Although Irene had important rights, it was her duty to obey me. And since I was head of the family, it was my business to learn ways of managing her. I scolded her harshly and then advised her with soft words. I teased her in public and compared her with other women who would make better wives and finer lovers. I sometimes was slack to provide food and fuel, stayed out of the house for a while, kept her unhappy with arguments, and struck her. I knew of several Hopi who beat their wives. I could have argued with Irene until I worried her into sickness, but that would have been a disgrace. I hated arguments and learned to manage her better with kind words, praise, and rewards. And I also learned that it was often better just to let her alone until she changed of her own accord; or if she didn't change, try to find some way to put up with her. Women are like the wind, blowing first from the east and then from the west. The sooner a man learns this the better. He must expect his wife to make quick changes from joy to sadness and back to joy, in spite of anything that we can do. She can be more stubborn than a mule and harder to control than either wind or weather.

There were many little ways to please and soften Irene. One of the best was to fail to scold her when she deserved it, and expected it. Whenever I had to be away, I made it a practice to tell her where I was going and when I would be back, naming a time a little later than I expected to return in order to avoid arguments. Whenever I was late for meals, I ate a bite with her, even though I had dined out and was full up to my neck—I could at least take a sip of coffee and tell her the news. At Katcina dances I saw that she was well fed in the houses of my relatives. Because of her weak legs, I often brought water for her, sometimes when I had to wrap my head in a scarf to protect my ears from mosquitoes. It was also a good plan to chop her wood and put it in a box back of the stove. Whenever I saw her with the axe, I took it. I took her to see her relatives and spoke highly of her in their presence. It was a good practice to praise Irene with jokes before these relatives. One day I went to see one of Irene's uncles, and joked with his boys, for I was their "grandfather." I told them that they were too lazy to get up at sunrise, or even to bathe, and that they would find themselves out of favor with all decent girls. I described myself as an early riser and a powerful man with women. Then to prove my point I remarked that everyone recognized that my wife was a prize worthy of any man.

One could also ridicule his wife before her relatives and friends if they thought he did not mean it. Sometimes when I met my wife's relatives and they asked me what they could do for me, I would remark, "Well, I want to have my head chopped off. My own squaw fails to satisfy me, and since I can't get any private wives, I might as well die." They would usually laugh and reply that I was such an ugly man that love-making was hopeless in any case. I taught myself many little turns to soften Irene and improve her treatment of me. Sometimes when she returned late from a visit or from work, she was surprised to find a fire in the stove and a meal under way. Whenever she was away for several days for a wedding or other reasons, I might wash my dirty dishes and keep the house in order. Then when she returned I tried to show that I had missed her good cooking.

I also made it a practice to tell Irene some of my dreams, whisper bits of information to her that others are not supposed to know, buy refreshments at the store—such as watermelons, fruit, and candy— and bring them home to eat. I almost always told her the news. I would wash her head in yucca suds, comb her hair for lice, and treat her scalp for sores. Generally, I excused her from intercourse when she was sick or even when she appeared too tired. Sometimes when she was restless, I sang her to sleep with my Wowochim songs. I also made it a rule to awaken her whenever she cried out in a bad dream; but I left her alone when she snored like a giant, even when I could hear the echoes in the rest of the house. And I never aroused her from a deep sleep for love-making, but waited until morning.

My greatest power of control over Irene was my threat to go back to my mother's house. For that reason I was glad I had been married in the Hopi way. The American marriage is too easy to make and too hard to break. It is difficult and expensive to get married the Hopi way, but if a man finds he has made a mistake it is easy to escape.

But I wanted to make a success of marriage. I knew I would not leave Irene for barrenness, for bobbing her hair, or for smoking. If I caught her in adultery, I would not fight her lover, but I would be terribly hurt and would speak to his relatives about it. I had never heard of a Hopi man killing his wife's lover, for adultery is not that important. I probably would not have left her for that, but I would have given her a good scolding, and I might even beat her. A husband can't often catch his wife in another man's arms and stay happy. I probably would not have divorced Irene even if she had a baby by another man. But I am sure I would have left her if she had become too lazy, or a drunkard. I often threatened to leave her for her quick temper, and also for gossip.

If my wife had not wished to live with me any longer and told me to get out, I would have gone. I could have taken my clothes, bedding, jewelry, tools, and masks, but that is about all. The corn in the house, even a two-year supply, would have belonged to her. I would have kept my sheep and horses. But if Irene had put me out, she would have been left in a worse fix than I—unless some other man supported her. Many Hopi women are glad to get back their husbands.

I had a number of complaints against Irene. She was too quick-tempered, sharp-tongued, and stubborn. Whenever she started a quarrel I would finally say, "I hope somebody will come in quickly, so that you will quiet down." If no one came and I could stand no more, I went to my mother's house and waited until she cooled off and the subject could be handled with soft words. I learned that unless one is sure of himself the last word with a wife is not worth the trouble.

My greatest complaint was Irene's love of gossip. I threatened to leave her more often for this than for anything else. Whenever I came home tired and hungry and heard her start an untrue story, I got angry. Women manufacture gossip in their idle moments and multiply it as they pass it along. Some of their false rumors in full bloom are big enough and bad enough to upset the whole village.

Here is a sample. Irene would go to a neighbor and say, "I have heard something that upsets me; and I hate to tell you. A few nights ago your husband was caught with —— ——. Whenever I see you, I feel so sorry to think such a woman could cut you out that I decided I must tell you." Now that's a lie, and it may be two lies. If Irene really pitied the woman she wouldn't worry her with the news. Furthermore, her husband may not have slept with the other woman yet. Such gossip seems to be a special trade with women. Two-Hearts must promote it. I warned Irene again and again that to peddle gossip is like playing checkers with an evil spirit. You win occasionally but you are more often trapped at your own game. I would scold Irene about this until she cried. She learned not to start a rumor but she still liked to keep track of whatever was on foot. I think it was because women were hanging around our place so much. But I was glad to see that Irene was popular; and I was polite to these women, for I knew better than to set them against me.

We worked very hard in summer but there were idle days in winter. For about two years I brought the mail weekly from Keams Canyon with horses and the trader's buckboard. Ira and my father joined herds with mine and took turns at the corral and in the care of the horses. Since I was not a silversmith and did not weave, sew, or make moccasins, I found enough time for other interests from October to April. The Katcina dances were a chief source of pleasure to me. I took part in them regularly and was often asked to do clown work.

Once I did clown work with a couple of Two-Hearts. Sometime after the death of my son the people in New Oraibi opened a new kiva and practiced for a dance. When I returned from work one evening, I was told to go to our Mongwi kiva for a special meeting. Kewanventewa was to be chief and Nathaniel decided to wear a mask and imitate a dog. On the day of the dance I felt anxious, went early to the edge of the mesa, and prayed for success. We painted our bodies, dressed, and went to New Oraibi just before noon. Nathaniel wore a mask with long cardboard ears resembling the face of a dog. When we reached the village, we looped a rope around Nathaniel's neck to lead him as a dog, climbed on a housetop, and sneaked to the edge of the plaza. There we sprang up and made comments on the "beautiful flowers in the valley," meaning the women and their colorful shawls. Slipping down a rope into the plaza, we made the usual speeches, built a "house" with ashes, placed our doll "sister" in it, and informed the people that we had a good watchdog who could do tricks. To prove it, we ordered him to urinate, which he did dog-fashion, and then told him to climb the roof and kiss a girl, which he tried to do. When we were tired of dog tricks, the clown chief, Irene's crafty uncle, told me that I was not built right and tied boards to my ankles, forcing my feet to point straight ahead. He then discovered a hump on my back, placed me on my belly, and weighted me down with stones until my aunts rushed out and rescued me. Then I kissed an aunt on the tongue, which caused laughter. Nathaniel cut his ears down to resemble a badger, treated the sick, and restored Kewanventewa's teeth with pumpkin seeds. Then we sang funny songs with double meanings. The theme of my song was: "My mare is very mean, she bucks and kicks. I have turned her loose dragging a rope. Whoever catches her may ride her." I explained that the song meant I had a cross, hot-tempered wife who was difficult to manage; that she had thrown and kicked me; and whoever caught her might ride. The people laughed and the leader cried, "Well, it is up to us men to break in our wild horses." At sundown we were soundly whipped to bring rain. In spite of my private feelings I had managed to get along very well with the Two-Hearts in the performance of my ceremonial duties.

I enjoyed clown work and often did it to help the people, but once in Shongopavi a painful joke was played on me. I was punished for adultery. Two comic "female" Katcinas charged us with this crime and offered us the choice between Hopi punishment now and the Christian's hell hereafter. When we decided in favor of Hopi justice, one of the Katcina "ladies" opened a bag and took out four pieces of prickly cactus attached to strings. The Katcinas led Kalnimptewa about forty steps away, and tied the string of cactus around his neck so that the thorny pieces dangled against his back and buttocks. Then they told him to run, which he tried to do in a sway-back position. But the Katcinas ordered him to stand upright like a man and proceeded to press the cactus thorns into his flesh. When he was relieved of his tortures, he said that he was very thankful that he had received his punishment now and was free of the fear of hell. The Katcina "ladies" led Kewanventewa—the old Two-Heart—to the same place, tied the cactus to hang on his chest, and, when he tried to run in a stooping position, one of them struck him a blow on the buttocks, causing him to straighten up quickly and swing the cactus against himself. Then it was my turn, and I could see broken cactus thorns sticking in the flesh of my partners. The "ladies" pulled me along to the starting place and, although I made pledges of strict virtue in the future, they told me that they knew my record at Moenkopi and advised me that it was far better to be punished now by fair-minded Hopi than to go to hell forever. Instead of tying the cactus to my neck, they fastened it to my G-string so that the prickly pieces swung between my legs. Although I ran spraddle-legged, it did little good, for the "ladies" followed close behind, striking the thorny balls to keep them swinging. I had a hell of a time, which the people, and even Irene, seemed to enjoy.

The clown work afforded a good opportunity to play jokes on people, chastise them for misbehavior, and even to take out spite on them. A clown could do or say almost anything and get away with it because his duty was sacred. Therefore we teased and joked the Christians in our clown work. Once during a dance at Bakabi a clown draped a bed sheet around his body, climbed to the housetop, and announced that he was Jesus Christ who had returned to judge the world. He said that it was the last chance to be saved, then let down a rope and invited the righteous to climb up to heaven. One clown accepted the invitation, seized the rope, and was struggling up when "Jesus" took a good look at him, shook his head, and let him drop back into hell.

It was also a good clown trick to put on spectacles and a longtail coat, fold a piece of cardboard to represent a Bible and hymnal, and stride pompously into the plaza to sing hymns and preach a sermon on hell fire. The Christians who did not like this could stay away, for then we could have a better time and probably get more rain.

I had more fun in clown work than anything else, but I did get some satisfaction out of teasing my "grandfathers," especially the old fellows who had joked me so terribly as a boy. I threatened to sleep with their wives, rolled them in the snow, and even threw them in mud puddles and spoiled their clothes. One day in 1919 we were building a warehouse at Hubbell's store. I was mixing cement in a large trough when my old "grandfather," Talasweoma, who had pretended to castrate me, came up with a small bag on his back. He said, "Well, Talayesva, I am old and quite ugly now, but I am sorry to see that you look even worse." I looked up and smiled, for he *was* ugly with a bent, bony frame, wrinkled hide, tangled hair, and little dim, squint eyes. I stepped over to him quietly, picked him up, and threw him into the sloppy mortar. As he scrambled out, he was pushed in again. He cried, "Please don't throw me back, I have learned my lesson, and I'll be good." The Hopi were laughing, but Mr. Hubbell, the trader, stepped up, looked cross, and scolded me for being too rough on the old man. He hobbled into the store, scraping mortar off himself. Later I walked in and said, "What is the matter, have you been crying?" "No," he replied, "I am very happy." Then I bought him fifty cents' worth of sugar and a pound of coffee. I had already begun to tease my own "grandchildren" and treat them pretty rough.

Next to the dance days with singing, feasting, and clown work, love-making with private wives was the greatest pleasure of my life. And for us who toil in the desert, these light affairs make life more interesting. Even married men prefer a private wife now and then. At any rate there are times when a wife is not interested, and then a man must find someone else or live a worried and uncomfortable life. People cannot think that a man is doing wrong if he finds a single woman or a widow so long as he uses her right and rewards her. I would not think hard of a decent man who went with my own sister, if he treated her fairly.

Women are very important to a man. They provide one of the greatest pleasures known, and it is through them that the people increase. We praised the women for their power to give pleasure and their importance in child-bearing, and whenever we heard one lament her lot we told her that she was more fortunate than we, for we did not even own the houses in which we live. We reminded women that we live harder lives, cultivating crops in toil and sweat and following herds in heat and storm, while all the food that we make belongs to them as soon as we bring it home, and they have the power to send us away empty-handed at will. We also pointed out that they should be able to enjoy love-making more than we, because they are rested, while we are tired, and they receive something while we sacrifice our strength. We put up a good argument to the ladies, but we didn't mean it, for when we were alone we laughed and said that we were lucky to be men.

We often talked of the types of women we liked best. I wanted one younger than myself and of medium height and weight; but I preferred an active skinny girl to a fat one who nearly sleeps. I preferred a light complexion, for we say that a woman with a dark skin may be half man. I never made love to an albino, but I thought I would like it. I was never particular about the color of a woman's eyes, provided they were shiny, but I wanted her to have thin lips and black hair. In my boyhood I did not care for body hair, but as a man I learned to like it on the pubes—never in the armpits. The old people said that Hopi women used to pluck out the pubic hairs and give them to their lovers as souvenirs. I also preferred broad hips, a medium-sized waist, and a soft, warm, moist body. In love I wanted my partner to be bold and lope right along like a horse that needs no spurs.

There are good and bad ways in love-making. My old uncle Kaya-yeptewa often told us about his own experience. We would ask him, in fun, how he managed to get so many private wives. His advice was to ask a woman in a polite way. He said, "She will first say no and scold you, but she may not mean it. Wait about four days and ask her again. She will say no, but scold you less. In four more days she may appear undecided, but on the fourth request she will probably say yes. If she is still cold, then leave her alone." We would laugh and say, "Gosh, you are a brave man." He advised that the best way to get a woman is to "win her with gifts." I think he was right, and I have never accepted a woman's favors without rewarding her.

I was not very bold, especially after marriage. I was more like Miles Standish—whom we had read about in school—afraid to ask unless I knew the answer would be yes. But most married men ask too much. I never entered a house and struggled with a woman, for I feared she might hate me the rest of her life. Hopi lovers hold hands, kiss, and caress the whole body, exchanging endearing remarks and complimenting each other on most everything. It is not right to kiss the pubes. It is not wrong for a man to force his way a little, if he is sure that his lover will consent in the end. Many Hopi do it anyway.

Although I tried a standing position, it is better to lie, and a self-respecting man stays on top. While it is a good thing to prolong the pleasures, a man should finish ahead of his partner, for she may watch the contortions of his face and later tease him. The best women will make excited, gasping noises at the right time, exert rapid pressures, and keep their eyes closed. I was able to last only about four minutes, and never practiced withdrawal, for that is indecent.

When I was young and rested, I liked love-making four times a week, but later I always skipped a night, and in summer I skipped two or three or more. Some careless people are said to double every night, and I have heard of men who boast five times. That is too much.

Night is the best time, for during the day Hopis are apt to walk in without knocking. My own mother walked in on Irene and me once, and when I showed embarrassment she said, "Never mind me, that's the way the world goes." When we were first married, Irene said she thought love-making was the "only life." But later she became less interested and did not seem to understand my side of the question. Wives often hold out on their husbands but they never say, "I want you to find a private lover and be happy." They just can't do that. Most men I have known will put up with a little denial and finally remark, "If you don't like this, I will find somebody else." That is usually enough. I would have left Irene if she had refused me too often and too long. On the other hand, if I could not satisfy her most of the time and she complained too much, I would suggest that we separate. But husbands and wives have to learn to be patient with each other.

Well, another little daughter was born to us about four years after the death of my son. I was pleased and thought that when she grew up I would send her to school to learn shorthand and typing, and get her a job in the office at Keams Canyon. But I said to myself that I would insist on her dressing in Hopi costume and wearing her hair in the "squash blossom." Then when the Whites came around, they could see a real Hopi girl and be surprised at her beauty and her ability.

I don't remember this child's name. She lived about four months, caught a cold, and coughed and coughed until she died. The white doctor and nurse did all they could, but their treatment was useless. The baby had to be taken to a Hopi medicine man, but it was too late. He tried to save her, but when she began to cough up blood we lost hope. It was in the month of November and I had gone for a load of wood. As I returned past the Shrine of Masau'u, I saw a man running to meet me. Joe, who had become my sheep partner, told me the baby was dead and offered to take charge of my wagon and team. I ran up the mesa by a short cut, and entered my house. Irene's relatives were there and had stopped crying, but when they saw me they began afresh. I knelt and uncovered my little daughter, running my hands over her cold body; and when I touched her chin, the mouth opened. Closing it again, I turned and said, "One of you relatives of my wife has killed this child. I hope whoever did it will die of the same disease. Examine yourselves from head to foot and uncover your own guilt. I don't want to cry for I am mad. Let the person who killed my baby bury her." I did not intend to let any Two-Heart bury my child, but I was speaking in anger.

My own grandfather had stepped into the house and he was not crying either. He said, "Talayesva, you are telling them right, and I am on your side." Turning to my wife's relatives, he said, "If you Fire Clan people don't like it, you may kill my grandson with your evil powers, but you will have to kill me first." Joe, who is a Grease-wood man married to a Fire Clan woman, came up with the wagon at about this time and joined my side of the argument. I talked plenty and didn't shed a tear, but I was crying in my heart.

I made some prayer feathers while Joe's wife bathed the body and wrapped it for burial. Joe went with me to the tomb where I lifted out the other two children and placed this one on the bottom, telling her to hurry back. The oldest bundle, containing my first daughter, was so decayed that the wrappings were falling to pieces, and the little bones were exposed.

The people talked more than ever. They said again and again that I was unlucky with children, and some of them tried to put all the blame on me, hinting that I was careless in the ceremonies, that I ran around with private wives, and that I had arguments with my wife which worried my babies and caused them to pine and die. I tried to defend myself from these charges, and sometimes I was very unhappy and even sick. I went out to herd one day with a very heavy heart. On the road I met Nathaniel, who had kind words for me and braced me up with good advice, which I appreciated. I told him that old Sequapa and my mother-in-law had accused me of the death of my own children. And as we talked together, tears rolled down my cheeks.

My people were having a hard time too. My oldest sister, Gladys, was expecting a baby, and her husband, Frank, went away trading with Navahos. Gladys went into labor in the evening, and the baby was not born until after sunrise next day. As I entered the village with my horses, people told me the news and said that the afterbirth would not come out. I hurried over and found my mother sitting on the floor holding Gladys in her arms. They had clipped the navel cord to save the baby and had fastened the other end to a stone. My mother told me to stand back of Gladys, lift her, and shake out the afterbirth. I raised her about eighteen inches and shook, while my mother caught hold of the stone and pulled. Gladys seemed dreamy, looked at me crossly, and said, "Leave me alone, I would rather die." When I laid her on the floor, she looked at me and died. Although she had treated me badly and had admitted that she did not want to live, I tried not to blame her too much, but persuaded myself that she had suffered a great deal and was out of her mind.

Ira and I carried her to the grave in a wagon to keep blood off our clothes and bad luck out of our lives. I dug the hole myself and when the burial was completed, I said, "Now, dear sister, go to your dead children and treat them well. Some day we will meet you with our dear ones." I could say no more, for I was crying. It was late in the day when I had hobbled my horses before I could free myself from sorrowful thoughts. Gladys had left four children for us to raise, Delia, who was about ten, two younger girls, and the new baby.

During the day Byron Adams, a Hopi missionary, and a white field nurse asked my mother to give the little boy to them for adoption, promising that when he grew up he might return to help our people. Since Frank was away, my mother decided to part with the baby. They took him to New Oraibi, and there the nurse untied the special string that we had bound to the navel cord. This let air into the baby's belly and caused it to swell up. The Whites also cut off a piece of the little boy's penis—calling the operation circumcision—something that we Hopi would never do. The child did not live very long, of course, and they buried him in a box in the Christian cemetery without a grave ladder and without food. I did not go near, but I felt like slapping the nurse who was supposed to be an expert but who had never learned the simplest things about babies. When I saw her afterwards, I wanted to give her hell, but realized that she would probably go to hell soon enough anyway, for surely her God would never let her get to heaven.

During these sorrows my uncle Talasquaptewa, who was very old and feeble, said to me: "My nephew, we have looked into your heart and chosen you to be the Sun Chief (Tawamongwi) instead of your brother Ira who is older. You will succeed me shortly in this office. I want you to watch me closely when I make the offerings so that you will know how to do it when I pass away." That meant that I was following in the line of succession—like a king—and would be Sun Chief of Moenkopi as well as Oraibi. He showed me the special place to stand or sit in guiding the rising sun in its journey to its summer house, and taught me all that I should know about the special office.

During his last years Talasquaptewa spent the summer in a little field house on a knoll about a mile west of Oraibi. He became very feeble and was visited and fed twice daily by my mother, who was always busy helping other people. When he could not eat, she would leave food and water beside him. One day in the summer of 1920, when I was working with others on a fence in the field at Batowe, Ira came with news that our uncle had been found dead. Chief Tewa-quaptewa, who had been raised by my uncle, and my father bathed and shrouded him for burial as a Special Officer. The Chief made a special speech asking him to send rain as soon as he reached the House of the Dead and took his place—for he was a Special Officer and could do that.

My uncle's remaining property was divided among us, except for a little which we buried with him. My mother got his share of the herd and his fruit trees. I received three very old sacred masks and became owner of the Mongwi kiva. I was thirty years old and glad to succeed my uncle in office. I resolved to do my best to serve my people and insure rains and a good life.

I also took more important parts in the Soyal. Since Lomavuy-aoma, my wife's uncle of the Fire Clan, was getting old and feeble, he asked me to take his place in depositing the special offerings on the shrine of Masau'u. This was a dangerous trip in the dark and many Hopi would never dare to take it for fear of meeting bloody Masau'u himself. At about two-thirty one morning during Soyal I sat by the fireplace and smoked while every member placed a paho on an old plaque, together with piki made by members of the Fire Clan and some raw rabbit meat, mountain tobacco, and corn meal. When I left the plaque to go, the people said in unison, "With your brave, happy heart, take our pahos over there and deliver our message to Masau'u."

As I left the kiva and walked down the mesa toward the shrine, the moon was almost down. I stepped bravely, sprinkled meal before the shrine, and prayed, "Great Masau'u, I have been sent over here to ask your help in our lives. Give us moisture and protect us; let the people increase, live to old age, and die without suffering." Placing the plaque on the shrine, I felt a breath of air rising like a gust of wind. Then I knew that Masau'u had accepted the gifts.

The moon was down and the night was dark when I sprinkled a path of corn meal and started back up the mesa. When I reached the second shelf, I heard a sound like heavy footsteps on the path below. I thought it was a messenger from another kiva on his way to a shrine. Thinking that I would test his courage, I picked up a rock and threw it near by. The steps stopped suddenly, and there was such complete silence that I knew it was a spirit and said to myself, "I never should have done this." Looking southeast, I saw what appeared to be another moon rising, but it was a big, red fire, blazing out of the ground about three feet high on the very edge of the mesa point. I stood by the stone wall and wondered what to do, whether to follow the trail toward the fire or make a short cut for home over the rocky ledge. Trembling with fear, I realized that Masau'u was making a test of me and expected me to prove my courage. So bracing myself, I walked as calmly as I could toward the light which burned down to about a foot in height. I walked about ten steps nearer, watched the flame die out, and then stepped lively toward the village, but my eyes seemed to fail me, and I lost my sense of direction. As I passed the little dam where I had seen my grandmother Bakabi, the naked Two-Heart, it seemed that something took hold of my coattail and pulled me back at every step. I tried to run and stumbled over a stone near the first building.

The guard at Mongwi kiva heard me and asked what was wrong. Without replying, I entered the kiva, sat down to smoke in silence, and asked forgiveness of the Fire god, resolving never again to play smart tricks on a mission to the shrine of Masau'u. To see the fire and to stumble and fall on such an occasion were unlucky signs. But I remembered that the first man ever to live in Oraibi had seen Masau'u himself without danger. The old Hopi say that Macheta used to see the fire in the evening at Oraibi Rock. Three times when he approached it, the light went out; but on the fourth time he saw a human form holding his great bloody head in his hands. The deity admitted that he was the god of Fire and Death who guards the mesa and assured our ancestor that he could stay and build his house near the Rock. The foundation of the old house could still be seen and I trusted that Masau'u would protect our lives.

In a short time my brother Perry, who had returned from school, died in New Oraibi. I carried his body to the grave, and while my father and a relative dug a hole, a large fly flew past and stopped in a bush. One of the men said, "That is the death fly[1] warning us of more trouble to come." I picked up a stick to throw at it, but my father

1. See Appendix, pp. 442–444.

cautioned me to leave it alone. We put many things into the grave with my dead brother—necklaces, turquoise earrings, bracelets, and dancing costumes—but sure enough, in twenty days my seven-year-old brother Glen died. I was at Bakabi helping my clan brother in his store. When I received the news, I hurried home too late, uncovered his face, and cried, for he was a quiet, happy little fellow, full of mischief, and a favorite with us—the same little boy whom I helped deliver. I remembered the fly, and ever after when I heard a large insect buzzing near by, I felt uneasy until I knew whether it was the death fly or a harmless bumblebee.

Misfortunes and signs of bad luck did not let up. One night soon after, as I came past North Mesa from Bakabi, someone threw a stone from a cliff, which landed just ahead of me. Looking up, I spied an owl flying eastward. I was aware, of course, that witches can turn themselves into owls and throw stones at people in the dark. I hurried home and told my wife and grandfather what had happened and he agreed that someone must be against us. All these things made me watch for signs and one night, when we were sleeping in the kiva for the Soyal, I started hiccoughing. Suddenly I was startled by feeling a hand placed on my heart, but a Soyal partner whispered, "Please don't think that I am a Two-Heart. I touched you for a quick surprise, for it is not right to name your private lover here, even to stop hiccoughs!"

The years passed quickly and finally my fourth and last child was born, probably in 1923 or 1924. It proved to be a boy. I was lucky in getting children, but unlucky in raising them. He looked like a white child and was one of the finest babies I had ever seen. At first I thought he was an albino, and although we gave him a Hopi name, I called him Alphonso—King Alphonso—and predicted that he would make a good sheepherder, a useful man, and a first-class lover of the girls. I was pleased and thought to myself, "Now this is the fourth child. Perhaps the underworld people will pity me and let the boy live." But within a few months, soon after the Niman dance, he became very sick. Irene's mother would have nothing to do with us and would hardly look at her daughter. She gave Irene no advice and did not seem to want her to have any more children; but I wanted children as much as ever. Irene's people were blaming me for the death of our children. Sequapa, who had had seven husbands—and would accept any man for pay—told my mother-in-law that I was causing the death of my own children by having intercourse with other women and failing to perform my ceremonial duties correctly. They even hinted that I was a Two-Heart, taking the lives of my children to save my own. When Irene heard about this gossip and got after me, I said, "It is a lie. I am not a Two-Heart and I have never met at their secret convention. I will stand on my own feet and question those women face to face."

I went for Sequapa and Irene's mother and brought them to our house. When they entered, I said to them in the presence of Irene, "You women must stand on your feet, look straight into my eyes and speak the truth. You are accusing me unfairly. I am not a Two-Heart and I have never been to their secret meetings. I have no power to defend myself from them. If they wish to kill me they can do it, and eat me too. I am only a common man and not worth very much. I can't even raise my own children. When I am dead, Irene can choose a new husband and get other children." Then I questioned them closely and argued like a white lawyer, saying much that I have forgotten. I seemed to have Sequapa in a bag from the start. She had no words at all, and soon hurried out. Then I turned to my mother-in-law and expressed myself fully. When I could think of no more to say, I concluded, "It seems that I have taken the best out of you in this argument." She also walked out without any back talk. I did not know whether Irene was on my side or not, for she only said, "I want to keep my baby, but I have lost hope." When her mother left, I said, "Irene, I am in an awful fix, out of step, and far from my Sun Trail. I don't believe I can save our baby from this trouble." We cried and cried and stayed up all night.

The next morning I took my wife and baby to my mother's house and started on foot to Hotavila for a Hopi doctor. As I ran along the road, I saw a dead horned toad before me. I stopped and said to it, "Well, you have told me that the little boy whom I have left behind is dead, but I will go on and get a doctor to discover who killed him."

In Hotavila the doctor said he would hobble his horses and come soon. I hurried home ahead of him, and when I reached the place where I had seen the dead toad, it had disappeared leaving no tracks—proof of an evil omen. At my mother's house relatives were crying and told me that the little boy had died soon after I left. I also learned that before I was out of sight Irene's old uncle came slyly to my mother's house and had a good chance to shoot another poison arrow into my sick child.

I took the dead baby and buried him in the tomb with his brother and sisters, but, oh, how I hated to do it. In bitterness and sorrow I said, "Now this is the last child that I shall have, for they all die. There are Two-Hearts against me, and it is no use to try any more." Those were wrong words to say, but I was upset and felt that mine was a hard life indeed. Long after, whenever I passed within sight of the grave of my children, a lump would rise in my throat, and it seemed that my anger and grief were more than I could bear.

One night in a dream my Guardian Spirit came to me and said, "Why do you worry? Don't you know that I am with you?" I apologized and told him that the false stories about me and the death of my children had put my steps on the wrong road. "This is the work of the Two-Hearts," he replied. "But troubled thoughts will do you no good. Brace up, and get back on the Sun Trail. I have been watching you day and night and have a complete record of your life. If you don't listen to me, I shall return, show you this record, and judge you. Don't ever get discouraged again or say that you are going to die. Remember that I am your Guide and that I will protect you. Now be good and be wise."

I awoke very happy and told Irene what I had seen and heard. She seemed to doubt me at first, but I showed her that life is important and that a man must have someone to watch over him. I pointed out to her that a man could never make up his mind to do a thing and suddenly change it for a better course in the nick of time if it were not for his Guardian Spirit. She admitted that it must be true and did not seem to blame me any more.

My health became poor. The lightning power which had entered my body years before when I passed the place of the dead horse had begun to take effect. My head ached, my eyes were streaked with red, and at times I shook from head to foot and foamed a little at the mouth, especially before a storm. Several medicines were tried, but none seemed to help. My grandfather advised me to drink my own fresh urine. I swallowed it eight times and received some relief. One evening I heard a roar in my head and felt that it would crack. I became dizzy and a little out of my mind, rolled on my sheepskin, pounded my forehead on the earthen floor, and cried like a child. Within a few days Polingyuama, a medicine man from Bakabi, came to see Ira who was suffering from the same trouble. We removed our shirts and sat on the floor before the doctor who sang four magic songs over us and washed our heads in yucca suds to remove the evil power. I gave the doctor a string of coral beads and a pair of polished turquoise earrings for myself and three strings of wampum beads for Ira. I recovered almost immediately but Ira improved very slowly. This was my first serious illness since my death experience at Sherman.

Life went on for two or three years with no important changes except that Irene's sister Barbara had trouble with her husband, Arthur, who was my clan brother. She lived with us part of the time and left her children with us even more. Irene and I got along all right, but I had no dealings whatever with her mother—not even speaking to her.

I also had some trouble with a Two-Heart. One of Nathaniel's children had died and he let the missionaries bury it. The people remembered his queer behavior and avoided him as a witch. He lived alone much of the time, teased children who came near him, threw stones at neighbors' dogs, and tried to be too familiar with some of the women when the men were away. He appeared less friendly to me, and once when I spoke to him at the store, he just stared at me and walked away. So I decided to keep a close watch on him.

Moenkopi remained a bright spot in my life. I went back from time to time to earn a little cash and to get some pleasure—seeing Mettie on the sly whenever I could. One trip turned out to be especially amusing. I stayed at Euella's house and helped Jimmie in the store for eight or ten days. Then we started to Flagstaff on a wagon with sheep pelts and Navaho blankets to exchange for merchandise. As we rode for more than a day, we discussed women to pass the time and Jimmie suggested that we visit some white ones. We reached town at noon on a hot dusty day and were very sweaty and dirty in the evening when we stopped peddling blankets from house to house. Finally, we entered a house with a reputation and found so many white men that we had no chance at all. I stepped outside and saw a half-breed Negro leave another house. Following him, I asked if it were a good place to go. He laughed and said, "Yes, for two dollars." I thanked him, stepped up to the door, and knocked. A woman opened it, and when I asked her where I could find some nice girls, she pointed to the house which I had left. I told her that it was full of customers and asked, "My friend, are you one of them?" "No," she answered. But I reported my conversation with the Negro and begged her to accept me. She said, "Well, I don't know, but I think I will not." Then I spoke in a soft voice: "I am a human being, too, and just as good as that Negro. My money is United States silver, not Mexican. Here is a dollar; see the lady's head on one side and an eagle on the other. Please take me." "You are very dirty," she replied. "You must take a bath." She led me to a bathroom where I stripped, washed, and waited. When she returned, she scrubbed my back herself with a rag and some good-smelling soap, and then examined me. As soon as I was dry, I called, "Can you give me something clean to wear?" "Here is a nightgown," she answered. As I pulled it over my head, I looked into the mirror and laughed, wondering whether I resembled the Holy Ghost.

I soon found her undressed on the bed; and as I joined her, I said, "Now it is my turn to examine you." She was fine, and when we had finished, she got up and washed me again. She was the cleanest woman I had ever seen. Then I put on my dirty clothes, told her good night, and found Jimmie waiting at the corner with a Mexican boy. He had had no luck at all. I told him my experience, and we had a big laugh about how some Whites think Indians are not even human beings.

The lightning trouble had been painful, but my greatest sorrow after the death of my children was a disease in my private parts. Red spots appeared on my penis, there was a foul discharge, and my testicles were badly swollen on both sides. I had slept with my wife the night before, but I had known no other women for more than a month, so I said to myself, "This can't be clap." The pain was so great that I could neither walk, sit, nor lie down, and when I tried to urinate a tiny trickle made me cry. I was sick for days and days, perhaps in 1927, and was seen by several Hopi doctors.

I was lying in my house on the earthen floor one day when my mother entered with Polingyuama and asked him to treat me. He looked me over from head to foot, took a long breath, and said, "Well, I will do what I can, but I may not be able to free this man from the power of the Two-Hearts. And if I do, then I will have to fight against them myself." Then he spat on his hands, rubbed them together, held them out toward the sun, inhaled a deep breath of spirit power, and began to examine my swollen organs. Finally, he extracted three poison arrows—a hooked devil's thorn that had bent my penis downward, and two porcupine quills that had caused the swelling. "You must stay away from women for a long time," he said. "There are some evil-minded people who are trying to kill you." My mother cried and said to the doctor, "Oh, please save my boy. He is the best child I have and helps me more than all the others. If I lose him, I don't know what I shall do. I will give him to you as a real son, and when he gets well he will help you too." "All right," said the doctor. "We will put our hearts together, banish unhappy thoughts, and pray for power to save him."

But I continued to suffer, and Jay from Mishongovi came to advise and treat me and plucked out a few stone splinters, a small piece of bone, and some antelope fur. Sammy from First Mesa also drove out some evil spirits with his magic songs. Yet no one seemed to get down to the main cause, for the pain grew worse. Then Kochwytewa, who had married a Sun Clan woman, came from Hotavila, made a brief examination, turned to Irene, and said, "You appear to be popular and a certain Two-Heart may be trying to get your husband out of the way and have you for himself. But you are not really very beautiful, and I advise you to stick to Talayesva and help save his life." He had a right to say this to her because he was her father's nephew and, therefore, her "father." Then as he examined me more carefully, he showed surprise in his face, glanced at my grandfather who was sitting near by, and suddenly removed several poison arrows. Turning to the old man, he said, "You knew very well that these arrows were in your grandson and did not try to remove them. Do you want him to die?" I watched my grandfather's face closely and was frightened when he appeared nervous and made no reply. Had he been innocent, he should have spoken up like a man and said, "You are a liar. I am not a Two-Heart and I am not the one who is killing my grandson."

I was sick and suffering. All good thoughts had departed from me, and I was facing west where the dead people live. My grandfather was old and feeble now, and I suspected that his time had come and that he had decided to kill me to prolong his own life. I knew I would have to watch him for the rest of his life.

This great illness occurred in February and it was May before I was free of pain. But even then my left testicle was very soft and shamefully small, and my penis was ruined. This impotence was a great disappointment to me, and even worried Irene. I was unhappy over it for a long time and felt that gladly would I give all my horses, or even my herd, for a renewal of my manhood. I tried to comfort myself with the thought that my misfortune was not as great as if I had lost my one good eye, an arm, or a leg, or even my life.

Except for that one time, my grandfather acted all right and was kind to me, but I kept a close watch on him. I knew he was a great doctor and realized that if I were kind and polite to him, he might regret the trouble he had caused me and decide to do me no more harm, even to save his own life.

My interest in children did not lag. Although I doubted that I could ever be a father again, I still wished for a son or a daughter and gave special attention to the small children in the village. I would let them ride on my wagon, take them into the kiva on my back, make toys for them, and give them choice bits of food. Sometimes I would take a baby boy on my lap and sing him to sleep while I played with his private parts to give him pleasure—just as others had played with me.

The people began to bring their babies to me when they were sick and unable to urinate. I found that the antelope power was still in me, although not quite so strong as formerly. I massaged the pubes of these suffering children, chewed up piki and fed it to them from my fingers, and was very happy when they recovered.

I dreaded to take the part of the Giant Nataska to frighten my nieces, nephews, and other children and make them behave. But Ira and I were requested to do this because we were the tallest men in Oraibi. The frightful mask was so large that my whole face could fit into the long bill with its jagged teeth. I painted my face black so that no child would be able to recognize me, and when we came into the village, I was very careful not to touch anyone in reaching for his gifts of meat and other food. As I leaped at one little boy and grabbed his piece of meat, I peeped through the teeth of my mask, saw him trembling with fear, and felt tears running down my own cheeks.

Almost all the children in the village liked me, and I had a very pleasant dream several times. Once, for example, I was sitting in my old home where I was born, when I heard a baby crying outside. As I stepped to the door, a voice spoke to me, "Pick up the child and feed it, for I can see in your heart that you are a good-natured man. Everyone has tried to comfort this child but failed, so please pick him up yourself." "Certainly, I will," I replied. "I don't know whether I am a goodhearted man or not, but I will do my best with this child." To my left was a baby lying in a grinding bin, and I noticed that it was a boy. Stepping quickly to him, I picked him up and said, "My son, stop crying and behave yourself." He quieted down immediately and smiled at me. Then I heard many babies crying, and looking about me I saw scores of them moving toward me on their little bellies. Gathering up as many as I could, I heard the voice saying, "Take them to your own house and feed them." "All right," I replied, "but I can't carry all of them. They may follow after me on their hands and knees." We had not reached my house when I awoke with a very happy heart, for I knew that it was my Guardian Spirit who had spoken to me.

13

Changes in Family Life:

1928–1938

I WAS IMPOTENT for a long time. Irene frequently reminded me of this—even when she was kind and gentle. We could also hear the chirping of a little spirit in the roof which made matters worse. Prayers failed to restore my spent powers and nothing else seemed to help. But I kept wanting children, and I needed them badly to prove that I was a good man who could raise a family—not a Two-Heart like Nathaniel who killed off his wife and children to prolong his life. Neighbors did not ask me to be a ceremonial father to their children; they said to one another, "Talayesva is unlucky with children." Sometimes there were rumors that Irene was not quite satisfied with me, and suspicions arose that other men were taking advantage of my weakness. I had no proof of this but was often worried.

In 1928 I got a son. When I returned from the herd one evening, Irene said that her sister Barbara wanted to see me in New Oraibi. I found her crying with a sick child on her lap. She and her husband had other lovers and quarreled a great deal. This was killing their two-year-old boy, sapping his strength and clogging his system with unhappy thoughts, for babies know what goes on and often worry over the misbehavior of their parents.

Since the father was a clan brother of mine, I felt partly responsible for the child's sickness. Looking at the little boy, I said, "Chusoma

(Snake Eater), I am here." He moved his head but would not open his eyes. He had refused food for several days, and his mother had lost hope.

"The child loves you," said Barbara. "If you will save his life, I will give him to you. I know you have been unlucky with your own babies, but you love children. If he lives he will stop your grief." I reminded her that I was not a doctor, and that the child might die in my hands. But I pitied the little fellow and finally said, "When a woman gives her sick child to a person and he recovers, she often takes him back. You might do the same thing." Weeping, she said, "I don't think I would do that. Irene and I are real sisters, and therefore she is the child's mother too." With strong feeling, I replied, "You and Arthur have enough sense to stop these private affairs, live right, and save the boy yourselves. You have failed and you want me to save him. If the baby dies, will you blame me?" "No," she answered. Then I agreed to do my best and said, "It is my wish that this boy may live. Tomorrow he will open his eyes and eat."

Although I was not a doctor, I could at least pray to my Sun god and try to save the dying child. I told Barbara to move up to my house and warned again, "If you stop seeing other men, that will help. I have been in this trouble myself and know how it is. Children get sick when their parents are unfaithful. Let's both pray and live right, and perhaps we will be lucky." I came home and told Irene that Barbara had given me her boy. That night I wished for a dream of guidance, but nothing happened.

I thought about the sick boy all next day, corralled the sheep early, hurried home, and found him there with his mother—still refusing to eat. After supper I took him in my arms, placed a silver dollar in his hand, and closed his fingers over it. He acted as if he still knew something and might want to live, for he held on to the dollar.

Then I remembered my grandfather's advice that when a child is sick and won't eat, he should be taken to the special Corn-and-Water Clan household, for in olden times these people had charge of the food and drink. I told Irene that I was taking the baby into the plaza for some fresh air, but I went straight to the house of Kawasie, the wife of my father Kalnimptewa. "Mother," said I, "this sick child has

been given to me. If I can save his life, he is mine." "Good," she replied, "you have been unlucky with your own children; but I hope you
can save him." Then she rubbed the boy's body and made motions to
drive off the evil spirits, shooing them away with her breath and with
both hands. Holding a cup of water to his lips, she urged, "Drink,
my grandson." He opened his eyes and looked at me. Kawasie said,
"Now open your mouth and drink." He did to the last drop. "Here
is piki and boiled liver," said Kawasie. "Please eat." She soaked the
piki in water and fed him. He ate and ate until I almost cried for joy.
Whenever she failed to feed him fast enough, he opened his mouth
like a young bird begging for another worm.

When the boy would eat no more, Kawasie placed him on my
back, pulled the blanket around him, and gave me the rest of the food.
As we entered the house, Barbara asked, "Where have you been?"
With a happy face I said, "We have been over there having a picnic."
Irene took the baby from my back, and as I looked at him, he opened
his eyes and said, "Tata," which means "Papa," and "Ma-ma," which
means "Eat more." Irene fed him again, and I laid him on a sheepskin,
telling him to rest. Soon he was sound asleep, still holding to the silver
dollar. I sat beside him and watched all night.

When the child awoke at sunrise, he crawled over into my lap and
said, "Tata, ma-ma." I was happy. He ate heartily, leaned back, rolled
his eyes up at the ceiling, and rested. I urged the women to keep him
quiet all day and then went out to herd. On the way I prayed to the
sun, moon, and stars and thanked them for my good luck. In the evening the little boy was better, talked more, and held on to my hand.
Barbara stayed with us four days more and spent part of the baby's
dollar. Then she went back to New Oraibi with the child. I shook
hands with him and hated to see him go, for it was I who had saved
his life.

For a few weeks I herded in the day and went every night to New
Oraibi to see my boy. He would climb upon my lap and eat. Then I
would bring him up to my house; but when it was time for him to go
to sleep he would cry for his mother, and I would take him back. The
double trip made me walk six miles. Once he decided to sleep with
me; but in the night he cried and cried until I took him home. He

finally got over this and spent the whole night with me. Soon he was a good little boy who seldom wanted to see his mother. I was proud of him and gave him an English name, Norman. In the evenings I would play with him to keep him happy, try to teach him little dancing steps, tell him stories that he could not understand, and sing him to sleep on my lap. I always gave him the choice bits of food and made little toys for him. I loved him better than anyone else except my mother, and was proud that the people saw him with me. Some of them praised me highly for saving his life and being such a good father to him. But my mother-in-law and I continued to pass each other without speaking. Nevertheless, I felt that my life had changed for the better and that I had more to live for. Even if I were impotent, I could live for my boy.

Another change for me began about 1929. For almost twenty years I had had little to do with Whites except traders, government agents, three prostitutes, a few tourists, and the field nurse. I used very little of the white man's food, except flour, sugar, and coffee; and I got along without his other goods except a little calico, some trousers, shirts, and shoes, a wagon and harness, a few farming tools, and some steel traps. A rifle, an oil lamp, and an iron stove were also useful to me. And with the assistance of the school principal I finally ordered some improved fruit trees from Utah.

I had avoided the missionaries, unless I could get something from them, and paid no attention to their Sabbath and their sermons. I resented the way they meddled in our private affairs, encouraged strife among us, destroyed our Hopi way of life, and brought on droughts and disease. While they pretended to care for our welfare, they made us feel that our gods were idols or devils, and that we were no better than dung. I usually took whatever they offered me and worked for them a little for cash, but I despised them for insulting our Katcinas, for interfering with our ceremonies, and for using their cheap gifts as bait to tempt weak-minded Hopi off the Sun Trail. They kept all the best things for themselves and were really hypocrites, for they rarely practiced what they preached. Whenever they worshiped in our plaza, I completely ignored them and sometimes chopped wood to interfere with their preaching. When my Bible was all gone, I got a Sears Roebuck catalogue and used its pages for toilet paper and for the protection of my young plants. It was also more interesting reading. I made less and less use of the English language, except when I talked to Whites or wanted to cuss. In fact, I was ashamed to be seen speaking with white people too much, especially at the dances. When disease and droughts came and when our crops were bad, we blamed the Whites—especially the missionaries—and cussed them to their backs.

Now I felt a little better toward the Whites and took more pains to be polite to them. A few would ask for me when they came to Oraibi, perhaps because I could speak a little English and would let them take my picture for a dollar. Some who called themselves "anthropologists" asked me to tell them stories and paid me very well. But I knew that Whites can see more sin than pleasure in sex, so I edited the old Hopi stories. I still did not care much for their company and was afraid to have them in my house because of Hopi gossip. But I found it much easier to talk in the shade for cash than to cultivate corn and herd sheep in the hot sun.

My first white friend of any importance was Mr. George D. Sachs of New York City, a very rich and religious man who distributed useless tracts on Christianity. I was drilling holes in turquoise beads in 1930 when this man approached me for the first time and asked permission to take my picture. I consented, and when he closed the camera I said, "Now come on with your dollar." He was free with his money and we became friends.

Norman did not have another serious illness but when he was about four a strange thing happened. He acted sad. I wondered if a spirit had warned him in a dream that trouble was near. One day after an early breakfast I went for my horses feeling very strange, for my ears rang every few minutes. I thought to myself, "Something is going to happen." I started to ride a horse but decided to be very careful and walked. As I watered the horses at the spring I looked up and saw a man beckoning to me in an excited manner. The ringing in my ears increased. It was Irene's brother Baldwin who said that my little boy was burned. While washing dishes in her mother's house Barbara had knocked over the coffee pot and scalded Norman. I thought to myself, "This shows that Barbara wants the boy back. She sees how healthy and happy he is with me and is jealous."

I had not been in my mother-in-law's house since the death of my last child. But I went straight to my boy. Barbara was holding him and both were crying. When Irene's mother saw me she cried too. The poor little fellow held out his hands to me. Taking him, I said, "Well, well, I never thought when I saved your life that this would happen." They had put kerosene on his face, but the worse burns were on his left arm and chest. I cried, "Poor boy, I have no way to save you from this suffering. It was not in my house that it happened." Then I turned to my mother-in-law, pointed my finger straight at her, and said, "It was in your house that this boy was burned. Now let's forget our quarrel, unite our hearts, and try to save the child." "I agree," she replied. "We will forget everything and work together. What shall we do?" We took the boy to our place, and Irene's mother and father came along.

The little fellow was in a dreadful plight. The white doctor's Unguentine helped, but some of his medicines did harm. The field nurse came, and after a few days I said to her, "Let's try both the Indian's and the white man's medicines. You have treated the boy four days, now rest and let me try Indian medicine for four days." She first argued and then agreed. Whenever she treated the sore, she always wrapped it tightly. I thought it should stay open so that cool air could get to it. On the tenth day Irene was treating the boy with the Indian medicine and both she and the child were crying. Then I also cried and said to Barbara, "We can't go on. You must help." We had a big quarrel and finally made up for the child's sake.

Norman improved a little, and on the twelfth day I let the nurse try her medicine again. It took about a month for the wounds to heal. I prayed daily and bought apples, oranges, and cornflakes for my boy. Piki was the best food of all, but the cornflakes were good too. He was eating my money every day.

When Norman got well Irene's parents moved back home, but Barbara stayed and I had to support her too. She remained with her two girls from March to May and then moved back where she belonged. One day when I butchered a sheep I helped Norman take a piece of the meat to his grandmother, Irene's mother, for her wishes had helped to save his life. We were glad to have anybody's wishes then.

We talked about the burn many times, and when Norman was older and more thoughtful he would say that he was glad that he had a father and mother who loved him. We taught him to say that when he grew up he would have a herd of his own and butcher sheep for us. Then I would reply, "That's right, my boy. You hold out your hands to us now, and we feed you. When we are old and feeble, we will hold out our hands to you and you will not forget us."

One day the children had an argument and someone said to Norman, "You had better go back to your real father. Don is not your real father and Irene is not your mother." He came home crying and asked me about this again and again. Finally I told him the truth. Then when he was angry he would say, "I shall go back to my real father and mother." Oh, how that upset me. "I don't think you will," I would say. "You are mine and the only child to my name. Your own father and mother would not care for you. I saved your life. Stay with me and I will give you candy. I will get many things for you, and when I die you will have my horses, herd, and other property. If you leave me now, you will suffer. Remember this, will you?" The boy would cry and promise to stay.

Norman was a quiet but playful little fellow, and was a great pleasure to me, especially when he tried to dance, shoot his tiny bow, spin his top, or ride my oldest horse. He liked to go to the field with me in a wagon. One day he caught some beetles and put them in a circle of sand, calling them his wild horses. When they escaped he cried a little but I made him laugh by saying over and over, "Alas, our lost horses!"

Once when I ploughed corn at Batowe Norman found a horned toad and said, "Now I will fool my mother. I will let her guess what I have and then tell her that I have found a dollar and put this toad into her hand." Irene guessed a wild potato and other things. Soon Norman said, "No, I have found a dollar. Hold your hand and close your eyes." When she felt the toad she screamed and threw it away. Norman laughed and laughed, but I apologized to the toad, explaining that it was just a joke, for toads are very wise.

In 1931 another white man became my friend. He was a Mr. Sutton from California who offered to buy a clay pipe from my little boy. I told Norman to give it to him, for I knew that he was a friend to our

Chief. To my surprise the man took a five-dollar bill out of his pocket and gave it to Norman. After that we were close friends, and I later gave his wife a fine finger ring. The Chief finally adopted Sutton as a son, and he joined my clan as an elder brother. He wrote often and remembered me every Christmas with bundles of clothing.

I also met a teacher from Oakland, California, and a writer whom we called "No Shirt" because he went around in nothing but shorts and was careless in his personal appearance, like women tourists. A bald-headed photographer came to Oraibi several times and once sent me a small album of pictures and some turkey feathers to make pahos. A Mrs. Miller came to see a Snake dance, met me, and later sent me some fine ostrich plumes which I used to decorate my masks for dancing. I was learning that Whites are like the Hopi, different in character, and that they should be studied separately and treated accordingly. Some of them were very low-class human beings—dumphole people, I called them—while others were respectable and made fine friends who could be trusted and who never discredited our Hopi beliefs and customs.

Although I had had bad luck with my own children, I was successful with Norman, and the people realized in the course of time that I was a reliable, upright man and would make a good ceremonial father. A few parents asked me to become the ceremonial father of their children and to sponsor them in the societies. Even the Chief asked me to be the ceremonial father of his adopted son Stanley. In the initiation of these boys and girls I remembered my own sufferings and permitted them to receive only two blows before pulling them out of reach of the Whipper Katcinas and presenting my own legs. I was very proud of two of my ceremonial sons, Ellis and Stanley.

It was a happy occasion in my life when I did the clown work in Moenkopi with my ceremonial sons as assistants. One day we heard that there was to be a Butterfly dance in Moenkopi and called a meeting in our own kiva where we decided to go over and surprise the people with a Buffalo dance. I was asked to take my ceremonial sons along and do the clown work.

On the day before the dance we sprinkled a path of sacred meal, placed the prayer feather on the road, loaded our big drum on a truck, and started to Moenkopi. There were about twenty-one men and boys and two girls for the special parts in the Buffalo dance. When we reached the stream near the village, we took a bath and waited for darkness. Then we entered the town in high speed, singing a Comanche song and surprising everybody.

A kiva was swept clean for us, and women brought in large quantities of food. After a feast the important men came, formed a circle about the fireplace, and smoked prayerfully until nearly midnight. Then we prepared for the Buffalo dance. We clowns striped our bodies with black and white, smeared black paint around our eyes and mouth, put on our headdress, and tied cornhusks to our paired horns to represent tassels.

When all were ready, we followed the drummer to the kiva of the Butterfly dancers, singing Comanche songs. Stepping to the kiva hole, I peeped in and saw the Butterfly dancers in their practice. We clowns yelled, and I asked two men to lower me into the kiva headfirst. Reaching almost to the floor, I cried, "Well, Butterflies, I don't think you will beat us Buffaloes in the dances." Everybody laughed and cheered as my men yanked me out again. Our drummer entered followed by the singers, while we clowns waited outside. I whispered to my boys to try hard to be funny. At the end of the first song I climbed down the ladder, followed by my little partners and a few side dancers dressed in war bonnets like Paiutes and Comanches. I danced about before the people in various positions and made funny noises. The little clowns imitated me and did very well. Whenever a boy or girl eyed me closely, I stared back, stuck out my tongue and made an ugly face, turned quickly, and presented my buttocks with bold gestures. As we finished our dances and started to leave the kiva, the leader of the Butterflies said, "Wait, we appreciate your performance. You have made us happy. Give us another dance tomorrow." We all said, "We are very glad," and returned to our kiva. There I sat and smoked prayerfully, for I was chief of the clowns.

In the morning the Moenkopi people invited us to their homes for breakfast. I was eating at the house of Talasvuyauoma, the War Chief, when we heard the announcement that all Butterfly dancers should dress. My clan sister Meggie—who once spied on me in love-making—sent for me. She was now married and had five children. As I entered her house I noticed a young girl about twelve who looked very familiar. I whispered to Meggie to tell me her name. "That's Elsie," she said, "the daughter of Euella who died recently. Will you please dress her for the Butterfly dance?"

I had never dressed a special performer for the Butterfly dance but I was willing to try. I put yellow paint on Elsie's feet to her ankles and on her hands to her elbows, took down her hair, combed it back, and placed a woven band on her forehead. I braided a lock of hair from the top of her head, put the fancy headframe in place, secured it with the braid, and tied strings under her chin. There were beautiful parrot feathers for the headframe and colorful yarn bands for the girl's ankles. I put necklaces and bracelets on her, attached my own inlaid turquoise earrings, rubbed sacred corn meal on the face of my little aunt, and fondly remembered how her dear mother was once my dancing partner and later favored me with many pleasures.

In the afternoon we dressed again for clown work and ran into the plaza yelling and leaping about, while the Buffaloes and the Butterflies danced to the beat of drums and strove to outdo each other. As I moved to and fro making faces at the people I felt a jerk on my G-string and discovered that Euella's blind old mother had been led into the plaza with her arms full of piki. I felt like crying when I saw this dear old aunt bringing me food. Just as I received the piki her old husband snatched at my G-string, tore it off, and waved it before the people. I stood in a stooping position with my hands full of piki while my loincloth lay on the ground. Oh, how the people laughed when one of my little clowns struck me on the buttocks, forcing me to straighten up quickly, and then pulled me around to face in all directions. Suddenly I thought to myself, "This will spread through all the villages, and when my wife hears about it she will make it hot for me." My old "grandfather" was still waving the G-string when Kochwytewa, the medicine man from Hotavila, buckled his silver belt around my waist and replaced my loincloth. Then my real mother, who had come to Moenkopi without my knowledge, ran to me with her blanket and placed it on the ground for my food. As I looked around my little partners were playing "horsy," and then doing the white man's hoochy-koochy dance. Feeling proud of them, I dropped my head for a minute, suddenly jumped high, yelled, and led them to the kiva where we ate and made plans for more tricks.

When we returned to the plaza the little clowns chased one another and jerked off their loincloths. The people laughed at our stunts until tears ran down their faces, while I smiled proudly to myself and watched the Whites. Some were smiling with us, but I heard later that one lady remarked, "I don't think these clowns will ever go to heaven."

At about six years of age Norman was initiated. Peter had been chosen for his ceremonial father. But Peter lived in New Oraibi, and we did not get along well with the people there. They were forsaking the Hopi religion and living like Whites, interested only in earning money. They were foolish, for a man should pray to his own gods and lead a good life. So when it came time for the initiation I decided to select another person to be Norman's ceremonial father, for I took care of him and had the right to choose. I selected Kayahongnewa, who was a member of the Katcina, the Wowochim, the Soyal, the women's Ooqol, and the Flute societies. In his early manhood he had been a prize runner and could wrestle with three men at once. He was nearly blind now but an important old man, and whenever he talked everyone listened closely. He knew most of the ceremonies, and people came to him to check the songs in their memories. I chose him partly because of his importance—since he would be able to put Norman into the leading societies—and partly because his wife, Kawamana, kept after me about the matter.

Norman was taken into the Powamu society where children are not whipped. It was my wish that he escape the flogging, for he had suffered enough by scalding and was a good little boy who had never needed a smoking. I took him to the house of the Rabbit Clan people, and from there he was led to the kiva. I don't know what happened, for I am not a member of that society and have no business prying into its secrets.

After the initiation Kayahongnewa made a bow and arrow for my boy, but never took much special interest in him. Perhaps it was because most of the ceremonies were dying out in Oraibi. Had these ceremonies remained strong, I think he would have taken Norman into the higher societies, perhaps into the Flute society.

Since Norman had been given to me, I wished to have my own mother name him in a head-washing ceremony which would make my adoption official by Hopi rules. Although he was seven or eight years old at this time, it was difficult to persuade him to go to the Sun Clan house for the ceremony because he was timid and shy. My mother washed his head and said, "Now, my grandson, I will wash away your old name, the weak one that caused your illness some years ago. I will give you a strong new name that will protect you from sickness. I will name you Tawaweseoma (Sun Journeying). I will make a road for you leading toward the Sun. Put your feet upon it and travel on to old age and into sleep." With these words she put the sacred meal on his face and gave him the mother-corn ear.

Norman usually was a quiet, obedient boy, but I had to whip him some. The first time was at the sheep corral when he was seven. Irene asked him to get some wood for her cooking, but he paid no attention to her. She asked him again and scolded him. He was offended, threatened to go home on foot, and actually started. I kept on shearing with the men until noon when Irene told me that the boy had left and that I had better follow him. I was tired and hot from shearing. I took up a cotton rope three or four feet long and tracked him to a cottonwood tree where I found him asleep. "You naughty boy. You ought to be ashamed," said I and whipped him a little. He cried, but did not move very fast. I followed after, striking him with the rope and saying, "Run, run."

In the summer of 1932 Professor Leslie A. White came to Oraibi with some anthropology students, Fred Eggan, Edward Kennard, and Mischa Titiev. They hired me to tell them about Hopi life and to act as interpreter when they talked with others. I liked this work very much and earned a good sum of money; but I was careful what I told them at first. The people criticized me for this work, but these were fine fellows—not at all like government agents, missionaries, and tourists— and I felt safe with the Chief on my side. It made me feel important and more comfortable to hire others to herd while I sat by a warm stove, smoked the white man's tobacco, and told Hopi stories. The students were full of jokes and even called me their teacher.

I had a big argument with Nathaniel. Luther, my father's sister's son, and Cecil, my father's brother's son, stole a watermelon from the Two-Heart's field and ate it. Cecil made a sketch of a woman's private parts in the sand by the melon vines as a joke. Nathaniel discovered it, was offended, and later claimed that he tracked Cecil and Luther to my field house where we were gathering sweet corn with my sister Mabel. We saw nothing of Nathaniel, but within a few days he started a rumor that when he passed our field house at night and peeped in, he spied Luther, my "father," having intercourse with my sister. He told a lot of details to Clara, Luther's wife, who was my wife's sister. Clara brought this awful story to Irene. I knew it could not be true, for I had slept under the same blanket with Luther and Cecil. If Luther had moved under Mabel's blanket, I would have known it. I even doubted that Nathaniel had seen us, but I knew that Two-Hearts often trail innocent people to get evil reports on them. We were so angry over this gossip that we sent for Mabel and decided to face Nathaniel with his lies.

Clara, Irene, Mabel, and I set out for the house of the Two-Heart. Our Chief came along with other men to listen, but stayed outside. Clara repeated to Nathaniel all that he had said to her. He tried to deny part of it, but he was trapped. I stood close by and got angrier by the minute. Finally I told Nathaniel to his face that he had lied. We passed hot words back and forth, and began to recite evil reports about each other. Then he reminded me that he had taken my side and helped me when I quarreled with my mother-in-law and was unhappy over the death of my last child. He exclaimed, "I met you on the road to your sheep camp and caught you crying. I took your side then and helped you free your mind of evil thoughts. Why are you against me now?" I told him that he had no right to call me a Two-Heart, that I had never attended a secret meeting of the underworld people, that I had not caused the death of my children, and that I had no power to defend myself. I reminded him that I had caught him crying in the field and that he had fled like a coward. "When was it?" he asked. I described the occasion about twenty years before and gave all the details. He could not deny this and was speechless for a moment. Then I out-talked him, reviewing his complete record for the people, how crazy he had acted, how his wife and children had died one after the other, and how he had even let the missionaries bury them without food and a grave ladder. My friends backed me and supported my statements with short sharp comments. Nathaniel threatened to strike me and pushed Mabel, almost causing her to fall. I was daring him to kill an innocent man and, expecting a blow, I raised my arm. In fact, I almost struck the Two-Heart; but my Guardian Spirit checked my fist before it fell and flashed a message to my mind to take the first blow like a man. I think Nathaniel read my mind by magic, for instead of striking me, he bowed his head and had no more to say. I had him cornered; the people cheered me, and a few spat at Nathaniel. The Chief had witnessed everything, but had not interfered, for he was afraid that the Two-Heart might take secret revenge on him as the most important man in the village.

After our quarrel Nathaniel seemed to be against me and my people more than ever, and for several years we exchanged hard looks and refused to speak. I kept a close check on his behavior, but caught him in no special mischief. Neither did I discover him using a strange language nor speaking big English words, as did the Two-Hearts in the Winslow store.

Mischa Titiev returned to Oraibi in 1933, rented a room in my house, and hired my sister Inez to cook for him. I was proud to have him with us, enjoyed working with him, and was glad to get so much money, but I knew other Hopi were jealous and that they might turn against me. But the Chief was on my side and Mischa made most of the people love him. I was also careful to teach him how to behave in the Hopi way.

My little boy loved Mischa too. I told him that if he would obey us I would get him a complete cowboy outfit for Christmas. He kept reminding me of this, saying, "Daddy, you said that you would get me a cowboy suit." I always replied, "Yes, if you keep on obeying us." Mischa helped me order the suit from Sears Roebuck. We also ordered presents for the other children—including a bucket of candy—and planned a Christmas tree. On December 23 the postmaster sent word for me to come with my wagon and get the goods. We made the trip next day and in the evening we opened the cowboy package. There were a "ten-gallon" hat, a red handkerchief, necktie, shirt, pants, rope, and toy pistol. When Norman came from school after dark, he put on everything, seemed quite a big man, and said, "Daddy, it is a good thing we have a father and mother." "Yes, it is," I replied. "You are the only child to our name, and when you grow up you will have all that we possess, goats, sheep, horses, and everything." Long afterward I kept reminding him of this.

While Mischa was with me, I had an awful argument with some unfriendly Hopis. Some of my neighbors did not like to see a white man living in the village and had it rumored that I was telling Hopi secrets, revealing the sacred ceremonies, selling idols from the shrines, and even parting with the special equipment of the Soyal ceremony. Some went so far as to claim that I dug up dead bodies and sold them to the Whites to put in their museums. Irene heard about this and cried, fearful that some bad luck would overtake us. Some of my friends advised me to have nothing more to do with the Whites, but I kept the Chief on my side and stood firm, for I was selling no sacred objects and revealing no ceremonial secrets. I enjoyed the company of Mischa, learned much from him, and received good pay. We became like brothers and he helped me with my work and even went with me to visit my friend Neschelles and have a Navaho sweat bath. Some of his questions seemed foolish to me, but most of them were easy to answer and did not touch on ceremonial secrets. Whenever I was in doubt, I put him off politely, looked up the Chief, and asked, "Do you think we had better tell this?" I discovered that the Chief was freer with his information than I, so I had nothing to fear from him.

But Barker[1] of the Badger Clan, who was the greatest "ladies' man" in Oraibi, stirred up more gossip than I could stand. He had gone to the Chicago Fair with his wife and others and visited the Field Museum. There he had found a showcase with exhibits of the Hopi

1. A fictitious name.

Soyal ceremony, with altars, costumes, all the sacred equipment, and even statues of the Hopi War god and special priests performing the most secret and sacred part of our ceremony. When Barker returned to Oraibi, he told many people that it was I who had sold this material to the Whites, that I had revealed all the Hopi secrets, and that in the exhibit he could recognize me in the special costume of the Star Priest and holding the sacred symbol of our Sun god. Barker told the Chief all that he had seen and said that these sacred Hopi objects were the most valuable possessions in the Museum. He also said that the Museum authorities had promised to send me a new automobile as part-payment. When I heard all this, I worried so much that I wondered if I might die soon. I knew that it was all a lie but it seemed true, and I did not know what to do. Finally, I decided to take the Chief to Barker's house and face this unfriendly man and his wife with all their lies. They gave us a detailed account of all they had seen in the Museum, but when I asked them to explain about the new car they looked embarrassed and said, "Who told you that?" When I pointed to the Chief himself, they quieted down. Although their daughter Clara[2] had not been to the Fair, she was present and talked so much that I wanted to slap her face, and when she died some time later I was very glad. Except for Clara, I did most of the talking and finally got them cornered where they had little more to say. The Chief stood by me and listened quietly; otherwise we would have had a worse argument. I knew I could depend upon his support, for although he was ten years older than I, he was my "son," and I had helped him a great deal when we were in school together, and had done whatever I could for him ever since, even writing his letters and serving as interpreter for him in his dealings with the Whites.

Mischa was also a great help to me. He typed for me a letter to the Director of the Field Museum, asking how they had obtained the Hopi exhibits. I sent the letter by air mail and did not have to wait very long for a reply which said: "The Field Museum never had any dealings with you, but only with the Rev. Voth who made the altars on exhibition. These altars are merely reconstructions, *not* originals.

2. Not Irene's sister.

The information for making them was secured by the Museum over thirty years ago."

That letter braced me up and provided a shield to protect me. The unfriendly Hopis were notified to come and read with their own eyes. They did not show up, but I spread the news around and decided to keep the letter for my protection as long as I lived.

Within a short time I had a dream in which my Guardian Spirit appeared to me in his customary dress and scolded me a little for keeping evil thoughts in my mind. He said, "Alas, you are getting off the Sun Trail again. You are now a middle-aged man and ought to know better, for nothing good can come from evil thoughts, arguments, and worry. Your Sun God, who is chief of all other gods, is getting weary at the way you worry over these things. So brace up and follow me." Then I realized that I should worry no more over what the people had said, and continued my work with Mischa in order to support my family. But I resolved to watch myself carefully and never reveal any ceremonial secrets.

Before Mischa left, the Chief adopted him as his son and I took him into the Sun Clan as my younger brother. I think he was the best-liked white man that had ever been to Oraibi. Some of the women even let him name their babies. I was sad when he left and was very gentle to his little dog which stayed with me. One of the finest things "Misch" ever did for me was to order medicine to treat my sore eyes. We were like real brothers.

Before very long my old uncle, Kayayeptewa, died. He had outlived three wives and was said to be a hundred years old. His first serious weakness of age had come in 1919 when I took over his herding. For eleven years longer he had been able to farm a little, bring wood on his back, look after his peach orchard, and weave blankets. Finally he gave up these jobs in the order named and spent most of his time spinning. He slept in the kiva but ate at my mother's house. Although he was somewhat deaf, he was still an important man in the Soyal, knew hundreds of stories about Hopi history, and could compose almost any kind of Katcina song. Whenever he talked we paid close attention, for he was a Special Officer. Most of his historical stories were too long, and the people grew tired and sleepy. But he had some first-rate stories on love-making, and the record of his life was proof of his right to speak on the subject.

By then the Hopi rule of respect for old age was breaking down and, except on ceremonial occasions, some of the children teased Kayayeptewa, treated him unkindly, and even played practical jokes on him, such as throwing sticks at him and tying dirty rags to his back. He would sometimes strike at them and warn, "If you want to live long, you had better respect old age." But during the last two or three years of his life he was of no use to anybody. He lay in the corner of my mother's house, very dirty and full of lice. My mother placed food beside him, sometimes fed him, and kept dirty rags tucked between his thighs which she changed like diapers.

One afternoon in November, probably in 1934, when the Wowo-chim ceremony was on and my mother had taken food to the kiva for some of the men, my sister Mabel came to tell me that our uncle was dying. Naquima was with him and said, "It is good that you came. Uncle has been dying since morning, but his heart still beats and there is a little breath left in him. I have covered his face with a blanket." I removed the cover, placed my ear close to his mouth, and listened. Then I said to Naquima, "His breath is about the length of my finger, and he is getting cold. He must be on the road to our dear ones. I hate to bury him in the dark. I will prop him up against the wall so that the breath will escape quickly. Let's not worry, for he is too old and weak to feel any pain; and it is better for him to be on his way." As I raised him, the last breath came out. Old Naquima was frightened and said, "This is the first time I have ever seen a person die. I think I had better go." He crawled out quickly and left me alone with the dead.

My brother Ira soon joined me. "You are just in time," said I, "and this is a good chance for you to help with the burial." I wondered if he were brave enough to do it. He smiled uneasily and said that while I prepared the body he would go hobble the horses and hurry back. I put water in a tub and washed the hands and face of our uncle and painted both arms and legs to the ankles with white dotted lines. I also made a white curve over his left eye with points turned up like a half-moon, to signify to the spirit people that uncle was a Special Officer. After washing his hair with yucca suds and combing it, I spun new string and fastened a soft prayer feather to the top of his head and to each hand, and placed one on his feet and one on his breast. Then I filled his hands with corn meal, closed his fingers, and tied them fast. Rubbing meal over his face, I covered it with a cotton mask with holes for his eyes and mouth. This represented the billowy clouds that would hide his face whenever he returned to drop rain upon our parched lands.

Before wrapping uncle in a blanket, I stood beside him, sprinkled corn meal over his body, and made an important speech, crying a little between words: "Well, dear Uncle, it is time for you to go. You are the only Special Officer in our Sun Clan and it will be hard for us to get along without you. I have dressed you for your journey to the House of the Dead. Lose no time in getting there. Our dear ones will welcome you gladly and show you to your special seat. Look after them as you have cared for us. Remember us and send rain. Visit us in December and sing the prayer songs again in our Soyal, for we still need your help. Be good and be wise in your future life."

Many of the people were in the kiva performing a short Wowochim ceremony, while others had gone into their houses with their children to escape the sight of the dead. Naquima had gone to the house of the Chief's brother. My mother had not returned, and Ira was slow in getting back. It was late afternoon, and I knew we must hurry or darkness would overtake us. So splitting some yucca stems, I bound the robes about the body in the old-fashioned way and bent uncle's knees so that he could sit in the grave. Then I collected the bedding, a shovel, pick, planting stick, food, water, and corn meal, and sat down to wait for Ira.

A nonrelative might have been willing to help me with the burial, but then he would have expected a share in my uncle's property, and we were opposed to that. I had bound a rope around the shoulders and thighs of the corpse and made a carrying loop to fit over the head of the bearer. It is best to bear the dead back to back, since the legs of the bearer are less encumbered in walking. When Ira finally came, I said, "We must hurry. I have been burying our relatives right along, and now it is your turn to take the corpse to the cemetery." Ira was older than I and was supposed to be braver, and I wished to test his courage. He smiled nervously and said, "All right, this will be the first dead body to ride on my back." I helped load him and told him that I would follow. I rolled the bedding tightly, tied a rope around it, took the digging tools and water, and set out, dragging the bundle behind me. There were no children in sight, and the two or three adults who were outside their houses looked off in the opposite direction.

As I reached the edge of the mesa, Ira was descending in a stooping trot. Approaching the grave spot, I saw him standing there staggering under his load. "Drop it," I called; "uncle will feel no more pain." Then I reminded him of the Hopi rule that the person who bears the body should make the "house" for it, but that I would start the hole for him. The clouds were heavy overhead and threatening a snow or hailstorm. While Ira collected stones, I dug a hole 4 feet long, 2½ feet wide, and 8 feet deep. On the west side I hollowed out a cave for the body, letting Ira throw out the last shovels of dirt. I handed him some corn meal to sprinkle on the bottom, dragged the body close, let it down into the hole, and pressed it back into the cave in a squatting position and facing east. We closed the cave with a large flat stone and chinked the cracks with pieces of bedding. We placed the rest of the bedding in the hole and sprinkled corn meal over it. Then we tried to get all the fresh dirt back into place, packing and pounding it with our feet, for to leave it lying around looks bad and may cause the death of a relative. We also piled stones on the mound so that coyotes and dogs could not get to the body, and so that no prowling White would be tempted to dig it up and take it away to a museum. When we had set a planting stick as a ladder, we placed food and water near by, emptied the sand out of our shoes, and turned our pockets inside out to rid ourselves of any loose dirt that might do damage to our lives.

As we returned to the Sun Clan house, Mabel and my mother were boiling juniper boughs. They poured the water into an earthen dish and took it outside to a special place where we removed our clothes and bathed. Mabel washed our backs and then bathed her own face and hands, and her feet up to the knees. We broke the pottery dish so that it could not be used again and bring bad luck upon anyone. Returning to the house, we placed a piece of piñon gum in a broken dish, lighted it with red-hot coals, and stood under a blanket so that the smoke could pass over our bodies and drive off the evil spirits. Then we washed our heads in yucca suds and put on clean clothes. The women should have washed the grave clothes that night, but since it was cold and dark they put it off until the next day. Ira and I went to our separate homes and tried to rid our minds of sorrowful thoughts. It is best to laugh and joke again as soon as possible, but now some of the people will say that you do not care much for the dead—which is a mistake.

Of course, neither Ira nor I had intercourse with our wives or any other woman for four days and would not have worked in the fields had it been crop season, but we could have herded our sheep. If anyone had heard dogs or coyotes barking near the grave at night, it would have been a noble deed to drive them off—but few men would have been brave enough to do it.[3]

On the third day at about ten o'clock in the morning I made two prayer sticks and five prayer feathers. Mabel boiled some beans, and I took them on a plaque with piki and went to the grave. Placing these offerings on the pile of stone, I made a path of corn meal leading eastward and left as quickly as possible, for I did not need to make another speech. On the next morning our uncle arose, no doubt, ate of the food, and departed for the House of the Dead. But I think he returned for Soyal in about two weeks, entered the kiva and helped us with the medicine-making ceremony. I made a special paho for him and resolved to do so at every Soyal for the rest of my life.

Our uncle had no horses, cattle, or sheep. He had turned his herd over to our mother several years before and had traded most of his property to get clothes, bedding, and other necessities in his old age. He had a son about sixty years old, but his peach orchard went to my sister Mabel and we divided his personal property among ourselves. Ira got a tanned buckskin for moccasins, my father got his weaving tools, and I received a coral necklace which I later traded for a horse.

Old Naquima was quite upset at the death of our uncle. Frederick, the Chief's brother, told me that when Naquima peeped out the

3. See Appendix, pp. 442–444.

door and saw us passing with the body, he cried, "Alas! we will never see our uncle again. It will be my turn to die next, for I am abused by my nieces and sometimes treated like a dog." Frederick tried to comfort him, reminding him that it was best for the old man to die, and that he would be happy with his loved ones. Naquima replied, "Yes, that is right, and in the next life I will not crawl in the dirt as I do here, but walk and run like a free man." "That is true," Frederick answered. "Now brace up. You are the oldest man left in the Sun Clan and should know better. You are the nephew of my father and therefore my clan father. You are not very old and will last a long time yet. We all love you, so get the evil thoughts out of your mind."

When there were Snake dances at Hotavila, Naquima sat by the roadside and begged from white tourists. Once I made a sign for him to wear which read: "Help the Poor." Sometimes he made as much as $5. Once we worked out a plan to make more money. I was to dress him like a wild Indian snake dancer, curl and tangle his hair, put bright red feathers on his head, draw a bull-snake design down the front of his body, and paint his face black with lips red. It was my plan to tie a red dyed angora goatskin around his waist, place him in a tent, and paint a sign: "This is a wild Indian captured in the Hopi forest. Tickets $.25 and $.50. Be careful, for the man is a cannibal." I worked out a speech for him to say whenever a White looked into the tent: "Fe-fi-fo-fum, I smell the blood of an Englishman." Then he was to squeal like a clown. We talked and laughed about our plan for many days, but were unable to carry it out because I could get no one to herd for me on the day of the Snake dance.

My grandfather died before very long. He was a great medicine man, but he could not save himself. I had gone for my horses, and Naquima was with him when he died. When I returned, Naquima cried, "Alas! I am left alone with no one to care for me." "Listen," I replied, "I have been advising you to brace up. My grandfather could not care for you, for he was too feeble. Our mothers and sisters will take care of you. Life is important. If you want to stay upon this earth, you must rid yourself of sorrowful thoughts. Pray to your Guardian Spirit to protect you, and if you don't get tired of your life, he will hold you tightly. Remember this, will you?" I helped to bury my grandfather just as I had our other dead relatives.

Naquima grew more feeble. He continued to live with my mother, Mabel, and my youngest sister, Inez, who was about eighteen years old. But he ate with my niece Delia, the oldest daughter of my dead sister Gladys. Delia had married Nelson from Hotavila. Sometimes Naquima would crawl down to the trading post where Mr. Hubbell gave him clothes and brought him home in his car. The knees of his trousers were always worn from crawling, but he tried to sew them with string from flour sacks. Sometimes the children would tease him, take things from him, mock him, and even kick or strike him. Most adults were kind to him, teased him about the girls, and pretended to punish him for misconduct in order to cheer him up. My sisters and nieces were careless and sometimes mistreated him, even threatening to give him no food. On cold days he managed to crawl down the ladder into the kiva and sit by the fire while the men worked. One day he fell from the ladder and landed on his head. Thereafter, he vomited frequently and became very thin, so I often took him into the kiva on my back.

Once when I returned with a load of wood, Irene said, "Naquima is sick." I found him on his back in Delia's house. He told me he had so much pain in his chest that he wished to die. He also said, "I am alone without father or mother and my nieces treat me unfairly. Food fails to stay down, and the Indian medicine does not stick." I mixed some corn meal in salt water, and as he drank it, I rubbed his stomach to make the food stay. He soon fell asleep, and I went home for my supper.

On the next day I found Naquima dead. My mother was sitting beside him crying, for she had cared for her crippled brother all her life. "Don't be too sad," said I. "Uncle has suffered for many years in a world that was sorrowful for him. Now he will go to our loved ones and be a free man." We dressed him for burial, and I told him to travel swiftly along a smooth and pleasant road to the home of our ancestors. I told him that his father and mother were expecting him and would treat him well. I did not cry, because he had suffered all his life and I was glad that his hardships were over. I carried him to the cemetery on my back and my father helped me bury him. Years later the people would ask me to tell them stories about Naquima and mock his funny speech.

In the summer of 1935 Norman went around with some lazy boys which spoiled him. One day we wanted him to do some work but he disappeared. I got a whip and struck him three blows, causing him to cry and say, "I'm going back to my real father." I scolded him soundly and told him to never say that again. Irene whipped him once with a paddle for staying out after dark. Whenever he got fresh after that, we would say, "Whip him," and look around as if to get hold of something, which was enough. I pointed out to him again and again that it was wrong for a boy ever to talk back. We were able to handle him with soft words most of the time, but occasionally he seemed to listen with his mouth and pay no attention with his ears. Whenever I told him to do anything, I liked to see him get up and do it quickly.

We scolded Norman often for sleeping late and explained that it is a disgrace for a boy to lie in bed after sunrise. Usually it was enough for us to wake and warn him. At bedtime I often said, "Be sure and get up before sunrise, or I will be after you with my water." One morning I went to the kiva to wake him for school, pulled his quilts off, and told him to hurry or I would drench him. Some time later he slept past breakfast again. I went over to the kiva with a pail of water, pulled the covers back, and wet him thoroughly. He yelled and came out.

Irene drenched Norman too. One day I went up to the housetop to wake him so that he could eat. I then went to my field and returned with melons and peaches by the time Irene prepared breakfast. Norman had not come down. She was suffering with an aching leg, was very angry, climbed on the roof, and doused him. He came down quickly and wide awake. When I got a chance, I talked to him with quiet words. Irene and Norman would have their little troubles, but that is the way mothers are with their children. Whenever he got too rough, I told him to cut it out. About all Irene wanted him to do was to obey her and go for wood and water.

I often advised Norman in a soft voice and urged him to be a good smart boy. I would say, "If, when you are older, the girls find out that you are lazy, the good-looking ones will have nothing to do with you; but if you work hard and help me, their parents will say, 'You marry Norman and he will support you well.'" I started some races so that he could run and reduce. I did not want him to be like those fat boys in New Oraibi who aren't fit for work. I told him that early morning runs would harden his flesh and cause him to live a long time. I was especially proud of him when he rode my horses.

I was happy with my little boy, gained a few more white friends such as schoolteachers, museum workers, artists, anthropologists, and botanists, and seemed to prosper in spite of my impotence. I kept as good a team as any man in the village, made enough to eat, and white friends gave me clothes enough to wear. I enlarged my fields, increased my herd, bought a new wagon, better harness, a cultivator, grubbing hoes, and an iron planting stick. Fewer trips were made to Moenkopi and I stopped seeing Mettie except at dances.

One night Irene discovered a change in me and asked in pleasant surprise, "What has happened?" I laughed and told her that I was renewing my youth. But I didn't become the man that I used to be. Love-making once a week or ten days was enough, and I found that I had better success in the early mornings, although the whole affair lasted less than five minutes. I realized that with age I would become useless again; so it was important to save my strength and prepare myself for a final end to these pleasures. I thought the best way to stay happy was to be more interested in my boy. Now Irene seemed more important for her good cooking than for love-making and I praised her for that. She seemed to appreciate this, and when her monthlies slowed up she said she was glad. But of course, she did not mean that all private pleasures were over for her, for Hopi women keep up love-making into very old age. I was kind to Irene but I loved Norman better, and if she had refused to keep him, I would have left her.

One night I surprised myself. I went for a load of wood and spent the night as usual at the hogan of my Navaho friend, Neschelles. He had gone away to treat a sick man, leaving his wife alone, except for small children. She was especially friendly. I slept with her and rejoiced to find my old powers fully restored. This was repeated on other trips whenever I was lucky enough to be the only man in the hogan. I knew that it was dangerous and that if Neschelles ever caught me, he would beat me. But he would do no more than that, and I thought the pleasure was worth the risk. I looked forward to wood hauling more than ever, and although my friend was usually at home, his wife managed to give me little thrills—at least by sly winks.

I continued buying and losing horses and had too many to describe in detail, although never more than five or six at a time. When they were too old or weak to work, I turned them loose to die. One stumbled over a stone and broke its leg. My brother Ira found one on its back in a gully and killed it with a stone. One horse kicked another and broke its leg. I killed the poor thing with an axe on the ledge north of the village. The women brought in the meat for food, and the Chief made a drum from the hide. Another horse ate locoweeds and went crazy. I was driving him to the wagon up a steep bank on the way to my cornfield when he acted strange and balky. As I struck him with my whip, he fell down, tried to roll over, and sprang up biting and kicking. I tried to work him to the cultivator in the field but could not do it. On the way home he ate by the roadside as he drew the wagon and caught the line between his feet, and as I tried to free it he reared up to bite me. Unhitching him quickly, I threw him with ropes, bound him head and foot, and cut his throat with my butcher knife. I hated to kill my best horse, but could not turn him loose to eat the crops of other people.

In July of perhaps 1936, I missed my favorite buckskin horse. The next morning I mounted a pony and went to Neschelles' hogan where I learned that a rider had passed on my horse in the early morning. Neschelles lent me his fastest saddle horse to overtake the thief. I left without food, trailed my horse beyond Blue Canyon, and camped for the night on an empty stomach. Riding fast next day, I entered a valley of juniper forest and luckily kept the trail. By noon I was so dizzy that I bound a rope about my waist to control my hunger, pressed on, and came to a field where there was one green pumpkin the size of my fist, which I ate. But I felt no better and feared that I might die in the desert.

I finally reached the hogan of Johokimn, a friend who had sold me horses. As I ate and told him my story, I noticed that his face was getting harder and sterner. Finally he volunteered to accompany me and thrash the thief, and urged me to eat more and get back my strength for a struggle. "Brace yourself and be a man," said he. I was glad to have his help, and as we left the hogan he told me to tighten my saddle girth, for we might have to fight on horseback. Following the trail up a mountainside, we came to another hogan where Johokimn announced harshly that we were out to catch a thief. A man informed us that he had seen the son of Fat Williams pass on a horse with a Hopi brand.

Hurrying on, we soon came upon an old man sitting beside a Navaho sweat house. Johokimn sprang from his horse, seized the old fellow, threw him on the ground, called him a horse thief, and threatened to kill him. But he was only teasing this old man, who was the grandfather of the real thief. Two Navahos came up and shook hands with us. One was Joe Isaac, a clan grandfather of mine, for he had married a Navaho Sand Clan woman who could be called my aunt.[4] He also offered to help us and said, "We will thrash that boy." From there we rode hard to another hogan, entered without invitation, and found several women staring at us. Johokimn scolded them and told them to talk to me. I stated that I had chased the thief for two days and that when I caught him I would put him in prison for ten or fifteen years. I said, "If you join that boy's side against me, you will all go to court and perhaps to jail." The mother of the boy cried and said that he had gone to the cattle corral.

We decided to go to a hogan near by where there was a medicine sing to heal a sick man, and to take up the matter with some Navaho judges who were present. There were ten or twelve men at this sing, and I discovered that my Navaho Sun Clan brother, Hotlotis, was

4. The Hopi claim kinship with Navahos who have clan names like their own whenever it is to their advantage.

the head doctor. Greeting me kindly, he asked how it happened that I was so far from home. Joe Isaac and Johokimn explained my presence to the crowd, and Hotlotis talked to the judges like a white lawyer, telling them that he was trying to save the life of a sick man, but that one of their people had stolen his clan brother's horse and thus might spoil the sing. He said, "You Navahos who live far from the Hopi are giving us who live near by a very bad name. You must return that horse." Then they argued back and forth for a long time and became so excited that I expected a fight and fixed my eye on a big stick, which might be used in self-defense. Some of the women cried. Finally the men cooled off and the judges said that the thief must be punished and that they would send a Navaho policeman for him the next day. But my friend Johokimn announced that he would get the boy himself, told me to wait at the sing, and left on his horse.

When night came, Hotlotis pulled me over beside him, gave me a gourd rattle, and told me to assist him in the healing ceremony. I did not know their medicine songs, but decided to try, although I noticed that some of the Navahos were smiling. By watching Hotlotis and imitating him, I did very well. We sang until midnight, ate a great deal, and went to sleep on the floor.

After breakfast next day I saw Johokimn coming with a boy bound in his saddle. He called to me, "Here is the thief. Kill him if you want to." I stepped up to the boy, looked at him closely, and could see that my friend had already whipped him. Johokimn jerked the boy from his horse, threw him on the ground with his hands still tied, and said to me, "Do what you please with him." The judges assembled and said, "It is up to you to do whatever you think best, but if you want the boy to look for your horse, he may go and fetch him while you wait here." I agreed, and the thief left humbly in search of my horse, while we sang again for the life of the sick man. During the day I also took a sweat bath with some Navahos, for it is a healthy treatment for rheumatism, a sore knee, or sore eyes. Before I entered the sweat house, I was told to draw the foreskin over my penis and tie it with a string for protection against the heat and the steam.

We stayed up a second night and sang until daylight. Then the wife of the poor sick man pleaded with us to sing until noon, and gave the medicine man a fine saddle blanket in addition to all the other gifts which he had received. In the afternoon the boy had not yet returned with my horse, so the judges promised me that they would compel him to bring it to the Snake dance at Hotavila. I agreed to this plan and, as we started away, my Navaho clan brother, Hotlotis, gave me part of the goods which he had earned at the sing. I received five pieces of calico, a saddle blanket, a Havasupai plaque, and some tobacco.

The doctor and I packed up our gifts, bade a friendly farewell to the Navahos who had attended the sing, and set out on horseback to the hogan of Johokimn. His wife had butchered a sheep and boiled half the mutton which she gave me as a present, for I had exchanged gifts with their family several times. Hotlotis said, as we rode away, "Now we will go to the hogan of one of my private wives, and if her husband is away, we will have pleasure, I first and you second." He boasted that he had many private wives in this part of the country and that he often visited them whenever he traveled to treat the sick or to look after his cattle. We soon reached a hogan, and to my surprise the woman was the daughter-in-law of my friend Johokimn. But we were unlucky, for her husband was there. From a distance I had noticed her sitting on a sheepskin in the hogan, but when we entered she was lying down as if asleep, probably because she did not wish to see her private lover in the presence of her husband. The man prepared food for us, and as we ate, I made occasional glances toward the woman, and once when I caught her eyes half open, I winked and was rewarded with a sly smile. When her husband and the medicine man stepped outside the hogan, I lingered a little. The young squaw arose quickly, moved over to the fire, and handed me two pieces of roasted mutton. As I accepted the gift, I squeezed her hand until she smiled sweetly. Then I hurried out to join my partner who was mounting his horse. After the farewell, we rode in silence until we were out of earshot of the hogan. Then I let out a big war whoop and told my partner that his friend was not asleep at all, for she had smiled at me and had shared her mutton with me.

Parting from my Navaho brother at Blue Canyon, I reached Neschelles' hogan by sunset. He met me with a broad smile and told me, to my surprise, that my horse had been delivered to him a few hours before. We had a fine feast that night, and his wife gave me a whole fresh mutton to take home. I departed next day and reached the hogan of Hotlotis by noon. He also had butchered a sheep which he tied on the back of my small horse. In the late afternoon, the fourth day after my departure from Oraibi, I proudly returned, riding into the village on my buckskin and leading my pony laden with fresh mutton and valuable gifts—clear proof of my courage. For few Hopi are brave enough to chase a Navaho thief.

I have never struck a Navaho, but once I had a big yellow dog that could lick their dogs. One day he followed me to Neschelles' hogan and was fighting Navaho dogs one by one, until eight dirty curs made a combined attack. When they all landed upon him, he slipped away from the fighting pack and left the other dogs biting each other. I laughed and laughed until a little Navaho boy's dog was so badly hurt that we had to kill him. The poor boy cried, and Neschelles finally asked me, "Will you give your dog to the boy?" "I can't spare my dog," I answered. "I will give you $5 for him," said my friend. When I declined this offer, he added two pairs of rawhide hobbles and a quirk. Finally I agreed. Then when I left on horseback and heard my dog crying to follow me, I almost cried myself—but I felt of my money, looked at my hobbles and quirk, and recovered quickly.

In the summer of 1937 I tore down part of Irene's old house and rebuilt it. My friend Mr. Sachs from New York came again that year and gave me $30 to purchase lumber for a board ceiling under the dirt roof. Almost everyone in the village helped me on the house. My dear old mother helped bring loads of dirt, and my blind old father did all that he could and wove a Hopi blanket for me. Then we all had a fine feast in the new house and the Fire Clan people praised me highly. After that I did not hear the chirping of my dead baby in the roof again and almost forgot some of the names of my lost children. The old Two-Heart who killed them had also died. But I was not happy in my new house very long.

The greatest sorrow of my life was the death of my mother. It was harder to bear than the loss of my children or my long sickness and years of impotence. I think I loved her more than anything. She was between sixty-five and seventy and was still leading a strong and useful life when, in January, 1938, she stepped on a sharp stick which pierced her heel. This was not very serious, but an evil person shot rattlesnake poison into the wound and caused her foot to swell badly to her knee. Poleyestewa treated her with the strongest medicine known to Hopi doctors, and the swelling in the foot went down, but her left arm became infected. A Two-Heart had shot ant poison into it, for another doctor removed a little red ant. My mother's system also was full of bad thoughts, and I think these were harder to overcome than the poison. While she was sick, I asked her about myself: "Have I scolded you thoughtlessly, or filled your heart with sorrow in any other way?" "No," she replied. "You talked crossly when you were a child, but you never scold me now. Neither does your brother, but your sisters talk back to me badly, and this has made me very sad. I think I had better die and go take care of our dear ones." Dropping my head in grief, I begged her to put aside such evil thoughts. "My mother," said I, "you are older than I and very wise. You have advised us how to live year after year. Now practice the same rules and face east with a brave heart." "I have thought of passing away for a long time," she replied. That remark made me angry, for it showed that she was killing herself. But I tried not to scold her. Instead, I reminded her that both good and bad thoughts present themselves to our minds and that we must choose the good. When she admitted that she was seeing dead relatives in her dreams and talking to them, I gave up hope and wondered if she was a Two-Heart herself. As the hours passed, she ate very little and seemed to be out of pain with her mind far away.

My mother died on the next day at sunrise. Ira, my father, Delia's husband, Mabel, and I were eating breakfast and watching her when her breath began to fail. I told the others to hurry with their meal and get out of danger. Soon after they left, my mother passed away in my arms. I cried, let her down on the floor, covered her face, and stepped outside to make water. As Nuvahunka, our mother's sister, arrived from New Oraibi, I said, "Our mother is dead and you do not have to see her." "She is my sister," she replied, "and I am not afraid."

Nuvahunka entered the house with me, uncovered my mother's face, cried, and said, "Well, my sister, this is the last time we will see you. You have been telling us how to preserve our lives and now you refuse to follow the good advice yourself. You have turned your face from us and stepped off the Sun Trail. I don't think I can look upon your grave after we bury you." She was angry and scolded my mother. We covered her face again and cried together. As I thought of all the good things that my mother had done for me, I wondered if I ever could be happy again.

I buried our mother with the aid of my brother. Since she was very heavy, we hitched horses to the wagon to take her to the cemetery. I had buried our dead ever since my marriage, and I did everything exactly right. In my tearful speech I gave her my very best wishes and urged her to go take care of our dead relatives, assuring her that we would get along all right, overcome our sorrow, and see her later.

My mother was the smartest and kindest person I ever knew and spent her life in keeping us well and happy. She whipped me some when I was a naughty boy, but I did not hold that against her. Some Hopi say that when their parents are old and feeble they will even the score with them for the thrashings that they have received in youth. I never felt that way. But my father refused to look upon our mother's face in death and had nothing to do with the burial. He stopped telling jokes, and later said that on several occasions she came to him in his dreams, but never tried to speak to him or touch him. He hated to see her in dreams because he was still angry with her for leaving him and his children, and he feared that she might call him to go with her. Whenever he passed the cemetery, he looked in the opposite direction, even though nearly blind. I never liked to talk about my mother's death, and when friends came around I would only say, "Our mother has passed away and we will not see her again until we leave this place."

But I kept seeing my mother at night in my dreams and greatly feared that she would touch me, for then I would have to go with her. It seemed that she would not stay with our dear ones, but kept returning. So I finally took some sacred corn meal and pahos out to the northwest ledge, sacrificed, scolded her, and told her to leave us alone and go back and stay where she belonged. And I wondered again if she were a Two-Heart.

14
New Crises:
1938–1939

IN JULY, 1938, another white man came into my life. Dr. Mischa Titiev of the University of Michigan wrote that Mr. Simmons from Yale University was coming to Oraibi and said that I might like to work with him and rent him a room. When he arrived, I stopped my work and went about with him. In two weeks he asked me to work for him, rented part of our house, hired my sister Inez to cook, and began questioning me about Hopi life. But he soon became more interested in my own life and taught me to write my diary, saying over and over that he wanted the complete record. He also helped me with my work at herding, farming, and care of horses, and used his car to take our friends to dances and sick children to Hopi doctors. When I knew him better, I agreed to tell him anything about myself except ceremonial secrets. Most of his questions were easy, but some were very hard, some were funny, and some even seemed foolish. But when I told him about the death of my mother, I broke down and cried. I was often surprised at myself for telling him things that I had never told any other person. This made me feel that my Guardian Spirit approved of our work; and I finally wondered if my Guide had brought us together.

The people also liked my friend, and Irene appreciated the rent money; but we feared that people might complain and start gossip, especially a man named Barker. I finally told Mr. Simmons about this, and then we took Barker to dances and were very nice to him in order to soften his spirit and tie his tongue. Myron, who was to become the Chief's successor, also complained a little. But when we took his sick baby to the doctor several times, he joined our side. The Chief liked my friend too, and when I asked him if he would consider him as a son, he seemed pleased. But we waited for Mr. Simmons to ask, which he finally did. Grace, the Chief's niece and the wife of Myron, was glad to become his aunt and godmother. On August 10 at about 8 A.M. I led Mr. Simmons to the Chief's house. The family and relatives gathered and Grace came with a dishpan of yucca suds. A sheepskin was placed on the floor and my friend was told to kneel. Grace wet two mother-ears of corn and rubbed them on his head. After she had washed his head, the Chief and all his family did likewise, including little Betty, an adopted daughter who was feebleminded. Then his hair was rinsed with clear water and Grace took sacred corn meal ground by the Chief's wife, Nasinonsi, and rubbed it on his wet face. Grace took the two mother-ears, waved them four times toward Mr. Simmons, and said, "Now we adopt you as a son. May you live from this day without sickness to very old age and pass away in sleep. You shall be called Honweseoma (Trailing Bear)." The Chief sat in front of Mr. Simmons, spoke to him in Hopi, and was interpreted by me. He introduced each member of his family and gave the term of address to be used. He advised him that one should always eat with relatives and feed relatives in return. He also instructed him in the proper respect for Katcinas and Hopi gods and shrines and promised to look out for his new son's interests. Then Honweseoma thanked his father and said he would try to be a worthy son, and a good Hopi.

I led the new "Hopi" to my mother's house where my sister Inez accepted his mother-corn ears, and I showed him our clan's sacred and secret Sun shield. That made him my younger brother and a member of the Sun Clan. He was told not to wash off the sacred meal; and I spent the rest of the day telling him about his new relatives and teaching him how to treat them.

But Irene still feared gossip from the people in New Oraibi, and one night I had a strange dream. I had come up with wood on my wagon, stopped near the door, and was unhitching the horses when I heard Irene crying. I stepped in quickly and found her leaning over the table, sobbing with her face in her hands. She said that the people in New Oraibi had scolded her for keeping another White in her house. I tried to comfort her and reminded her that we were not under the control of the Hopi Council in New Oraibi, but took our orders from the Chief. I said, "Don't worry, they want to keep all the Whites and get their money. Our Chief will defend us." Then a big, yellow automobile came up, loaded with Whites. My friend, George D. Sachs from New York City, was driving the car, and I knew all his companions. Mr. Sachs came in with an important paper and said, "We have brought this to protect you from unfriendly Hopis. You have nothing to fear, for we will fight for your rights." As the other Whites entered the room, my new brother came in through the back door. I said to all, "This is the man who lives with us and he has become my brother." Then as everyone shook hands, I said, "We will all stick together so that no one can win against us." My wife stopped crying and said, "Thank you, my friends. Now we are safe." I awoke feeling happy, but with bells ringing in my head. When I realized that we were alone, I looked around to make sure that we were safe; then I lay awake, thinking of my dream. And at sunrise I went to the east edge of the mesa with corn meal and prayed.

In a few days we had trouble with Nathaniel. During the summer another daughter had died at Phoenix. Although she was far from home, I felt sure that Nathaniel killed her, like his other children, to prolong his life. And when they brought the dead girl home, her father ran off like a coward and let the missionaries bury her in the wrong way. I also heard reports of Nathaniel's mistreatment of children. One day he caught Norman by the shirt, accused him of damaging his house, and threatened to strike him. Lilly, Herbert's wife, complained to the field nurse that Nathaniel had caught one of her boys and tried to choke him. The field nurse asked Dr. Paul W. Preu, a psychiatrist who was with Mr. Simmons, to investigate. The doctor and Mr. Simmons questioned me closely about Nathaniel, but I tried to avoid the subject and refused to go with the doctor to see either Lilly or Nathaniel. But he called on Lilly and wrote down what information he could get. When I passed Lilly's house in the evening, she called me and said that she regretted telling the doctor anything. She was especially worried because her words had been written down. She was a relative of the Two-Heart, and feared that he would take revenge on her children. I was uneasy, told Mr. Simmons how worried we were, and asked him to help us get the paper. He agreed to coöperate, and I asked Lilly's husband to come to my house. When he came, he wanted to get the paper immediately. We drove to New Oraibi and all three of us went into the doctor's room, for Herbert would agree to nothing that might give anyone a chance to copy the report. I explained our troubles, asked for the paper, and got it. Herbert took it home and destroyed it, for we wanted the matter dropped.

My white brother wanted to meet Nathaniel and asked me to introduce him, but I was afraid to do it, even for pay. I felt that it was the duty of the government agents to protect the children, but I decided that if I caught him mistreating anyone, I would walk up to him like a man and tell him to stop. Then if he wanted to fight and struck the first blow, I would defend myself. He was a weak old man with only one good arm, and his collarbone had been broken, but I was afraid of his power. It was dangerous for me to say that I wished for his death, but I knew that when it happened I might say that I was glad. I didn't think I would help bury him, unless his relatives refused and let me take his property, and then I could sing a war song over his dead body.

My white brother left in September with instructions for me to keep a complete diary, and in a few weeks I had a terrible dream in which I visited the secret meeting place of the Two-Hearts. I was sitting in the door of the third story of my house, removing my shoes, when my Guardian Spirit suddenly appeared and told me to follow him. I replaced my shoes quickly and followed about fifty steps behind my Guide. He led me past the old stone church and disappeared over the southeast edge of the mesa. When I overtook him on the lower shelf near a shrine, he said, "Step on this water shield with me and prepare for a ride." The shield resembled a woven plaque such as the women make on Second Mesa. It was about thirty-six inches wide with a three-inch outer rim. The shield was half red and half yellow, but the border was black with prayer feathers fastened at the six cardinal points. We stepped upon the plaque, and each of us seized a propeller stick tipped with a prayer feather. The shield arose and floated with us northeast like a cloud, moving over desert and high mesas. Finally my Guide said, "I am taking you to the secret meeting place of the underworld people. Perhaps you will recognize some old friends. Remember that I am your Guardian Spirit. Don't be afraid, for I will protect you."

As we moved swiftly through the air, we saw a big red mountain about three miles off. We drew near, landed on the roof of a large white house, climbed down, and started toward the foot of Red Cliff Mesa. My Guide reached into his tobacco pouch, drew out a root, took a bite, and handed it to me, saying, "Chew this, spit into your hands, and rub them over your body." The medicine disguised my appearance so that no one could recognize me.

At the very top of Red Cliff Mesa we saw a cave resembling a kiva, with a looped yucca rope for a ladder. I climbed down with my Guide and found a great underground kiva, where Two-Hearts from all tribes and nations were gathered to enjoy the dances. As we took our seats, my Guide whispered, "Look to the right." Close by the fire sat a Ute woman in a love-making mood who smiled brightly at me. She was very pretty and seemed eager to have me, but I resolved with effort to dismiss such thoughts and watch the dances.

There were eight pairs of Katcinas who danced and sang very beautifully. During the seventh dance, my Guide said, "After the eighth, it will be our turn. You will be able to make these steps." I had never tried this kind of dance, but I promised to do my best. All these Katcinas had strange designs on their masks, carried yucca whips in their hands, and danced slowly at first, but very rapidly near the end. I wondered whether I would be able to take such fast steps, but my Guide assured me that they would be easy. "You are a young man yet," he whispered.

We climbed out of the kiva, went back to our water shield, and found masks and costumes lying on the floor in the big white house. We quickly dressed in moccasins, dancing skirt, sash, belt, armbands, and other things that Katcinas wear, put on our masks, and practiced a few steps. I made four quick steps, whirled around, shook my mask, and made a Katcina noise. My Guide said, "Very good, follow me and do whatever I do."

When we were back at the kiva, I peeped through the hole at the top and made the Katcina noise. Then we circled the kiva four times and were ready to enter. I was surprised at the speed with which my Guide descended the yucca ladder. But when I tried it, I swooped down like a bird. The Two-Hearts were greatly surprised to see two new, strange dancers. I could see them asking questions of one another concerning us. Soon the drummer took his place and all the people sang a tune for us to dance. The songs were new and the finest I had ever heard. In the ceiling were little bells which rang with the beating of the drum. I followed my Guide in his steps and tried to memorize the songs. I found it very easy to take the steps, for the spirit within my mask seemed to direct me. As we danced for the third song, my Guide whispered, "These people would like to make prisoners of us. We must flee before we get caught." Just as the dance ended, we raced up the yucca ladder and rushed to the big white house, where we discarded our Katcina outfit, climbed to the roof, stepped on our water shield, and quickly floated away. But as we sailed along, I looked back and saw many Two-Hearts chasing us. When I warned my Guide that we were in danger, he said, "I have a medicine that will help." He withdrew a root from his pouch, took a bite, and handed it to me, saying, "Let's chew this medicine and spit it straight at the Two-Hearts." This we did. The wicked people began stumbling and falling to the ground on their faces. In surprise I asked my Guide what the medicine was. "It's rainbow medicine," he replied, "the same kind that witches use to keep back the clouds and cause droughts." Looking back again, I saw a mighty rainbow appear between us and the Two-Hearts, which blocked them from further pursuit. "Now we are safe," said my Guardian Spirit. We were moving smoothly and swiftly through the air, but before we had gone another mile, I awoke and felt that I was still upon the easy-gliding water shield. I was happy for, although I had at last attended a meeting of the underworld people, I felt safer than before. I felt sure that as long as I remained under the protection of my Guardian Spirit the wicked Two-Hearts would never catch me.

Within a few months, however, a Two-Heart forced me to challenge him face to face. I was working on my diary when my dogs barked and a stone struck my house. When a second rock nearly broke a window, I rushed out, saw Nathaniel, and said, "Here! Here! You damn fool! What are you doing?" "You have mean dogs," said he, "and some day I am going to kill them." "Well, kill them now and be done with it," I challenged. "Go ahead and kill them." I dared him again and again and called him a coward in strong language. Then he hit a dog on the hip with a stone, so that he ran off yelping. I grabbed the old Two-Heart by the collar and said, "We are all afraid of you because you are a witch. You are not supposed to be afraid of anybody, but you are trembling. Now stand up and prove your courage. I will expose myself to your evil powers. I can die bravely. Go ahead and kill me, for I have only one heart and no power to protect myself." I challenged him four times; but he backed down. Then I called him an evil-minded troublemaker who raises hell with women, children, and dogs. "But when it comes to a showdown, you won't fight," said I. "You are not a man. You are a weak old woman." I turned him loose and told those who had gathered to laugh at him—and I hoped they would spit at him. He walked off and I went back to the house—trembling and too upset to work. It took me a long time to overcome my anger, and even then I was afraid for myself and family.

A few weeks later I had a dream that just saved my boy from the Two-Heart's revenge. Four men came to me with lively steps, with faces painted black, and in Snake dancer's costumes. They told me that a certain Hopi witch had asked them to bring rain and a hailstorm. Then they left as quickly as they had come, and I awoke with bells ringing in my ears. I had planned for Norman to herd the next day, but quickly changed my mind.

After breakfast I saddled my horse, tied on two blankets, and rode down the mesa, thinking of my dream. In New Oraibi I said to Joe, my herding partner, "Bring these blankets to our camp when you come. It may rain or hail today, for four Snake dancers warned me in a dream last night that they were bringing a storm. The clouds are already gathering—see them coming like warriors on a warpath. We must be watchful." Moving on in an easy gallop, I overtook a wagon with a man and his two sons who were going out to plant beans. "Why don't you take along coats and blankets?" I asked, "Don't you know it is going to rain or hail?" They laughed and replied, "Well, we will see what happens." "Don't you realize that I am a medicine man who can predict rains?" I asked. They laughed again and said, "No, we don't know anything about that, but if it does rain we'll say you are a weather prophet, and perhaps a witch too."

I herded all morning, keeping a watchful eye on the clouds which were rushing together with lightning and thunder. The herd and I were racing for the corral when the storm broke with fierce winds and pelted us with hailstones the size of my thumb. The sheep and goats cried for their lives and crawled under some greasewood bushes for shelter. I sat in my saddle with a blanket over my head and thought about the Hopi gods—and of life, death, and Two-Hearts. But for the protecting bushes some of my freshly sheared sheep would have died, and indeed, one mother did deliver a lamb at the peak of the storm. After the hail, the wind blew more sharply, causing my sheep to shiver in the cold. I rescued the wet lamb, led my flock to the corral under the bank of the wash, and buried the little newborn thing in warm sand up to its eyes. Then I collected some dry cedar bark and built a fire, for I was wet to the skin. As I ate my lunch, I thought of my dream, knew that Nathaniel had called up the storm, and felt thankful that Norman was safe at home. But I pitied the poor fellows who ignored my warnings and went without blankets.

Joe came in a wagon with his family in late afternoon and called, "Talayesva, are you still alive?" "Yes, just a little," I answered. "I nearly passed on to our dear ones, but my Spirit Guide saved me and my flock." "I pitied you in the storm and I'm glad you are safe," said Joe. As we made camp and butchered a fat goat, I told him about my dream. He was surprised and said that some day I would be a medicine man. I did not know about that, but as I lay in camp that night, I thanked my Guardian Spirit for saving my boy from the wrath of that old witch.

I had made Norman a fine Katcina mask, praised his voice, and encouraged him to be a good dancer, for that is more important to the Hopi than an education. In a few days he danced at New Oraibi and did very well. When he came home I said, "Thank you for dancing. But don't think that it is for pleasure. When you dance, watch your steps carefully and keep wishing for rain. Now is the time to fix this in your mind. Put away your childish thoughts and dance and pray like a man. You are not alone. Your Guardian Spirit watches over you, and the Six-Point-Cloud-People will hear your prayers. From now on I shall teach you these important things." He looked straight into my eyes and seemed to be wondering.

Ten days later there was another dance. In the morning after break-fast Norman came home with his little nephew. They had some piki wrapped in a towel and said that they had received much good food. I reminded him again that he danced for rain and not for pleasure and said, "Do your best and pray to your mask for strength." He listened closely and promised to try. I told him that it was the only way to be a worshipful dancer, and that he must learn these things now and later pass them on to his children.

I went in the afternoon to New Oraibi and entered the house of my clan sister Jennie, where Norman stayed to practice the dances. She had company and we talked about our schooldays at Sherman, the hard time we had learning to read and cipher, and the good times at the socials. I made her laugh by saying, "Now we are getting old and cannot swing our partners." When the visitors had gone, I talked about my son, asking Jennie not to tell him untrue stories nor let him loaf with lazy boys. I said, "It will be better for him to herd for you. We will teach him to be a smart boy and when he marries we will share our property with him. We will urge him to pay close attention to the old people in the kiva and try to be a good Katcina."

I went to Hotavila a few nights later to see the Eshau Katcinas dance. They are the spirit gods who look after spinach and other wild plants which the Hopi used to eat. They danced and sang about how disappointed they were to see the people neglecting the old foods for new-fangled things like canned goods, wheat bread, cakes, and pies.

They urged us to go back to the food of our fathers so that in summer the fields would be green again, the crops flourish, and wild flowers bloom everywhere. It grieved me to hear this song, for we are spoiled by the white man's fancy foods and foolish clothes. Now the Hopi turns up his nose at the old-fashioned foods, and the day will come when no woman will dress in a decent Hopi way. I realized that the good old days are gone and that it is too late to bring them back. As the Katcinas danced, my mind was filled with these thoughts and I was so upset that tears ran down my face. It was clear that we could never be good Hopis again with our religion neglected and our ceremonies dying out. It is no wonder that we are weakened by disease and that death comes early—we are no longer Hopi, but kahopi.

When I ate breakfast next day at my clan sister's house, I was glad to get old-fashioned Hopi dumplings made of blue corn meal. Some time later, as my wife cooked, I thought to myself, "I am tired of this fancy stuff." When she called me to eat, I said, "I would like some Hopi food." "What is the matter with you?" she asked. "Don't you like my cooking?" "Yes," I replied quickly, "but I am a full-blood Hopi and feel a need for old-fashioned foods. Please give me some piki and some water in a bowl." Handing it to me, she said sharply, "Here is your food," and ate her fried potatoes, eggs, chili, and coffee with canned milk. Later we had Hopi dumplings and fried chilis for supper. Norman remarked that he did not think he could live very long on that. I reminded him that the old people outlived us who eat the white man's stuff, and that if the white farmers have a bad year, we may be forced back to the food of our ancestors. I said, "You must be careful with our food. Our great uncles have told us of the dreadful famines in their times when whole families died of starvation. Now, my boy, these talks have been handed down from them to us, and it is my turn to tell you."

Once when Norman did not want to herd on account of bad weather, he was persuaded to drive the horses to the wash for water. In the afternoon I took them out and hobbled them, and, returning to the village, entered Claude James's store where a group of men and boys were talking about women. The Chief was telling about his private life, how he used to work on the Santa Fe Railroad, made plenty of money, and spent it on women. He was giving all the details of love-making. Norman was there and was what I call a greenhorn on this subject. But he was learning, for he was leaning forward to hear every word, and he had his mouth and eyes wide open—filling himself with jokes.

Some time later I found two large pieces of cardboard in the kiva where Norman slept with other boys. On them were vivid drawings of the sex act and examples of masturbation. I teased Norman about the pictures and asked him to name the artist. We had a good laugh, and he said, "Don't let any white man see them." I had never caught him masturbating. If I do some time, I shall warn him that the white doctors say it will ruin his mind and health, but the Hopi doctors doubt it; and that they are probably right.

I soon heard that Norman was writing love letters to the school-girls and that he had a special friend with whom he slipped out at night. I hoped the girl would not get a baby too soon and wondered whether I should advise him to see her in private only occasionally and then not too near her monthlies. But I realized that since he was getting into the habit, I probably could not stop it. He was growing up then, almost fourteen and oversize, and I knew that love-making would become about as important to him as eating.

One night Ross, who owns a small store in Oraibi, saw Norman and Myron's stepson, Lorenza, trying to break the lock on the door of the building. They were arrested and had to go to trial charged with attempted theft. I advised Norman to admit that he tried to enter the store by force, but that his purpose was not to take any property but to reach two girls who were sleeping there. He could not be blamed too much for that.

I made up my mind that if Norman started a baby somewhere, I would tell him that he should marry the girl—if she belonged to a clan into which he could marry. It was my duty to give him the same advice that the old people gave me. I thought that if he went too steady with one girl, I should investigate her. If she proved to be lazy, too old, or too ugly, a common flirt, cross-tempered, gossipy, or tubercular, I would warn him against her. I wanted him to get a quiet, good-looking, hard-working young woman who was good-natured, patient, and peaceable; one who was neither stingy nor a spendthrift, who had the respect of her neighbors, and who would leave other men alone after marriage.

One day I was very anxious for Norman. I had asked him to herd, and since it was very cold I had told him to put on another sweater, an overcoat, and two pairs of socks, and had loaned him my scarf. After he was gone, I took a pail of water to our kiva to sprinkle my bean plants for the Powamu ceremony. Later I returned to the house to carve a doll for Irene out of a cottonwood root. I worked on into the afternoon, but did not get along very well, for the wind and snow were coming fast and causing me to worry about my boy. I knew I should have herded myself. Then I thought, "Perhaps his grand-parents at Lolomi Spring will have sense enough to give him a blanket to cover his face." I wondered if they would tell him to spend the night with them, but decided that if he failed to show up by sunset I would search for him. As the storm increased, these thoughts multi-plied until I could stand them no longer. I put away my work, pulled on an extra pair of socks, stuck matches in my pocket, took a blanket, and set out to find him. I traveled about a mile and a quarter, saw snow dust in the distance, and thought it was a whirlwind; but it was a horseman riding fast. It was Norman, and I was happy.

A worse thing happened in the summer. Norman went out with his uncle Baldwin, riding a mean horse. At about sunset the horse ran past our door dragging the saddle. I ran in the direction whence he came, fearing that Norman had been thrown and killed. He came up the path bringing the saddle blanket and crying with a sprained wrist. I could see that a bone was out of place and was frightened, feeling much like a man on a narrow path who fears to take the next step. We were planning to walk to Hotavila to see a bone doctor when a car came up. It was Fred Eggan and his wife. Norman was still crying and we were excited and unhappy. Fred gave him some little white but-tons which he called aspirin and offered to take him to the hospital at Keams Canyon. But I decided to go to a good Hopi doctor.

We reached Hotavila in the afterglow and stopped at the door of the old blind doctor. When I explained our trouble, he said, "That is too bad. Come close so that I can see if the bone is broken." He felt over the wrist and said to Norman, "When I press the bone back into place it will hurt; be brave while I work." Norman braced himself and did not even whimper, but I was trembling. In about twenty minutes the job was done, and the doctor said, "My son, you are brave, no child can stand that and many men would have cried." I paid him twenty-five cents, and thanked him too. The treatment would have been free at the hospital, but this was better.

Two days later Norman went with me to spray plants. As we stopped at the spring for water, I spied a little boy hiding in the wagon, David, the son of Julius. "Where are you going?" I asked. "With you if you will let me," he answered. We drove to the field and Norman soaked the medicine—roots, rabbit intestines, and dog dung—while I hoed weeds. As I worked I looked up and saw the boys spraying plants. David was holding the can of medicine and following Norman who was using the broom in his left hand. I was proud of my boy for being willing to help me with his one good hand.

A few days later I returned from herding, found Norman working in my melon field, and thought to myself, "It is a good thing for a man to have a son. Mine is a good planter and weeder and a fine little herder. I am proud to have a boy who will make a useful man. Even now he works without my telling him." I had tried to do my duty in teaching Norman to be a hard worker. Many times I had said, "Now you are learning to herd. I have given you a few sheep since you were a little boy. It is my plan that some day the herd will be yours, but if you are lazy, you will lose it. Be square with me, and I will be square with you." He had often replied, "Well, father, your talk about the sheep business suits me fine. It is better than hoeing weeds, for you don't have to use your arms so much. I know that if I had not been given to you I would not be alive now." Then I always said, "Remember that, my boy, it is important. I saved your life and I love you. You are the only child to my name, and all that I have will be yours. So when I tell you to do something, obey me."

But I had taught Norman to be a good field worker too. I said time after time, "Work fast so that you will be trained that way." I advised him to keep on working when he was tired, in order to toughen him. That very spring, 1939, when we were planting corn, Norman seemed tired, but I said, "You don't have to quit, just take your time. This is the way we did when we were boys. Our fathers taught us to stick to the job and said that when we got used to work it would be as easy as eating pie." The sun was very hot, we were tired, and our hands were blistered, but every plant counted. Norman kept working with me. Finally I had said, "Sonny, how would you like to go on with your planting?" "Well," he had replied, "my back and hands are sore, my tongue is parched, my throat is dry, and I can't spit." Then we rested.

I knew the kind of manhood I wished to see in Norman. I wanted him to grow strong and be industrious, mild-tempered, good-natured, and popular with men as well as women. I hoped that he would be wise and that his deeds would fit his words. I wanted him to be kind, quiet, and sociable, but full of jokes and able to wear a smile when things go wrong. I hoped he would keep out of arguments, never gossip, never strike anyone, and use firm words with a soft voice even with anger. I was glad for him to be educated, but I hoped he would stay home and be a good herder, in my own footsteps. I wanted him to take good care of our property, keep the respect of the neighbors, know the teachings of our ancestors, follow the good life, and escape the Two-Hearts.

It was a good thing for me to have a hard-working son during my illness a few weeks later. While I lay upon my bed, Norman offered to go down to the melon field and work. I said, "I am thankful that you want to help me in my sickness. Will you herd for me tomorrow and next day?" "Certainly I will," he answered. "You have had a hard time to raise me. Now I am old enough to repay you." That was what I wanted to hear, and I almost cried at the way that brave boy said it. I replied, "I'm very thankful that I have a son who helps his dad when he is sick." He hobbled my horses, went to the field, and worked all morning. On the evening of the second day I was dozing when I heard Irene call out to him, "Thank you, dear sonny, thank you ever so much." He handed her six cottontails. I had bought a box of cartridges for him that very day and I was proud that he was getting to be a good hunter and a sharpshooter.

Norman kept his health but more sickness came to me. Once I had a very sore ankle and went to see a medicine man at Bakabi. When I limped into his house, he fed me, took my corn meal, prayed outside, and returned quickly, breathing upon his hands. He examined me closely, looked worried, and said, "Last night in my dream, a Snake man came and said that I was treating too many people who had been struck by poison arrows. He challenged me to fight and said that if I won I would also save a man who would come limping to me. I wrestled and won, so you are safe." Then he felt over my ankle again, jerked out a poison arrow which he threw outside, and said: "As you herded some days ago, your horse stepped on the tracks of a male and a female rattlesnake coiled in intercourse. You know that when they are doing that, they will stand for no teasing. You got off your horse and stepped on the tracks also. Then snake poison entered your ankle." "That is true," I answered. "I discovered the tracks after I had stepped on them, and said to myself, 'Some day something will happen to me.' Soon my ankle felt sore, and it seemed that snakes were coiling themselves around it and striking upward on my leg." He removed the poison and said, "Well, I will never let two snakes get the best of you." I thanked him and set out for home in a slow gait.

In a short time the ankle was well and I was able to wrestle with Poleyestewa. One morning as he rounded up his horses and was taking them to the spring, I drove mine in a fast trot to overtake him. Just before he looked around, I jumped from horseback, rushed my horses past him, and called back, "Why don't you run like I do, you lazybones?" "I don't think you have run very far," he replied, "for I know very well that you never walk when you can ride, and your pants are full of hair. I am going to thrash you." Then the fun began. He jumped from his horse and wrestled with me until he was out of breath. Then I picked him up, carried him to a pool of water on the rocks, and set him down in it. We continued to struggle until we were wet to the skin and our shirts were torn to shreds. The day was cold, and when we reached the village we were shivering. I put on my last good shirt, went to the store, and bought a dollar shirt for my pesty "grandfather," for I knew that I had gotten the best of him.

The snakes did not bother me again, but as I herded one day in summer, my dog stuck his nose into a sage bush, cried, jumped back, and ran around rubbing his face with his paws. There were two blood spots on his upper lip. I rushed to the bush, looked under it, and heard the rattle of a snake. Beating it with a stick, I said, "You mean devil, I shall split you wide open." I pried the snake's mouth open with two sticks and with my knife quickly split it down to its tail. There were the two blood spots. If this had not been done, my dog would have died. Whenever a snake is crazy enough to bite a person or animal, the first thing to do is to kill the snake and split him open. The blood that the snake sucks from the wound will move rapidly to the end of its tail and disappear. If it is not overtaken and exposed, the wounded man or beast will die. One should never harm a good, wise snake, for it is sacred and a blessing to the people, but evil and foolish ones must pay with their lives. My dog's head was swelling fast, so I washed his face in my urine.

For several weeks I had felt that trouble was near. Once I found a jack rabbit dragging a steel trap and, when I heard ringing in my ears, I thought it was a sign that Norman would get hurt. Then one night I dreamed that a Hopi goddess attacked me and tried to seduce me. I was sitting under a cottonwood tree, beating a five-gallon can and shouting to frighten crows from my cornfield. There was a soft wind from the west, and I wondered if it would bring rain clouds. As it was near noon, I gathered some dry sticks and picked green corn for a roast. Then I saw a shadow moving toward me, but thought it was a cloud and did not look up. It stopped, and suddenly a powerful being jumped upon me and caught me around the waist. I fell backward and tried to look upon the face of my opponent, but could see only a white cottonlike mask. I soon knew that it was a female spirit. And as she locked my arms in a powerful embrace, my memory faded, my breath weakened, and my body became limp. But memory and strength returned quickly and I exclaimed, "Well, I never thought that any good spirit would struggle with me while I did my duty. Now I must fight." I tried to roll over and get on top of the spirit, but she was too much for me. As we wrestled, I came on top once, got a glimpse of her face, and discovered that she was the Mother god of wild game such as deer, buffalos, and rabbits.[1] As she swung herself on top again, she turned

1. See Appendix, pp. 440–442.

her face from me and said, "I came to have intercourse with you, but you don't seem to want it. Do you wish to be a good hunter?" "Yes," I replied. "If you had come to me in an open, friendly way, I would not wrestle with you. But when you sneak up and capture me, it is my duty to defend myself. Please let me go; and if you will give me game, I will make a paho for you at Soyal." She agreed, got up, and started behind my field house. I followed about fifty yards back and noticed that she wore a fresh deerskin as a blanket with the forearms tied across her breast. She also wore some long grass from each ear and two tassels on her head. Finally she looked back at me, sat down, spun herself round like a top, and disappeared into the ground. I ran to the spot, but saw no hole. There were four dead rabbits near by, and I heard a voice saying, "Don't be afraid. Take them home with you, for they are your reward." Then I awoke with bells ringing in my ears, found my body wet with sweat, and feared that something was going to happen.

Some time later my friend, Professor Fred Eggan of the University of Chicago, came one afternoon and found me resting on a sheepskin. He promised to return after supper with a special book for me to see. "All right," I replied, "I would like to see an interesting book." And I noticed that he smiled as he got into his car.

While I corrected my diary in the evening Fred returned, placed a large volume on the table, and said, "Here is the book that I was telling you about." "All right," I answered, "I'll finish this page and then we will look at it." He said that it was published in 1901 by the Rev. Voth and remarked, "You remember that in 1933 some Hopis from here were at the World's Fair in Chicago, went to the Field Museum, and saw what they thought was a statue of you dressed in a ceremonial costume used in the Soyal. You know that when they returned they claimed that you had sold the secrets and ceremonial equipment and made much trouble for you. Now I will let you see this book." When he opened it, I was surprised to see pictures of secret altars, how the members of the Soyal dressed, and what they did. This evil man Voth had written out all the secrets, not only of the Soyal but of other ceremonies. I saw the names and pictures of the Soyal officers, those old timers, and recognized every one of them. Now at that time

I was only a little boy and had not been initiated into the Wowochim. Fred also showed me altars of the Snake and the Antelope ceremonies. These things were of greater value to the Hopi than anything else in the world and the Whites had gotten them away from us. I felt very badly. But I did not blame the Whites for buying them as much as I blamed the old Hopis, the head Soyal Priest, Shokhungyoma, and Chief Lolulomai. There was even a picture of my great-uncle, Talasquaptewa, who acted as Star Priest. If those chiefs had not permitted Voth to take the pictures and watch the ceremonies, they would never have been published. Fred urged me not to feel badly about it. When he closed the book, I asked how much it would cost. The only good thing about it was the fact that it was clear proof that I was not the one who had sold the secrets. I wanted it, for if any Hopi ever charged me again with selling secrets all I would need to defend myself was this book. Fred left about nine-thirty, and I went to bed. But I was so worried that I never slept until one-thirty in the morning. With all our ceremonial secrets out, it is no wonder that our gods are offended and fail to send us enough snow and rain, and that sickness, droughts, and other misfortunes come upon us.

In June, 1939, Kochwytewa, the best doctor in Hotavila, got into trouble and lost his life. His son, who is my clan brother, told me that the old man had been persuaded to join a society of Fire Doctors at Mishongovi in order to renew his powers with the women. But he was trapped into joining a society of Two-Hearts who caused him to burn up with fever and lose his flesh and strength in less than a month. He also became discouraged about everything and advised the people that there was no use to plant their crops, for droughts and evil winds would destroy them. When his son returned from his field and heard the bad-luck arguments, he scolded his father and said, "Well, you Two-Hearts are against us. I don't want to neglect my farm and look for trouble. Most men nourish happy thoughts, expect good crops, and try to prolong the lives of their families. When you were healing the people, you were wise and full of good advice. If you wanted to live now, you know that your Spirit Guide would not drop you, for you have preached that all your life. But if you want to die it is up to you. I am going to fight for life and for my family, and we will see who wins. This is the last time I shall advise you, for I am through with you." The old doctor died a few days later and the son told his family not to cry, "for it was his own fault."

When I heard these things I said, "Well, my brother, we are no longer babies or even children; we are grown men who support families. Let's push each other forward in our fight against the underworld people. Let's plant our crops with confidence and if we are lucky, we will get a little rain. It is the business of our Guardian Spirit to protect and guide us. We will forget about the dead and be very careful to escape the traps which Two-Hearts set for us."

But on July 1 I nearly lost my life. I had hitched my horses to the wagon to leave my field at Batowe when I heard a woman's voice calling from the west, "Talayesva, come; Talayesva, come." I could see no one and was frightened when I realized that it was a death call. Dropping my head, I said to myself, "I don't want to die. I am still middle-aged and strong, so I will brace myself and fight." Then I drove home hurriedly and very worried, but kept the news from my wife. On the next day, which was Sunday, I got up before sunrise with a very sore throat, drank a cup of water, and rounded up my horses. Then I lay down until breakfast, still keeping my troubles to myself. I could eat nothing but bread soaked in coffee, while Irene and Norman had mutton ribs, piki, apricots, and coffee. Although every swallow was like a sharp knife in my throat, I forced down three cups of coffee, for I feared that by the next meal the pain would be worse. Norman went with me to the melon field to remove sand from our plants. After two hours of work I started up the mesa, feeling very sick. I was wet with sweat, my breath was short, and I felt choked. Staggering into my door in a dazed condition, I motioned to my wife for a bed. As my memory came back, I told her that on the day before I had heard a woman's voice calling from the west and thought that it was my mother. She cried and fixed food, while Norman went to hobble the horses.

Irene brought me some corn gruel and, although I did not want it, I remembered my grandfather's advice always to eat when sick. So

I managed to take a little, closing my eyes in pain with every swallow. When I lay back on my blanket again, I was out of breath, and it seemed that even my spittle would choke me. I spat every few seconds but tried not to groan, for that would have frightened Irene.

Feeling very uneasy, I made plans to go to Bakabi and see Jack Sekayaoma, the doctor who had treated my ankle. There was no car in the village at the time, so when I grew tired of my bed I went to my sister's house and took some of the white man's Mentholatum. I returned to my house at four-thirty and found Irene very gentle and kind, and preparing more food for me. I knew that I would not be able to swallow it, but I was pleased to see her trying to feed me, for it showed that she did not want me to die. I felt grateful for such a good wife and was reminded of my dear mother. Brushing aside a tear or two, I said to Irene, "Since my mother passed away, you are stepping into her shoes and taking care of me like she did." Then I tried to put bad thoughts out of my mind, drank a little of the gruel, leaned back against a roll of sheepskins, and rested. When I heard a car, I drew on my shoes quickly and asked Irene to put some sugar in a can and get me some corn meal for the doctor to use in his prayers. The pain was increasing and my breath was short and weak.

We started to Bakabi in high speed and as we approached the Hotavila foothills the pain got worse. My breath was still shorter, and my memory was fading fast. From my heart I begged my Guardian Spirit to please not drop me on the road to the doctor. Then as the car sped along, I reached out my hand and sprinkled a little meal.

When we reached the doctor's house, I entered quickly, handed him the sugar as a gift, lay down on a sheepskin, and gave him the corn meal. "Well, my son, you did right in bringing this meal," said he. "Some sick people come without corn meal, which makes it harder for me to get power from the gods to heal them." When he returned from prayers, he placed his thumb and index finger back of my jaw, examined me carefully, and said, "An evil woman has shot poison arrows into your throat." Then he jerked out the quill of a porcupine a half-inch long, showed it to me, and hurried out with it. He returned quickly and removed another arrow that looked like the bone of a snake or a lizard. After a closer inspection he said, "There is a poison arrow next to your jaw bone which I am unable to get without the use of a medicine song." He sang, worked very fast, and got it. "Now you will get well and wear your pleasant smile again," he said. Even then I felt better and thanked him, saying, "Hereafter, I want to call you my father and your good wife my mother, for my ceremonial father died recently in a distant town." As I told him about my death call in the cornfield, I felt a need to cry, but feared that it would hurt my throat. "Cry," said he, "even if it hurts, for it will drive out the evil thoughts." We came home quickly and my good wife put me to bed, for I was much better already and wanted to sleep.

The next morning Irene washed my face and hands for breakfast, but I could eat only gravy. Norman offered to do my work and pleased me greatly. Later in the day Chief Kewanimptewa of Bakabi came to buy a small turtle from me and commented on my pale face. As I described my death call, he dropped his head but finally said, "Well, my son, you are no longer a boy, but a full-grown man. You know that when one gets upset with his wife or children, or about anything else, he brings sickness upon himself. I don't want you to confess your faults before your family, but you must drive out your bad thoughts. Just say, 'Get away, evil spirits,' and then pull yourself out of their hands like a free man." "All right," I replied, "I will take your advice. I have had some bad thoughts, but I will throw them out." I was glad that there was no need for me to make a confession in public like the Christians have to do for their Holy God.

After a short nap I opened my eyes and saw Irene's sister Clara sitting beside me with a sad face. When she inquired for my health, I said, "I have been without sleep and food, am weak, and my throat still hurts, but I think I will be better tomorrow." She told me that she had the same trouble eight years before, and advised me to think good thoughts and get well quickly. I assured her, "I will come out all right, for I am not alone. My Guardian Spirit watches over me day and night and he has permitted me to suffer only because I have been careless. Now I shall put my steps back on the right road and get well." After supper I took another nap, but within two hours I coughed myself awake. Irene was sitting beside me and asked me to let her soften my bed with three or four more sheepskins. The next morning I was better and able to write down the details of my sickness.

On the following day my doctor came. When I told him that I was better, he advised, "Don't go out-of-doors for another day. I have had a dream about the voice that called you at Batowe. It was not your mother. There were two women, but not your dear ones. They are alive and working against you. If I told you their names, they might kill you. So just forget about them."

After the doctor had lunched with us, I moved my seat close to his and asked him to see if any more poison arrows had been shot into my neck. He reached into his medicine pouch for a piece of root, bit it, and frowned like a man who sucks a lemon. Then he sang a medicine song, pulled out a poison arrow from my neck and said, "Now, I have outdone your enemies and your throat will soon be well." He gave me a teaspoonful of corn pollen to swallow at bedtime, a small piece of bitter root to chew, and two leaves to place on my right cheek. When he had advised me to keep happy thoughts in my mind, I thanked him and promised to go to Bakabi for the Niman dance—but I did not tell him that I planned to take him a nice fat mutton.

On the following Saturday I sprinkled meal at the east edge of the mesa, thanked my Sun god for deliverance from the Two-Hearts, and set out with relatives Shongopavi to attend a wedding feast and a Katcina dance. After the feast I visited our great-grandmother's old house—whence our family migrated to Oraibi—and there advised a sick man to try the treatments of Poleyestewa, who was becoming a good doctor. Then I attended the dance which proved a sad failure. Thirty-five Katcinas, two Side dancers, a Drummer Katcina, and several clowns had arrived from First Mesa. As I watched the performance in the plaza, I was unhappy, for I noticed that the drummer beat too fast and spoiled the songs. When the clowns appeared, they behaved too roughly and even burst some of the watermelons that the Katcinas had brought for the people. A further fault was that the Katcinas wore no spruce boughs around their necks and carried none in their hands. The Side dancers also made a mistake by whipping the clowns too hard, for a Katcina should never come into the plaza to harm the people. When the clowns were whipped, sure enough, a bad wind arose and a little girl fell from a roof and "died." A man carried her into a house, where many people followed, and some of them were crying. I worked my way into the crowded room and saw the father's face filled with sorrow as he held the child on his lap. Finally the little girl showed signs of life again, and the father said that if she had remained dead, the dance would have ended. He then sent for the clowns and told them: "Brothers, you are put here to make the people happy. Now unite your hearts and pray for the life of my child." "All right," they replied, and each laid his hands on the body of the four-year-old girl and went out. I felt very sad and left for home.

It was a bad year for sickness and misfortune. The last week of July I had an attack of stomach trouble which made me rush out to the toilet so often that I lay down in the shade of a chicken house and spent the whole afternoon waiting for emergencies. The trouble continued during the night and I got little sleep.

Ira informed me on the next day that there were many weeds in my cornfield at Batowe. So setting out with the wagon, I reached my farm by noon, cultivated my corn until dark, ate a light supper, and went to bed in the field house. During the night I heard two female owls call mournfully from my rooftop, and a male bird answered in the distance. Never before had owls perched on my roof at night and moaned like a sick person. I realized that this was an evil omen, became very uneasy, and drove them off. The next day at lunch I felt a sudden pain at the base of my spine, and instead of easing up, it grew sharper and made me jump. I remembered the owls, thought of the two women who had damaged my throat, and decided that they were after me again. I was wet with sweat and quickly made up my mind to hurry home, leaving my cornfield full of weeds. When I reached Oraibi, I went to bed immediately but suffered too great pain to lie still very long. Irene fetched Poleyestewa, who rubbed me thoroughly and listened to my story of the owls. He told me that the tenderloins in my buttocks were out of place.

The next day I managed to go with Norman in the wagon to the sheep camp and get a nice mutton for my doctor at Bakabi. After a lunch at the doctor's house he had me lie on a sheepskin and examined my back, saying, "You have been struck with a poison arrow at the very tip of your spine." When I told him of the owls, he nodded his head and said that they were the two women and a man from New Oraibi who wished to kill me, but that they would fail, for he could outdo them. Then he removed the poison arrow with his usual skill.

There was a dance at Bakabi which I was able to attend on the next day. I ate lunch with the Katcinas, smoked with their Father, and prayed for rain and health. Then I returned to the plaza and sat down in the shade with my old uncle from Shipaulovi. He inquired, "Why didn't you come to see our Niman dance?" "My tenderloins were damaged and I had cramps in my buttocks," I answered. When he told me that he danced himself and led the tunes, I showed surprise. Then he remarked, "You think I am getting old, but I never have cramps like you youngsters. My nerves and muscles are still elastic. I never get very tired." "Well," said I, "you old-timers were trained to run in the early morning, to bathe in the springs, and to eat the good old Hopi foods. Our flesh is soft, and though we are younger in years, we are older in body. The good lessons that the old people taught us are dying out." "That is true," he replied. "The next generation of our people will be as weak as Whites, and our ceremonies will be wiped out."

I had suffered enough sickness to be glad to do what I could to treat others. In August (1939) there was a dance in New Oraibi in which Ira and Norman took part. I butchered a sheep and we moved down and stayed in a house that belongs to Norman's mother. As we ate supper on the day before the dance, a woman called at the door and said, "Your friend, Kalmanimptewa, has not urinated for two days. He is suffering great pain and wants you to come quickly. He was treated at the hospital two weeks ago, but now he is worse than ever." I went immediately and found his wife, who was the mother of my first sweetheart, Louise, standing in the door. She said, "I'm glad to see you, for my husband needs you badly. But first let me feed you." After eating a little, I said to the sick man, "My friend, I was glad to advise you two years ago. It was my wish then to set your feet back on the Sun Trail. Now you are off again. You are old enough to listen to your Guardian Spirit who directs your steps. I don't want you to make a confession before your family, but please get rid of any bad thoughts in your mind. Your children are looking to you for guidance and support, and if you pass away what will become of them? Please brace up for their sake. Pray to the Sun god every morning and to the moon and stars at night. Unless you listen to this, you are lost. What do you say?" "Your advice is very good," he replied, and began to cry. "That is all right," I encouraged. "Don't be afraid to cry. It will free your mind of sorrowful thoughts." Finally he said, "My friend, I do not question your words. I know I am old enough to brace up. I was thinking too much of myself when I got sick, and I could not get my mind off our dear ones in the west. Now you have turned me around to face east again. Thank you." With that he shook my hand, pleasing me greatly. I moved my seat closer and found a large, hard lump below his belly button which I massaged for a long time, while he suffered and groaned. Finally the lump disappeared as though it had melted, and I chewed some piki and fed him, feeling happy to know that there was a little Antelope power left in my hands. When I had done my duty, I told him good night and came home. But before I slept that night I remembered some strong root medicine up at Old Oraibi that might help my sick friend. In the morning I got the medicine and returned. My patient was in a chair at the table with a broad smile on his face, for he had urinated and slept very well. I gave him the medicine, told him how to take it, and advised him to keep happy.

Sickness struck our family again within a few weeks. My niece Delia, who was married to Nelson and had moved to Hotavila, had a baby in her womb and both legs were swollen to her hips. When I went to visit her, Polingyauma, a Hopi doctor, was waving an eagle's wing over her and singing a medicine song. By his side lay two new shirts and $3 in cash as rewards for treatment. When he finished, I said, "Thank you, father, you are the doctor I would have chosen for my niece. You know that you adopted me when I was very sick several years ago. Now I want to give my niece to you so that you can save her life. When she is well, she will be your daughter and you may eat at her house whenever you like." "Thank you," he replied. "Now you are both mine and we will be happy." When I asked him the trouble with Delia, he explained, "There was a poison arrow, the bone of a bull snake, in each leg, which caused the swelling, but my song will soften the legs and reduce them by morning. I have cured many cases like this, so you may tell your people not to worry." While we ate, the doctor was called to a woman whose baby was still-born some time ago.

Delia's father-in-law, an old crippled man, put some mountain tobacco in his pipe and smoked, saying, "Now, my grandson, since you are the uncle of my daughter-in-law, I want you to tell all the people that belong to your clan to unite their hearts with ours and pray. I treat your niece like a real daughter and try to keep her well and happy." "Thank you, my grandfather," I replied. "Your words touch my heart." Then shaking hands with him, I continued, "I am not an underworld person. My heart is single and I face the east prayerfully. I will take your message to my people. Let us live and be happy." Then I left, for I was a little suspicious of this old man. We had had a quarrel several years ago. Ira and I chased his folks from our sheep-watering place because they never tried to bring rain and good luck on the Oraibi people, but only on themselves. Later he had been opposed to the marriage of Nelson to my niece but was unable to stop it.

Within a week and while we were working on a fence at Batowe, we saw a car coming from Oraibi at full speed. A man jumped out and said, "Don, I have come for you. Your niece Delia has twins and the afterbirth won't come out." We reached Oraibi at sunset, took my sister Mabel and my niece Geneva, the sister of Delia, and hurried to Hotavila. As I jumped from the car, a neighbor called Geneva to come to her house, and then I knew that Delia was dead. Our clan mother, the widow of Kochwytewa, was sitting in the door with eyes red from weeping. As I rushed in, Nelson said, "Sit down, my children's mother passed away twenty minutes ago." Stepping to Delia who lay in the corner, I uncovered her face, placed my hand on her cold forehead, and cried. Mabel came and cried with me, but we sent word for Geneva not to come, for we feared that it would take her a long time to overcome her grief.

It was getting dark and we had to hurry with the burial. Our clan mother bathed the body and Nelson made prayer feathers. A wagon was brought and we took the body with bedding, shovels, and picks to a place beyond the peach orchard, where we buried it by flashlight. When we had returned and purified ourselves, we ate and went to bed at about midnight, while our clan mother bathed the twins. I slept fitfully and had a sad dream in which my own dear mother was holding out her hands and begging me to come. I had to wave her back and tell her to go away without touching me.

We arose at sunrise, washed our heads in yucca suds, and had breakfast. I walked to Bakabi, entered my uncle's house, and wiped tears from my eyes. When my uncle came and shook hands with me, I told him the sad story. The old man cried and advised me. I thanked him and invited him to come to Oraibi and advise my people. Although I tried to brace up, it was three or four days before I could laugh again or joke with my friends.

On the fifth day I arose early in the morning, gathered my horses, greased my wagon, and set out for Hotavila to attend the birth feast. Since the mother of the twins had died, we were having their naming ceremony fifteen days earlier. Mabel and my nieces were already there. I took the wagon to bring home Delia's other children and all her possessions for, contrary to old Hopi rules, she was living with her husband's people. Ira and I had decided that it was best to give the babies to some Hopi missionaries, for all Hopis know that it is very hard to raise twins. They almost always die. But Ira pointed out that since these babies were strong enough to kill their mother, they might be able to live.

I reached Hotavila while the feast was on, washed my face and hands, and ate the pudding, mutton stew, piki, and coffee. After breakfast I said to my people, "Will any of our Hotavila clan mothers take a baby?" Sewequapnim, the widow of Kochwytewa, said that she would like to but that she could not support it. Then I turned the question to the twins' aunts, Nelson's sisters. No one seemed to want an extra baby. Finally I said, "Well, you have all refused. Now, I will tell you my plan, and no one has a right to interfere with it. Unless somebody takes a baby before sundown, we shall give them to the missionaries." The women dropped their heads, but said nothing. I knew they hated to see the twins go even to Hopi missionaries, but I thought that if we were lucky the babies might live and still would be among our people.

I told my kinsfolk to put all Delia's belongings into the wagon— clothes, corn, beans, sugar, potatoes, pots, pans, and everything. When the loading was completed, I made another speech: "Well, aunts and grandmothers, don't let this parting grieve you. We are not going home for good. Let's all try to take care of Delia's children and make them happy. Come to see them, but don't cry when you come." They all cried a little then. When their grief was under control, I said to Nelson, "I have given a few sheep to your wife, and if any of them are still alive, I wish you would give one to our clan mother, the widow of Kochwytewa. Save the rest and let them multiply for your children. If you still have the wampum beads that I gave Delia, give them to your oldest son when he is grown. Now, Nelson, come to Oraibi and see your children at any time. You have helped my folks a great deal in hauling wood and coal and I hope you will continue to do so. I love you and never thought this would come upon us. Let's stay happy for our children's sakes. This is all I have to say." Then we drove past the mission house near Bakabi and left the babies, but one of them died within a few days.

I kept wondering what actually caused the death of Delia, for I knew that the doctor had successfully treated the bull-snake poison. Finally Nelson's older brother told Irene that Delia had also been sick with the lightning disease which causes a person to shake, feel dizzy, and foam at the mouth. While in this condition her father-in-law scolded her unfairly for neglecting her children and thus filled her mind with bad thoughts and set her feet on the path of sorrow that led to the grave.

Within a few days I had a pleasant surprise. My old friend, a high-school principal in Oakland, California, sent me a little live turtle about an inch long and with a beautiful picture of the Golden Gate Bridge across San Francisco Bay painted on its back in turquoise blue. It was a fine present and pleased me greatly, for I also found my name "Don" printed on it. My wife was so pleased with the little thing that I wondered whether she could wear it as a pin on the front of her dress. In the afternoon some of Neschelles' Navaho friends came and looked at my turtle with their eyes wide open. When they asked me if some turtles always have pictures painted upon their backs, I said, "Yes," and smiled to myself, for I think they believed it. After they had gone and I was working on my diary, Norman came in, spied our pet, and wanted to know where I got it. Like his mother, he was greatly pleased with it and finally said, "Well, I am the only child to your name, therefore I will have this turtle." Irene looked at me quickly but I said, "O.K.," and kept busy with my diary.

We celebrated Norman's birthday on September 29, 1939. Our relatives were invited to a party like a white man's affair. Every man, woman, and child brought a small gift—a few cents, a melon, or some candy. Irene had baked a cake but since we had no candles, we stuck fourteen matches into the cake and helped one another light them at the same time. When we were ready, I struck Norman fourteen blows on the back, then told him to blow out the lights and taste the food first. Irene took small bits of food from every dish and placed them to one side to feed the spirit gods. We had a feast of bread, three kinds of cake, stew, cookies, doughnuts, two kinds of pie, muskmelon, water-melon, cocoa, and coffee. There was so much food left over that all were invited back for breakfast.

My boy was now fourteen and I wished to get him a special riding horse. But this led to a big argument with a Navaho. One came to me and said: "I have two horses for sale, one is a fine mare four years old and so gentle that the children ride her. I will trade her for anything of value." When I invited him into the house to examine a pair of turquoise earrings, Julius came to the door and said to me in Hopi, "Don, you know the government is compelling the Navahos to dispose of their horses because of the drought and is paying them only $2 per head to kill the old ones. Try to get both horses for your earrings." Thanking him, I turned to the Navaho and said in his language, "My friend, these earrings are of great value. You have to get rid of your horses anyway, or the government will kill them. Give me both horses, or there will be no trade." He hung his head for a minute and then asked, "Have you no other earrings?" "No," I replied, "but if you give me both horses for this set, we will be good friends." He finally reached out his hand to signify agreement, and I invited him to breakfast. Then he left with the earrings, and I corralled the horses.

When I returned from Bakabi in the late afternoon, Irene said that she had been looking everywhere for me. She explained, "That crazy Navaho has returned and is going to sell one of your horses to another man." I hurried to the corral and found him with several Hopi. "What do you mean by such conduct?" I demanded. "We traded and made friends this morning." "I have learned that your earrings are not worth both horses," he replied. "Well, I don't want a friend who is too crazy to keep a bargain," I answered. "I know your father very well. He is an old man now with gray hair and a wise head, but you seem to be a damn fool." I stepped into the corral, unhobbled both horses, and told the Navaho to leave with them as soon as he returned my earrings.

In surprise he asked, "Aren't you going to keep one horse?" "No, you can take them home and let the government kill them," I snapped, as I started back to my house. Very soon he entered my door with Andrew and several other Hopi who came along to listen. Reaching out his hand, the Navaho said, "I am sorry I broke our friendship. Please keep the horses." "Nothing doing," said I, "you can stop this monkey business, take your horses, and clear out." Andrew told me in Hopi that he had already given the man a silver bracelet for one of the horses. "Well, brother," said I, "it is you who encouraged this Navaho to cheat. I don't want anyone to buy his horses, let him take them home and kill them." Then Andrew got his bracelet and went out. I said to the Navaho in a softer voice, "This man has caused our trouble." He stuck out his hand again, but I shook my head and said in Hopi to the others, "I am teaching him a lesson." He seemed worried and sat with his head down. After a very long silence, I said, "You had better go." Finally he replied, "My friend, if you will keep the horses, I will return soon with a fresh mutton to cheer you up." "Well, I will give you one more chance," I answered. And when I stepped over to shake his hand, I saw tears in his eyes. He started out, but I said, "Wait, we will eat." My Hopi partners smiled but said nothing. As soon as the food was on the floor, I said, "Well, judges, let's eat," and we all laughed. After supper, the Navaho helped me take the horses out on the mesa and hobble them before he said good-by. I returned to the house and asked Irene to fix my bed, for the long argument had worn me out. But before going to sleep, I said to my family, "I hope that damn Navaho doesn't return tonight and steal our new horses."

I also wanted a new saddle for Norman and for over a year I had watched a small one hanging in Hubbell's store. But the price was $52. Then one day Claude James got a good saddle from a Navaho for $40 and let me buy it for $5 down and $5 a month. It was a happy moment for me when my boy rode out to herd on his new horse and saddle and with a broad smile on his face.

But Norman was careless in his horsemanship. He let others use his saddle and even left it out in the weather or at the houses of other people. He neglected his horse in the early mornings, rode her too hard in the rabbit hunts, and let her cut her foot on barbed wire. Once when he tried to saddle her, she jumped away. He jerked her in anger and lost hold of the rope. I pointed out to him that his ill temper had frightened the horse and captured her myself with kind words. I said, "Handle her gently and she will love you."

One night I struck Norman and nearly lost my life. After supper on October 22, 1939, I asked my wife where Norman had left his saddle. She told me that he had left it at her sister Clara's. I went for the saddle and discovered that it was not Norman's new saddle, but an old one belonging to my nephew, Lorenza, at New Oraibi. I was angry, for it made me think that Norman did not care much for the things that I bought for him. I was also afraid Lorenza would leave the new saddle out to get wet or be stolen by the Navahos. I went to Cecil's house to find Norman and met him coming out the door. "Where did you leave your saddle?" I asked sharply. "At my aunt's house," he replied.

I scolded him and said, "Why did you leave it there? It seems that you don't care for the things I buy for you. Go down and get it to-morrow. If you don't obey me better, I shall thrash you." Norman got angry and retorted, "Well, kill me now and be done with it, then I won't be of any more trouble to you."

"What did you say?" I asked; I stepped lively after him and slapped him on both cheeks. Then as suddenly I changed my mind and said, "Sonny, you have no right to say that to me. You are the only son to my name. I saved your life when your mother and father neglected you. I never thought you would say such bad things to me. You have angered me, and now you are killing me, for I can't stand this treatment."

Leaving him standing there, I went back to my house; but oh, how my heart was crying, and I could feel my death hour drawing near. I was trembling all over, and my limbs and mouth were getting numb. I entered the house and lay down, thinking to myself, "What can I do to save my life?" I saw no way to free myself of the sad and bitter thoughts that were crowding into my mind and settling in my belly. My stomach was getting hard like a rock. Irene asked me what was wrong, and when I told her part of it, she began rubbing my belly. Now my lips were getting cold and stiff, my eyes were rolling in their sockets, and my breath was getting very short. I glanced at the door which seemed to be in the west corner of the room and saw it move backward and forward. Then I saw my dear mother who had died two years before standing at the door and holding out her hands to me. When I told Irene what I saw, she cried and said, "We had better get a medicine man."

I replied with broken words, "Well, if you want to keep me alive, it is up to you." She ran outside crying and set out to find Poleyestewa, the best doctor in Oraibi. While I waited alone, I heard my mother calling me to go with her. For a moment I wished to follow her where there is no sickness or sorrow. My thoughts were killing me and the pain in my belly was so severe that I thought I could not stand it; so I sat up and was facing west and thinking about going with my mother when Irene returned with the doctor. He hurried to me and said, "What is the matter, my grandson?" I tried to speak, but could not. They lay me back on the sheepskin and the doctor rolled up his sleeves and began rubbing my belly. When he again asked what was troubling me, I moved my hand toward my mouth with rubbing motions. He understood that I could not speak, and began massaging my mouth. When my lips were limbered, I confessed, telling him all my troubles and that I had seen my dear mother who held out her hands and called to me to come. I told him that I knew my bad thoughts were killing me. I confessed first and then cried, for among the Hopi a person cries after his confession to clear evil thoughts from his system.

As I cried and the doctor rubbed my belly, I felt a need to vomit. Poleyestewa held my head and Irene held a wash basin which I filled almost twice with yellow, bitter stuff. My belly was now soft, my breathing was getting longer, and I felt sleepy. I thanked the doctor for saving my life, promised to keep bad thoughts out of my mind, face east, and keep thinking of my living friends instead of my dead relatives. The doctor helped my wife put me to bed. I asked Irene what time it was, and she said, "Two-thirty in the morning." I prayed in my heart that my Guardian Spirit would watch over me in sleep and drive off any evil spirits that might be lurking in the dark to attack me. I went to sleep immediately and don't know when Poleyestewa left and my wife went to bed.

I awoke before sunrise, feeling a little better, and decided to go and work on my farm to keep bad thoughts out of my mind. So I arose and went out to look for my horses. When I returned to the house, Poleyestewa was there waiting for me and asked how I felt. I told him that I was much better and that my belly needed no more rubbing, for it was worn out, and that I had greased it with vaseline. He told me he was glad to find me well, and assured me that he would pray for my life. He then advised me to keep happy thoughts in my mind while I worked in my field. As we sat down to breakfast, my father's sister, Poleyestewa's wife, came to inquire for my health. When I told her that I was better, she said, "Well, we were anxious for your life last night, but now we are happy." She cried a little as she talked to me, and I almost cried myself while we ate our breakfast.

Norman had not come home, even to eat. I decided that he had gone to his aunt's in New Oraibi. I wanted him to come back, but I made up my mind that I would not send for him. I thought to myself, "Now he is like a prodigal son journeying in a far country. When he returns, I will have a right to talk to him and teach him a lesson. I don't think he will talk back to me again. I will advise him and forget about slapping him."

I started to Batowe in the wagon with Irene and stopped at New Oraibi. There I looked up Norman's real father, Arthur Pohoqua, and asked him to talk to our boy. We then drove to our field to harvest my crop. On the second day I wrapped myself in a heavy coat to protect my belly from the wind and we drove to New Oraibi with a load of corn. There I stopped for Norman's saddle, but decided to leave it alone lest I upset him again.

In the late afternoon I returned to New Oraibi to get my rope that Norman had left but I did not touch the saddle. I had a good chance to talk to Norman's Aunt Jennie and let her know that while I would not ask Norman to return, I hoped to see him soon. In the evening I went to Cecil's house and got Norman's bedding, for I suspected that Cecil had encouraged Norman to talk back to me.

In three days Rudolph, a bone doctor, stopped at my house. I told him the full story of my trouble with Norman and said, "Now, my son, you are a big clan brother to Norman. I want you to give him a good strong talk and warn him never again to endanger my life with his back talk." He replied, "I will do that. Now, father, if you want to live, put all evil thoughts behind you and the evil spirits will cease to trouble you. You have been facing west, I will turn you to face the rising sun and he will lead you along the trail of life." I thanked him and told him the complete story of my death at Sherman and how I visited the House of the Dead. When I finished, he said, "That is true, many have told us how they have died and returned to life."

While the doctor and I were talking, Norman came in looking sad and shamefaced. I did not speak to him, but Rudolph told him to sit down. Just then Irene entered with some good food for supper and exclaimed to Rudolph, "Father, are you here? As soon as I can cook, we will eat." We told Norman to have some melon, and as I could see that he was crying in his heart, I whispered to Rudolph, "Wait until another time to talk to him."

After supper the bone doctor was called to another household. When I noticed that Norman was ready to go to bed, I moved my seat next to his and talked to him in a soft voice for about an hour. He confessed that he was sorry he had said such hard things to me. I advised him on what he should and should not do and warned him, "If you want to keep your father alive, you will have to be careful, for too much back talk will kill me." He promised never to do it again and went off to bed.

Norman was a good boy for a long time after our talk. On my next trip to Winslow I bought him a new pair of overalls and a high-grade silk shirt dyed red, with flowers painted on the breast and both pockets, and within a few weeks I bought him another shirt, a pair of shoes, a red silk handkerchief, a white sweater, a fine dancing sash, a pair of moccasins, fancy buckskin ankle bands, and a beautiful bow guard. I also bought him a seven-dollar hat for half price, a rifle, and a pair of high top boots. With a big smile over his face Norman said, "Thanks for these things." I replied, "Well, as long as you obey me, do right, and work hard, I will buy many more things for you." "I will try," he promised. I seemed to love Norman more and more and I realized that he could come nearer breaking my heart than any other person.

15
Life Goes On:
1939–1940

I WAS ALMOST FIFTY and living well in spite of sickness, droughts, and poor crops. Checks came regularly for my diary—about $20 a month—and I felt like a rich man who could trade in Winslow and buy flour, sugar, and lard by the hundred pounds. I was also getting heavy and soft from eating rich foods and writing in an easy chair instead of following my herd in rough weather. When I killed a sheep, I could not carry it home on my shoulder, which showed that I was growing old and weak.

But the people were jealous of me. Some said that I sat in the cars of my white friends like a little god, and others claimed that the checks came from officials of a museum in payment for the bodies of dead Hopis which I stole from graves and sent to them. The head man in the Hopi Council in New Oraibi ordered me to take no more white friends to the Katcina dances, and one well-educated Hopi warned me that my brother at Yale was a German spy and that I might be arrested. This worried me until I got letters from the University which I could show as proof that Mr. Simmons was a citizen and a safe man.

A rumor was started also that I was a Two-Heart. I had told my clan uncle, Jasper of Shongopavi, the story of my dream trip to the underworld kiva, and he repeated it to others in his village. Pat, the

Hopi doctor there, heard about it and said that it was not a dream but that I had actually attended a meeting of the witch society, for two of the songs which I had described were real underworld songs. Myron got wind of this and told me. One day Jennie, my clan sister in New Oraibi, called me into her house, urged me to talk no more about this dream, and warned that someone might use it against me.

A few weeks later I received a letter with a check and took it to my brother's house, where Laura, a former wife of Myron, was visiting. When she saw it, she said, "I think you have received something from a museum in payment for dead bodies." "You are not speaking the truth," I replied. "Read the letter and see for yourself." She looked at the check, but ignored the letter. Then I said, "This proves that I have only one heart and am not hiding my work from anyone like some of you people do. I try to do right, but someone is always against me. However, I have a shield to protect myself, so I am safe. None of your lies can harm me, for my future life will prove that your stories are false. If I were stealing dead bodies and selling them to Whites, I am sure that I would be punished by a bad sickness, which would kill me. That would be the proof of my evil ways. Think this over and correct yourself." Then I stuck the letter in my hip pocket, climbed on my horse, and came home. Whatever the people say, I have no fear of becoming a Two-Heart, for I know that my Guardian Spirit will protect me until I die, and the Hopi gods are my witness that I have never sold sacred objects used in the ceremonies, nor revealed ceremonial secrets that were not known before. My Spirit Guide would drop me if I tried to do that. I felt impatient with those New Oraibians who crave to be like Whites themselves, profess to be Christians, and act as crazy as chickens with their heads chopped off. They were jealous of my white friends, and I was more determined than ever to continue my work with them.

In the first week of December (1939) my wife's brother Baldwin was married and had a wedding feast in his parents' home at Loloma spring. Irene and I went in the wagon with twenty watermelons, two boilers full of stew, a sack of flour, and a package of coffee, for we were to furnish a feast to the bride's relatives. Many people of the Fire and Parrot clans were there. The bride was very nice and friendly, and kept herself busy making everybody happy and showing that she was a good housewife. After supper the women who were baking piki in another room sent for me to tell them a story. I felt timid but thought to myself, "I am a man and must brace up." So I washed my face, combed my hair, tied a silk handkerchief around my forehead, and walked in. They fixed a soft seat for me and asked for a story. Baldwin's aunt said, "Go ahead with your story or we will send you to the same place that we are sending the groom's people tomorrow—we are going to put up a big mud fight and send them all to their dear ones." I replied in fun, "Well, I will be able to be with my loved ones where there is no sorrow or sickness, no arguments, and no hard work." One of the women asked, "Is it really true that the dead are happy?" "Yes, I have been there and know," I replied. Then I told what I had seen on my death journey, especially about the Two-Hearts, and watched the faces of two of the women who looked worried. They may have been the women who turned themselves into owls, called from my housetop, and shot poison arrows into the base of my spine. I thought to myself, "Sometime I may have a dream and find out."

I had not been much of a lady's man for two or three years, for I had come to see that spending my money on women is like throwing it away. Both Irene and I seemed to enjoy food better. I had actually made love to no one but my wife for some time and then only briefly every two weeks. But I still liked to joke about the subject. For example, when our neighbors got linoleum for their floor, I ordered one for Irene. When it came, we finished supper quickly and put it on the earthen floor while Irene's sister Clara was present. Irene looked very pleased and I said in fun, "Hereafter you will treat me better or I will walk out and get another squaw." She laughed and said, "You think you have paid up, but today I bought a new Spanish shawl at the trading post. The trader said that you could pay $10 now and $8 next fall." That made me feel funny, but I did not want to say anything before Clara. Irene had never put me so much in debt before, and I wondered if she was getting a little fussy and extravagant. But it was a beautiful shawl. When the linoleum was laid, Clara asked me the price and said that some day she hoped to have one. I said, "Well, if you will work hard with your husband at night, like Irene does with me, perhaps he will get one. Irene moves right along in a gallop." They both laughed and said, "Don't put this in your diary for your white brother." "He doesn't scold me," I replied. We were only joking, of course, but jokes have truth in them.

One day Neschelles stopped with his family and ate with us. During the meal his wife asked, "Why don't you have two wives like our men?" "That would be fine," I replied, "but whom can I get?" She smiled and said, "Just pick out any good-looking, hard-working woman." "In this village," I answered, "all the women are lazy. I think I would like a Navaho squaw, and I have a fancy for your sister." Then Irene caught on—even though we were speaking in Navaho—and said, "If my husband gets that Navaho woman, I shall use a club on her." We laughed and Neschelles remarked, "Nobody wants to marry my wife's sister because she is a widow." His wife replied, "My husband has a private wife near the spring. At first I thought I could not stand it, but later decided that she could help me work." "I too am in need of a private wife," said I, "for my squaw is not very good any more. She does not keep up with me in movements, and sometimes she lies so quiet and still that I wonder whether she is dead. Then I look closely at her face, and she winks." After a laugh, I glanced at Irene and saw that our jokes were too sharp for her, so I said, "Let's change the subject. My wife is quick-tempered. If she ever beats me up, I will go to your place."

Although I was not the man that I used to be, the little things in love-making continued to interest me. I got a chance to hug a young Navaho squaw and enjoyed it too. As I returned from my field at Ba-towe one day a good-looking woman was watering her horses at the windmill. I jumped off my wagon, shook hands with her, and asked her where she lived. She was from Piñon, about twenty-seven miles away. When she learned that I was from Oraibi, she said, "I don't know you, but if I should happen to go to your place, would you take care of me?" "Certainly," I answered, "especially if you agreed to a little loving, for I am in need of a nice squaw." With that I closed my arms about her and drew her close to me. She said nothing at first, but quivered a little. Just then two small children raised their heads in her wagon and stared at us, but they did not cry. My friend freed herself gently and said, "Perhaps we will meet next week." Then we smiled at each other and I climbed on my wagon. When I had gone about fifty yards, I looked back and saw her watching me. So I waved my hand and received a ready reply. Then, with a happy heart, I whirled my whip over my head and set my team into a fast trot.

I had a dream that reminded me of my first school day. I was hitching my horses to a wagon when two horsemen came in uniform, handcuffed me, and took me to jail in a big white house, charging that I was writing false reports to Washington. I declared my innocence and defended myself so well before the superintendent that he asked me if I would like to go back to school and become a lawyer. When I told him my age, he said, "Fifty is not very old. Perhaps you will even become a judge." Then he led me to the back room of a school where I could take a bath. And a white woman came to help me, put her arms around my neck, and kissed me. I placed my right hand on her breast and returned her kisses, while I let the fingers of my left hand find their way about. I awoke all too soon, and without any bells ringing in my ears, for I was not afraid this time.

I also had a little excitement with a white woman at the Walpi Snake dance. The people were so crowded in the plaza that hundreds were on the roofs of houses. I stood against a wall. Just above me sat a white woman with her legs dangling by my shoulder; and whenever I glanced up, I noticed them. As the performance began and the people pressed closer together, my shoulder got wedged between the woman's knees. The Antelope dancers had marched into the plaza and were circling the snake "house" when I placed my hand on the lady's knee and said, "Sister, do you mind the way my shoulder presses here?" "No, we are crowded and it is all right," she replied; but I noticed that her companions were smiling. At the height of the dance, she said, "My friend, I have a cramp in my left leg. How can I stop it?" "If you don't mind, I can help," said I. "Go ahead," she nodded. I took hold of her toes with my right hand, put my left hand back of her leg, and pressed up very hard. Then I rubbed the calf of her leg up to her knee and a little more, finishing just as the dance ended. She seemed to appreciate my treatment and thanked me. And as the people departed, she and her friends shook hands with me, and we all laughed.

In my fiftieth year I had a long light love affair with Molly Juan of Hotavila which proved a disappointment. Molly's husband, Latimer[1] (my wife's clan brother), was sick and I visited him frequently to advise and cheer him up, and to slip young Molly a dollar or two, squeeze her hand, and exchange understanding glances—all of which started very casually. But her eyes said more and more, and I began to cultivate her like a tender plant until, finally, she was beckoning for me to stop whenever I drove past.

One day Molly came to New Oraibi to attend a Katcina dance and was treated very coldly by my wife. I soon made it my business to go to Hotavila and passed my friend's house, which appeared to be empty. I walked over, peeped in, and heard a splashing noise which sounded like someone taking a bath. I entered quickly and discovered Molly alone with her hands full of wet clay, and plastering. Greeting her gently, I said, "I am sorry my wife treated you unfairly." I took her soiled hands in mine, drew her to me, and held her tightly. She seemed so happy that I thought my reward was at hand. But just then I heard the patter of small feet, quickly kissed her, sat down on a box, and started some small talk. Her children rushed in to say that lunch was ready at her clan house. I knew that she was mine for the taking; but I realized more than ever that I had to be careful lest Latimer discover my interest in his wife, become worse, and cause me to get a bad name. As I journeyed home, I felt disappointed and impatient, for I calculated that I had cultivated Molly for more than a year and at a price of more than $10. So I made plans to visit her during a ceremony when her husband would spend the night in the kiva. But when that night came and I set out for Hotavila, a bad storm came up and drove me back.

One afternoon a month later, January 1, 1940, I got up from a nap and started to the horse corral when Walter from Bakabi passed. Whistling to him, I called, "Merry Christmas and Happy New Year." Then I asked him to take a message to my friend. Laughing, he said,

1. Both names are fictitious and the first was Don's own selection.

"I know about you and that woman. You have been monkeying with her for more than a year." "That is true," I replied, "but see here, my friend, I have always stopped short of the last step. Therefore, I am not afraid of any news." Then I had a chance to tease him. "Say," said I, "how are you getting along with my niece R——?" I watched him closely, and when his face flushed, I teased, "Oh, Walter, you are a man; stop blushing. Now I know for sure." "Yes, it is true," said he, "but I have told no one. If there is a dance at New Oraibi, please invite me to her place." I promised to see what I could do for him, and as he started to go, I said, "Remember my message to Molly." He slapped me on the back and we both laughed. Although I had slept with my wife the night before, I kept thinking of Molly, and I was proud of this old feeling of manhood.

A few weeks later I decided to go to Bakabi for a Katcina dance and asked Irene to wash my hair in yucca suds. Then I took scissors and went among my neighbors seeking a barber. I said to an old couple, "I must get my hair cut, for it is touching my shoulders and I have noticed that my private wives are slighting me." After a laugh Tom Jenkins said, "You are too ugly for the ladies any longer, so you had as well wear it long." I reminded him that he was more hopeless than I, for he looked worse and was older. Finally I set out for Bakabi without a haircut, and as I passed the Buffalo shrine, a car overtook me and the driver stopped about ten steps ahead. Whenever I ran, he started up again and kept just out of my reach. There were five people in the car watching me and laughing. At last I caught on and climbed in. The driver was Irene's uncle's son, Perry, whom I had teased for years. When I got off at Bakabi, he looked around and laughed as if to say, "I am squaring accounts for what I have suffered from you." I stepped around to the driver's seat, took hold of him, and said, "You devil, what do you mean, treating me unfairly?" He laughed and said, "I was not treating you unfairly, I was training you to run." Then he put his mouth close to my ear and whispered, "When you get caught some night with Molly, it will pay you well to know how to run." He slapped me on the back and we both laughed. I did not want the matter discussed in public, so I left him holding the better end of the joke. I entered the kiva, took a piece of mountain tobacco, smoked it, and prayed with the Special Officers. After a supper with my clan father, Kewanimptewa, the Governor of Bakabi, I went back to the kiva, remained for all the dances, and then came home without having seen Molly at all.

Some months later I went again to Hotavila with a white man who wished to buy some souvenirs, and we stopped at Latimer's house. To my surprise Molly had delivered a premature baby which had died two weeks before. As she served us piki and wild-root Hopi tea, I kept wondering how she got the baby, for I felt sure that her husband was too weak. I was glad for once that I was innocent and wondered who had been meddling in this family.

Men are in a position to help each other in the management of their wives. If a woman should ask me about the love affairs of her husband, I would be prepared to know nothing about them or even to tell a frank lie. For I think my Guardian Spirit would forgive me and even help to make the lie more useful than the truth. Whenever a neighbor is having trouble with his wife who is in the wrong, it is a good time for a man to warn his own wife and treat her a little better. I help support my neighbor whenever he is in the right, and I am willing to go and talk to the troublesome wife if there are any kinship ties that give me a right to do so.

One night in January, 1940, when I blew out the light and got into bed, I noticed that Irene was unhappy. "What is on your mind?" I asked. "Can you tell me?" Irene cried and said, "Grace has left Myron and gone back to Shongopavi for good.[2] You know that at the last night dance Myron came home and caught a man sneaking from the door. He followed this night lover, caught him by the shoulder, and discovered that he was W— from Bakabi. Myron was very jealous and had a big argument with his wife. Grace told me that she did not especially care for W—'s attention but that Myron had made it so hot for her that she was going back to her people to stay. Today her relatives came for all her possessions. Grace has given her bean plants to me to harvest." "Well, you don't have to feel so badly about it," I

2. Since Grace had come to Oraibi to live with Myron, she did not own the house and had fewer rights. She could not drive Myron out.

replied, "Grace has left Myron once before. They will probably be back together in three or four months. Many people seem to be separating now, but I hope there never will be such trouble between us."

Two months later Grace came tagging back with her children, and Myron came to my house to talk about his wife. I took his side and agreed that Grace never accepts the advice of anyone. I said, "Since I am her father's nephew, and therefore her 'father,' I have a right to advise her. If she were my real daughter, I think I would give her a thrashing." I assured Myron that he is a good farmer and has made his wife a rich woman, while her first husband was a lazy man. I praised him for giving his wife a better life than she had ever known before, and pointed out that in spite of his fine treatment she was seeking something still better in the arms of other men. I agreed that this behavior should be stopped and said, "Myron, you are in the right, I have lost confidence in Grace on account of these private affairs. I have a good notion to go to her once more and scold her soundly. This time I shall not believe her and will not take her side when you make it hot for her. Whenever she comes to my house again, I will have a chance to scold her. Then if she talks back, I will have nothing more to do with her and tell her that she is no longer fit to call me 'father.'"

Myron replied, "I hope you will give her a stiff talk. When she was sick at Shongopavi she sent for me and told me that she was coming back home. I was angry and made her cry. I reminded her that I never ordered her to leave in the first place. She said that when you came to the dance, she watched you closely and noticed that you had no kind words for her. I informed her that everybody felt the same way about her." "Well, Myron," I replied, "she is causing you and your people much trouble. From now on, you must watch her closely and make her behave. At present she is tame like a lean, tired horse and you have a good halter on her. But when she has gained a little fat and spirit again, she will lift her head like a wild mare, be as crazy as ever, and kick up her heels in the face of you and your friends." "That's right," Myron admitted. "I told her the same thing when she came back to me. But at present I have trapped her in a deep gorge and I have closed the passage so that she is my prisoner. So I think that I shall be able to manage her for a little while."

I had a very bad dream about Irene. It seemed that I was living about four miles from Oraibi and that there was to be a dance in the old village. Irene had gone with her brother Baldwin to prepare food so that the people could eat and be happy. When evening came, I did my own cooking and ate supper alone, but Solemana, my old ceremonial mother, came in to wash the dishes. I set out for Oraibi, reached my old house after dark, and found no one there. Lighting a match, I discovered that Irene had made our bed for use and had then disappeared. I went to more than fifteen households inquiring for my wife, but all my friends shook their heads. In a house of Irene's sister and her close relatives, I found a group of women who fed me; but when I asked for my wife again, they looked at each other, blushed, and said nothing. Then I knew that Irene was hiding from me with a private lover and that her sisters were shielding her. I arose from my seat and hurried out, hot with anger, and sweating.

Seeing a dim light in our house at last, I rushed in, found Irene making piki, and asked, "Where have you been?" When she said that she had been there all the time, I knew it was a lie, slapped her on the right cheek, and exclaimed, "You crazy woman, I understand you now and know all the dirty tricks that you are playing on me." As Irene cried, her sister Barbara, Norman's mother, entered and said, "Don't kill her, she has suffered enough. I hate you for the way you treat her." Irene added that she hated me too. Then Barbara said, "Irene tells me that you are getting too old for love-making and cannot even have an erection." Greatly grieved, I replied, "All right, Barbara, you may support Irene yourself. I can't stand this foolish talk. I know your record of loose living, and you ought to be ashamed of yourself. You are a foolish woman who never listens to anyone. I have treated you and Irene fairly. Now I am through with you both. If I cannot satisfy Irene in love-making, I will leave her to a younger man." Just then Irene's sister Edna came in, scolded Barbara, took my side, and praised me highly as a good provider. She concluded by saying, "My brother-in-law, please stay with your wife." My heart was crying, and I was planning to take all my things over to my Sun Clan house. I awoke feeling very unhappy, lay still on my bed, and studied my dream carefully, wondering about it. Irene had arisen to build a fire, noticed the sorrow on my face, and asked me what had happened. As I told her, she did not pay much attention at first; but when she noticed that I was getting sadder and sadder, she spoke kindly and said that she hoped the unlucky dream would never come true.

I kept seeing Whites from time to time. A stranger came to Oraibi and Betty, my little ceremonial daughter, ran to tell me that our Chief wished to see me. I found an old artist with him who said that the Chief had agreed to pose for a portrait for $3 and that he wanted me to pose for $2. "Why not $3?" I asked. "You are not the head chief," he argued. "I am an officer and head of the Sun Clan in line with chiefs," I answered. He turned to our Chief and asked, "Is he also a chief like you?" "Why, yes, yes, he is a chief," was the answer. The artist eyed me closely and said, "All right, tie an eagle feather in your hair and don't wear a headband." Two days later I put on my turquoise earrings, coral and wampum beads, and a soft eagle feather, and went down to the school to pose. I wanted the artist to take plenty of time and make the painting fit my looks exactly. A few days later this old man took me to First Mesa to see a dance and was very impatient because I ate with friends and returned to his car a little late. So he drove in high speed—like a mad dog—for a while and then slowed down. When I saw that he had cooled off, I told him why I was late. He smiled and said, "Forget it." We reached the Teachers' Club in New Oraibi ahead of all the others, and as I got out of the car I remarked, "I will walk up the mesa. You are ahead of everybody else, so perhaps you will cook their supper." I wanted to remind him of his impatient manner, for I have never liked hurry-up people.

"No Shirt" also came back, but he already had a new name. He had failed to pay me for some work on a Hopi corn story and had written many letters urging me to be patient. After that I had called him "Patient Man" and had thought of having him arrested if he ever came to Hopiland again. He came nearer cheating me than any white friend I ever had, but I finally got my pay. One evening when I returned from work, my wife said, "Patient Man came today with a number of white women, called me 'Mrs. Talayesva,' and gave me a little pot." When I asked her if he wore any shirt, she said, "Yes, he was dressed like a gentleman." "Well, I hope he will act like one," I remarked. The next day I saw him and he gave me some white shells and glass beads. He said that the beads as well as the shells came out of the ocean, but I didn't believe it. He later returned and spent the night with us, saying that some old clothes would pay for his board and lodging. But when the Chief refused to let him take pictures for less than $1 each, he grew very impatient, said he would send no more clothes, and asked me to let him take my picture, insisting that I smile. I knew I was wasting my time, so I told him to make himself at home in the village and went back to my diary. Some days later a friend asked me how I liked this man. "Not much," I replied, "certainly not from my heart. He does not have a good mind and he is not one of my special friends." I made no pahos for him at our Soyal.

The high-school principal who had sent me the little turtle also returned and ate a meal with me. He wanted to take some pictures in the village, but our Chief refused to permit it for anything less than the regular price of "one dollar a snap." The next day I took him to New Oraibi to visit a highly educated Hopi lady who was a school-teacher and ran a little hotel. She told him that she was the only Hopi teacher on the reservation; and as they talked together, they used such big words that I felt left out and as if I were deaf, for all I could do was to look around the room like a dumb animal. Finally I went with my friend to the school building where he took out a paper and asked me many questions; but I could not answer some of them because they were about ceremonial secrets. This man painted a picture of our house and surprised me with a gift of personal stationery with my picture, full name and address, and some cloud symbols printed upon it.

One day a white woman came to our house and said she was from Ann Arbor, Michigan. I said, "Perhaps you know my friends there, Professors Mischa Titiev and Volney Jones?" She knew them well and I explained that I had helped Volney get his degree in botany and Mischa his in anthropology. I said, "Quite a number of students have been picked from the universities and sent out here, and I am proud to say that some of them call me a teacher." When she asked me to take her through the village, I quickly put on my shoes and first showed her the room in which Dr. Mischa Titiev had lived and where, later, my white brother from Yale also lived and worked with me on a complete record of my life.

I was proud of my white friends and wrote to them regularly to cheer them up, and every year after Soyal I sent them sacred corn meal and prayer feathers to protect their lives. Whenever I receive letters from them, I consider myself lucky and sometimes say, "Now the stars shine brighter." When the new postmaster handed out five letters to me at one time, he said in surprise, "You must have many white friends all over the United States." "Yes," I answered, "I have lots of friends from the different universities and I am proud of them." He stood staring at me for a while, thinking, perhaps, that I was a big man.

On January 1, 1940, my white brother returned from the East to check on my life. I had used up almost three-dozen pencils on my diary, but he wanted to know more. So I hired a man to herd my sheep and for fifteen days I did nothing but eat, sleep, and talk. When on the sixteenth he asked me for details about the ceremonies, I had to say, "What I did in the Soyal is secret. When you ask me about that, it sets the people against me." He seemed very disappointed, settled accounts with me, shook hands, and said that he would have to leave Oraibi three days ahead of schedule and study about the ceremony in Voth's book. When he left, I was very sad, and I think he was too.

At six o'clock I went to the post office to get my mail, hoping to see Mr. Simmons there. He came up to me and offered to drive me home. On the way I told him I was sorry to disappoint him and offered to read the Voth book through with him, point out the errors, and talk only of myself. He returned and we studied the record for two days, but we had to watch carefully and hide it whenever anyone came in. I told him no secrets that Voth had not already published, but that damned missionary was a smart man. When my brother left for home, I wrote him a long letter on just what I thought of Voth.

Jauneta, Cecil's wife, was sick with tuberculosis, and Cecil was neglecting her so badly that the Hopi Council in New Oraibi sent an officer up to talk to him. She had married Cecil when she was quite young and children came too fast. When her last baby was born in the summer of 1938, her pelvic bones had not gone back into place. Furthermore, she worried because Cecil denied that the baby was his and ran around with other girls. They had many arguments and Cecil whipped his wife several times. She eventually neglected her children and had an affair with a strange man. When the little boy was eleven months old, Jauneta's mother had brought him to me twice to be treated with my Antelope power. I had said, "This baby has discovered that his mother does not care for him and is sleeping out of wedlock." The child died six months later.

I advised Jauneta many times, but she became weaker day by day and soon was unable to walk. The Hopi doctor who had treated my niece Delia said that she was too far gone for anyone to save. It was wrong for him to say that to her relatives and worry them. Members of the Ah1 society took Jauneta to Hotavila and treated her for "knotted intestines," but brought her back no better in March. I decided to advise her once more, and when I entered her house, two white missionaries were on their knees begging Jesus to do something while old Buhumana held her daughter on the floor. The poor girl's strength was spent, for her head hung down and her eyes were half-closed. I thought the missionaries were carrying things too far and, when they left, I advised Jauneta. But I could see that my words were not touching her heart.

In two or three weeks a Hopi missionary and his wife came to our house and asked Irene to join the sewing circle at the old stone church and receive some Christian cheer. When Irene asked them if they had been able to cheer up Jauneta, they admitted that she was worse. I told the missionaries that we had been advising Jauneta and praying to our Hopi gods for her health. They said, "If she gets on the Christian Road and gives her heart to Jesus Christ, her name will be written in the Lord's book of life. Have you never heard the story of Nicodemus, a ruler of the Jews, who came to Jesus by night and was told that in order to be saved he must be born again?" "Oh, yes," I replied, "I was taught that in the Y.M.C.A. before you were born." The woman asked me if my name was in the Lord's book. "I don't think so," I replied. "When I returned from Sherman I examined our own religion and found it good enough. Now I am fifty and will never take on Christianity." The missionaries preached a lot of Bible to me, but I kept replying, "I knew that before you were born." When they departed, I laughed and thought that I would have treated them a little better if they had not preached down to me.

About a month later Buhumana told me that her daughter was much worse, and that her lips were too numb to speak. I said, "I think I had better advise her once more." "You may do whatever you please with her," said the old lady sharply. I found the sick girl on a blanket, half covered and with her private parts exposed. "Jauneta," said I, "your body is worth more than anything else to you. Please cover it." "I can't," she replied. "My arms and hands are numb." I pulled a blanket over her and sat down beside her. "I'm not so well," she complained. "Instead of getting better, I am growing weaker. My mother scolds me often. I hear much good advice, but I keep thinking of dying. I guess it is up to me. If I can't wish strongly to live, I suppose I will die." This made me unhappy and I asked, "How about your husband, does he help you?" "Not much," she replied. "But the day before yesterday my mother beat me and said she would have nothing more to do with me, and then my husband drove her out of the room and has taken care of me since." "That sounds bad," said I. "It is the duty of your mother and your husband to care for you, and your mother should never tell you to die. Now brace up. Ask your Sun god for help and remember that you can live if you want to. I love you and don't want you to sacrifice your young life." Just then Cecil came in and urged his wife to take my advice. I told him to watch over her closely. He replied, "That is what I am doing. Since the old woman left, I have done the cooking." But Jauneta had made up her mind to die. Within two days she passed away, and the missionaries buried her in the Christian cemetery—and baptized old Buhumana. Jauneta thought that by dying she would cause her husband to worry over her. But she was mistaken for he had other girl friends who could keep him happy.

One day I visited Kalnimptewa, my father's old blind brother, and said: "Father, as I stood in my door I saw a Hopi missionary preaching to you from a Bible." "Yes," the old man answered. "He talked a great deal, but his words failed to touch me. He warned me that it would not be long before Jesus Christ would come down from the sky, say a few sharp words, and destroy all disbelievers. He said that my only chance to escape destruction was to confess and pray to his holy God. He urged me to hurry before it was too late, for a great flood was coming to Oraibi. I told him that I had prayed for rain all my life and nobody expected a flood in Oraibi. I also said that I was an old man and would not live very long, so he could not frighten me that way. I told him that I did not want to start an argument, but that I was much older than he and believed my thoughts on this subject were better than his." He concluded, "Now, Talayesva, my son, you are a full-grown man, a herder and a farmer who supports a family, and such work means a happy life. When our ceremonies come round, pray faithfully to our gods and increase the good life of your family, and in this way you will stay happy." I thanked him and went home feeling confident that I would never pay any serious attention to the Christians. Other gods may help some people, but my only chance for a good life is with the gods of my fathers. I will never forsake them, even though their ceremonies die out before my eyes and all their shrines are neglected.

When the missionaries preached the Gospel to me, I almost always got tired, and often felt sick in my stomach and wanted to vomit. I tried to change the subject, find something interesting to do, or just walked off—unless they made me angry. Then I out-quoted them and tried to trap them with catchwords from their own Holy Book. I think the Mormon preachers had better manners than the Protestants, but they could be tiresome too. One day two Mormons ate with me and said, "We would like to tell you that your history states that the Spider Woman had five grandsons and that she made for them a cloak of mouse skins in many colors. That is the same story that we have in our Bible. You Hopi are also descendants of Joseph, whom his brother sold into Egypt. His father made a coat for him of many colors. Our great-, great-, great-grandfather was Joseph, and we are all brothers." It was a good little story, but I doubted its truth.

Once I had the same dream about missionaries three times in one month, and it differed only in small details. A strange person came and informed me that the Hopi Christians wanted to destroy our ceremonies and invited me to go along with him to a meeting. He assured me that he was my Spirit Guide and that he would protect me. We speedily reached a great roundhouse with many rows of seats about the walls. In the center stood two men in ceremonial costumes, Tom Pavatea and Travis, a Tewa Indian from First Mesa. My Guide explained to me that we were fighting for the right to keep our ceremonies and customs and to be free to worship our gods. Then Tom held up his hand with a broken pot in it and invited all to speak who were willing to defend Hopi religion and liberty. He said, "We must have freedom to perform our ceremonies." A Tewa woman spoke in her language, and Travis nodded his head to signify that it was a good speech. As she dropped some money into the pot, I stepped up to her and told her that I was glad to hear such fine words, and that I was on her side. In surprise she asked, "How did you understand my language?" I explained that my Spirit Guide had put understanding into my mind. Then I heard another speaker, and my Guide told me to look closely at him. He was Myron, the new Governor of Old Oraibi, holding his son by the hand and making such a fine speech that everyone clapped. When Myron dropped his money into the broken pot, all others followed in turn. The collection was counted, and Tom called out that he had $2,000. "We win," he cried. "The missionaries don't have that much money, so they will leave our religion alone and we can support the poor and the old people." We were rejoicing to know that we were a free people when my Guide said, "Let's go," and made four quick steps. I followed him in the same manner and awoke wet with sweat, and heard bells ringing. My wife had heard me groaning and shook me; otherwise, I might have gotten more of the dream.

Some time later I had a frightful dream. As I picked up four bridles and started to the corral for my horses, Irene called and told me that white soldiers had surrounded the village. I soon learned that the missionaries had reported our Chief, Tewaquaptewa, to the government at Washington for performing his ceremonial duties in the Soyal, and that the soldiers had come to kill him for disobedience. I discovered that they already had him surrounded out near the Buffalo shrine and rushed to his aid. Irene called for me to come back, saying that I had already spoken strong words that displeased the people and that

I might get into trouble. Looking back as I ran, I replied, "But I love our Chief. He is my 'son,' and I don't want him to die before the people." Some Christian Hopis and soldiers who had gathered about the Chief said, "Here comes that old fool whom we hate so much. We know he will do something." I urged the crowd to let me get to the Chief. When they refused, I used my full strength and pushed them aside, knocking some down who called me bad names. Reaching the center of the crowd, I found our Chief imprisoned in a large box with his head sticking out a hole, and a man was standing over it with a big, sharp knife, ready to chop it off. I quickly said to the white officer, "Brother, please put your weapon away and don't kill an innocent man. Our Chief is only trying to be true to his religion like other people are true to theirs. You know that if a person has no religion to follow he lives no better than a dog, so please let me take him back to his house." Opening the lid of the box, I pulled him out of danger. Then the white officer turned and said to the people, "Talayesva says that the Chief is innocent, that he only wants to be true to his religion, and pray to his gods in order to get a good life for his people. You missionaries who wanted us to come to Oraibi and do away with the Chief are really the bad people. Now we will let the Chief go free." I took hold of him and led him through the crowd, but I awoke before we reached the house. The dream seemed real and may actually happen, but I hope not.

Within a short time we gathered at Hotavila for the Snake dance. My old uncle, Dan Coochongva, made a speech to the crowd of Indians and Whites. He reminded them that in former times white and red men of all races and nations lived happily together in the underworld. When Two-Hearts spoiled the good life below, our ancestors escaped through a hole in the ground near what is now the Grand Canyon. But, alas, Two-Hearts came up with the people and have caused untold trouble upon the earth. He told the Whites that their ancestors had hurried eastward, but that now they had returned as our brothers, according to prophecy. He also reminded them that we Hopi have a promise from the first white man that some day, when the Two-Hearts have become too powerful, a great white brother will return to the Hopi villages, cut off the heads of all Two-Hearts, and destroy them completely. He ended by saying, "Only then will Hopis and Whites be united as one people and live in peace and prosperity, such as once existed in the underworld. My father, Chief Yokeoma, expected the powerful white man to return and slay the Hopi Two-Hearts in his time, but he was disappointed. I am still looking forward to the coming of our Chosen White Brother."

As I sat on the west side of the plaza and listened, I wondered whether the Chosen White Brother would ever come and free us from the curse of the Two-Hearts. I knew this wise old man had been telling the people that Hitler is the Chosen White Brother who will slay all the wicked and deliver the righteous, but I didn't believe it could be true. Misfortunes, strife, sickness, and death—all of which are caused by the underworld people—are our greatest problems. I fear them more than anything else and sometimes I doubt whether anyone will ever be able to destroy these powers of evil, unite us into one race, and restore the good old Hopi life.

We might be better off if the Whites had never come to Oraibi, but that was impossible, for the world is full of them, while in numbers we Hopi are as nothing. Now we have learned to get along with them, in a manner, and we would probably live much worse if they left us to ourselves and to the Navahos. We need Uncle Sam to protect us and to feed us in famines, but I wish the United States Government would send us better agent employees, for they are supposed to come out here and help us. There is not much that I want from the Whites except my special friends, and I hope they will never forsake me. I do not care for fancy clothes and fine living. If I had thousands of dollars, I would give most of it to my boy, but I might buy a pick-up truck and build a little Hopi house down in New Oraibi where I could live with my family in winter. I would like an iron stove, some chairs, and perhaps running water piped into the house, but I would not have electric lights or a radio. I would like a victrola, however, so that I could hear the songs that I have recorded. In summer I would move back into our house in Old Oraibi and I would always return for the Soyal.

One night I had a very good dream, and I hope it will come true in my future life. I was walking along a trail and came to a junction in the path. There I saw the fresh tracks of a strange man leading

Don C. Talayesva, August 26, 1940.
Photographed by Dr. Fred Eggan.

westward. Following them, I came to a ranch with a fine brick house and a large porch facing east. The tracks led on into the front door, but I stood staring. Soon I heard a friendly voice say, "Follow the tracks into the house, for it is prepared for you." Happily I stepped into my new house, but found no one there. I left my lunch and other things on a table, walked out into the yard, and looked west at the red walls of a mesa which were striped with white at the base. Near my house was a fine flock of sheep in a corral, and lo! there by the gate stood my Guardian Spirit, beckoning to me. When I reached him, he said, "My son, I am the Guide who has protected you all your life. I have built this house and provided this herd for you. Open the gate and let out your sheep. They will graze, find water, and return in the evening without a shepherd." As they passed through the gate, I counted at least nine hundred. Then my Guide said, "The grazing and the farming lands that you see are all yours. You will need them for your family, so never let any white man get them away from you. Come with me and I will show you water." I followed him 440 steps to a place where he stopped and said, "Dig here and you will find a spring." I looked up and saw someone coming with a flock of sheep. My Guide said, "That is Sekaheptewa, one of your old grandfathers." "But he died many years ago," I exclaimed. Sure enough it was he, but he turned off toward the southwest and disappeared. When I turned to my Guide again, he was sinking into the ground. Then I heard a dog bark and awoke with bells ringing in my head, and with a very happy heart.

It is a pleasant future to look forward to; but until then, I want to stay in Oraibi and have plenty to eat—especially flour, sugar, coffee, and the good old Hopi foods. When I am too old and feeble to follow my sheep or cultivate my corn, I plan to sit in the house, carve Katcina dolls, and tell my nephews and nieces the story of my life. And I would like to keep on writing my diary as long as my mind holds out. Finally, when I have reached the helpless stage, I hope to die in my sleep and without any pain. Then I want to be buried in the Hopi way. Perhaps my boy will dress me in the costume of a Special Officer, place a few beads around my neck, put a paho and some sacred corn meal in my hand, and fasten inlaid turquoise to my ears. If he wishes to put me in a coffin, he may do even that, but he must leave the lid unlocked, place food near by, and set up a grave ladder so that I can climb out. I shall hasten to my dear ones, but I will return with good rains and dance as a Katcina in the plaza with my ancestors—even if Oraibi is in ruins.

Concerning the Analysis
of Life Histories

Concerning the Analysis of Life Histories

A LIFE HISTORY is a detailed account of the behavior of an individual in his environment. It may also attempt to be a dynamic account which casts the individual in bold relief, explains how it happens that he behaves in a certain manner at a given time, and predicts how he will behave in a series of similar situations. The purpose of the present study has been exploratory in the dynamic sense, but it is too early to attempt comprehensive and neatly fitting formulas which adequately explain and interrelate all the facts. Indeed, it may be that an extensive life history is so extremely complex that it cannot be analyzed as a single unit in which all the variables are properly accounted for. But this has not been demonstrated.

We assume that something can be learned of the dynamic interpretation and prediction of human behavior in life-history perspective. This assumption is based upon the belief that every individual is born in an environment that requires adaptations, that many of his adjustments are continually manifested, and that some of them may be investigated, interpreted, and predicted—at least in terms of discernible limitations imposed upon his behavior.

In general, there are four types of limitations to behavior which are subject to systematic investigation: limitations inherent in biological endowments; restrictions conditioned by the physical environment;

restraints imposed by members of society; and taboos stipulated by the culture or mores of a given group. Biologically determined individual differences are established facts with respect to sex, physique, rate of maturation, potential life span, intelligence, energy output, endocrine secretion, temperament, and all other characteristics for which there are developed anything like accurate techniques of estimate and measurement. Certain insights into the interpretation and prediction of individual behavior are achieved to the degree that relevant biological potentials can be reliably evaluated. An obvious example is the fact that Don was born anatomically male, not female, was endowed with a normal potential span of life, and possessed feet that were somewhat abnormal. These facts established limits to his behavior in the sense that it was certain that he would never bear a child, and highly improbable that he would ever engage in certain types of women's work such as pottery making or compete successfully in the races. On the other hand, the fact that he grew to be above average in height made it very likely that he would occasionally play the role of the Giant Katcina in the discipline of children.

Likewise, the physical environment established limitations to the behavior of Don almost from the moment of birth, and the semiarid desert has continued to exert strong influences upon his adaptations. This factor must be kept constantly in mind in any comprehensive interpretation of his life experience.

Furthermore, the members of Don's society—particularly his intimate associates in the family, such as mother, father, grandfather, uncles, siblings, wife, and son, and certain key persons in Oraibi, such as the Chief, medicine men, Special Officers, and Two-Hearts—exerted a tremendous restraining and directive influence upon his conduct. A clear conception of the statuses and roles of these personalities and their relationships to Don is extremely helpful, indeed indispensable, in gauging the range of behavior permitted to Don and in specifying the status and role which he may be expected to fulfill. These influential associates must be kept in mind for any extensive analysis of his behavior. Indeed their influence is reflected in almost every act, thought, and feeling tone or sentiment.

A knowledge of the vivid projection of Hopi personalities into an imaginary environment peopled with ancestral spirits, friendly and unfriendly, and with demons and deities who are believed to control good and bad luck—the aleatory element—is also essential to the understanding of much that goes on in Don's life. It is awareness of these factors which gives the ceremonies their significance in his life and makes for very detailed prediction of his conduct in ceremonial roles. The coercive and restraining influence of the spirits and gods—projected personalities—is a very realistic extension of the strong arm of society into the realm of religious determination of behavior. And it should not be overlooked that the religious sanctions are strongly reinforced by the treatment which Don receives from his associates. The enforcement agents of religion are often one's own contemporaries. With a knowledge of Hopi religion and the personalities of Don's associates, a great deal of his behavior may be anticipated in minute details, for these numerous contemporaries see to it that he performs in a specified manner.

Finally the culture, or the commonly recognized mores of Hopi society at Oraibi, provide the idealized rules for Don's behavior in a very extensive range of responses. They not infrequently also qualify the margin of permissible deviations. With certain biological potentialities granted, a knowledge of these mores is perhaps the best single guide to the interpretation and prediction of his behavior, certainly the portion of his behavior which may be regarded as normal by his contemporaries.[1]

But in Don's case a knowledge of Hopi customs is not enough. It is important to remember that his childhood occurred at the turn of the century when the Oraibians were confronted with a clash of cultures and with conflicting systems of mores which vied for the loyalty of individuals. A central conflict seems to have been established in his life with its roots essentially in this historical phenomenon. The task of interpretation would have been much simpler if the Oraibians had not

1. For an extensive treatment of the mores, see William Graham Sumner, *Folkways,* Ginn & Co., Boston, 1906.

come in contact with Whites and an alien culture. This difficulty is not insurmountable, however, and in this connection it also must be remembered that until ten Don's life situations were dominated almost continuously by the native environment and that Hopi mores became deeply ingrained in his "style of life." The general assumption that the early years are more important in the formation of persistent patterns of behavior is amply verified in this record.

It can be established beyond question that with the easily accessible knowledge of the mores of Hopi society it is possible to anticipate some of Don's conduct. For example, if one knew the standard norms of behavior and the statistical incidence of deviation therefrom, he could state with reliable probability, at least in negative terms, that Don as an adult would never make love to a Sun Clan woman, wed two wives at the same time, develop a distaste for piki, commit murder, grow corn without prayers, show contempt for the Katcinas, have intercourse with any woman during the time that he participated in the Soyal ceremony, or show a tendency to make favorable comments about the weather on sunny days and unfavorable comments on rainy days. While the predictions cannot be mathematically certain on single items of behavior, the odds are very high in favor of probabilities, and certainly such conduct is not difficult to interpret in the light of Hopi customs.

The relationship of Don to the mores of his society is illuminating. It is constantly evident that Don is a *creature* of his culture in the sense that his behavior—his acts, thoughts, and feeling tones or sentiments—are largely molded by it; and it is probably impossible to understand him without recognition of this fundamental fact. But in a certain sense he is also a *creator* of his culture in that he can never quite perfectly match up to the idealized standards, and may occasionally even initiate a variation—by accident, invention, or borrowing—and see it imitated by others until it has become a folkway or *mos*. Furthermore, Don is a professed *carrier* of his culture in that he exemplifies it and persistently endeavors to transmit and inculcate it in the younger generation, particularly his son. While these roles of the individual as *creature, creator,* and *carrier* of culture are recognized and well documented in social-science literature,[2] there is a fourth role for Don, and for every individual, which is largely neglected in life-history studies. He is a *manipulator* of the mores, or of his culture. By good luck or ingenuity he may utilize the mores to his own advantage. He may marshal them to strengthen his position or to coerce associates into fulfillment of his requirements; or he may even inspire other persons to make sacrifices. If he finds himself in situations of compromise, he may flaunt folkways, ignore mores, and take refuge in "higher principles," arguments of expediency, or supernatural indorsements. When motivated by self-interest and fortunately aligned with popular mores which give him an advantage, he may elbow competitors to one side and win coveted prizes in terms of authority, position, and other prerogatives. He may also endeavor to manipulate the mores to manage the dead as well as the living and thus outwit the spirits, placate the higher gods, and control what he considers to be the aleatory element. An individual who is a first-rate manipulator of the mores is in a position of considerable advantage.

In a life-history study it is instructive—knowing the mores—to watch the individual override obstacles and manipulate his way to goals; or becoming trapped, wriggle and worm his way out, sometimes badly scarred. The individual is rare, in fact, who can wear his culture and get his way without some chafing. The dilemma for him is to achieve his goals by means of his mores with as much success and as little friction as possible—and that is in part a manipulative role. It is a very useful cue to interpretation to be able roughly to differentiate in any given situation whether the individual is acting more in the role of *creature, creator, carrier,* or *manipulator* of the mores.

A study of behavior also implies some theory of adjustment and certain principles of learning in the adaptive process. It is obvious that the individual is not born with instincts that teach him how to behave

2. See William Graham Sumner and Albert G. Keller, *The Science of Society* (4 vols.), 1927, New Haven, Yale University Press.

John Dollard, *Criteria for Life History,* Yale University Press, New Haven, 1935.

A. Kardiner, *The Individual and His Society,* Columbia University Press, 1939.

in varied situations. He is instigated by drives, either primary or derived, and learns to adjust through trial and error and through the temporal coincidence of reinforcements, positive or negative. Discriminative principles and rules of adjustment and learning are essential to a systematic interpretation of behavior and these life-history data were gathered with many of them in mind, but space prohibits any systematic presentation of the principles of learning at this time.[3]

It is the opinion of the writer that the concepts listed above must be elaborated and kept consistently in mind for any satisfactory analysis of a life history. But even if a systematic analysis of data as complex as a life history fails to explain adequately all the related phenomena, something can be done by a technique of situational analysis. If it proves unprofitable to attempt to explain a whole personality over an extended period of time by means of a few sweeping and simplified formulas, the life course from birth to death may yet be viewed as a successive series of linked situations in which the individual makes adjustments, and these adjustments may be studied in single units.

The simplest situation, of course, is one in which the individual, entirely apart from the influence of associates, is incited to behavior by some stimulus, either within or without, experiences maladjustment, and makes an innate, random, or self-initiated adaptation such as a kick or cry in earliest infancy. But on the human level of adjustment few situations are so simple, since processes of socialization begin at birth. In fact, it is doubtful whether the identification of such situations is often possible, for the vast majority is infinitely more complex due to the impact of experience, society, and culture.

Although the simplest situations are rare and of little use in the study of personality development, it is possible to break up the extended life course into more or less natural situational units of normal complexity, but small and simple enough for more systematic investigation. The advantage of this procedure lies in the fact that such a

3. For a summary of the principles of learning, see Neal E. Miller and John Dollard, *Social Learning and Imitation*, Yale University Press, New Haven, 1941, and E. R. Hilgard and D. G. Marquis, *Conditioning and Learning*, D. Appleton-Century Co., New York, 1940.

situation when viewed as a unit, even with temporal boundaries more or less arbitrarily established, can be subjected to more accurate and detailed analysis; the individual can often be observed in the process of adaptation and he can report on many of his experiences when they are fresh in his memory. A still more important advantage is apparent in the possibility of using everything that can be gathered about the previous behavior of the individual in similar situations as guides to an understanding of the particular item of conduct under scrutiny. A tiny part of the life course is thus framed and keyed by all that has gone before instead of making an evaluation of the whole personality based on knowledge of a few fragments of behavior. Hence, instead of using a few scattered bits of conduct as keys to countless situational responses, it is possible to utilize scores or even hundreds of previous accounts in varying combinations to gain insight into a single limited and well-defined situational adjustment. The plan of analysis is actually a systematic and comprehensive reversal of the popular practice of evaluating individuals on the basis of casual and very limited contacts or references; and the ratio of reliability is proportionally raised.

Furthermore, the analysis of separate successive adjustments to particular situations builds up verifiable indices of patterned responses to similar circumstances which check one another. These type adjustments, when assembled in sufficient quantities, may suggest clear and deeply ingrained configurations of conduct in the individual's "style of life."

The process of situational analysis can be illustrated by an example in the life of Don. In July, 1938, he took the investigator to a certain rock southeast of the village and there displayed an attitude of reverence, caution, and considerable anxiety. He explained that a powerful spirit, the Spider Woman, had resided beneath the rock for centuries and could harm or injure any person at will. When the investigator carelessly approached the large stone and attempted to place a hand upon it, Don seized him by the arm, pulled him away quickly, and exclaimed, "Be careful, you might be captured!" Then he gathered twigs, placed them by the shrine as a sacrifice to the deity, and cautiously withdrew. The situation was confined within a period of fifteen minutes and some of the specific problems raised are: Why the cautious approach to the rock, the reverence and the anxiety? Why the excited rescue, and why the sacrifice and withdrawal? The answers are simple in the light of literally hundreds of sampled sections of experience throughout the course of Don's fifty years. In summary, the particular visit to the shrine was made in response to an urgent request, in addition to the promise of financial reward. From early childhood Don had heard stories of how the Spider Woman had performed miracles for people who gained her good will, but had captured and destroyed many persons, even giants, who dared to arouse her displeasure. Many individuals in authority had told him how they had seen the old woman sitting on the shrine, and that any person who went too near her "house" would surely be captured in her web like a fly and be drawn underground. Or that if she captured the spirit of anyone, even though he escaped in person, he would soon sicken and die. It was a common belief that she captured and punished people who failed to make annual sacrifices of prayer feathers. Cases could be cited of individuals who had died because of their neglect of this duty. All children had been warned to stay away from the shrine lest the old woman capture them or entangle their spirits in her web and cause their death. When Don was four, he followed his father off the mesa against orders and stopped near the shrine. Suddenly he saw what he thought was the old woman sitting upon the stone and felt a strange power drawing him to her. He had reached the edge of the shrine in a dazed, helpless state, when a villager saw him, shouted warnings, rushed up, snatched him out of danger, and took him home. Don became sick and delirious, and during the night he saw visions of the old woman prowling about the house seeking to capture him. His father, mother, and grandfather feared for his life and frankly discussed their anxiety in his presence. They sought out a highly respected medicine man, who advised the father to make his belated sacrifices and prescribed how he might redeem the captured spirit of his son and thus save his life. The sick, frightened boy witnessed the dramatic recovery of his spirit by his father and never went near the shrine again until he was a grown man. All his life he has seen men and women sacrifice at the shrine, his father has never since neglected this duty, and, ever since he became a full-fledged Hopi man at twenty, Don has performed his obligations to the deity. This accumulative account, greatly elaborated in the record, sheds light on Don's behavior in the specific situation and is useful in indicating probable responses under similar circumstances.

As illustrated, the methodological procedure in situational analysis is to select out tiny but puzzling bits of observed or carefully reported behavior in the life course and assemble about them all available and relevant data from the life history for the purpose of gaining new insights. Since one can rarely utilize laboratory techniques and demonstrations in life-history analysis, his only opportunity to appear at all convincing is to marshal sufficient evidence, bit by bit, to interpret satisfactorily the behavior and solve the problem.

Such a situational analysis of case-history data may be likened to the solution of a jigsaw puzzle. One receives a package of oddly assorted bits of cardboard with fragmentary sketches of design upon them. He is confident that a picture will emerge in clear outline when the pieces are properly arranged. Finally, the patterns so dovetail as to provide clearcut and conclusive proof that the job is done correctly. Even when a few scraps are correctly pieced, a suggestive pattern of design may appear which makes it progressively easier to fill in odd bits of data. Moreover, if a few parts are missing they may be spotted by the gaps in design and often described in detail as, for example, the missing head of a horse, leg of a man, or trunk of a tree. But in any life history gathered with present techniques, only a mere fraction of the total picture can be reconstructed. However, by a liberal selection and careful assortment of sample fragments one may discover rather clear designs, typed patterns of adjustment; and often it is possible to trace their development in the experiential account.

But it is in the meaning of experience for the individual, the subjective implications of behavior, that both difficulties and advantages appear for the investigator. The question inevitably arises as to how an experience shall be defined or labeled for interpretation in the life history; and multiple implications are possible. There are at least four ways that an experience may be defined, recorded, and later utilized for purposes of analysis.

1. There may be a purely objective account of a situational adjustment—a record of stimuli, responses, and following effects—such as might be received through totally unacculturated eyes and ears, or by mechanical cinema and sound-recording devices. Such an account would be invaluable for its objectivity, but would fall far short of the whole story in terms of experiential implications, and might prove quite misleading.

2. An experience may also be recorded in terms of the labeled or customary meaning which the contemporary culture stamps upon it. It may be recorded with the implications that the average Tom, Dick, or Harry would see in it. A certain black fly, a dead toad, or a ringing noise in the ears might then mean the death of a relative. It has been pointed out already that cultural controls over an individual's *behavior* are limited by biological capabilities; no culture or society can survive and completely prohibit eating, breathing, elimination, and cohabitation. But when it comes to the cultural control of the *meaning* of experience there is no limit. A ringing sound in one's ears, for example, can be made to mean anything. This is a fact which is very important for individual behavior. For all cultures select particular experiences and endow them with disproportionate meaning or significance. A life-history account will prove misleading if the investigator fails to record the meaning which the culture stamps on a particularly significant experience.

3. In addition to cultural implications, certain events will take on *unique* personal meaning for an individual as a result of previous highly conditioning experiences; and their pronounced effect upon his behavior can be understood only in the light of the previous circumstances—Don's fear of the Spider Woman for example. This is one of the most important facts to observe in life-history studies, for it establishes a level of continuity in individual behavior which cannot be touched by purely cultural analysis and which, no doubt, underlies much so-called "abnormal" behavior. The most expertly devised cultural chart for experiential ratings in terms of their customary significance for behavior completely misses the point and can go no further than gauge the degree of deviation from normal expectations, and

possibly indicate the type of experience which set off the "abnormal" or irregular responses.

4. The significance of a previous experience for the individual may become greatly modified by succeeding circumstances. Probably few, if any, experiential implications are stamped letter-perfect once and for all into the personality of the individual on their initial introduction. They are more likely to change, to become conditioned by and integrated with successive qualifying experiences. Indeed, the implications of an early painful experience may undergo considerable change and develop into something quite different and even contrary to initial impressions. An adult's attitude toward his childhood punishments, or pranks which were played upon him in his youth, are common examples. The individual may very soon find a way to interpret a critical experience more in his favor. An alert self-interest, protective conscience, or "guiding spirit" may manipulate the meaning of experience to considerable advantage, within cultural limits, and steer a course of action which reinforces the more favorable personal interpretation. Rationalization or even retrospective falsification[4] may alter the implications of the original experience; or it may become partially or perhaps wholly forgotten. On the other hand, the experience may at a later date attain excessive prominence in consciousness, become a topic of preoccupation, take on such ominous meaning as to prompt great anxieties, feelings of hostility toward others, or self-derogatory and disabling attitudes which not infrequently lead to self-destructive behavior. Individuals do "work over" much previous experience in some sort of integrative process, but the trend that an event will take in the life course in terms of meaning is very difficult to anticipate. Although it is socially and culturally cued and limited as a rule, it may also be very definitely dependent upon somatic factors such as those which apparently influence mood swings between the extremes of elation and depression; and finally it is dependent upon the unique experience of the particular individual. But, however that may be, the fact to emphasize here is that within the life

4. Term contributed by Geoffrey Gorer.

course something happens to previous experience—it is recondi-tioned—and that the personal significance of past events often does not remain constant. They are indeed highly modifiable, may take on variable meanings or "faces," and greatly complicate the problem of interpretation and prediction, making it necessary to identify the ap-propriate "face" in order to fill out the design of continuity within the life of the individual—in other words, these separate experiences themselves have "life histories."

These potential variables in the meaning of experience suggest that if we are minutely to work out design and continuity in a life history, we must not only record a fair sampling of experiences but date their appearance, catalogue their meanings at least in terms of the culture and the implications for the individual at the time, and keep a chrono-logical record of their change of meaning along the life course. In the manifold minutiae of life experience such a program appears ut-terly perplexing, and one may ask whether any reliable order, consis-tency, and continuity in life-history data can ever be achieved even for the more modest and partial assignment of situational analysis. There is, however, one impressive saving factor. We may discover a family likeness to the various meanings which an experience may take for an individual and an astonishing continuity to the meaning of manifold experiences and their influence upon the behavior of the individual throughout his life course. Indeed, comprehensive studies of life histories strongly suggest the hypothesis of a basic underlying continuity to all the individual's experience and behavior, however variable, unusual, and "abnormal" it may appear to be on superficial inspection. The thesis is that if we knew enough about the previous record of an individual, any behavior which we might find him per-forming would fit neatly and naturally into the sequence of responses. He is found to be consistent even in his "inconsistencies." Such an assumption holds out the scientific challenge that when we have de-veloped detailed and reliable techniques of life-history investigation we may discover a foundation of order, design, and consistency in the data which is sufficiently stable and clear-cut to reveal the manifold and interrelated elements; and which, when properly pieced together, will demonstrate true continuity in the life course and make it possible to trace with confidence how an individual comes to be the person that he is, and how it happens that he thinks, feels, and behaves as he does. Then granted certain circumstances, one should be able to predict within limits the kind of person that he will come to be at a future date. It is here that detailed life-history studies may make their chief contribution to the understanding of individual conduct. They tend to establish a level of continuity in behavior that is more fundamental than either biological, environmental, societal, or cultural determinants, being in fact a synthesis of all four.

But such a scientific achievement, if ever possible, will require most exacting and painstaking procedures. It is certain that before we can reliably interpret a whole life course in terms of simple formulas, we must become proficient in the accumulation and careful manipulation of masses of experiential data in the analysis of limited and well-documented situational adjustments. We shall not be able to understand how an individual comes to be the person that he is until we can explain segments of his behavior, how it happens that he behaves as he does in specific situations. We must gather masses of data about sampled individuals, break up the problem of human behavior into limited, well-documented situational adjustments, and fit all known relevant data about them for the light that they may shed upon the narrowly confined problem, and for the principles of behavior and adjustment which may evolve. A more or less automatic check on the procedure and the data is provided in the fact that items of experience must fit neatly and naturally about the various situational points in analytical focus. The same data will be used again and again in the interpretation of different situational adjustments in the same life history and if the information is not reliable, inconsistencies will be revealed. But that is a distinct advantage, for the best test of systematic procedure is that it be self-checking.

In summary, we shall endeavor to focus the lens of investigation upon the individual pivoted on the points of maladjustment and influenced by four fundamental variables which must be integrated for the achievement of at least sufficient balance and poise for continued survival. The concept of adjustment is proposed as a balancing principle—a sort of operational gyroscope which embraces within its orbits biological capabilities, physical environment, society, and culture, and somehow holds the individual in relative equilibrium for careful scrutiny and analysis. We shall endeavor to limit the program of analysis and more finely focus our attention on the individual's process of adjustment in concrete situations and in terms of well-known principles of learning, but always in the light of all relevant data which can be assembled and fitted about the particular problem. These situational analyses will check and countercheck one another and lay a solid foundation for an attempted interpretation of the whole life course. And it is hoped that the study may provide some additional basis for a further formulation of principles of human behavior in social settings which may have wider application.

Appendices

APPENDIX A

An Example of Situational Analysis

In a recent laboratory experiment[1] a rat in a grilled cage bit a rubber tube at every sound of a buzzer—very odd behavior for a rat. But it was explained that the animal had been subjected to electric shocks which were turned off whenever it hit upon and performed this particular response, and that later the rat had been conditioned to respond to the buzzer signal as a *cue* to escape shocks. In the light of this information which was sketched in detail, the behavior of the rat made sense. When once the buzzer sounded in the absence of the rubber tube and the rat in desperation bit its tail, and again when the excited animal bit a finger that had been left within easy reach, its behavior was still understandable—in fact, the animal was referred to as "the rat which had been trained to bite." A tiny section of the life history of the rat had been presented as a problem—why did it bite at the sound of the buzzer? And it had been quite satisfactorily explained by examining other relevant sections of the rat's life history and by the utilization of certain well-known principles of conditioning. If one could present strange bits of human behavior in such illuminating frames of reference, they might often appear as understandable. And that is exactly what must be attempted. Limited situations with significant items of behavior must be selected from the individual's life history, expressed in terms of well-defined problems, and interpreted by the aid of sound principles of conditioning and the utilization of enough related

1. Conducted by Dr. Neal Miller.

life-history materials to explain the "problem behavior." There is no excuse for life-history students to dodge this duty to make sense of their data. The fact that human behavior is more complicated and difficult to explain than is the conduct of rats must be accepted as a challenge for hard work rather than an alibi for short-cut formulas and easy guesswork.

In the case for analysis an experience has been selected which is complicated but is not too fantastic or incredible for a general reader unfamiliar with Hopi life. Don is permitted to relate how he felt, thought, and behaved for one night of the eighteen thousand that he has lived. This account is recorded in his diary three days after the events occurred and without additional information, the text being altered only for brevity, clarity, and grammar.[2]

In order to make this one night's behavior more understandable, it is necessary to assemble additional information on a number of inquiries. *First*, there is the problem of motivation—why did Don slap his adopted son? *Second*, why did Don take the situation so seriously? Instead of spending a miserable half-night and almost dying, there were other alternatives—at least theoretical ones. He could have apologized to Norman and let it go at that, proceeded to give him a sound thrashing, or walked away and thought no more about the matter. Actually, these alternatives were impossible for Don, were probably very impractical, and may have resulted in more lasting maladjustments. The reasons for taking the situation with utmost gravity are entirely obvious to Don as it will appear later. *Third*, how may one explain the pronounced symptoms of trembling body, numbness of lips and limbs, choking sensations, shortening of breath, hardening of stomach, the need to vomit, and the death call? *Fourth*, how successful was Don in working out a satisfactory solution in this difficult dilemma? Is his behavior to be classified as entirely "abnormal" and beyond comprehension, or is it largely understandable in the light of Don's previous experiences and in terms of an attempt to manipulate the mores to his own advantage? To what extent did his adjustments in this situation relieve anxieties and insure security? Did he successfully escape the major penalties and achieve maximal reinforcements?

On first sight, the question of motivation for the apparently simple acts of violence appears obvious; but to Don it seems mysterious, and it may indeed prove to be the most difficult problem to solve. Some insight is possible, however, and perhaps enough to emphasize the fact that the question is crucial.

2. The reader will refer to pages 357–361.

Before attempting to answer it, the character of Don should be reviewed, particularly the traits of personality that are most relevant to this behavior. It should be remembered that Don is not a weakling but one of the largest and strongest men in Oraibi, and possesses sufficient strength and stamina to administer punishment to an insolent half-grown son. Furthermore, he is not a tenderfoot. In childhood he was regarded as "tough" and one of the "meanest" boys in the village. At his initiation into the Katcina society, he stood a usual whipping without a whimper, broke down only when the flogging was more than doubled, and has since been proud of the scars which resulted from that ordeal. In the Agency school he was slapped for pulling the ears of a Navaho lad, had his mouth washed with soap for talking too much, stood in the corner of the classroom for misbehavior, and was soundly spanked for imitating Christ. Later at Sherman he deliberately chose to be lashed with a rawhide, and with his trousers down, in preference to debating in public. He has the reputation for horseplay in clowning and has been willing to run about in the plaza with cactus dangling between his bare legs and against his back and chest, and to have the thorns broken off in his flesh.

Don can draw blood without flinching. He pierces his own brow and the eyes of his sheep to let out "bad blood," slits the tails and ears of his lambs, and puts salt into their wounds. He has slaughtered probably two thousand sheep, also stretched a cow and severed its throat. He killed his favorite horse which had a broken leg by knocking it on the head with an axe; and when his most valuable horse ate locoweed and acted crazy on the road, Don tied it up, threw it, and cut its throat with a butcher knife. He split the body of a sacred rattlesnake from mouth to tail in order to save the life of his dog. He assisted his own mother in the birth of his youngest brother, and on another occasion he tried to shake the afterbirth from his oldest sister until she died in his arms. Therefore, for Don to slap a disobedient boy would not seem to be too delicate a matter.

Don also has fighting propensities. As a boy he was in constant conflict with others, particularly his elder brother, and was "nearly killed" by him. He bought a revolver with the first money he ever earned. After marriage he threw a stick at his wife on one occasion and slapped her on another. He wrestles with gods and spirits in his dreams. And he is hardly a coward. As a young man he crawled into the den of a wounded coyote, and once chased a Navaho thief for three days to regain his stolen horse, a feat which few Hopi will dare attempt. He can bury the dead and drive dogs and coyotes from fresh graves at night. He has taken offerings to the shrine of Masau'u in the dead of night, and repeated this performance, although terribly frightened by the god of death. He asserts that he could spend the night in a white man's cemetery: "I would place a little food on each grave, ask the spirits to do me no harm, lie down, and snore like a hog." He has a reputation for courage in Oraibi and is very proud of it. He once seized a prominent missionary by the lapel of his coat and ordered him out of his mother's house. On three occasions he has faced witches in public, accused them of their evil works, and dared them to strike him.

Don also has some social justification for chastising his adopted son. A boy is expected to obey his father and never talk back to him. Hopi fathers do sometimes punish their very young sons. Don whipped Norman with a cotton rope when he was a small boy. Furthermore, Don is an important person in Oraibi and head of the Sun Clan. Therefore, he has a right to exercise some authority and deserves respect. In addition to this, he is familiar with the fact that Whites condone the punishment of irresponsible and disrespectful boys.

In summary, Don is a strong, oversize, middle-aged man, somewhat courageous, tough-minded, and aggressive in conflict, and in a position to be angered by Norman's conduct. It can be added that Don is not feeling well at this time. He is suffering from a stomach disorder which is a periodic and chronic complaint of long standing. These facts about Don provide some explanation for the slapping of his son; but they certainly are not justifying to Don in retrospect, and they do not afford adequate explanation to anyone familiar with Hopi society and culture.

A still better case can be made out for Don's conduct, but it, too, will fail to justify his behavior in his own eyes. Norman is Don's favorite object of affection. He has stated on many occasions that he cares more for this boy than for anybody else in the world; that he would leave his wife if she refused to let Norman stay with them; and that his adopted son could come nearer breaking his heart than any other person. This emotional dependence upon Norman is borne out by a long record of pampering him. A few weeks before Don had traded a valuable string of beads for a riding horse for his son. Norman had neglected the horse and let it become entangled in a barbed-wire fence, cutting its legs badly. Don had recently scolded Norman for further rough treatment of the horse. Don had also watched a saddle at the trading post for more than a year, wishing to buy it for Norman. He finally purchased one for $40, was paying $5 a month on it, and still owed about half the price. Two weeks before Norman had left this saddle out in the field twice. He had also exchanged it with a boy who is reputed to be careless with property. Now, for a second time, he has exchanged saddles and his new one is probably left out to be damaged by the weather or stolen by a Navaho. Don meets Norman coming from Cecil's house and remarks angrily, "You don't seem to care for the things that I buy for you." Norman is saucy, which is very unusual behavior from a youth to his father. Furthermore, he uses about the sharpest words that one Hopi ever speaks to another, "Kill me now and be done with it."

On previous occasions Don had successfully cowed his enemies in public by daring them to strike him dead; proceeded to ridicule them as cowards for not doing it; and then persuaded friendly spectators to boo at them, and even urged that they spit upon them. In addition to showing that he does not care for the things that his father buys for him, Norman has talked back to him in the most contemptible and challenging manner possible for a Hopi. He has placed Don in the dilemma of either striking his son or admitting that he is a coward—and Don takes great pride in his courage. Norman has cut Don to the quick by throwing into his face the very taunt that Don has often used himself to out-do witches. Norman may really be implying, "Kill me if you dare, you Old Witch"—and to be accused of witchcraft, even indirectly, is a grave stigma to any Hopi. Don loses control momentarily, and slaps Norman twice before he comes to himself with a quick thought.

It should be emphasized again that, although for the reader there may appear ample grounds for Don to slap his son, there is not sufficient justification in Hopi eyes, and most certainly not in Don's mind. The motivation for these acts is still much more of a mystery than the simple demonstration of the electric shock on the behavior of the rat. If the test were repeated, Don probably would not slap his son. Therefore it is necessary to leave this question unanswered in part, and to seek more light upon it.

Why did Don take the situation so seriously? It is in an effort to answer this question that problems of motivation become clearer. According to the Hopi kinship system, a son never belongs to the clan of his father; and a father never has a very strong official hold on his son. It is the boy's mother's brothers who are chiefly responsible for his conduct and who have the authority to punish him without public censure and without loss of rights over their nephew. If a father wishes to secure his son's loyalty, his coöperation in labor, and his care and support in old age, it is distinctly to his advantage to lure rather than coerce him. A father has a great deal to lose in antagonizing a half-grown son, and relatively little to gain in disciplining him, since that responsibility normally lies with his wife's brothers. It is far wiser to let them do the chastising. He may even gain their hostility if he takes too much initiative in disciplining their nephews.

Furthermore, there is a strong cultural taboo against Hopi adults resorting to physical violence—except perhaps against their wives—so strong, in fact, that such behavior practically never occurs, and certainly not between a father and his half-grown son. The following chart roughly signifies the extent of restraint upon physical violence in adult males. The perpendicular lines represent the normal status changes in the life of a Hopi male with the exception of the fact that they do not all become Special Officers, clan chiefs, or medicine men, although most adult males achieve some official status as wise old men at least. Listed numerically from one to thirteen are the types of violence which are prohibited and the positions in life when they are permitted. A dotted line under an item in the list indicates the time in life when that particular type of violence is theoretically permissible and occasionally occurs. For example, in number 12, anyone is theoretically permitted to fight in order to save his life after the first blow has been passed, but such behavior almost never occurs. A single heavy line under an item indicates that this form of violence does occur but is not very common, as illustrated in number 6, "Wife beating for adultery." Two heavy lines under an item indicate that for that period of life the form of violence which is listed is regarded as normal. Three heavy lines under an item indicate that it is more or less expected behavior. This chart was constructed from the pooled information of various informants rather than as a result of statistical findings. The significant items to note are numbers 6 to 9. A man may strike his wife for adultery; and he may punish his son before he is initiated into the Katcina society, but after that he is not expected to use physical force. On the other hand, an uncle may continue to discipline his nephews. In general, violence is prohibited to a remarkable degree; and Don resorted to it under conditions that are prohibited, making his acts of violence more serious, for example, than when he struck his wife.

Don's behavior is more serious for him than the same acts would be for a normal father since Don has a weaker hold on Norman than the average father has over his sons. Norman is Don's only son and an adopted one at that. He has full right to leave Don and go to live with his real mother or one of her sisters. Furthermore, he is a good worker and they would like to have him. Don has no lineage nephews old enough to work for him, although he has a sister and three small children of a dead niece to support. He very definitely needs Norman's support and loyalty.

Don also has an exceptionally strong personal need for Norman which must be elaborated in some detail. Offspring are greatly desired by Hopi and often arrive before marriage. Don had intercourse with Irene for several months before marriage, but a baby appeared over a year after marriage and

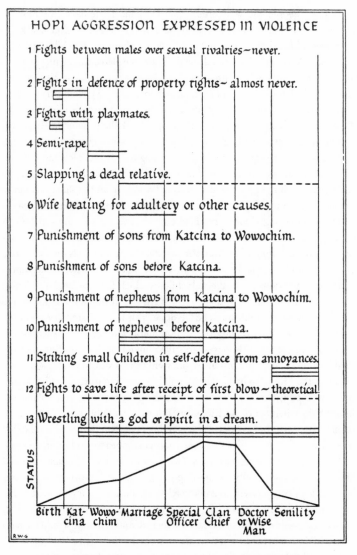

HOPI AGGRESSION EXPRESSED IN VIOLENCE

1 Fights between males over sexual rivalries ~ never.

2 Fights in defence of property rights ~ almost never.

3 Fights with playmates.

4 Semi-rape.

5 Slapping a dead relative.

6 Wife beating for adultery or other causes.

7 Punishment of sons from Katcina to Wowochim.

8 Punishment of sons before Katcina.

9 Punishment of nephews from Katcina to Wowochim.

10 Punishment of nephews before Katcina.

11 Striking small Children in self-defence from annoyances.

12 Fights to save life after receipt of first blow ~ theoretical.

13 Wrestling with a god or spirit in a dream.

STATUS

Birth · Kat-cina · Wowo-chim · Marriage · Special Officer · Clan Chief · Doctor or Wise Man · Senility

R W G

A Chart of Social Status and Restraints on Physical Violence
with Respect to Situations and Stages in the Life Course.

soon died. People had wondered, "Can Don and Irene have children?" A medicine man informed Don that Irene's mother's clan brother had killed the baby. This grieved Don, but also kept the blame for no children on the Fire Clan. Another baby arrived and died, and the blame was again placed on the old Fire Clan uncle. A great-uncle of Irene's confessed on his deathbed that a Fire Clan man was killing Don's children. Irene gave birth to a third child which lived about four months and died. A quarrel resulted in which Don publicly blamed the Fire Clan people for killing his child. In accusing them, he was defending himself against a possible charge of witchcraft and the killing of his own children to prolong his life. People constantly remarked, "Don is unlucky with children." Three deaths in a row could be used against him as proof that he was a Two-Heart in the same manner in which he accounted for the death of Nathaniel's children. Indeed, Nathaniel caught Don crying alone in the field one day and tried to comfort him. A fourth child was born and became very sick. Sequapa and Don's mother-in-law told Irene frankly that Don was causing the death of his own children, pointedly implying that he was a Two-Heart. There was a heated argument in Irene's own house over the sick child in which Don vehemently denied that he was a Two-Heart or that he had killed any of his children, and dared these two women to kill him and be done with it—a customary and courageous method of reversing the accusation of witchcraft. He successfully squelched his accusers by this aggressive nonviolent defense. But the baby died next day under circumstances that were clear proof to Don that a Two-Heart of the Fire Clan had killed his child. According to Hopi belief, someone was responsible for its death, and it was up to Don to keep the blame off him and on a member of the Fire Clan. But Irene was not entirely convinced of his innocence. In his hours of travail his Guardian Spirit, whom he had trusted since his death experience at Sherman, appeared to him in a dream and assured him that he was not a Two-Heart and that the witch who had killed his child was really of the Fire Clan. With this information he won back the loyalty of his wife, but his own best friends, including the wife of his father's brother, often remarked, "Don has no luck with children." Now in his sorrow over the death of his last son he had vowed that he would have no more children and sometime thereafter he became impotent. Yet he wanted children greatly, and needed them to exonerate his character, heard their chirping voices in the ceiling of his house, and dreamed of babies—arms full of them. The fact that he was the father of four dead children and was yet childless afforded easy proof to the Fire Clan that he was a Two-Heart. So strong was this anxiety that in dreams he needed the reassurance of his

Guardian Spirit that he was a man of one heart. But he refused to speak to his mother-in-law again for nearly three years.

In the course of time Irene's sister married Don's clan brother and bore a son. When the child was two, his parents became involved in extramarital affairs which, it is thought, grieved the baby so badly that he refused to eat and was at the point of death. The mother sent for Don and offered the child to him, begging him to save it. This was the chance of Don's life to vindicate himself. A Fire Clan woman in her distress had given Don, who was known to be "unlucky with children," a chance to prove that he could save a sick child from death and raise it to manhood, and was, therefore, really a good man and of one heart. He took very great pains with the baby, named him Norman, had his own mother adopt him to bind the tie more securely, and did everything he could to draw the child away from its mother and make him his own son. He even selected a new ceremonial father for him, and his vindication was almost complete when the child's own mother let him get severely burned, for then even the mother-in-law was reconciled with Don. He spent thirteen years more or less pampering the boy and never let him forget that he had saved his life. Don probably does need Norman more than any other person in the world, for he is the man's only chance to have a son, a chief security of his old age, and living proof to the Fire Clan people and the whole village that he can raise children and is not a Two-Heart. Norman's health and good life with Don have even encouraged other families in Oraibi to select Don as the ceremonial father of their children, a high honor and an additional proof that Don is an upright man with a good heart. Much more data could be assembled to indicate that Don has special needs for Norman and that he also has great fear of becoming a Two-Heart. His chief security against this anxiety is the belief that his Guardian Spirit may never "drop him." In this light it is rather obvious that Don believes his best chance to keep Norman is to lure him.

To review the situation: It is to the advantage of all Hopi fathers to attach their sons to them by kind treatment, and for any father to strike his half-grown son is taboo and almost never occurs. Don has a greater need for Norman than the average Hopi father has for his son, and at the same time he has a weaker hold upon him. Don cares more for Norman than for any other person, and the boy is living proof that Don is an honorable, upright man who can raise children and has nothing to do with Two-Hearts. But in the face of all this Norman is careless with the gifts that Don buys him, and of all people, he challenges Don to "Kill me and be done with it." He hurls at Don the very charge that Don has often used with success in defending himself in the presence of witches, and indeed the charge that is customarily made against Two-Hearts.

In a significant lapse of self-control Don slaps Norman twice. And he virtually accepts the challenge to kill his son, for it is common knowledge in Hopi society and endorsed by Hopi doctors that a child struck in the dark is likely to die.[3]

Don is in a most difficult situation. It should be recalled that he is more than an ordinary man, has served as a Special Officer in the Soyal, and is clan chief, and certainly knows better. He has struck the last person in the world that any Hopi father should strike, his half-grown son, the only son that he can ever have, at the most dangerous time, at night, and in direct response to a recognized Two-Heart challenge. If Norman gets sick now, or within a few days, any good Hopi doctor can easily explain the cause and few Hopi will doubt it, especially if they wish to believe it. And it would be to their advantage to believe, for some of them want the services of Norman and many of them are jealous of Don's work with the Whites. Therefore Norman may die or leave Don and go live with his Fire Clan people, and in either case Don loses the person he needs most. The situation cannot be taken lightly by Don, and he has very good reason to wonder why he ever slapped Norman in the first place.

But there is a further cause for regarding the situation with gravity. Don is in danger of death himself. To bring this fact into focus, it is necessary to summarize Don's experience with his Guardian Spirit. As a boy he had tried to dance with a snake in his mouth, had thrown the snake to the ground, seized a stone, and raised his arm to strike it when suddenly he changed his mind and held the blow, thus sparing the life of a sacred snake and saving himself from further danger. This quick change of mind was later recalled by Don as a miracle. When Don had tried to commit suicide by digging a hole in the sand and later got out just as the walls caved in, that, too, was viewed as a miracle at a later time. When at Sherman Don suffered pneumonia, became delirious, and believed that he died and journeyed to the home of the dead, he met for the first time his Guardian Spirit. This spirit assured him that he would watch over him for the rest of his life if he proved to be a good man. But he warned, "I hold you lightly as between two fingers and if you don't obey me, some day I will drop you." After this experience all Don's "miraculous" escapes from danger, including previous ones, were interpreted

3. See Wayne Dennis, *The Hopi Child*, p. 46. D. Appleton-Century Co., New York, 1940.

by him as due to the protection of his Spirit Guide. On at least five other occasions after he returned to Hopiland, this Spirit Guide warned him in the nick of time, particularly when in the act of using the penis plant and twice when he had raised his arm to strike a Two-Heart. Now what has happened on this fateful night when he is in an argument with his son and has raised his arm to strike in response to an implied Two-Heart challenge—where is his Guardian Spirit? Indeed, the Spirit Guide must have failed him, for he actually strikes twice, something that even Two-Hearts refrain from doing when challenged. Has Don's Guardian Spirit dropped him at last, as he threatened to do? Is his death hour really approaching? And if both lives are endangered, both Norman's and Don's, is it not to the advantage of Don to get sick first? He is indeed trapped, but he still has some possible advantage over Norman. He is older, has more experience, and has a much higher position in Hopi society. If he acts immediately, he has a chance to determine in part the *meaning* that the situation shall have. Therefore, in the role of both sufferer and manipulator, he speaks quickly, "Sonny, you are killing me." That is a significant advantage—to take the initiative and stamp the most favorable meaning upon a difficult experience.

It is quite obvious that the situation should be taken seriously when it is considered in the light of Hopi culture and Don's personal experience. But a better test of the proposed interpretation may lie in an analysis of the symptoms—numbness, shortness of breath, a hard stomach, need to vomit, and the appearance of his deceased mother. Mirrored in life history, these experiences may appear quite understandable and provide significant cues to the correct explanation of what goes on.

There is much material in the life history which suggests that Don was early conditioned to associate these symptoms with states of helplessness and danger. During the first year of his life he was almost continuously bound on a cradle with little opportunity for movement. In his second year he was subject to seizures. When he was four, five, and six, he was choked several times with cedar smoke until he was limp and unable to cry, had stomach trouble, and vomited. When he had pneumonia at Sherman, his hands and feet grew numb, he was unable to speak, and he believed that he stopped breathing. After he returned to Oraibi, both he and his brother suffered from "lightning disease" which caused numbness, shortness of breath, and foaming at the mouth. When he was twenty-two his brother's sick wife, showing the same symptoms, died with her head in his lap. Old Masenimka, his godmother, became ill and sent for Don, and while giving him her blessing, her lips grew numb, her breath short, and she died that night. When his old uncle Kayayeptewa was dying, his breath was the "length of a finger," and he could not talk, and when Don propped him up against the wall he died. Whenever Don is sick with any complaint, or filled with anxiety, he is almost certain to feel numb, to have trouble with his throat, and to suffer shortness of breath, and he reports that the majority of poison arrows are extracted from his throat. These symptoms are so commonly associated with crises in his life that their appearance are cues to increase his anxiety.

A fundamental doctrine among the Hopi is that disease and death are caused by worry. The accepted theory is that if bad thoughts which settle in the stomach and cause it to harden are not expelled by confession and vomiting, death will ensue. This belief is uppermost in almost all illness. Don has vomited for relief since he was smoked as a child, and customarily resorts to confession, crying, massage, the drinking of warm water or urine, and tickling his throat with a buzzard feather or his fingers—standard Hopi remedies which get good results. Therefore, in this situation he is following long-established responses to anxiety and is pursuing customary Hopi practice in treatment.

The death call is also a common Hopi experience and most persons receive it several times during life, usually from Masau'u, witches, or their own dead relatives. Don has seen Masau'u, has heard witches in the form of "owls" calling him to die just six months before, and more recently heard a call from the west saying, "Talayesva, come, come." In every case he had suffered great anxiety, and with similar symptoms.

Now a Hopi man's mother and her house are his security in the fullest sense. This is especially true when a man is in trouble with his wife and her people. He may always return to his mother. Don had followed this practice since when a child he ran crying to her when he was punished for bedwetting, threatened with castration, or frightened by the fire of Masau'u near the Oraibi Rock. In his death journey he first came home to his mother and never forgot the fact that she failed to notice him. When in trouble with girls at Shipaulovi and Moenkopi, he came back to mother. She was present at the birth of all of his children; when his last child was dying he took it to her house, and when he was very ill with "penis trouble," he sent for her. Whenever he has had trouble with Irene he has threatened to return to his mother—a typical Hopi way of managing wives. Sometimes when he is sick and wishes to encourage Irene in her care of him, he compares her favorably with his "dear mother who has passed away."

Now in his death hour, while Irene rubs his stomach and he feels a deep need to justify his acts of violence, insure the loyalty of his wife, and regain his wayward son, a door opens and closes in the west like the door in the hospital at the time of his "death." And there stands his dear mother with outstretched arms calling him to come with her where there is no more sorrow and suffering. It is a most opportune moment for favorable effect upon his wife and for later disciplinary advantage over his son. Telling Irene what he sees behind her, he adds pointedly, "If you want to keep me alive, it is up to you." In other words, "Mother is here, and if you don't do something quickly I shall go with her, and it will be your own fault." This is the second time within a little more than a year that Don has produced very loyal behavior on the part of Irene by means of a death call, and the first time on record that he has used the call of his dead mother to coerce his wife. But this is a very critical situation which justifies strong measures. Crying, Irene hurries to fetch a doctor and save Don's life as a good, loyal wife should do.

Additional supporting evidence for the interpretation of symptoms could be produced, but it appears unnecessary, since their explanation is the simplest part of the problem. The more pertinent question is: How successful was Don in working out a satisfactory adjustment to this difficult and hazardous situation? How skillful was he—either consciously or unconsciously—in manipulating the mores to his own advantage? For these rather irregular adjustments to prove adequate, both immediate and long-term results should be realized. Don must quickly extricate himself from the blame and consequences of an unusual act of violence. In other words, he must escape public censure if possible, get back in favor with his Spirit Guide—his conscience—and save his life which seems endangered. As he puts it, he must "forget about the slapping" as soon as possible and see that others do not use it against him. In long-term perspective, he must stay in the good graces of his wife and of her relatives, if that is possible, and regain the obedience and loyalty of his son. If he accomplishes these results, there are grounds for regarding the adjustments as appropriate for the situation, or at least one would be cautious in ranking them as unappropriate. At any rate the behavior becomes more understandable.

Don did secure almost immediate results. He shifted the responsibility of murderous aggression from himself to Norman and became the suffering father whose life was endangered. Furthermore, he gained the immediate care and loyalty of his wife; in fact, he placed her in the position where any service less than the best she could render might be interpreted as causing his death. She has no time to look for Norman but hurries out in tears to get a doctor for Don. It is interesting to note that when Norman goes off to his aunt's house, Don borrows a bit of alien (Christian) culture and classifies him as a "prodigal son." It may also be said that Don's mother, the security-symbol of his life, did not fail him in his hour of need; she came and called but she did not touch him. In death she provided perhaps a greater reinforcement than she could have rendered in life. Moreover, the bad thoughts were all successfully expelled according to Hopi standards—two basins full—and Don was purged of evil. Poleyestewa, who is Don's father's sister's husband, was definitely allied with Don, and he is an important person to have on one's side, a doctor whose diagnosis is highly regarded, a Special Officer in the Soyal, and the Crier Chief who makes all important announcements. On second thought the Guardian Spirit did not drop Don after all, for did he not receive a sudden insight just after the second blow, and was he not inspired to make a most opportune remark, "Sonny, you are killing me." Now Don can thank his Spirit Guide for protection and pray for him to keep off all evil spirits while he sleeps in peace. In fact, these adjustments turned out so satisfactorily that Don was tucked into bed by a devoted wife and the loyal doctor, and fell asleep before they left his side.

In the morning there was the good doctor to rub him, advise him, and pray for him, the doctor's wife, Kewanmainim, to shed tears of joy for his narrow escape, and his own dear wife who was so concerned about his health that she accompanied him to his field eleven miles away and helped him harvest his corn. Don was also in a position to reprimand his "prodigal son," when he returned home. And even then he thought over appropriate words for the occasion.

It appears that the critical problem was rather satisfactorily resolved for the moment, but much more manipulation was necessary for lasting results. The prodigal must return home and become a dutiful and loyal son. Otherwise the chief goal would be lost. Don got his clan sister, Norman's aunt, to talk to the boy. He also urged his clan brother, the real father of Norman, to advise him on how he should treat his adopted father. Furthermore, Don persuades his clan son, Rudolph, a prominent medicine man at Mishongovi, to talk to Norman. Rudolph was a particularly strategic person to advise the "prodigal" for he is a clan father to Irene and an elder clan brother to Norman. It is also Norman's duty to listen to his elder brother, especially when he is a wise and important doctor. It is not recorded that Don discussed this matter with any members of the Fire Clan except his wife.

When Norman returned home five days later, Don had a long talk with him and warned him that such back talk, if repeated, would surely kill his father. Norman apologized and promised never to do it again. Furthermore, Norman returned to sheepherding for Don, and cared for his horses. And some months later Don was able to say of his son: "Norman has remained a very good boy. Although he had made plans to go to Shipaulovi to see the Lakon dance, he readily agreed to herd so that I could go instead. On my next trip to Winslow I bought him a pair of overalls and a high-grade red silk shirt with flowers painted on the breast and both pockets. Within the following months I bought Norman another shirt, a pair of shoes, a red silk handkerchief, a white sweater, a fine dancing sash, a pair of moccasins, a pair of fancy buckskin ankle bands, and a beautiful bowguard. I also bought him a seven-dollar hat for half price, a rifle, and a pair of high top boots. That brought a big smile over his face." Norman promised to obey.

One may reflect upon what role this night's events may take in Don's "stream of life experience," what particular meaning it will come to have for him, and what use he will make of it in future adjustments to his wife and son. It is suggested that Don will probably never strike his son again, certainly not at night, and that he will never let Norman forget that insolence and back talk are likely to cause his father's sickness and death. He may even forget that he slapped Norman. But on the other hand, should Norman become disrespectful and insolent again, Don will probably worry, get a bad stomach, perhaps vomit, and may even hear another death call.

Although the present sample of situational analysis is incomplete and not entirely satisfactory, it appears reasonable to conclude that it makes this small section of Don's behavior more understandable. It is also possible that it provides some useful insight into other situational adjustments in the life course. Finally, when numerous situations are selected and analyzed in this manner, it may be possible that the interpretation of each will check the others and thus build up an inductive foundation for an interpretation of the whole personality in terms of defining how Don came to be the person that he is and how it happens that he feels, thinks, and behaves as he does.

Legends and Myths of the Hopi

The legends and myths are to the Hopi what Scripture, science, history, and literature are to us; and they are frequently related for both instruction and entertainment. Those which Don heard as a boy help to explain much of his behavior as an adult. A small sample is recorded here in very much abbreviated form. Many of the same legends were reported by H. R. Voth in the decade of Don's childhood and are greatly elaborated in his text, *The Traditions of the Hopi*.[1] To Don the legends are not "myths and tales," but true accounts of his people and his gods. He was much concerned with correcting details in the manuscript and often insisted that the stories were too greatly condensed and had important items left out.

The gravity with which Don takes the legendary accounts may be illustrated in his attitude toward the first one, which tells of Hurung Wuhti and the beginning of life. While in New Haven, he made a special request for an opportunity to worship the "Lady of the Eastern Ocean." When he was taken to the beach, he walked reverently to the water and prayed: "Our Mother of the Ocean, I have arrived from afar to pray to you. I thank you for all your blessings and have come to tell you about life among the Hopi. We have been suffering from much sickness. Please drive off all disease so that our people will increase. Notify your spirit people to hasten with clouds and give us moisture for our crops. Let them arise and go ahead of me over

1. Field Columbian Museum (Anthrop. Series, Pub. 96), Vol. VIII. 1905.

the mountains, drop rain on Oraibi, and refresh my people so they will be in good health when I return. I ask this in the name of my God, the Sun. May our lives be good." He then stooped and splashed water four times toward his home, wet his hands, and rubbed them over his heart to make himself "good and strong." Soon thereafter he smoked to send a message to the Six-Point-Cloud-People.

THE BEGINNING

In the beginning water almost covered the flat world below the present earth. Far away in the east there lived a goddess (Hurung Wuhti) in a kiva with a tall ladder from which hung a gray and a yellow foxskin. In the west was a similar goddess, and to the ladder of her kiva was attached a turtle-shell rattle. Daily the Sun god put on first the skin of the gray fox for the early dawn and then the skin of the yellow fox for the golden glow. He would rise from an opening in the north end of the kiva, pass over the waters to the kiva in the west, touch the turtle shell on the ladder there, enter the kiva, and depart through an opening in the north end, move underneath, and rise again from the kiva in the east.

Eventually the deities of the east and the west caused some dry land to rise up out of the water. The Sun god noticed this in passing over the world and mentioned it to the goddess in the east, saying that he had observed no signs of life on it. She journeyed west over a rainbow to confer with her partner, and together they made a little bird of clay. Having covered it with a cloth on the floor of the kiva, they sang over it to impart life, and instructed the wren to fly over the land in search of some living thing. The bird flew far and wide, but without success, for it failed to go to the southwest where the Spider Woman lived in a kiva at the edge of the water.

Upon receiving this second report that the land was barren, the goddess in the west created many birds and animals in the same manner in which the wren was formed and sent them out to inhabit the earth. The goddess of the east, still visiting in the west, made a woman of clay first, and then a man, and covered them with a cloth. Together the deities sang over them to instill life, taught them a language, and told them to occupy the earth. The goddess led them over the rainbow to her home in the east where they stayed for four days and then left to found a home of their own.

The Spider Woman in the southwest gathered some clay and created people in pairs, giving them a language and sending them forth. But once she forgot to create a woman, and this is the reason for single men. Later she made a spare woman, and advised her, "Somewhere there is a single man; try to find him and live with him. Do the best you can." They finally found each other and started life together, but quarreled, separated, and came together again repeatedly. Other people learned quarreling from them and this accounts for domestic strife today.

After some time the goddess in the west called to her partner in the east to come over again and help her make some more people, but always in pairs. These people lived in peace, except when they quarreled with the people of the Spider Woman over game. Finally, the deity in the west said to them, "You may remain here. I'm going to move farther out into the ocean. Whenever you want anything, pray to me there." The other goddess moved eastward, and that is the reason no one ever sees them now. Whenever the Hopis want anything from them, they deposit prayer offerings in the village and send out their prayers.

THE ESCAPE TO THE UPPER WORLD

Life in the underworld was very good for a while; it rained all the time, everything grew, and there were blossoms everywhere. By and by things changed; the people became wicked, strife arose, and evil men seduced good women. Then it stopped raining, bad winds arose, and the crops failed. Two-Hearts were everywhere, and few were left whose hearts were single and good.

The good chiefs met to devise some means of escape. They had heard sounds like heavy footsteps above. So they decided to investigate, and made a small bird of clay, which came to life under the charm of their songs. They said to it, "Our hearts are heavy here; above somebody seems to be walking; perhaps you can find out for us." The bird agreed, whereupon the chiefs planted first a pine tree and later a reed, hoping to pierce the dome of their sky. When the reed pushed its way through, the little bird spiraled aloft, passed through the opening, circled about for a long time, and returned exhausted and without any news. Then a hummingbird was made, and later a hawk, but they failed to find anybody in their flights. So the chiefs made a catbird and said to it, "We are living here in trouble, with children who won't obey, and with people whose hearts are bad, so we want to leave. We have heard footsteps up there. You go and find out for us. And if you find someone who has a good heart, ask him if we may join him."

The catbird flew up through the opening and searched everywhere. Finally it flew over the place which is now Oraibi and saw a man sitting beside a great rock and leaning forward. When the bird drew nearer, the man moved his head a little and said, "Sit down; certainly you have come for some purpose." This was Masau'u, the bloody-headed god of Fire and Death. The catbird said, "We are not living very well down below, and the chiefs sent me to ask if they may come and live with you." "I am living in poverty, but in peace," replied Masau'u. "If they wish to share such a life, they may."

The bird returned with Masau'u's message. At that time there were many peoples living below—white men, Paiutes, Navahos, Havasupais, and others. Some of them planned to leave with the good chiefs and, on the fourth day, they began climbing up the tall reed. Many Hopi chiefs climbed out: The Village Chief (Kik-mongwi, who was also the Soyalmongwi, and leader of his people), the Flute Chief (Lan-mongwi), Horn Chief (Al-mongwi), Agave Chief (Kwan-mongwi), Singer Chief (Tao-mongwi), Wowochim Chief (Kel-mongwi), Rattlesnake Chief (Tcu-mongwi), Antelope Chief (Tcob-mongwi), Marau Chief (Marau-mongwi), Lakon Chief (Lakon-mongwi), and the Warrior Chief (Kalehtak-mongwi or Pookong). So many came crowding up the reed stalk that the chiefs feared a Two-Heart might follow them in disguise and start trouble in the new world. So they began to shake the reed from the top and many people dropped back.

All those who managed to reach the top gathered at the edge of the opening, and the Village Chief addressed them: "Now that we have escaped from the underworld, let us live with single hearts." But soon his little daughter became sick and died. The Chief cried, "A Two-Heart has followed us. I will toss up a ball of fine meal and let it fall on the guilty person." It fell on the head of a young maiden. The Chief rushed up to her, crying, "So you are the one who has caused the death of my child. I shall throw you back again." As he carried her to the opening (*sipapu*), she begged to remain in the upper world and told the Chief that his child was alive down below. He looked through the opening and saw his little girl running around with the others. "That is the way it will be," said the Two-Heart to the Chief. "If anyone dies, he will go down there and remain four days and come back again as a Katcina to live with his people." Then the Chief caused yellow water to fill the opening and prevent communications between the two worlds. He allowed the young Two-Heart to remain in the upper world, but ordered her to follow along far behind.

The upper world was still dark, so the Spider Woman, who had escaped with the others, assisted by the Flute Chief, took a piece of white cloth (*owa*) and cut out a large circle upon which she made a drawing of the moon symbol. After they had sung over it, the Spider Woman took the disc away toward the east. Soon the moon arose, but it was a pale light. The two then cut a circular piece of buckskin, sketched a Sun symbol, and sang over it. The

Spider Woman carried it away, and in a little while it rose in the east, making the upper world light and warm. The Spider Woman and the Flute Chief had also rubbed the yolks of eggs over the Sun symbol, and that is what makes it so very bright, and why cocks know when to crow before dawn.

The chiefs created plants and living things and decided to scatter out over the earth. Their language was Hopi, which the Village Chief wanted to keep for himself and his people, so he asked a mockingbird (*Yahpa*), who spoke all languages, to teach them to the different peoples. When this was done, everybody sat down to a farewell feast. The Chief laid out a great many corn ears of different lengths which they had brought up from the underworld. "Now," said he, "choose of these before you start." There was a great wrangle, for each wanted the best ears. Such people as the Navaho, Ute, and Apache struggled and got the longest ears, leaving the little ones for the Hopi. The Chief took these up and said, "You selected the longest ears for yourselves and you shall live on them; but they are not corn, they are only grasses." That is the reason these people now rub out the tassels of many grasses and live on them, while the Hopi have corn, for this is what the smaller ears really were.

The head Chief had an elder brother who said that he was going toward sunrise with a party and that he would touch the sun, at least with his forehead. It was agreed that if he stayed in the east, he would always remember his people in the west. He promised the Chief that if his Hopi brothers should ever get into trouble and live again as they did in the underworld, he would return, capture any Two-Hearts who had caused the trouble, cut off their heads, and restore peace and prosperity to the people. As this elder brother and his party journeyed eastward, the Spider Woman made horses and burros for them to ride. So they became far more successful than others, and they are the white people who come to us now. But our elder brother has not yet returned to punish the Two-Hearts and deliver us from our misery.

THE EARLY SETTLEMENTS

The different parties set out to find homes. The Chief and his party, followed by the young Two-Heart, traveled eastward and settled for short intervals wherever they found fields and springs. Sometimes they made springs by planting perforated vessels in which were certain herbs, stones, shells, pahos, and a small snake. Within a year, a spring would come forth. In the meantime they used rain water, for they understood how to make rain.

Some of the party finally arrived at Moenkopi, where they lived for a while, claiming that land. Others came along what is now called the Little

Colorado River and the Great Lakes, arriving at last at Shongopavi and starting in the plain a village which is now in ruins.

One day in Shongopavi, while the people were eating, the Chief's brother, Machito, held a sweet corn ear between each two fingers of one hand, at the same time eating from the other hand. As corn was very scarce, the people complained to him about his greediness. At this he became angry and left, taking with him the Aototo and the Aholi Katcinas. He came to Oraibi and built a house near the Rock and later brought his wife of the Parrot Clan from Shongopavi.

When Machito had lived at Oraibi for some time, a group of Shongopavi rabbit hunters passed Oraibi Rock and tried to persuade him to return with them. He refused and carved in the rock some picture writing which the Hopi cannot now read, and which was covered recently by a falling stone. Since he feared attack, he finally built his house on the mesa by the Oraibi Rock. The old wall is still there. He also took a big stone and made a landmark between his place and the Shongopavi land. From time to time other Bear people joined him.

One day Masau'u, the Fire God at Oraibi, revealed himself to Machito and his associates. He readily agreed to give them what land they needed, but would not consent to be their chief, because, he said, "You will return to your old life; you will become the same here as you were in the underworld. Someone who is a Two-Heart came out with you. An evil society will be formed on earth. When the white man, your elder brother, returns and cuts off the heads of all the Two-Hearts, then I shall have my land back. Until then, I will not be chief." He did promise, however, to guard the village by night with a firebrand and to keep off enemies, disease, and pestilence.

Other peoples began to arrive. Whenever a new clan came, a member of the party would go to the Chief and ask permission to settle in the village. The Chief usually inquired whether they were able to produce rain. If they had any means of doing this, they would say, "Yes, this and this we have, and when we assemble for this ceremony or when we have this dance, it rains. With this we have been traveling and taking care of our children." The Chief would then admit them to the village.

An early arrival was the Bow Clan. When the Village Chief asked the leader what he had brought with him to make rain, he replied, "I have the Shaalako Katcinas, the Tangik Katcinas, and others. When they dance, it rains." He was asked to demonstrate. Even on the day before the dance it rained a little, and on the dance day it rained torrents. Then the Chief invited them to move into the village, gave them a large tract of land, and told them that they could hold their ceremonies first. Therefore the Wowochim ceremony, led by the Chief of the Bow Clan, came first, followed by the Soyal ceremony, in charge of the Village Chief from the Bear Clan, and the Snake and Flute ceremonies, which were held in alternate years. The Snake cult was brought by the Snake Clan, the Antelope by the Bluebird Clan, and the Flute by the Spider Clan. The Lizard Clan came from the northwest with the Marau society, the Parrot Clan brought the Lakon, and the Badger Clan proved that they understood medicine and could make the charmed liquids for the Flute, Snake, Marau, and other societies.

At that time everything was good, and no evil person lived in the village. There was much rain, good crops, and plenty to eat. It was a golden age. Many of the gods could be seen face to face. The Katcinas lived within or near the village, and whenever they danced or the people held their ceremonies, it always rained. Everybody was happy.

Finally, however, the young Two-Heart who had escaped from the underworld seduced others and taught them her evil magic. Then it was learned that Two-Hearts lived in a village to the west. These people became so wicked that the Great Serpent, the God of Waters, produced a flood and destroyed most of them. But a few were saved, traveled eastward, and settled near Oraibi. Soon they scattered to the different Hopi villages and initiated others into their evil society, even stealing babies from their cradles for this purpose. For a long time there was more or less open strife between evil spirits and Two-Hearts on one side and the Hopi gods and good spirits on the other. The gods and Katcinas who lived in or near the village sometimes fought open battles with the evil powers, and even the animals, birds, and insects took active parts and revealed their true human characters to the Hopis.

THE TWIN WAR GODS

In those days the Twin War gods (Pookonghoya and his younger brother Balongahoya) lived with their grandmother, the Spider Woman, just north of the village where the Achamali shrine now stands. They had a race track between their house and the village, where they could be seen running and playing shinny in the early morning. They were on good terms with the people, helped them in their battles with evil spirits and Two-Hearts, and sometimes made love to the Oraibi girls.

Once a large monster called Shita, who lived in the west, came often to Oraibi to devour children and even adults. The Chief asked the War Twins to help defend the village and made two arrows for them, fastening bluebird feathers to the shafts. The War gods met the monster at the Oraibi Rock and engaged him in battle, but he swallowed them both. The brothers laughed as they slipped down the monster's gullet, shot an arrow into his heart at close range, and killed him. In his stomach they found many people of other nationalities whom he had devoured in different parts of the world. They all climbed back into the monster's mouth only to find escape barred by his teeth which were firmly set in death, but they finally came out through his nose.

A cannibal giant and his wife (Cooyoko and Cooyok Wuhti) built their house on a mesa east of Oraibi and began to kill and eat the old men and women who went out to gather wood. So the Chief asked the War gods to destroy them. They went to the mesa, discovered the giantess picking lice off her dress, and shot a lightning arrow at her, shattering her to bits. Soon her husband came up the mesa singing, but the War gods had concealed themselves in his house, and as he entered, shot two lightning arrows into him. Then they scalped the giants and returned home, swinging the trophies and singing. After that, whenever the old people went after wood they returned safely.

THE WAR GOD MARRIES A HOPI MAIDEN

One day the Twin War gods heard that two beautiful maidens were watching a field near Mount Beautiful. They decided to go hunting and visited the maidens. The girls greeted them joyfully and in a half-jesting manner said to their suitors, "Let us cut off an arm from each of you, and if you do not die we will marry you." The younger brother said to the elder, "They are beautiful; let's try it." He held his arm over the edge of the mealing trough, and one of them struck it with the upper mealing stone, cutting it off. The other maiden did the same to the elder brother. "If we recover," said the twins, "we shall come for you." They left for home with their severed arms and told their grandmother, the Spider Woman, what had happened. "Very well," said she, "I will knit your arms back again." So she had them lie down, placed an arm beside each twin, covered them with a cotton cloth, and sang until the arms were restored. On the next night the twins went to the house of the maidens and slept with them until the cocks crew in the early morning.

There was another beautiful maiden who refused all offers of marriage. The War Twins were entranced with her and asked their grandmother for advice. She said, "You poor ones, you are too small and unsightly; she certainly will not want you." But that evening they went to the village to set mousetraps near where the maiden lived, and put a squash seed under each stone trap. The maiden invited them to set traps in her house, for the mice were very bad. They set them near the mealing bin, asked for a piki tray, and made a trap of it. They told the maiden to watch the traps, and during the night they killed an antelope, brought it to the house, and placed it under the piki tray. The next day the maiden and her father were pleased to have the twins return and set more traps. This time the War gods killed a deer and placed it under the tray.

On the following evening the twins quarreled over who should visit the maiden first. Finally the elder brother dressed, called on her, and found her grinding corn. Since he was such a good hunter and trapper, her parents were pleased with his interest in their daughter and hinted that he would be welcomed as a son-in-law. So the War god took the young girl home with him, and the Spider Woman gave her a little food which increased in her mouth so that her hunger was satisfied whenever she chewed. The old woman slept with the girl that night while her grandson had to sleep with his twin brother.

Early the next morning the grandmother and the maiden went out to sacrifice corn meal to the Sun. Then the Spider Woman shelled corn and told the maiden to grind for four days, as all Hopi brides do. On the fourth day at yellow dawn the grandmother stepped outside and called for help to wash the heads of the young couple. She brought out the War god and his bride and told them to sit down and wait. Soon a great many clouds gathered overhead and dropped rain upon them. "Thanks for bathing our bride and groom," said the Spider Woman. The maiden ground corn again all day and in the evening prepared a meal. This was repeated for many days, but the girl felt disgraced because no one was carding and spinning cotton for the bridal costume. Even the War Twins were out playing shinny and shooting feathered arrows through cornhusk hoops instead of working on the wedding outfit like respectable Hopis. The maiden noticed, however, that the Spider Woman often went into an inner room and said, "Thanks, thanks," to someone. So one morning the Spider Woman prepared yucca suds and washed the heads of the Elder War Twin and his bride. Then she brought forth a complete bridal costume made by spiders that had been carding cotton, spinning, and weaving in the secret room. The maiden was dressed and sent home, followed by the groom with a large quantity of meat on his back. Later the Spider Woman asked the clouds to drop extra rain on the fields of the bride's father.

The bride soon bore a little son, who grew up and played with the other children. His father made him a bow with which he learned to shoot, but he killed the Oraibi children with his lightning arrows, which made the people very angry. So the War god placed the little boy on his back, left his wife in Oraibi, and returned to live with the Spider Woman.

There once lived in Oraibi two girls who were close friends and often ground corn together. But they fell in love with the same young man and became bitter enemies. Now the Yellow-Corn Maiden, who was a witch in disguise, wished to destroy her friend and rival. So one evening as they returned from the Spider spring northeast of the village, the Yellow-Corn Maiden suggested that they rest on a sand hill. Pretending to play, she drew from her bosom a little wheel tinted with the colors of the rainbow and threw it at her friend. As the innocent girl caught it, she fell down and was changed into a coyote. The evil girl laughed, picked up her jug, and returned to the village.

The poor maiden, who was now a coyote, was chased away from the village by the dogs. She wandered all day, and at night came to a Katcina hut and found some rabbit meat which she ate; after that she fell asleep. Two Katcinas came from their hunting and found the coyote. They drew their bows to shoot, when they heard the coyote sob and saw tears on her cheeks. So they bound her and took her to the Katcina Gap northwest of Oraibi, where the Spider Woman lived.

The Spider Woman recognized the poor creature and sent one Katcina into the village for some special herbs (*tomoala*) and the other to the woods for juniper boughs. She boiled some water and poured it into a vessel, then thrust a hook from a tomoala pod into the coyote's neck and another into her back, dipped her in the water under a cloth, and, by twisting the two hooks, pulled off the coyote skin. The restored maiden was neatly dressed with her hair in whorls just as she had left the village. The Spider Woman listened to the girl's story and comforted her, saying, "You poor thing, that cruel girl is a Two-Heart, but we will fix her." She took the maiden into another room, put juniper boughs into water, bathed her, and gave her some corn to grind.

After a few days the Spider Woman told the maiden that her mother was lonely and that she should return to her home. The old woman climbed to the housetop and called to her neighbors, the Katcinas. They came and agreed to take the maiden home. The Spider Woman dressed her beautifully, arranged her hair in whorls, placed a blanket over her shoulder, and told her to ask her father to make prayer feathers for the Katcinas. She also instructed her how to take revenge on the witch girl. They proceeded to the village in the early morning, the maiden following a line of Katcinas. Some of the people recognized the girl and ran to tell her parents, who welcomed her with outstretched arms.

The next day she ground corn and told about her experience in a little song. The Yellow-Corn Maiden heard the song, visited the girl, and was treated kindly. They ground together all day as if nothing had happened, and in the evening went after water. As they filled their jugs, the witch girl noticed that her friend dipped water with a beautiful cup which the Spider Woman had given to her, and that water flowing from it reflected the colors of a rainbow. She took the cup, drank from it, and was turned into a bull snake on the spot. Then it was the good maiden's turn to laugh.

The bull snake wandered about for many days, became very hungry, and lived on rabbits, mice, and birds. Later it crawled into the village and was killed by the girl's parents, who did not know that they were slaying their own daughter. Her soul was thus liberated and started to the House of the Dead. Ever since, Two-Hearts have left their graves in the form of bull snakes, still wrapped in the yucca leaves with which they were buried; and whenever these snakes are killed, the souls of the sorcerers are set free to go west for their punishment.

THE BLOODY MAIDEN WHO LOOKS AFTER THE ANIMALS

In Oraibi there once lived a youth who passed the house of a certain maiden on the way to watch his father's fields. The maiden took piki in a blanket, followed him, and invited him to lunch with her in the shade of a house near the cornfield. After eating, she said, "Let us play hide and seek, and the one who is found four times shall be killed." "All right," he said, "but you hide first, for you suggested it." She spread her blanket over him, and warning him not to look, ran through the growing corn, where she hid under the leaves of a plant. He searched for her in vain. When his turn came, he hid under a bush, but she found him with ease. The second time she pulled out the tassel of a cornstalk, crawled into the opening, and drew the tassel back into place. He hunted throughout the cornfield, but again failed to find her.

As he wandered about discouraged, seeking a hiding place for himself, he heard a voice: "Come up here," it said. "I have pity on you. She has already found you once and will certainly find you again." It was the Sun god, who let down a rainbow and told the boy to climb up and hide behind his back, adding, "Here you will be safe." The maiden searched a long time without success, then pressed a few drops of milk from her breast and, holding them in her hand, saw the sun reflected in them and spied the boy hiding behind it. So the youth came down and covered himself again while the maiden went to hide. Although he lifted the corner of the blanket and tried to watch her, he had no better success. When he gave up, a watermelon burst and the girl stepped out, challenging him to hide again. As he traveled through the corn with a heavy heart, he heard another voice saying, "I pity you; come in here." Looking down, he saw a small hole by the side of a cornstalk, the house of the spider, which he entered quickly, while she spun a web across the opening. But the maiden came and found him easily with the aid of a crystal which she drew from her bosom. Then she hid again—in a ditch filled with rain water—and turned herself into a tadpole, which completely escaped the boy's notice. When he went to hide a fourth time, a worm took him into its house in a piece of dead wood. But the maiden found him almost immediately.

Returning together to the field house, they sat down on the north side. Here the maiden dug a hole close to the corner post and said to the youth, "I have defeated you; take off your shirt and beads." Thereupon she seized him by the hair, jerked a knife from behind her belt, bent him over, and cut his throat so that the blood ran into the hole. Covering it, she dug another hole somewhat to the north, buried his body, and returned to the village with his shirt and beads.

When the young man did not return home, his parents were very sad and ate only a little of the meat which they had. As the mother tried to drive the flies away from the mutton with a broom, one of them spoke to her, "Why do you drive us off? When we have sucked this meat, we will go and look for your son." Soon they flew away to the cornfield and tracked the youth to his grave. Here they uncovered both the blood and the body, sucked up the former, and injected it into the latter. The heart of the youth began to beat, so that he raised himself up and followed the flies into the village.

Going to the maiden's house, the young man found his shirt and beads in a room filled with wealth filched from other slain youths. He shook his shirt in the face of the maiden and thereby caused an evil charm to enter her body and change her into a pregnant woman (*Tihkuy Wuhti*). She immediately entered an inner room and came out dressed in a white robe, with her hair tied up like that of a married woman, and her face and clothes covered with blood. The costumes of the slain youths hanging in the room transformed themselves quickly into deer, antelopes, and rabbits, and dashed from the house. The maiden tried to stop them. Seizing the last animal, an antelope, she wiped her hand first over her own genitalia and then over the antelope's face, and let it go after twisting its nose. She then turned to the people who had gathered outside and said, "After this, you shall have great difficulty in hunting these animals." Then she left the house and disappeared, trailing after the game. She still lives with the animals, and Hopi hunters sometimes see her wrapped in the white robe and covered with blood. They still make prayer offerings to her because she controls the game, and sometimes they wrestle with her in their dreams.

THE GIRL WHO WAS RESCUED FROM THE TWO-HEARTS

There lived in the village a beautiful White-Corn Maiden who stubbornly refused all offers of marriage and love-making. Finally the members of a certain kiva, who were Two-Hearts, decided to rape the virgin even if they had to kill her to do it. These men met one night in Skeleton Gulch, where a great number of corpses had been thrown after a battle. They planned to make a wheel of cornhusks, such as children still use in play, and then capture the breath of the maiden and wrap it in the wheel. They also made a number of feathered arrows, one of which was dipped in rattlesnake poison. The next day a number of young men were playing with the wheel and arrows near the maiden's house when she came down the ladder on an errand and passed them. The youth with the poisoned arrow pretended to shoot it at the wheel, but instead, struck her in the foot. That night she died. Meanwhile the Two-Hearts had assembled again at Skeleton Gulch, scheming to do more mischief. As soon as the girl had been buried, they changed themselves into coyotes, wolves, and foxes and went to the grave to steal her body. The brother of the maiden, who was deeply grieved at the death of his sister, had gone to the west edge of the mesa and was sitting there looking at the grave when he saw the animals approach it. He was about to shoot an arrow into the pack when he heard one of them speak and discovered that they were Two-Hearts. After they had dug out the body, the one who had transformed himself into a gray wolf slung the corpse upon his back and carried it away, followed by the others. The young man trailed them in a roundabout way to their kiva, where he peeped in and saw the body lying north of the fireplace. He hurried back to the village and went to the War Chief for assistance.

When the old warrior had heard the story, he took down two war costumes, giving one to the youth and putting on the other himself. Then he stepped outside the house and blew a bone whistle very loudly. A great noise was heard in the sky and a small man stood beside them—the Star and Cloud Deity (*Cotukvnangwuu*). The warrior again whistled shrilly and called the Hawk Deity, who flew down and offered his assistance. The old man spat into his hands and whistled again, calling a great number of skeleton flies, harbingers of death, who came and drank his spittle until he closed his hands upon them. Thus fortified, they proceeded to the meeting place of the Two-Hearts and entered the kiva unobserved.

The Two-Hearts had transformed themselves into men again. They had undressed the maiden, covered her with a piece of cloth, and were singing to revive her. The oldest one took her breath from the cornhusk wheel and put it back into her body. She came to life, sat up, looked at the evil men, and began to cry. An old female Two-Heart washed the maiden's face and rubbed corn meal over it, combed her hair in whorls, and placed her upon a sheepskin in the center of the kiva. The Two-Hearts lined up in the order of their age and with the intention of raping her, each in turn.

At this very moment, however, the old Warrior Chief liberated a skeleton fly. Its buzzing quickly turned the thoughts of the Two-Hearts from the expectation of rape to the fear of death. The leader, who was nearly upon the maiden, looked up, saw the fly, and halted in dismay. At that instant the Hawk Deity rushed into the kiva, threw the man aside, seized the maiden, swung her on his back, and flew away. Her brother and the Warrior Chief then made themselves known and challenged the Two-Hearts to mortal combat. The sorcerers quickly extinguished the fire and began to shoot poison arrows at the youth and the warrior, who protected themselves with their shields. The warrior drew from his pocket a little bag of stinging bees and let them loose upon the Two-Hearts, who soon cried for mercy. The Star and Cloud Deity then shot a ray of lightning among them and shattered them to pieces. When the lightning flash had done its work and the kiva was dark again, the warrior waited with the young man until they felt the warm blood of their victims bathing their feet. Then the old Chief said to the vanquished Two-Hearts, "This has happened to you for your misdeeds. Because of your evil ways you do not deserve to live, but being very skillful, you will doubtless restore yourselves again." Thereupon he and the young man left the kiva and returned to the village, replacing the war costumes in the special house.

The Star and Cloud god ascended into the sky, where he found the beautiful virgin living in a house with the Eagle and Hawk Deity. The skin of an eagle's body hung on the north wall of her room, and a hawk's skin on the east wall. The girl ground corn daily, preparing food for the warriors. After some time they announced that she could visit her parents. So the hawk took her on his back and flew swiftly to earth, setting her down near Oraibi. When she reached her home, she told everyone that she had died and was now living with the warriors above and could only visit Oraibi occasionally. After a short time she disappeared but returned in four days, saying that she had returned above to look after the War Chiefs. She continued to live with her parents, making frequent trips to the upper world, but one night she fell asleep for the last time. Then her relatives treated her body as eagles are treated when they are sent home and buried her on the west side of the village. Her brother again watched the grave for four days, but this time it was not disturbed.

In the meantime important events had occurred in the kiva of the Two-Hearts. The Star and Cloud Deity had returned, entered the kiva, and restored his victims, but as a punishment he had given back to the several individuals different parts than those torn from their bodies. Before leaving, he said, "You are evil and this shall be your punishment. You shall be ridiculed by the people." In the morning when it became light, the Two-Hearts observed with great consternation what had happened to them. An old man found that he had only one of his own legs, while the other was a woman's; another man had one arm of natural size, and for the other that of a child; a third found a woman's head on his body; and so on.

They were all discouraged, and one of the old men suggested at once that they had better not live very long. He thought he would drop from the ladder to the floor of the kiva and die. When the Two-Hearts came out of the kiva into the village, they were the laughing-stock of the people.

GOOD AND EVIL SPIRITS WHO INFLUENCE THE PEOPLE

There had long existed two powers in the world, one evil and the other good. Once the evil power lived in the form of a crow on the high mesa southeast of Oraibi, where the Sun shrine is located. He would walk up and down on the edge of the mesa watching the people plant their corn in the valley. Noting the fields that were planted first, he would later eat the young plants. Occasionally he flew around the village of Oraibi, observing the people. He had a power to influence those who did not possess strong hearts. He could project sickness into their bodies and evil thoughts into their hearts, and caused some of them to steal and gossip. Regretting their conduct afterwards, they would say, "What is it that makes me so bad? I was not formerly this way." Good people were thus turned into evil under the influence of the crow, but the old people told them that there was a good power in the world striving to overcome evil. They assured one another that every person had a Guardian Spirit who is trying to lead him along the right path and keep him from falling. It was said that the evil and good powers constantly wrangle over a man. Sometimes he senses a sudden shock and a quick change of mind under the influence of his Spirit Guide. If a man pays no attention to his Guide, he will be dropped.

A FAMINE AND THE GOD OF GERMINATION

It had not rained in Oraibi for four or five years. The people moved away in search of food or died of starvation until only a boy and his sister were left in the village. He formed a little bird of the pith of a sunflower stalk which transformed itself into a live hummingbird and flew away. It returned next day and entered an opening in the wall. There the boy found a small ear of corn which he roasted and divided with his sister. The bird continued to bring corn for four days, but on the fifth day it entered the hole as usual and the boy drew out the original piece of sunflower pith. Holding it in his hand he said, "You are a living thing; go and hunt for our parents."

Returning to life, the bird flew to a hill three miles south of Oraibi (Tuwashabe), where it found a cactus plant with a red blossom. Below the plant was an opening which the bird entered and found itself in a kiva where grass and herbs were growing. At the north end was an opening leading to a second kiva with growing corn. At the north end of this kiva was an opening leading to a third where the bird found grass, herbs, and corn of all kinds. Here lived the god of Germination and Growth (Muyingwa), and with him were all the birds.

The hummingbird alighted on the god's arm and said, "Why have you listened to the Two-Hearts who wanted you to retire to this place and forget the people up there. It has not rained for a long time, and nothing grows. In Oraibi there remain only a couple of poor children. Come and look after the things up there." "All right, I shall consider the matter," replied the god. "Take something to the children." The bird broke off a nice roasting ear and took it; and it saved their lives.

The bird then flew away to seek the parents, and found them at Taho where the Hopi secure black paint to this day. They were living on cactus and were very much emaciated. In the meantime Muyingwa had decided to return to the earth and look after things. He ascended to the kiva above him where he stayed four days while it rained a little at Oraibi. Then he ascended to the next kiva and it rained considerably. When, after four more days, he emerged from the last kiva, he found grasses and herbs growing in abundance. The parents had seen clouds approaching Oraibi and resolved to return to the village, unaware that their children were still alive. Other Oraibians, who had not perished, also heard that it was raining at home and returned. When the children grew up, they, and after them their descendants, became the Village Chiefs and owners of Oraibi.

THE REVENGE OF THE KATCINAS

A long time ago many Hopi lived in a village somewhere east of Oraibi. West of this was a large mountain like the San Francisco Mountains, where many Katcinas dwelt. The Hopi in the village sometimes had ceremonies, but they did not yet know the Katcinas. One night some of the Katcinas assembled in their kiva in the mountains, put on their regalia, and came to the village, where they began to dance in the plaza. The people, hearing the sound of the dance, awoke from their sleep and came out to see. By the line of dancers was a Katcina Uncle (Katcina *Taha*). Not knowing who the dancers were, the people became angry and decided to kill them, but the Katcinas got wind of the plot and ran away. West of the village they jumped from a bluff into a large crack in the earth. Here their pursuers set fire to them and burned them up. All were killed except the Katcina Uncle, who had landed at the bottom of the pile. Early in the morning he crept out and returned to his home in the mountains, singing a song of lamentation.

Now the Katcinas who lived in the mountains were planting corn and watermelons in their fields among the foothills. All at once the Hehea Katcina, who was hoeing with a wooden hoe such as is still used by the Hehea Katcinas in their dances, heard someone singing and sobbing. Raising his hoe, he listened and saw a Hototo coming. "Why are you walking along muttering and crying?" he inquired. Between sobs the Hototo replied, "We were there in the Hopi village dancing, when they came out and threatened to kill us, so we ran away and jumped into a gulch west of the village, where we were all burned except myself." The Hehea Katcina called his companions and they all began to moan. Together they returned to their homes in the mountains, where there were a great many Katcinas, men, women, youths, and maidens.

When they heard of the deaths of the Katcinas, they determined to take revenge. At the order of their chiefs, the Katcinas dressed and assembled. For three days they made it hail. Early in the morning of the fourth day they called a cloud to rise and hover over the mountains while they ate their breakfast in the kiva. This was their emblem or standard—a very beautiful cloud.

The people in the village saw the cloud and went out into the fields to work their crops. During the morning many more clouds began to rise above the mountains, towering one upon another. They gathered from all four points. Now the corn of the Hopi had begun to mature, and the people felt very happy over the clouds, expecting good rains. Toward noon it began to thunder and rain in the mountains and the clouds began to move toward the Hopi village. When they arrived, thunder boomed and lightning flashed, but great hailstones fell instead of rain. All the crops were destroyed, and people were killed, even though they had left their homes and fled to the kivas. Only one man and one woman remained alive. When everything had been destroyed, the clouds said one to another, "We will stop now and return." Then they began to disperse in all directions. The Katcinas in the mountains rejoiced, saying, "Now we have avenged ourselves; let it be thus." The woman who had been spared bore children, and the village was eventually populated again.

THE SALT JOURNEY[2]

When the Shongopavi people lived at the foot of the mesa and the War Twins lived north of Oraibi with their grandmother, the Spider Woman, they noticed many Hopi traveling west to Blue Canyon for a Locust dance. The Twins decided to go with their grandmother to see the dance. They played shinny on the way to pass the time and reached the village by noon. There they watched the dance until they became very hungry, but no one invited them to eat because of their untidy appearance. Finally, a girl did call them to her house, and they noticed that her food was without seasoning, for salt was then unknown to the Hopi. But the Twins themselves were salty, since they were sweaty and unwashed; in fact the only clean spots on them were the backs of their hands, with which they constantly wiped their running noses. When the girl noticed that the Twins were running their hands across their noses and dipping them into the stew to season it, she was offended and whispered to her family that the stew would be fit only for dogs, and that she would never invite the boys again.

The Twins hurriedly ate and returned to the plaza, where they grew hungry again in the late afternoon; but reports of their bad manners had spread among the people, and no one would invite them to eat. They grew angry and told their old grandmother to go westward from the village, because they were going to take revenge on the people. Then they shot arrows into the sacred shrines in the plaza, causing the people to protest angrily: "You gods are supposed to protect us and should know better. We will teach you a lesson." As the crowd rushed upon them, the Twins chewed some powerful medicine

2. See Mischa Titiev, *A Hopi Salt Expedition* (American Anthropologist, n.s.), Vol. 89, pp. 244–258. 1937.

and spurted it over their opponents and the village, turning everything into stone. They followed the grandmother past what is now Moenkopi and set up a shrine at the spring, Pau'kuku. Then they proceeded westward to establish a new settlement at Salt Canyon and to prepare a trail for the good Hopi to follow in going for salt. They stopped at Tutuveni to carve their emblems, as Hopi have done ever since, and soon overtook their grandmother, who was weary. They urged her to hurry on, saying, "Our enemies may return to human forms and follow us." At Totolospi they let her go on while they stopped to play a game of checkers. When they overtook the grandmother again she was exhausted so that they had to half-drag her along. Finally, when she complained that she could not take another step, they dug a narrow trench and told her to rest in it upon her back. They removed her dress, saying, "Now your private parts will show, and when the Hopi pass, every man will get into you. In this way we will trade with each other, because, on their return, the Hopi will leave salt for you." Then they chewed medicine and spurted it upon the Spider Woman, turning her to stone.

The Twins hurried on to the mouth of the canyon where the elder god said to his brother, "You stay here so that when the Hopi come for salt they will pray to you for rain as their reward for beating us at checkers." Thus the younger War Twin was turned to stone, and his elder brother traveled on past the place that spreads the buttocks, past the home assigned to the Reed Clan, the stone with the fur carvings, and the Chicken shrine. When he came to the home of Masau'u, the Head Chief of the Canyon, he very fortunately secured this powerful god's promise to help any Hopi who passed that way in the future. At the home of the Coyemsie he received a similar promise. Beside the Sipapu he said, "When salt gatherers come here they will deposit their offerings and pray." After leaving instructions for the proper procedure in removing the yellow clay (*pavisa*), he went to the edge of the cliff, picked a place to descend, and dropped to the ridge below. There he established the home of the Kwans, set up the stone basin for the medicine water, and walked along the ledge rubbing his fists against the walls of the canyon and turning everything he touched to salt. Finally, he climbed back on the shelf and turned himself into stone, the chest-shaped rock that has ever since assisted the Hopi in their descent to the salt.

VISITS TO THE HOUSE OF THE DEAD

Once a youth sat at the edge of the mesa looking down upon the graves and wondering whether those who died continued to live somewhere. At last he took some corn meal, sprinkled it at the edge of the mesa, and prayed to the

Sun god: "If somewhere you have seen those who have died, please inform me." Having prayed thus for four successive days, he sat down and observed what appeared to be a man ascending the mesa and approaching him. "Why do you want me?" he asked. "Because," said the youth, "I am always thinking about those who are buried here, whether it is true that they are living in some other life." "Yes," replied the stranger, "they are living. If you are anxious to see them, I shall give you this." Then the Sun god, for it was he in the form of a man, handed some medicine to the youth. By eating it, he could fall into a deep sleep and die. After taking this medicine, the youth actually died, visited the House of the Dead, and returned to tell others how the dead live. Since then many people in Oraibi have had similar experiences, traveled far, and returned to recount what they have seen.

Various people report different details, but all their stories are much the same. After dying, they set out on a path leading westward. On the way they overtake unfortunate people traveling with great difficulty, tired and thirsty, begging for food or drink, and asking to be carried at least a few steps. They pass people carrying heavy loads with burden bands consisting of a single bow string which cuts into the forehead. Cactus plants are attached to tender parts of their bodies to prick them afresh at every step. Some are naked and forlorn, dragging themselves along a rugged path infested with vipers that often raise their heads to hiss and strike. These sufferers are neighbors and relatives from Oraibi who are being punished for their sins. They are the people who have not wanted it to rain, who have done something offensive to the clouds to drive them away, or who have invited bad winds and hailstorms to harass the people. They are those who have not listened to the advice of the old men, have failed to follow the straight road, have stolen private property, or have started ugly lies, causing others to worry. They are Two-Hearts, who have projected lizard tails, biting ants, snake venom, poisoned arrows, or evil thoughts into other people to cause their death. Theirs is a long and tortuous journey, sometimes lasting centuries before they reach the House of the Dead.

But the upright, those who have heeded the advice of the old people and have faithfully followed the Sun Trail, are permitted to take a broad, smooth highway patrolled by members of the Warrior society (Kwanitakas), who wear a big horn for a headdress and ring a bell to attract attention as they escort the righteous travelers over difficult passes and provide direction for the rest of the journey. Ofttimes a good person is placed on his own kilt, lifted up by a steady breeze, and carried smoothly over the rough road as if flying.

At last the righteous reach a place where the wicked are punished in smouldering pits, and from this horrible sight pass on into a large village of white houses where their departed relatives are living in peace and plenty. They find that those who were good on the earth hold the same ranks and positions that they had enjoyed in Oraibi. These ancestors do not eat ordinary food but only its aroma or soul, so that they are not heavy when they are transformed into clouds and float in the air. They smile at even the idea of eating solid food and say to the visitors, "You must go back again. You cannot stay with us here yet, because your flesh is strong and salty. You must work for us at home making prayer feathers (*nakwakwosis*) at the Soyal ceremony. As you see, these feathers are tied around our foreheads to represent falling rain. Then we also will work for you here. We will send you rain and good crops. You must wrap up the women in the white blanket (*owa*) and tie the big knotted belt around them when they die, because owas are not tightly woven and when we skeletons move along on them through the sky, thin raindrops fall from the fringes of these belts." They advise the visitors that after they have returned to Oraibi and told the people what they have seen and have assured them of life after death, it will be better for them not to think about death any more, but to perform the ceremonies regularly, live peaceably, and keep their feet faithfully upon the Hopi Sun Trail that leads to life.

Guide to Hopi Kinship and the
Identification of Don's Relatives

In the Hopi kinship system, which is of the Crow type,[1] the individual may claim relationship to seven large groups of persons through what will be called "connecting relatives": mother, father, both grandfathers, a ceremonial father, wife, and one or more "doctor fathers" to whom he may be given for treatment when sick. It is also possible to describe relationship through brother, sister, son, or daughter as the connecting relative.

The following abbreviations are used in the expression of certain common and primary terms of address:

Fa = father	Da = daughter
Mo = mother	C.Fa = ceremonial father
Br = brother	C.Mo = ceremonial mother

1. A chief characteristic of the Crow type is that cross-cousins on the paternal side, ego's father's sister's children, are classed with the parent's generation and called by a term signifying father or father's sister; and cross-cousins on the maternal side, ego's mother's brother's children, are classed with descendants one generation below ego and called by a term signifying son or daughter. See Robert H. Lowe, *Hopi Kinship* (Anthrop. Papers of the Amer. Mus. of Nat. Hist., 1929), XXX, 361–397.

Si = sister	C.So = ceremonial son
Hu = husband	C.Da = ceremonial daughter
Wi =wife	D.Fa = doctor father
So = son	

In Don's case the kinship groups may be plotted in five major divisions since his father and mother's father belonged to the Sand-Lizard-Snake phratry and his wife and father's father belonged to the same linked clans. It will be noted that he has two "doctor fathers" of separate linked-clan groups.

No effort is made to include all known clans in the linked-clan group. For example, the Moon, Star, Turkey, and Quala clans could be included with the Sun, Eagle, and Hawk, but no persons are mentioned in the narrative from these clans.

A chart-index system has been devised which lists in alphabetical order the names of all Hopi persons who appear in the narrative, indicates their clan affiliation, their place of residence, their generation classification with respect to Don as nearly as this could be ascertained, the degree of relationship to Don, the term of address which Don uses in speaking to them, and the reciprocal term used by them in addressing Don. In addition, there are references to pages in the text where these persons are mentioned. Many more clans appear than are listed in the chart above, due chiefly to kinship ties resulting from marital connections.

The following abbreviations are employed to identify place of residence in terms of either village or mesa and are listed in the third column from the right.

B. = Bakabi
F.M. = First Mesa
H. = Hotavila
K.C. = Keams Canyon
M. = Moenkopi
Mis. = Mishongovi
N.O. = New Oraibi
O. = Oraibi
Shi. = Shipaulovi
Sho. = Shongopavi

At least five generations were recognized and will be referred to by the following symbols:

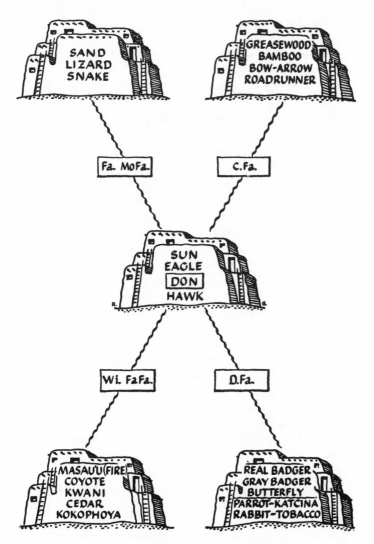

Don's Clan Affiliations through Connecting Relatives.

+3 = Grandparents' generation
+2 = Parents' generation
 1 = Don's own generation
−2 = Children's generation
−3 = Grandchildren's generation

These are listed in the fourth column under "generation," although Don was not always definite on this point.

The connecting relatives, when relationship is traced through them, are listed by identifying symbols in column five. When it is a primary relationship with Don, such as Fa, Mo, Br, C.Fa, etc., no connecting relative is given.

The same kinship terms are often used for many relationships established through blood, marriage, ceremonial, or doctor-father adoption, and irrespective of place of residence or personal acquaintance. But the use of them does not imply the same closeness of kinship and mutual obligation. The Hopi distinguish the following degrees of relationship which will be referred to hereafter by symbols indicated below and listed in column 6.

A blank space on the chart indicates a primary relationship such as Fa, Mo, Br, Si, etc., with respect to Don or with respect to his connecting relative when one is given.

Number 1 signifies persons one degree removed from a primary relationship to Don or the connecting relative, MoBr, for example.

Number 2 signifies more remote lineage relatives of Don or the connecting relative.

Number 3 signifies clan relations of Don or the connecting relative which are not covered by the above categories.

Number 4 signifies linked-clan relations of Don or the connecting relative.

The letter *a* indicates that the relationship to Don or the connecting relative is that of regular adoption, such as Don's adoption of Norman.

The letter *c* indicates that the relationship to Don or the connecting relative is through ceremonial adoption.

The letter *m* indicates that the relationship to Don or the connecting relative is through marriage.

The Hopi kinship terms of address are given the following numerical symbols:

1. ina'a = Fa.
2. ingi'i = Mo.

3. ibaba = Elder Br.
3a. itupko = Younger Br.
4. ikoko = Elder Si.
4a. isiwa = Younger Si.
5. iBisingwa = Hu ("sleeping partner") igonya used by outsiders.
6. iwuhtu = Wi ("my woman") inima used by outsiders.
7. iti'i = So or Da ("my child").
8. ikwa'a = FaFa.
9. iso'o = FaMo.
10. ikaya'a = FaSi.
11. itaha = MoBr.
12. imiwi = BrWi, applied to all female relatives-in-law, lineage especially.
13. imi'iangwa = SiHu, applied to all male relatives-in-law in ego's clan in generations below mother, but not men marrying into his father's clan. Pookonghoya ("Little War God") used sometimes.
14. itiwaya = SiSo or SiDa.
15. imiyi = SoSo, SoDa, DaSo, DaDa.
16. imi'ianansingwa = WiSiHu ("partners").

1	2	3	4	5	6	7	8	
NAME	CLAN	Residence	Generation	Connecting Relative	Degree of Kinship	Term of Address	Reciprocal Term	Page
Ada	Snake	O.	+2	Fa	4	9	15	175, 223
Adam	Sun	F.M.	+2	Mo	3	11	14	106–107
Adolph Hoye	Parrot	O.	1	D.Fa	3	1	7	121, see Index
Alice	Corn	O.	1	C.So	m	12	1	209
Andrew	Badger	O.	1	D.Fa	3	3a	3	368
Archie	Sun	O.	1	Mo	2	3a	3	76, 106–108
Arpa	Real Badger	F.M.	+3	D.Fa		1	7	212, 217
Arthur	Sun	N.O.	1	Mo	3	3	3a	302, see Index
Bakabi	Sun	O.	+3	Mo	3	9	15	216–218, 298
Baldwin	Masau'u (Fire)	O.	1	Wi	1	3a	13	311, see Index
Barbara	Masau'u	N.O.	1	Wi	1	4	13	307–309, 311–312
				Br	m	12	3	
Barker	Real Badger	O.	+2	D.Fa	3	8	15	321–322, 340
				Wi	3	15	8	
Bechangwa	Sparrow Hawk	O.	+3	Mo	2	7	1	71, 75
Betty	Parrot	O.	-2	Da	c	7	1	340, 384
Billy	Rabbit-Tobacco	M.	+2	D.Fa	3	1	7	
				Mo	3	3	3a	
Blanche	Masau'u	O.	1	Fa	3	3	3a	161, 163–164
				Wi	3	4	13	
Buhumana	Gray Badger	O.	+2	Br	m	12	3	223, see Index
Byron Adams	Grass	F.M.	1	D.Fa	No Kin	10	15	387–388
Carl	Sun	O.	1	Mo	3	3	3a	296, 260

Name	Clan		Gen.	Rel.				Pages
Cecil	Corn-Water	O.	1	Fa	2	3a	3	319, *see* Index
Clara	Masau'u	O.	1	D.Fa	3	8	15	106, *see* Index
				Wi	1	4	13	
Clarence	Water	O.	1	Fa	1	2	7	155–156
Claude James	Rabbit-Tobacco	O.	–2	C.Fa	3	3	3a	
				C.So		7	1	
				D.Fa	4	1	7	
Dan Coochongva	Sun	H.	+2	Wi	2	15	8	143, *see* Index
David	?	Shi.?		Mo	3	11	14	116, 391
Delia	Sun	O.	–2	Si	1	14	11	112, 351
Dennis	Masau'u	H.	1	Wi	2	3a	3	142, *see* Index
				Fa	1c	3a	3	
Dick	Coyote	O.	1	Fa	2	8	15	225–226, 258–260
Edna	Masau'u	O.	1	Wi	1	4	13	106
Edwin	Rabbit-Tobacco	O.	+2	Fa	3	3a?	3?	383
Ellis	Snake	O.	+2	Fa	4	8	15	103, 219
Elsie (Louis's Girl)	Corn-Water	M.	1	C.So		7	1	314
Elsie (Euella's Da.)	Lizard	M.	–2	Fa	3	10	15	145–146, *see* Index
Esau	Gray Hawk	?.		C.Fa	2	4a	3	316
Esther	Squash	?.	1	Mo	4	3	3a	121
Euella	Lizard	M.	1	Fa	4	10	15	147–149
Eva	Bamboo	M.	1	C.Fa	4	10	15	155–157, *see* Index
Felix	Butterfly	O.	1	D.Fa	3	1	7	153–154, 228
								83–84

NAME	CLAN	Residence	Generation	Connecting Relative	Degree of Kinship	Term of Address	Reciprocal Term	Page
Frances	Sand	M.	+2	Fa	3	10	15	151, *see* Index
Frank (Masaquaptewa)	Bear	Shi.	1	Si	m	13	3a	139–142 *see* Index
				Mo	3	7	1	Index
Frank (Siemptewa)	Corn	M.	+2	Wi	3	15	8	120, *see* Index
Freddie	Rabbit-Tobacco	M.	+2	Wi	3	1	7	207, 273–275
Frederic (Charles)	Bear	O.	1	Fa	3c	3	3a	327–328
				Wi	3	15	8	
Gladys	Sun	O.	1	Si		4	3a	26, *see* Index
Glen	Sun	O.	1	Br		3a	3	299
Grace	Bear	O.	1	Mo	3	7	1	340, 381–382
Hahaye (mother)	Sun	O.	+2	Mo		2	7	25, *see* Index
Harry Kopi	Sand	O.	+2	Fa	2	1	7	71, *see* Index
Harry McClain	Gray Hawk	F.M.	1	Mo	4	3	3a	122
Hattie	Sun	M.	1	Mo	3	4	3a	120–121, 241
Herbert	Coyote	O.	1	Wi	3	3a	3	204, 341–342
Henry	?	M.	1					161
Herman	Water-Coyote	O.	1	Wi	3	3	3a	
				Fa	4	8	15	98
Hicks	Tewa Tribe	F.M.						
Homikniwa	Lizard	O.	+3	Mo	1	8	15	104
				Fa	4	8	15	
Honwuhti	Lizard	O.	+3	Fa	3	9	15	39, 89, 110

	2	3	4	5	6	7	8	
NAME	CLAN	Residence	Generation	Connecting Relative	Degree of Kinship	Term of Address	Reciprocal Term	Page
Kalmanimptewa	Badger	N.O.	+2	C.Fa	2	3	3a	117, 362–363
Kalnimptewa	Sand	O.	+2	Fa	1	1	7	71, see Index
Kamaoyousie	Greasewood	O.	+2	C.Fa	3	10	15	109
Kawamana	Bamboo	O.	+2	C.Fa	3	10	15	317
Kawasie	Corn	O.	+2	Fa	2m	2	7	308–309
Kayahongnewa	Rabbit-Tobacco	O.	+2	So	c	8	15	317–318
Kayahongva	Sand	O.	+2	Fa	1	1	7	112
Kayayeptewa	Sun	O.	+3	Mo	2	11	14	71, see Index
Kelhongneowa	Sun	O.	+2	Mo	2	11	14	75–76
						3	3a	
Kelmaisie	Rabbit-Tobacco	O.	+2	Mo	3m	12	3a	117
						4	3a	
Kewalecheoma	Badger	O.	+2	D.Fa	3	1	7	194
Kewanimptewa	Sand	B.	+2	Fa	3	1	7	359, 381
Kewanmainim	Sand	O.	+2	Fa		10	15	31, 269
Kewanventewa	Masau'u	O.	+2	Wi	2	11	13	272–273, see Index
Kochwytewa	Badger	H.	+2	Mo	3m	1	7	304, 316, 356
Koyonainiwa	Badger	O.	+2	D.Fa	3	1	7	110
Latimer	Greasewood	H.	1	C.Fa	3	1	7	379–380
Laura	Navaho Badger	N.O.	1	Fa	3	4a	3	375
Lillian	Water	O.	1	C.Fa	3	4	3a	147–149
Lilly	Greasewood	O.	1	C.Fa	3	10	14	341–342
Logan	Water-Coyote	O.	1	Mo	c	3a	3	193–198, 210

Name	Clan							Pages
Lolulomai (Chief)	Bear	O.	+3	Wi	2	1	7	68, *see* Index
Lomaleteotewa	Masau'u	O.	+3	Wi	3	11	13	272
Lomavuyaoma	Masau'u	O.	+2	Wi	2	11	13	183, 297
Lomayeptewa	Kokophoya	O.	+3	Fa	1	8	15	74
Lorenza	Bear	O.	−1	Mo	3	7	1	349, 369
Louis Hoye	Greasewood	M.	1	C.Fa	3	1	7	120, *see* Index
Louise	Rabbit-Tobacco	O.	1	Mo	3	7	7	116–119, 120–122
Luther	Sand	O.	1	Fa	2	1	7	98, 319
Mabel	Sun	O.	1	Si		4a	3	201, *see* Index
Mae	Greasewood	O.	1	C.Fa	3	10	15	108–109
Margaret	Water-Coyote	O.	1	Fa	3	9	15	98
Mark	Rabbit-Tobacco	O.	1	Mo	3	3	3a	211, 216, 241–242
Masahongneowa (Nice Man)	Snake	O.	1	Fa	4	1	7	238
Masatewa	Lizard	O.	+2	Mo	3	8	1	270
Masawyestewa	Parrot-Katcina	O.	+2	Mo	m	1	15	151, 273
Masenimka	Sand	O.	+3	Fa	1	9	7	28, *see* Index
Mattima	Lizard	O.	1	Fa	3	1	15	89
Maud	Parrot	F.M.	1	D.Fa	3	10	7	111
Meggie	Sun	M.	1	Mo	3	4a	15	153, *see* Index
Mettie	Rabbit-Tobacco	M.	1	C.Fa	3	4a	3	138, *see* Index
Minnie	Bear	O.	1	Mo	3	15	8	
Molly Jaun	Coyote	H.	1	Fa	4	9	15	379–381
Mtuute	Sun	O.	+3	Mo	3	11	14	62, 71

NAME	CLAN	Residence	Generation	Connecting Relative	Degree of Kinship	Term of Address	Reciprocal Term	Page
Myron	Parrot	O.	1	Mo	3m	13	3	
				Wi	3	15	8	
				D.Fa	3	1	7	340, 375–382
Namostewa (Ira)	Sun	N.O.	1	Br.		3	3a	see Ira
Nannie	Bear	N.O.	1	D.Fa	3	4a	3	111
Naquima	Sun	O.	+3	Mo	2	11	14	34, see Index
						3	3a	
Naseyouaoma	Gray Badger	M.	+2	Mo	3m	8	15	
				D.Fa	3	1	7	192
Nash	Grass	F.M.	1		No Kin			100–103, 218
Nashingemptewa	Masau'u	O.	+2	Wi	3	11	13	208
Nasinonsi	Parrot	O.	+2	Mo	3m	12	3	
				D.Fa	3	10	15	175, 340
Nathaniel	Bow	O.	+2	C.Fa	3	1	7	266, see Index
Nawesoa	Masau'u	O.	+2	Wi		2	13	222, see Index
Nelson	Sand	H.	-2	Si	2m	13	11	329, see Index
				Fa	3	1	7	
Norman	Masau'u	O.	-2	So	a	7	1	
				Wi	2	7	13	310, see Index
Nuvahunka	Sun	N.O.	+2	Mo	1	2	7	39, see Index
Nuvaiumsie	Water-Coyote	O.	+3	Fa	3	9	15	26
Pat	Bluebird	Sho.	1?	Mo	m	13	3a	374
				Mo	3c	7	1	
Pavatea (Tom)	Ahl	F.M.	+2	Fa	a	1	7	111–112, 390

Name	Clan		±	Relation	3	10	15	Reference
Pavingyesnim (Frances)	Sand	M.	+2	Fa	3	3	3a	*see* Frances
Perry	Greasewood	N.O.	−2	C.Fa / Wi	3 / 3	15	8 / 3	380
Perry (Br)	Sun	O.	1	Br	3	3a	3	96, *see* Index
Philip	Katcina	Shi.?	+2	Mo	3	7	1	138
Pierce	Corn	O.	1	D.Fa	3	3a	3	207, 211
Pole	Lizard	M.	1	Fa	3	10	15	158
Polehongsie	Greasewood	M.		C.Fa	3	10	15	207, *see* Index
Poleyestewa	Greasewood	O.	+2	C.Fa / Fa	3 / 1m	1 / 11	7 / 15	167, *see* Index
Polingyuama	Parrot	B.	+2	D.Fa		1	7	302–304, 363
Ponyangetewa	Corn	M.	+2	Mo	3m	13	7	212
Punnamousi	Bear	O.	+2	Mo	2m	12	3a?	68, 175
Ralph	Masau'u	O.	1	Wi	3	2	7	96
Rex Moona	?	O.	1	No Kin		3	13	107
Robert Selema	Masau'u	O.	1	Wi	3	3	13	221
Robert Talas	Sun	M.	1	Mo	3	3	3a	159, *see* Index
Roger	Greasewood	M.	+2	Fa	2m	8	15	151, *see* Index
Ross	Rabbit-Tobacco	O.	1	D.Fa / C.Fa	3 / 3	1 / 3a	7	349
Rudolph	Squash	Sho.?		Mo	3	7	3	372
Sadie	Parrot	O.	1	D.Fa	3	10	1	175–177
Sadie	Coyote	M.	1	Fa	3	10	15	155, 160
Saknimptewa	Water	O.	+3				15	233
Sam (Second Mesa)	Sun	Shi.	1	Mo	2	11	14	113, 145–148

1	2	3	4	5	6	7	8	
NAME	CLAN	Residence	Generation	Connecting Relative	Degree of Kinship	Term of Address	Reciprocal Term	Page
Sam (Poweka)	Rabbit-Tobacco	O.	+2	D.Fa	3	1	7	95
Sammy	Yucca	F.M.	+2	Wi	3	8	15	304
Saul	Gray Hawk	O.?	1	Mo	3	3	3a	121
Secaletscheoma	Greasewood	O.	+2	C.Fa	3	1	7	206
Secavaima	Sun	Shi.	+2	Mo	3	11	14	106
Sekahongeoma	Greasewood	O.	+2	C.Fa	c	1	7	84, *see* Index
Seletzwa	Badger	O.	1	Fa	3c	3	3a	203
Sequapa	Coyote	O.	+2	Fa	3	9	15	295–300
Sewequapnim	Sun	H.	+2	Mo	3	2	7	365
Singumsie	Sun	M.	+2	Mo	3	2	7	216
Solemana	Greasewood	O.	+2	C.Fa	1	10	15	71, *see* Index
Sophie	Bear	Shi.	1	Mo	3	7	1	139, 144, 147–148
Stanley	Parrot	O.	−2	C.So	c	7	1	314–316
Susie	Rabbit-Tobacco	M.		D.Fa	3	8	15	120–122
Talasemptewa	Rabbit-Tobacco	O.	+2	Mo	3	3	3a	41, 62
				Fa	3m	8	15	
				D.Fa	3	1	7	
Talashungnewa	Sun	O.	+3	Mo	2	11	14	71, 112
Talasquaptewa	Sun	O.	+3	Mo	2	11	14	46, *see* Index
Talasveyma	Gray Hawk	O.	+2	Mo	3	3	3a	117

APPENDIX D

A Sample of Don's Composition

1. My father was present in the room when I was born. he look after my mother when my mother is going to have baby.

2 It was a custom to let the woman stay by herself withoug any children around bothering her even a 3 year old child. only those that is going to help her when the woman is going to have a baby such as Doctor or a husband or a lady that must be relative.

3 The sand is put on the floor for the mother when she getting near to have a child so she could stay upon. When the pain stop when she get tired she can lean herself sidewise on some kind soft pile of bedding and rest on it until the pain started she can set on the floor with her knees.

4 In childbirth the mother will be on her side so the bone below her vulva will fit back to its place. if she dont do that the bone will not fit tight back to it place and that will hurt the woman and will trouble her right along, then the bone Doctor will replace it back and he will hurt her. but that is the only we to cure her.

5 yet the Hopi Doctor have examine my mother and fix the child or straighten the baby so the baby will come out without doing her much harm We were twins in our mothers wome so the Doctor twist the black and white yarn and and put it around our mother wrist in that way we come together.

when I was born Im the biggest baby that was born because we are two. I cause let of trouble to my mother it takes me long while to come out.

6 It was a custom for some person to look after the mother to get behind and put their arm around the upper belly button and shake her so the baby will come out.

7 The lady that help my mother when I was born is Nu-va-un-sie a special old lady that knows how to work on it and the after birth she know how to do these things. She cut my naval cord on a piece of an arrow and tie a string that she cut from my mother's hair string at the end of the naval cord so the air cannot go in to the belly button and troubles the baby.

8 It is a custom to feed the mother the special kind of food after the birth. unsalt gravy so that gravy will help to mother to have a good milk in her breast. but not feed her before the birth of a baby.

9 I was born with my head first, but not with my feet.

10 this question I got a hard time in answering it. I ask my own people about this question, but none of them seems to know it. it might be the custom for the Oraibi people to take the spit out of the baby's mouth and put it on the back of the baby's neck. I think that over and then I think I will go to Grace and ask her about it. she is belong to the Shimopovi people. perhaps they might have a custom about that. I went to her and ask her and she said it is she told me that by taking a spit out of the baby's mouth and put it on the back of the baby's neck. it means by doing that, some times the baby cry too much and putting the spit on the back of the neck, is to hide the baby cries so the baby will not cry too much. I think that is ture. I believe I answer your question rightly.

The Soyal Ceremony

DATE, 12–17 TO 21–38.

Next day December 17th starting again early in the morning we got up from our bed put on our Shoes or moccacine and we went out to the edge of the Oraibi massa toward east and say our morning prayer. then we all come back it was not so cold we dont have to put on our clothing as we go and pray in the morning. Coming back to our kiva we stay there untile breakfast time we all went out and go to our houses and took our food back to our kiva and eat. I have piki and a little coffee for our breakfast when we finish our breakfast I went out and took my dish and took it back to our house then I went out to my sheep correl to herd I try to hire some one to herd for me but no one seems willing to herd for me of course I got to pay a $1.00 to some one that herd sheep for me when I get there I open the gate and turn them out and I herd all day. but I don't have to hunt or kill any rabbit because Im in our Soyal Ceremony we members are not al low to kill or hurt any game we have attend our ceremony and to pray and in our wishes to have lots of crops next coming summer. Every living creature will be multiply or increase rabbit birds and so forth It seems the day is too long because I dont hunt rabbit by hunting rabbit thats make the days much shorter I did not watered my sheep. Every time I try to drive my sheep toward the Oraibi wash they turn around and go the opposite direction that makes me think the other sheep herder has watered them yesterday it was Norman. in the evening I took them back to the correl and put them in and close the gate and then come home just in time when the Soyal members are taking their food to the kiva I take off my over coat and took my blanket and my food and went to the kiva and eat supper with the rest of my partnership I have unsalted flat bread and coffee for my supper after supper we took our dishes back to our homes and return back to our kiva and stay there singing our prayer songs untile 9.30 oclock. then we make up our bed and have a nap untile next morning while Im in the kiva my wish is that my Guardian Angle will bring a good dreams to me, but no dream, scinse 3 days have pass. perhaps some times yet. Early in the morning we all went out at the edge of the massa and pray as we use to pray so our prayers will reaches to the 6 points to the cloud people so as to renew our lives that is bring some rain. It was Sunday morning then December the 18th we come back and stay in our kiva untile breakfast time we all come out and get our food for our breakfast then we had our breakfast I have Hopi dumpling and coffee for my breakfast when we get through with our breakfast we took our dishes back to our homes then we are ready with our work making our pahos we work all day there are many many thing we have to make paho for them human being animals birds Spirit Gods Cloud Gods springs rivers Oceans every living creature nature and our dear ones that have pass away We work from morning untile sunset it is a hard work too our back are tired and we are hungry too. we put away our paho work and go to our houses and wash our hands and faces and took our food and went to our kiva and eat our supper We ate hartely for we are hungry the food seems have a good tasteing too after we had our supper we took our dishes to our houses and go back and stay there singing our prayer songs. then we have to go to bed little earlier because next day at night we have to stay up all night no sleeping untile sunrise so we make up our bed and go to sleep. Next morning we get up early in the morning and then that time we dont go to the sun and pray we work for a while untile breakfast time it was December 19th Monday morning when breakfast time we bring our food to our kiva and eat our breakfast that time I had oatmeal, and piki for my breakfast when we finished our meal we took our dishes and took them back to our houses and then go back and work we got to do all we can smoke pray and sing our ceremony songs and do lots of other thing it seems when we do all those things and get busy the day is much shorter after we get through then! it is time for us to eat our boil meat mix with homany and season with salt. We took our good food to our kiva and began to eat our breakfast. oh! how good the food taste it seems our eyes shines more brighter after supper we gather up all the food and put them in a same dish and basket and took them to our Chief house save that food for another day such as going hunting rabbit and coming back we can eat that food when our Chief wife warm them up. then we took out dishes to our homes and go back at stay there from sunset all through the night smoke pray sing and do lots of other things wishing to have another rain and snow so as to have a good moisture in our farms. the night seems quite long finealy it is getting dawn on the east direction it is getting gray. then we took our pahos to every household telling them that we make those things for them so they will be well protected I know I make pahos for every Hopi that is living in Old Oraibi and all of my white friends then by the time when the sun is about rising all the Hopis took their pahos and take them out to the east directions and put them on the ground and do a worshiping stick them in the ground the men took their pahos to the antelope shrine and pray there so as to be well protected and be a good hunter

When the sun rise from the east it was then Tuesday December the 20th. We Soyal members asembel to our kiva and sing our song then we are dismiss from the ceremony. We that live at Old Oraibi took those Moenkopi men that attend our Soyal we invited them to our homes for breakfast each of us has to take one man so as to have enough men to go around to each men that is we are in every house hold there are Hopi pudding boil mutton mix with homany for us to eat everybody seems happy because we have had a good celabration for the coming of the new year starting from the beginning of the new year every body have had a paho and they are welcome. when we eat our breakfast I took my man to my ralatieves and have him eat in my Sun Clan homes. then when we go all over my clan folks I turn him loose and then I put my paho that I made for my dog I put that around his neck and he seems to be well please. then I go after my horses I meet them coming into the village they are halfway to the village I put them in their carrel and I hang their pahos on every tail of my horses telling them to be happy and be healthy for I make a paho for them Then I took another paho to my orchard and hang them on every tree branches and when I come back I hang some more paho in my room down stairs and up stairs. after that is done I took my mask to the kiva and the men are busy painting their mask in Soyal day as a rule the Hopis put up a dance so we are busy working dressing our mask after I paint my mask and fix a head dress I hang a paho on my mask that I made for him you know Kachena is a living spirit to whom we pray to. when I finish dressing the mask it was noon time I went to my house and eat my dinner and I gather all my dancing custam outfit in my bag and my corn meal and go back to the kiva and put them in my blanket and my mask wrapped them up then we all went to a place where the Kachena shrine and the home where we dress I dount the Kachena mask and I found out they are 17 so we are quite a bunch. we dress up and started from there into the village. It was a first day for a Kachena to dance for the people in December Soyal celabration when the dancers went into the Plazza they saw lots of people at the Plazza quite a number of the Hopis come up to the village from New Oraibi the dance started in the afternoon about 3 oclock P.M. and quit just in time when it is 5 oclock P.M. and go back home where they belong as our believe is. We change our dancing custom outfit put them in our bags and return to our kiva when we are all asemble then Chief Tewaquaptewa make a prayer feather for the rabbits. that is next day we are going to put up a rabbit hunting the feast is going to be on the 4th day from that day on December 24th Saturday on that day the sun started back to his summer home. After we make a prayer feather. he took them to a place to which direction we should go next day going out hunting then he announce it that is it will be next day evary men are happy because it is much fun and they love to hunt. After sunset we all come out of the kiva and went to our homes and eat our supper we had the same thing which we have had only we add coffee milk and bread to it I was very sleepy because we didn't sleep for a whole night so just as soon as I eat I went to our kiva and sleep there are quite a bunch of men lying on their bed snoring like a dikens I make up my bed and joines with them I wake up once and went out during the night and it was cloudy it snow I look around for a while and went into the kiva after I take a leak and go on with my sleeping hours. we woke up early in the morning before sun rise, roll up our bed went to the edge of the massa and pray to the sun and come back to our kiva It was Wednesday morning December the 21st. I did not stay there long but came out and go to my house I shear one of my sheep pelt and throw it outside where the snow is put some on the skin so it will get wet then we had our breakfast we had the same thing for our breakfast which we had right after our meal is over I started working on making my snow shoes from off the sheep skin. during that morning the fog is too thick and it makes me think the rabbit hunting wont be successful.

Part of a Letter

DATE 11—4—41

Oraibi Ariz., Nov. 4, 1941.

Dear brother Honweseoma.

I would like to Answer your nice letter and thank you for the check enclosed I was very much pleased to have them Im now broke. We havent got a cent in our purse and couldnt buy any grocery Thank you very much.

The picture that Mr. Grosman has gotten is very nice. Im proud to say that my picture will be placed in the Yales mans book and soon it will be all over the world.

I have gotten lot of letters from the white people saying that they wanted to get a book that was published. I think the books are passing out from the Yale University and scatter all over the U.S. to most of the people whom I never met. I think the way it sounds to me is pretty soon Ill be a great man. I dont really mean that I like to be but the white people will call me great man. When they put my address they write Chief Don C. Talayesva you remember I dont like to be Chief or Mr. Talayesva. Don is good enough for me. . . .

Sincerely
your brother
DON C. TALAYESVA.

INDEX

DT in the index stands for Don Talayesva. Page numbers in **boldface** refer to illustrations.

473

and DT's children's deaths, 271–72,
294; and DT's death journey, 128,
143; and DT's return to Oraibi, 142;
and DT's school years, 105–6; and
DT's wedding, 224–25; kinship chart,
458t; as medicine man, 26, 43, 51, 61,
227, 268, 269–70, 302; and the Ooqol
ceremony, 22, 257; stories told by,
48–50, 90; suspected of being a Two-
Heart, 304–5

Honweseoma. *See* Simmons, Leo

Honwuhti, 39, 110, 458t

Hopi medicine: burns, 19, 39, 312; death
call illness, 357–60; Delia's pregnancy and death, 363–64, 366; and
DT's children's deaths, 271, 280, 294,
300–301; DT's mother's death, 337;
DT's powers, 33, 70, 305, 362–63,
387–88; Homikniwa as doctor, 26,
43, 51, 61, 227, 268, 269–70, 302;
Jauneta's illness, 387–88; lizard
poisoning, 212–14; as men's province,
13; Naquima's illness, 329; origin
story, 435; owl omen, illness after,
361–62; in pregnancy, 25, 268–70 (*see
also* childbirth; pregnancy); ribs out
of joint, 216–18; sore ankle, 352–53;
Spider Woman illness, 51–52, 406;
swollen genitals, 303–5; Tuvenga,
38–39; twins twisted into one, 25, 270,
466; urine as medicine, 61, 302, 354;
worry as cause of illness, 426; wrist
injury, 350–51. *See also* illness; *and
specific doctors*

Hopi people: characteristics, 10, 54; DT's
pride in, xiii, 187; DT's relationship to
cultural norms, 401–3; factional split,
xxii, 22, 64, 72, 93–94, 106, 115–16,
143; food (*see* food); gendered division
of labor, 12–14 (*see also* men; women);
history, 9–10; language, 10, 123;
medicine (*see* Hopi medicine); origin

stories, 433, 435–36; religion (*see*
Hopi religion); social organization,
14–17, 72, 230; suspicious of DT,
xiii–xiv, 318, 321–23, 340–41, 375;
today, xiv–xv; traditional way of
life, xxiii, 9–14, 232–33, 347–48 (*see
also specific topics*); traditions dying,
347–48, 362

Hopi religion: central to Hopi life, 14–15,
17–18, 401; ceremonial year, 19–22
(*see also specific ceremonies*); ceremonies observed by whites, xvii, 45, 157,
198–99, 378–79; DT's commitment
to, xix, 215, 220, 232–33, 387–89,
394–95; dying out, 317–18, 348; gods,
17–18, 57, 66, 430–50 (*see also specific
deities*); Katcinas (*see* Katcina dances;
Katcinas); prayer feathers (*see* pahos;
prayer feathers); secrecy of ceremonies, xiii–xiv, 5–7, 15, 19, 172, 261,
321–23, 339, 355–56, 375, 386; stories
(*see* stories). *See also* kivas

horned toads, 65, 300–301, 313

horses: buying/trading for, 211, 367–69;
caring for, 275–76, 278; death of DT's
horses, 276–78, 332, 417; introduced
by Spanish, 12; lightning-struck, 240–
41; lost or stolen, 258, 332–36, 417;
meat, 58; Norman's horse, 367–69,
418–19; origin story, 434; races, 159,
242; sold for shawl, 283

hospitality, 56–57, 278

Hostiles (faction), xxii, 22, 64, 72, 94, 106,
116, 143

Hotlotis (Navaho doctor), 333–35

house of DT and Irene, 257, 336, 376–77

Howard, 145–46, 459t

Hoye, Adolph. *See* Adolph Hoye

Hoye, Louis. *See* Louis Hoye

Hubbell, Mr., 290, 329

Huminquima (Irene's father), 222, 231,
459t